# EASY GUIDE TO
# SEWING

**Tops and T-Shirts, Skirts, and Pants**

The Taunton Press, Inc., 63 South Main Street, PO Box 5507, Newtown, CT 06470-5506
e-mail: tp@taunton.com

Front Cover Photographer: Boyd Hagan
Layout Artists: Rosalie Vaccaro pp. 2–119; Cathy Cassidy pp. 120–223; Susan Fazekas pp. 224–373
Photographers: Scott Phillips pp. 2–119, 225, 239, 251, 295, 307, 345; Boyd Hagan pp. iii, 120–223;
Susan Kahn pp. 224–373 except where noted above
Illustrators: Robert La Pointe pp. 2–119; Steve Buchanan pp. 120–223; Christine Erikson pp. 224–373
Indexer: Lynda Stannard

**Library of Congress Cataloging-in-Publication Data**

Tilton, Marcy.
  Easy guide to sewing tops and t-shirts, skirts, and pants /
Marcy Tilton and Lynn MacIntyre.
     p. cm.
  Includes bibliographical references and index.
  ISBN 978-1-60085-072-1
  1. Dressmaking. 2. Machine sewing. 3. Clothing and dress
measurements. I. MacIntyre, Lynn. II. Title.
  TT515.T52 2009
  646.4'04--dc22
                         2008036642

Printed in the United States of America
10 9 8 7 6 5 4 3 2 1

# EASY GUIDE TO
# SEWING

## Tops
## and
## T-Shirts,
## Skirts,
## and
## Pants

LYNN MACINTYRE
AND
MARCY TILTON

The Taunton Press

# 1 $\vert$ Which Top to Make?

Tops make good starter-level projects for beginners or quick wardrobe additions for sewers with experience. You'll find tops patterns sprinkled throughout the pages of pattern books—shown alone, with sportswear, combined with suits, and in the designer and easy-sewing sections.

Train your eye by going through pattern books, clothing catalogs, and fashion magazines, looking only at tops and T-shirts. Notice what shapes, silhouettes, and necklines reflect current fashion and the combinations designers have chosen to put together. See what you like and note what changes you'd make to personalize the pattern for yourself.

In this chapter, you'll learn to determine which styles enhance your face and figure, and how to combine pattern and fabric with each other and with your skill level. You'll also understand how to build a collection of tops in your best colors, necklines, and shapes that will fit into and extend your wardrobe.

The combination of a beautiful fabric and simple, well-fitting shape is unbeatable. If quick sewing is your goal, use a pattern, style, fabric, and the sewing techniques you are familiar with. When you want to "grow" your skills, you can gradually add new elements. Tops that are challenging and time-consuming are ones that have complex construction details like piping or tucks, are cut on the bias, or use hard-to-handle fabrics such as charmeuse or georgette, and require fitting skills.

## Choosing the Best Style

Begin at home—try on the tops you already own with other pieces in your wardrobe to see what works and what else you need. Perhaps you have a jacket or pants that you'd wear more often if you had the

Keep a record/design journal of detail ideas and measurements of favorite garments. Measure the width at the underarm and hem, the back length, the depth of the armhole, and the width of neck and shoulder seam.

right top to pull the look together. With notebook and tape measure in hand, do some design research in your own closet or discreetly in your favorite clothing store, taking key measurements of the tops you like best. Note the fit and overall shape, the back length (measure from neckline to hem), the depth of the armhole (with the garment flat, measure in a straight line from underarm to shoulder seam), and necklines (see the photo at left).

Look for hem depth, edge finishes, topstitching length and width, and fabric types. I keep a file folder full of design details I have admired on ready-made garments. Incorporate the results of your design research into your pattern and fabric selection.

## Wardrobing and color tips

The following are guidelines I use in planning my own wardrobe and sewing projects. Add pieces that go with at least three to four others already in your wardrobe. Sew in color modules each season, adding related colors in succession. For example, one spring/summer, I sewed everything in ivory, black, and coral, the next year in oatmeal, brown, and teal, adding a few prints that had all of these colors. I take inventory at the end of a season and list the items I wish I had, then use this list to start my projects the next year.

It can be discouraging to make a top that does not fit beneath favorite sweaters or jackets. Make sure the tops you make relate to the garments you'll wear over them in shape, neckline, depth of armhole, and length. The silhouette and length of the top must complement the skirt or pants as well. I rely on the "rule of bigness": If one piece (top or bottom) is big—like an oversized tunic or long, flowing skirt—then the proportion will balance if the other element is small, like a fitted top with a long, full skirt or an oversized tunic with slim pants (see the illustration at left).

Tops frame the face. Color draws the eye. Use color in the tops

### Balancing proportions

For balanced proportions, follow the "rule of bigness": Combine big tops with leggings or fitted tops with full skirts.

you sew for maximum impact by harmonizing with your natural coloring, skin tone, and hair and eye color. Contrast is the difference in lightness and darkness of your skin compared with your hair, and is an important factor in determining whether you will look best in bright or muted colors. If your skin is very fair and your hair is black, you would be considered high contrast, and you'll look best in high-contrast, clear colors; if your skin is pale and your hair a medium brown, you would be low contrast and be flattered by midrange, muted colors. Extend your wardrobe by using neutrals in jackets and sweaters, and adding the drama of color in tops.

## Style and proportion

The tops that will look best and feel the most comfortable on you will enhance your figure and face shape. Since tops hang from the shoulders, the style, cut, and fit in the shoulders and upper chest—along with the shape and width of the neckline—are significant. How well a style works for you often depends on your body type. You'll want a style that complements your figure in size, shape, and length. A slim, well-proportioned figure can wear almost any style of top. Statistics reveal that the average American woman is 5 ft. 3 in. and weighs 148 pounds.

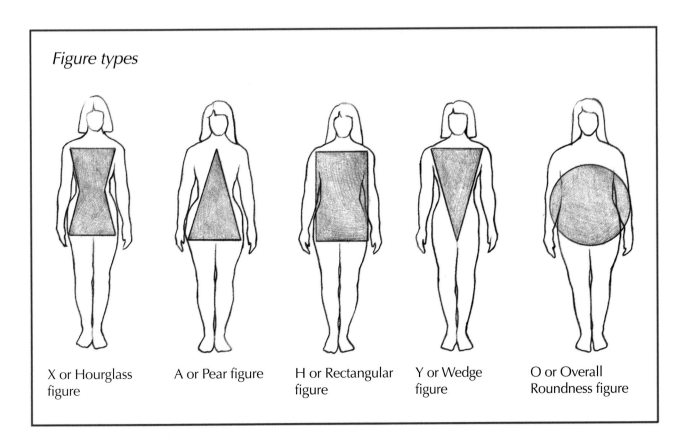

### Figure types

X or Hourglass figure

A or Pear figure

H or Rectangular figure

Y or Wedge figure

O or Overall Roundness figure

## Silhouettes and body types

Understanding your figure type will help simplify your choices in selecting styles that maximize your assets and result in fewer mistakes and greater confidence. The following guidelines describe figure types and the styles of tops best suited to each (see the illustration on p. 5). If you have a hard time deciding, work with a friend. It is easier to visualize for another than yourself.

**A or Pear figure**  The shoulders appear narrow and the bust and waist are small in proportion to the hips and thighs. If you are pear shaped, and the majority of women are, create fullness and width above the waist while minimizing hips and thighs.

- Look for tops with wide or extended shoulders, straight-line tops with shoulder pads, and upper-body details like pleats or tucks, and wide or scoop necklines.
- Allow the length to be above or below the fullest part of the hips.
- Look for lightly fitted tops that end at the high hip.
- Avoid tank tops, raglan sleeves, and design details that draw the eye downward.
- Avoid horizontal details at the hipline.

**H or Rectangular figure**  The rectangular figure is angular, with few curves and no defined waist.

The hips and shoulders are about the same, the silhouette is straight up and down, and there is little difference between the waist and hip. Many fashion models fall into this category, and much ready-to-wear clothing is produced with this figure in mind.

- Look for set-in and dolman sleeves, extended shoulders, tank tops, and raglan sleeves.
- Wear semifitted styles to create the illusion of a waist.
- Find long tunics, over blouses, and tops with center-front seaming.
- Avoid boxy or square shapes.

**X or Hourglass figure**  Hips and shoulders are about the same width with a defined waist, and full bust and hips. The "drop," or difference, between bust and hip is from about 10 in. to 12 in. If an hourglass is slender, she can wear most styles. If full figured, she should seek out straight lines that minimize curves.

- Make fitting easy with princess and vertical seaming, which also divide the figure in a pleasing way.
- Look for set-in sleeves, extended shoulders, and dolman sleeves.
- Choose tunic tops, semifitted styles, and wrap details to flatter the figure.
- Use darts to make most tops fit and look better, which also eliminate excess fabric.

- Use soft fabrics with drape over the bust. Crisp, heavy, or textured fabrics can add bulk.
- Avoid tight tops, pockets, or horizontal seams at the bust. Watch for pocket placement at the bust.

**Y or Wedge figure**  The wedge figure, or inverted triangle, is wide in the shoulders, full-busted, and narrow in the hips. The upper arm may be heavy. Some women develop this figure as they age.

- Look for raglan and dolman sleeves, extended shoulders, and cap sleeves.
- Choose loose-fitting, fluid tops, long tunics, and straight, simple architectural lines. Diagonal seaming and asymmetrical details that divide the upper torso are visually pleasing.
- Avoid tops with horizontal lines, patch pockets, or oversized sleeves.

**O or Overall Roundness figure**  Often a mature figure, an O has a full upper body, wide waist and hips, and a prominent tummy.

- Elongate and visually slim down this figure with a relaxed fit in styles that are hip length or longer.
- Choose straight lines and angles to contrast with the round figure, and direct attention to the face.

- Create a vertical effect with tunics that hang straight, with two-layer twin sets, and with center seams.
- Camouflage rounded shoulders and arms with small, angular shoulder pads.
- Use gabardines, silk linens, rayons, and crepes. They are light- to mid-weight fabrics with flat to medium textures and have some drape. Stripes and small-scale prints also work well.
- Avoid tight styles, heavy or textured fabrics, horizontal lines, and patch pockets.

## Necklines and face shapes

Principles of contrast and repetition work well in choosing the necklines on the tops you sew. Repetition exaggerates and contrast softens the effect. If your face or figure is round, then using round necklines can emphasize that roundness. If your face is angular, V necklines will make it appear more so. By placing a round neck next to an angular face, or a V neck next to a round face, you'll discover that the contrast minimizes those characteristics (see the photos on p. 8).

The following exercise is fun to do with a friend; I teach this to help students develop an eye for their own best necklines: Using plain-colored, scrap fabric, cut out shapes (cut freehand or use pattern necklines as a guide) in jewel, scoop, V, and square

*Notice how Cherilyn's angular features are emphasized by the V neck (left photo) and are softened by a round neck (right photo). Ellen's round features appear more so with a round neck (left photo), but the openness and the shape of the V are subtly flattering for her (right photo).*

necklines. Hold the various shapes against your figure, raising and lowering the neck and noting which shape and proportion is best for you.

# Marriage of Pattern and Fabric

Mystics search for the meaning of life, romantics search for true love, and sewers are ever on the hunt for the perfect combo of pattern, fabric, and themselves. The right blend of pattern and fabric is a creative challenge to the designer in every sewer, and lies within every sewing project. In the ready-to-wear industry, a designer will try a garment in several fabrics before selecting the best one to put into the line, and to determine techniques and the order of construction. For home sewers, there is one chance to put all the elements together

into one garment. That makes you the designer, fitter, sample maker, presser, and finisher all in one. Even if you paid attention in sewing class, have read the suggestions on the pattern envelope, and have some sewing experience, there is always the possibility of something running amok: The fabric is too stiff, too flimsy, wrinkles easily, makes me feel fat, doesn't go with anything else; the litany goes on.

When selecting a pattern, consider how to simplify, customize, or change it to be completely your own. Ignore the color or fabric used on the pattern envelope, looking at it in black and white. Scrutinize the technical sketches on the envelope and in the guide sheet.

Listen to your inner voice: Pay attention to your instinctive reaction to a piece of fabric or pattern. It is better to recognize a potential problem before you get into a project. Some of your most important decisions are made in the fabric store. As fabrics get more costly and time more scarce and precious, it is crucial to make clear decisions. Play with the fabric. When you find one to consider, take the bolt to the mirror and unfurl a length that simulates the garment you want to make. For tops, work with one layer, draping the cloth over your shoulder to visualize it as a completed garment. If there is any shred of evidence that it is too crisp, it probably is, and no amount of washing will soften it. One of my criteria for drape is that I want to see the curve of the body beneath the fabric. Crush it to see if it wrinkles, and poke your thumb into it to see if it stretches and recovers. Stand back a few feet from the mirror and squint. Does the color change, get muddy, or does it light up your face?

I do not believe in the axiom "She who dies with the most fabric wins." Be discriminating about the fabrics you purchase so you can enjoy sewing and appreciate wearing every garment you make. A mountain of unused fabric can be overwhelming rather than inspiring.

I frequently buy a ⅛-yard sample to take home to check with my wardrobe and shoes, hanging it in the closet and visualizing to see if it were already made into a garment how often I would wear it. Next I cut the sample into pieces, testing laundering, fusing, and seams. Sometimes just having ⅛ yard is enough and keeps me from making more costly mistakes. I collect swatches and keep them from one season to the next to help see what I should have made and did not.

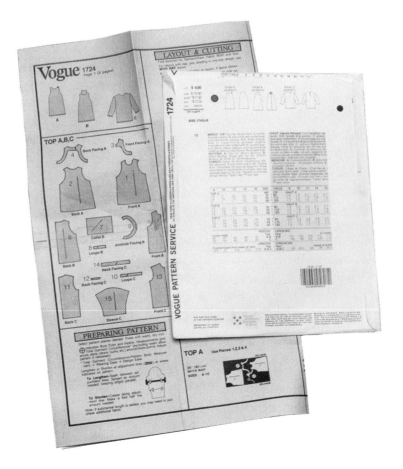

*The line drawings and pattern shapes show silhouette, scale, and details. In this instance note the bias collar, all-in-one facings, and flat cap on the sleeve.*

Which Top to Make?    9

# 2 Selecting the Pattern

Choose your pattern based on your skills, your wardrobe, and your figure, but most of all what you love. Patterns labeled "easy to sew" may have fewer pattern pieces and are theoretically easier to make, but they might lack the style or fit of a similar style with more complex seams or techniques that suit you better. Look for patterns with the intent to make more than one garment from the same style. The first time I work with a pattern, I discover many possibilities for the next version. Build your skills gradually, adding new techniques and fitting expertise with each garment. For example, once you have made a simple shell with a faced neck and 1-in., machine-stitched hem in linen, you might want to try the same pattern in silk broadcloth with a bound neckline, French seams, and a ¼-in., narrow, rolled, machine-sewn hem. Then you'll be ready to try changing the neckline, cutting it on the bias, or adding a piped edge. I usually have a half dozen or more projects in the works at one time—a blend of challenging and simple garments—so if I'm stuck or stale or bored with one thing, I can move to another.

## Hard vs. Easy Tops

The design, details, cut, and fit of a pattern design and choice of fabric combine to contribute to the degree of difficulty and amount of time it will take to complete the top. Garments that are fitted take more time and skill than loosely fitted styles. Construction details like neck finishes, closures, vents, and buttonholes add to the complexity of a garment. For instance, a facing is easier to apply than bias binding, and a single-bias binding is easier to execute than double bias. A dropped-shoulder sleeve is easier than a set-in sleeve, and loops are simpler to make than buttonholes.

*This garment illustrated in each of these patterns is called a sloper, used by patternmakers to draft patterns, and it is used by sewers for fitting. In theory, if you adjust the sloper to fit and make the same changes on the pattern, it should fit as the designer intended.*

# About the Pattern Companies

As you gain sewing experience, you'll want to use patterns from all sources, ranging from well-known, large American companies to European ones and to the growing selection of U.S. small-studio companies. When I was learning to sew, I can remember wondering if I would *ever* feel confident enough to tackle "designer" patterns… and I can also remember the thrill when I realized that I could sew any pattern in the book!

## Slopers

Each pattern company has its own sloper, which accounts for the variances in fit. A sloper is a fitted garment with darts, defined waist, and set-in sleeves, that is used as a map from which all patterns in the pattern book are drafted. For instance, all Vogue patterns are drafted from the Vogue sloper, and all McCall's patterns are drafted from the McCall's sloper. American pattern companies allow more ease (the difference between your measurement and the pattern) in their patterns than do their European and small-studio counterparts, so I use a different method to determine size for Butterick, McCall's, Simplicity, and Vogue than for Burda, Neue Mode, Style, New Look, and studio patterns.

American companies use standardized measurements in creating their patterns, yet each company has its own distinct fit, look, and customer. All the patterns in their pattern books are drafted using the size 10 sloper and are graded (made larger or smaller) from it.

## Determining your pattern size

In U. S. patterns, use the high-bust measurement to determine pattern size. To take a high-bust measurement, measure under the arms, over the chest, and above the bustline. This method is used to determine the size pattern you will start with, and will correspond to the bust measurement in the pattern. For instance, if your high-bust measures 32 in. yet your full bust is 35 in., you'll use a size 10 pattern, which shows the full-bust measurement as 32 in. The high-bust measurement is used because American patterns tend to run large in this area. The upper chest is difficult to alter, and if it doesn't fit, the garment will look out of proportion. If you are between sizes, buy the larger size if you are large boned and the smaller size if you are small boned. The width you need to have the garment fit around your body can be easily added at the side seams, as discussed on pp. 36-37.

Determine your size for European companies and American small-studio companies by using your true body measurements. For most people this means you'll use more than one size. If you measure a 36-in. bust, 29-in. waist, and 43-in. hip, you'll follow the cutting lines indicated for each of those measurements, blending the lines from one size to another.

# Measurements for Sewing Tops

The six essential measurements you'll need for sewing tops are: high bust, full bust, waist, hip, finished length, and bicep. The first step in personalizing your pattern is to take a set of your body measurements and then compare your measurements with the pattern; see the charts on pp. 30-31. Take measurements wearing undergarments you'll wear with your top for an accurate fit.

1. Tie a narrow, ¼-in. piece of elastic to mark your waist. Measure the high bust as described on the facing page (see the top left photo above).

*Use the high-bust measurement to determine pattern size with American patterns.*

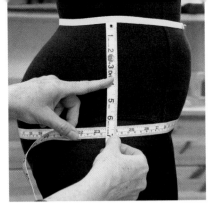

*Measure the hip at the fullest point, then measure how far down from the waist.*

2. Measure the bust at the fullest part.
3. Measure the waist at the elastic.
4. Measure the hip at the fullest part, then measure how far down this point is from the waist (see the top right photo).
5. Finally, measure the biceps at the fullest part; this is usually at the underarm (see the photo at right).

# Selecting a Pattern for Knits

As with regular tops discussed in Chapter 1, begin with a pattern whose basic measurements and details are right for you. Examine the pattern for shape of the body, the ease across bust and hip, length, neck shape and width, depth of armhole, and shoulder width. If you have a favorite garment in your wardrobe, use it as a guide, or go shopping and try on a variety of knit tops. Assume that any pattern you choose will be changed and customized to get the fit and effect you want.

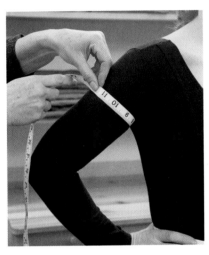

*Measure the bicep at the fullest part, usually at the underarm.*

A word about knits-only patterns: You can use a pattern designed for a woven fabric with a knit, but do not use a woven fabric for a knits-only pattern. Knit patterns have a stretch guide on the pattern envelope to show how much a knit should stretch for that design. Some knit patterns are designed to use the stretch of the knit for fit, like a body suit or snug top. The pattern measurement is smaller than the body and uses the stretch for fit.

# 3 | *Working with Fabrics*

Making the best fabric choices for your sewing level is a skill just as important as learning to sew a straight seam. Some fabrics are a pleasure to sew and press, responding to your touch and resulting in exactly what you want. Napped fabrics, slippery fabrics, and plaids and designs that require matching take more time and skill.

## Easy vs. Challenging Fabrics

An easy-to-sew fabric is stable: It does not shift when cutting or sewing, and it has a quality called "tooth," which means that the fabric has a tendency to stick to itself and stay where you pin it. I find natural fibers easier to handle and more pleasurable to work with than synthetics. Foolproof fabrics for tops are usually natural fibers that are slightly crisp yet not stiff, such as mid-weight linen, shirting cotton, Liberty cotton, silk noil, silk broadcloth, jacquard, wool challis, wool double knit, wool jersey, and Austrian cotton knits.

What makes a fabric hard to sew? Challenging fabrics take more time and require more experience and skill in cutting, sewing, pressing, and handling. Drapey or sheer fabrics may shift while cutting and sewing, and require stabilizing. Plaids require mindful placement, one-layer cutting, and care in stitching so the plaids match. Though ethnic hand-woven fabrics make beautiful tops, matching plaids and stripes can be tricky because they are often woven unevenly. Beware of printed plaids and stripes; they are rarely printed on grain, so they are impossible to match and are a sure source of frustration. Velvet must be cut in a one-way direction, the pile shifts when sewing so seams must be hand-basted, and it requires special pressing tools and techniques. Synthetic silkies, microfibers, and sheers shift, pucker, and demand even more expertise in pressing and stitching than their natural-fiber counterparts. Wool gabardine and men's-wear worsteds need an experienced hand with pressing and precise topstitching.

*Foolproof fabrics are crisp, but not stiff, with a pattern or texture that makes it hard to spot mistakes.*

The surest formula for success for beginners is to start with a crisp fabric you know you can work with easily, like cotton shirting or linen, and an uncomplicated pattern design for the first garment. Gradually move on to making similar patterns in rayon challis or silk broadcloth. As skills and confidence develop, move up to slippery, fluid fabrics like silk crepe de chine or charmeuse, and last, to the final frontier of challenging fabrics like georgette and chiffon. The following list will help you decide which fabric to start with.

## Easiest fabrics

The easiest fabrics are a natural fiber, in a mid-weight, and slightly crisp with some pattern or texture that camouflages glitches and are a pleasure to press and sew.

**Linen** This fabric is most often cited by experts as being user-friendly. It is crisp, comes in a wide range of weights, the wrinkles hide mistakes, and it gets better with age. But linen can be stiff and add bulk, so choosing the right weight and quality is important. Also blending linen with silk and rayon adds drape.

**Cotton** Shirting cottons like those made by Liberty of London are light but crisp and easy to sew, and are perfect for tops. Search out cottons that do not wrinkle easily.

**Wool** Wool double knits are a snap to sew. They do not ravel and don't stretch out of shape.

## Easier-to-sew fabrics

The variety of fabrics in this category require a little more skill.

**Cotton** Austrian cotton knits are stable double knits. Other good choices include fleece and brushed denim.

**Silk** Cotton-like silks such as silk noil, raw silk, silk broadcloth, and silk and linen blends work well.

**Wool** Wool challis, wool jersey, and wool crepe are good, but not all wool crepe is created equal. This generic category can refer to light, fluid, drapey fabrics and heavier weights better for jackets or pants than tops.

## Challenging fabrics

Once you've mastered the fabrics above, you can move on to more demanding ones.

**Silk** The more slippery, silky, and sheer the fabric, the more expertise you need. Look for silk crepe, silk charmeuse, jacquard, silk velvet, chiffon, and georgette.

**Wool** Wool gabardine and men's-wear worsteds are called "hard finish" wools, which means that they are firmly woven with a flat surface and take skill in pressing and topstitching because mistakes show easily.

**Synthetic silkies and microfibers**
These fabrics are tightly woven so they slip and shift as you cut. The seams pucker as you sew, so they need careful pressing and precise topstitching.

I confess to a fondness for soft, drapey fabrics, and recognize that they take more skill and experience to sew with. The bottom line is experience: Cut your teeth on easy-to-work-with fabrics, and gradually work up to the more challenging ones. I learned to work on challenging fabrics by making mistakes and by taking lots of time, patience, paying attention to grain, and hand-basting whenever the fabric seemed to be getting away from me.

Test each fabric you use, and keep a record of what worked for your future reference. I keep a notebook of ideas gleaned from examining ready-made garments. I have made T-shirts from cotton, wool, velour, cashmere, panne velvet, Lycra blends, and fleece, and these are among my favorite garments.

## Choosing Knits

The word "T-shirt" might conjure up images of white-cotton men's underwear, but the customized couture version you

*Challenging fabrics that shift in cutting and sewing require experienced handling and take more time and patience to get professional results.*

can sew has its roots in fine ready-to-wear, where a price tag of $200 and up isn't uncommon. If a T-shirt is well made and beautifully shaped, it can be the glue that holds your wardrobe together and worn just as easily with a suit as with jeans. When you sew your own versatile T-shirts, you can refine the fit, alter necklines and shaping to flatter your figure, use beautiful fabrics, and add fine details. If you make a few T-shirts each season, you'll have a collection of tops and tuned-up patterns to use and wear again and again.

To sew a knit top that looks like fine ready-to-wear, seek out good-quality knit fabrics. Since knits don't have much appeal on the bolt, keep an eye out for fine or unusual ones. They're among

*Knits may appear "flat" on the bolt, but they come alive when worn. I look for interesting textures and colors in every fabric opportunity.*

Wool jersey is not washable. I always preshrink white, cream, or ivory wool knits at the dry-cleaners because they have never been dyed and may shrink at an alarming rate in pressing during construction.

the few fabrics I stockpile. I've made T-shirts from many knit fabrics, including wool jersey, Austrian cotton knits, velour, cashmere, Lycra blends, stretch velvet, linen, and fleece. I look for knits with good recovery and drape, and appealing color, feel, and texture. I love Lycra blended with any other fiber (especially cotton, linen, wool, or rayon) because it improves the drape and adds stability along with stretch. Cotton interlock is one of the most readily available natural-fiber knits, but is not a great favorite of mine. It takes more fussing during construction, doesn't have good recovery, doesn't take well to pressing and shaping, and doesn't wear well. My interlock T-shirts usually last only one season. Wool jersey has good drape, comes in beautiful colors, is easy to sew, and translates well into many designs. Donna Karan has said that if she had to choose only

one fabric to work with, it would be wool jersey. It is dry-clean only, so be sure to send it to the cleaner's for preshrinking before sewing. If you machine-wash wool jersey, it shrinks down to a thick, felted, soft fabric that can be used for embellishment, or warm jackets or vests. Look for knit stripes to use as bindings and accents.

# Interfacing Guidelines

Interfacing is an in-between, extra layer that is used to add stability to edges and openings, and to control stretch. In tops and T-shirts, you'll use interfacing to reinforce beneath buttons and buttonholes, on facings, collars, and occasionally in hems. Interfacing should be the same weight or lighter than the outer fabric, and never visible or obvious from the right side. You may purchase interfacings specifically designed for this purpose, use self-fabric, or choose a fabric not necessarily intended for interfacing.

## *Available types*

There are so many kinds of commercial interfacings available, it can be confusing to choose. The market for over-the-counter interfacings designed especially for the home-sewing market is always changing, and products come and go under different names. Interfacings are categorized in two ways: the construction of the fabric (woven, nonwoven, knit, weft) and by how they are applied (sew-in and fusible). Sew-in interfacings may be woven or nonwoven and are machine- or hand-basted into the seam allowance, then caught into the seam itself. Fusibles have a resin or glue on one side that bonds the interfacing to the outer layer with a combination of heat, moisture, and pressure. The resin will add varying amounts of body or stiffness to the outer fabric, depending on how much resin there is on it. All four varieties—wovens, nonwovens, knits, and weft—are available as sew-ins and as fusibles.

***Fusible or sew-in?*** Unsure of whether to use a fusible or sew-in interfacing? Here are a few pros and cons of each. Fusibles have been developed and perfected by the ready-to-wear clothing industry and are quick and easy to apply. They work best with porous fabrics that allow the heat and steam to permeate the resin, melt it, and bond the interfacing to the outer layer. If your ironing board cover is made of Teflon, you may have problems because the surface does not absorb the steam, and the Teflon bounces the steam back, creating air bubbles. The same thing can happen with nonporous fabrics like gabardines or firmly woven fabrics. When considering a fusible, examine the amount of resin on the fabric. If the

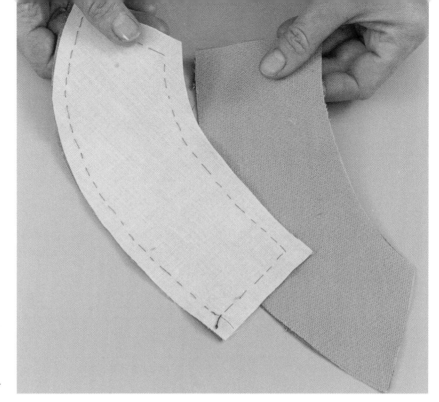

*Hand-basting a sew-in interfacing gives control and a fine finish.*

bonding agent is thick or obvious, the interfacing may be too heavy. If the fusible has not been preshrunk, it may shrink as it is being applied, causing air bubbles. However, if the right fusible is chosen and applied correctly, it is quick and easy: It stabilizes the area, keeps it flat, and prevents stretching or raveling. Sew-in interfacings, on the other hand, are the purist's choice. It takes more time and care to use a sew-in and to keep the layers smooth. I often find commercial sew-in interfacings too stiff, and prefer to use cotton batiste, silk organza, soft-washed muslin, or self-fabric.

***My preferred interfacings*** In my studio, I've narrowed down the field to a few favorites, though I am always eager to test new

| Interfacing | Type | Works with | Attributes |
|---|---|---|---|
| Fuse Knit* | Fusible knit | Mid-weight fabrics | Stable on lengthwise grain such as linen. |
| Sof Knit* | All-bias (stretch in all directions) | Crepes, light knits silk, rayon | Good for a soft and drapey effect. |
| So Sheer* | Fusible knit | Crisp, light fabrics like handkerchief linen | Very sheer; structure and resin adds crispness; stable on lengthwise grain. |
| Sof Brush* | Fusible knit | Microfibers | Termed "cool fuse," a signal to use cooler iron temperatures than other interfacings; stable on lengthwise grain. Called a weft insertion, which is a knit with a thread woven in on the weft, making it more stable than a knit and more supple than a woven. |
| Soft Shape** | Nonwoven all-bias (stretch in all directions) | Velours, velvet, velveteen | Melts into outer fabric without adding thickness or stiffness. |

\* Manufactured by HTC.
\*\* Manufactured by Pellon.

If you are using a light or soft fabric, you want a light, drapey interfacing. Stability is important behind zippers and buttonholes. Use the non-stretchy, stable direction parallel to the buttonhole or zipper.

products. I use fusible interfacings for most projects. The characteristics I look for in an interfacing are drape and stability. I like the interfacings listed in the chart above because they are light, fluid, and do not make the fabric too stiff. The bonding agent melts into the fabric and blends with it, not making it "more." I stockpile in 5-yard to 10-yard cuts and buy my three favorites by the bolt in black and natural. White interfacing shows through light and dark colors easily, so I rarely use it.

The interfacings I use most often are: Fuse Knit, (the generic term is fusible tricot), Sof Knit, So Sheer, Sof Brush (all manufactured by HTC), and Soft Shape by Pellon. Fuse Knit, Sof

Brush, and So Sheer are fusible-knit interfacings that are stable on the lengthwise grain. Sof Knit and Soft Shape are "all bias," which means they stretch in all directions. Fuse Knit is perfect for mid-weight fabrics such as linen. It is stable on the lengthwise grain, so when adding behind buttonholes or zippers, you should position the stable direction in the same direction as the buttonholes. So Sheer is a very sheer fusible tricot that appears light but the large amount of resin adds crispness. I use it behind buttonholes and zippers or with crisp, light fabrics like handkerchief linen. Sof Knit is the interfacing I reach for when I am working with crepes, light knits, silk, or rayon, and when I want something soft and drapey. Sof Shape is a nonwoven all-bias fusible that melts into the outer fabric without adding thickness or stiffness. It is perfect for velours, velvet, and velveteen. Sof Brush was designed to be used with micro-fibers, a recent breed of very-fine man-made fabrics. It is termed "cool fuse," a signal to use a cooler iron temperature than for the other interfacings. It is a weft insertion, which is a knit with a thread woven in on the weft, making it more stable than a knit and more supple than a woven.

***Using fashion fabric as interfacing*** Sometimes I use alternatives to a purchased interfacing such as a layer of fashion fabric, cotton batiste, or washed muslin. Silk or polyester organza are good options for sheers. Use polyester organza if you want a crisp effect. Silk organza is best hand-washed before using. Hand-washing removes the sizing and makes it softer, which will happen over time anyway, so you can see if the weight of interfacing and garment are compatible.

## Interfacing knits

As a rule, interfacings do not play a major role with knits, but two are indispensable in my studio for unconventional reasons. Sof Knit is a very soft, all-bias, knit-fusible interfacing. I apply a narrow strip in hems on knit tops to prevent rippling.

Fusible tricot, which stretches in the crosswise and is stable lengthwise, is perfect for stabilizing openings or behind buttonholes. Always test compatibility on a scrap. Clear elastic is perfect for stabilizing shoulder seams.

## Pretreating interfacing

All interfacings will shrink, so preshrink everything before you apply or you run the risk of having the layers of fabric shrink or form bubbles on the surface that are nearly impossible to fix. Pretreat all interfacings—fusibles, nonfusibles, wovens, and nonwovens—in the same way. Hand-wash by dipping the folded interfacing in hot tap water for 10 minutes. Hang to air-dry. I usually "steam shrink" small pieces of fusible interfacing just before fusing by holding an iron 1 in. above it and giving it a shot of steam.

## Applying interfacing

Applying fusible and sew-in interfacings are a snap if you follow these easy directions.

***Fusible interfacing*** Follow temperature, steam, and timing instructions on the plastic interleaving instruction sheet sold with your interfacing. Cut the interfacing the same size and on the same grain as your fabric. At the ironing board, position the fabric wrong side up, and place the interfacing with resin

There is a vast world of interfacings made for the clothing industry that never makes its way into fabric stores. If you live near or visit areas that have a garment industry, you may find useful interfacings from designers, jobbers, and fabric vendors selling overruns.

# TESTING INTERFACING

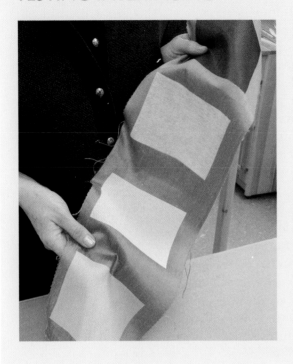

The key to success with any interfacing is to test it with your fabric scraps after cutting out the garment. Test more than one kind of interfacing to see which works best. Use a large enough sample of interfacing to get an accurate reading of its performance. Can you see a ridge where the interfacing ends from the right side? Test for drapability, thickness, stability, and appearance. If you can't tell the difference between two interfacings, then it probably does not make a difference which one you use.

*Test all the interfacings you are considering, leaving space between to check for weight and to see the results from the right side.*

I do not recommend trimming away the seam allowances on fusible interfacing as is sometimes advised. The uninterfaced seam allowance can cause a wavy distortion along the edge.

side down. If fusing a number of small pieces, line them up on the ironing board and fuse at the same time. Spray lightly with water, cover with a see-through press cloth, and press, using an up-and-down (not a back-and-forth) motion, keeping the iron in place 10 full seconds. If fusing a long or large piece, begin in the center and work outward to keep the pieces from stretching or shifting. Turn the pieces over, and press from the right side to melt any residual glue. Trim any interfacing that peeks over the edge. When fusing, I keep a

piece of washed muslin on the ironing board to keep the cover fresh.

***Sew-in interfacing*** Cut interfacing the same size and grain as your fabric. If the fabric and interfacing are stable, machine-baste around all edges just inside the seamline. If your fabrics are slippery or stretchy, hand-baste with one strand of thread, using a running stitch just inside the seamline. Trim the interfacing close to the stitching. Press.

# Preparing the Fabric

Be consistent about preparing all fabric as you buy it. I pretreat all fabrics as I purchase them so everything in my collection is ready to sew.

## Prewashing the fabric

Prewashing not only shrinks the fabric but removes sizing or finishes. One of my favorite fabric stores, Fabric Temptations, in Arcata, California, prewashes a sample of all its fabrics, and attaches it to every bolt with information about shrinkage. Some fabrics such as wools, linen, silks, and blends get more interest and character with washing. If you are not sure whether to toss the entire piece of fabric in the washer and dryer, cut off ⅛ yard, then cut that strip into three pieces. If the fabric ravels, serge the edges. Hand-launder and line-dry one piece; machine-wash and line-dry the second; machine-wash and machine-dry the third; then compare the results. I hand-wash and air-dry my handmade clothes because they look fresh longer (the action of machines wears them out more quickly than I do), but machine-wash and dry most fabrics before cutting out the pattern. If the fabric is going into my stash, I smooth out the wrinkles and fold it away.

The washer and dryer also age knits more rapidly than wearing. I recommend hand-washing, air-drying, and touch-up pressing for handmade T-shirts. Use stain remover and an occasional wash on the delicate cycle for tough spots, but avoid the dryer if possible. Machine-wash velours and stretch velvets on gentle, air-dry until barely damp, then toss in the dryer to remove wrinkles.

Prepare a washed-and-dried piece of fabric for cutting by finding the crosswise grain. Tear across the fabric if it allows, or pull a crosswise thread, cutting along the thread from selvage to selvage. Press one layer of the fabric on the wrong side. This takes a bit of juggling at the ironing board. Spread out a sheet on the floor to keep the fabric draping over the ironing board clean. Take a bit of extra time at this stage to get familiar with the fabric. Spray-mist it as you press if necessary. Hang the fabric on a padded hanger if you will not be cutting immediately.

## Truing the grain

Grain. Grain. Grain. Getting your fabric squared and true so the woven threads are lined up and at right angles to each other is one of the most basic and important elements in creating great clothes.

After a linen, cotton, or silk top is laundered, hang it dripping wet on a shaped hanger, pulling the seams flat and hems taut. Let the garment air-dry and wear as is, or press from the wrong side, touching it up on the right side while it's slightly damp.

Consider trying this option on ready-to-wear: Do the shrinking *after* the garment is constructed for a prewashed look. Cut your top one to two sizes larger than your size and 1 in. to 2 in. longer. After construction is complete, machine-wash and dry. This technique works well with linens, which get soft and evenly wrinkled and really do not need ironing afterward.

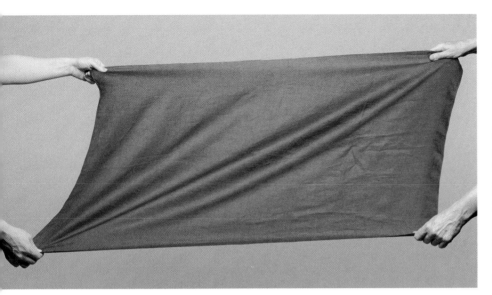

*When a fabric is off grain, realign the threads by pulling on the bias to straighten it.*

# Laying Out and Cutting the Fabric

In the clothing industry, cutters are among the most highly paid because the layout of the pattern pieces determines how much fabric is used. Many small designers insist on doing their own cutting even if others do the actual sewing. Cutting is a crucial and creative part of the sewing process, so do it at a time when you feel relaxed and alert. I am consistent about cutting with right sides together to protect the fabric and to make transferring markings easy. I usually consult the pattern-cutting guidelines, but I use my common sense in arranging the pattern pieces. I like to get all the pieces positioned, then pin in place on the straight of grain. It's best to position the large pieces first, filling in with the smaller ones. When I'm laying out many pieces on a length of fabric, I position the large pieces, rolling up the fabric length as I go to be sure everything fits, then go back and pin everything in place.

A cutting mat is handy, but you can use the edge of a table to line up the selvages and crossgrain. Fold the fabric in half lengthwise, right sides together, and check to see if the corners match up evenly. If the edges refuse to square up, the fabric is "off grain." If a fabric is off grain by more than an inch or two, it is necessary to coax it back into alignment. Often fabric is torqued as it is rolled onto the bolt, and straightening it is a simple process. If you have someone to assist you, one person pulls on the corner at the short side, and the other pulls on the bias (see the photo above). Continue gently tugging every foot or so along the length of the cloth. If you are alone, take the fabric to the ironing board and press along the bias to correct the off-grain alignment. Touch-up pressing may be necessary after straightening.

## Laying out wovens

Place each pattern piece precisely on the straight of grain. Eyeball the grainline on each pattern piece so it looks parallel with the fold or selvage, and pin at one end. Measure the distance from the grainline to the edge. Then pin the other end of the grainline exactly the same distance from the edge so the pattern grainline is parallel with the edge of the fabric (see the photo at right). If the piece is cut along a fold, turn under the pattern tissue along the foldline and then line it up along the fabric fold. With stable fabrics like linen, I use a combination of a few pins and pattern weights to hold the pattern in place, then cut with a rotary cutter, which I find quicker and more accurate than shears.

Cutting with a layer of paper beneath the fabric makes working with slippery, moving, or unstable fabrics much easier. When I learned this technique from Margaret Islander, an industrial techniques expert, I felt instantly more confident about using challenging fabrics. Use this method for cutting silks, silkies, sheers, and bias. The paper can be newsprint, medical examining-table paper, or patternmaking paper. It must be the same width as your fabric or wider, so tape widths together as needed. Square off the ends of the paper so you can line up lengthwise and crossgrain with the paper's edge. In this case, use pins, not weights, pinning the pattern through both the fabric and the layer of paper. The paper helps stabilize the fabric, so once cut, leave the pieces pinned to the paper until you are ready to sew.

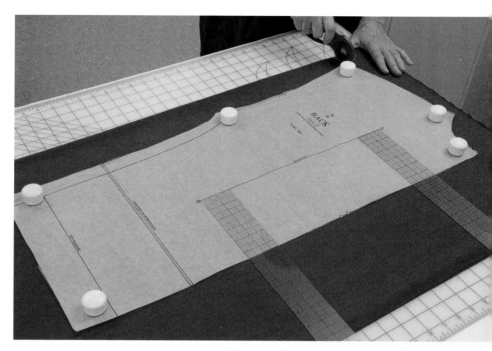

*Place each pattern piece precisely on the grain before cutting.*

## Laying out knits

Knit garments are usually cut on the lengthwise grain (follow a rib of the knit as a grainline), but you may occasionally prefer a fabric's design or stripe on the crossgrain, which is fine if the fabric has enough stretch going around the body. Since many knits have a subtle directional shading (they're knitted from one end to the other), use a "with nap" layout whenever possible. Mark the center front and back with tiny snips, and mark the wrong side and notches with a chalk pencil (see the photo at right).

*Mark center front and back neck with a tiny snip.*

*Use chalk, a chalk marker, a dressmaker's pencil, or tracing paper to transfer markings to the wrong side of the fabric.*

# Marking Your Fabric

I often use a combination of marking techniques on one garment, always choosing the simplest and the most accurate for the fabric and pattern. Transfer markings as soon as cutting is complete.

## Tools and techniques for marking

Use the following tools to mark the wrong side of the fabric only.

- Chalk wheel: This makes a thin, fine line of chalk, and is good for marking darts and stitching lines. One of my most used sewing tools, I keep it handy in several colors.
- Chalk: This is available in small squares in a few colors and in white, and also available in pencil form, called dressmaker's pencils. You'll want both varieties. Use the squares to indicate the wrong side of a fabric. Use the pencils to make a small, precise dot. If you are using a serger to finish seams before construction, mark notches with chalk on the wrong side.
- Tracing paper and tracing wheel: This works best with plain, not light, colors and flat textures. This is the marking tool I use the least often, but

when I do use it, I prefer Saral and Clover paper because the colors stand out without bleeding through to the right side.

Use the following tools when you want to mark the right side of your fabric:

- Clo-chalk: This disappears when ironed or washed or within 24 hours. I love this tool for marking precise topstitching.
- Tailor's tacks: These are the purist's way to mark. Once you try this quick technique, you'll find it is the most reliable way to transfer markings. Use four strands of embroidery floss in a contrasting color and thread it through a chenille needle, which has a large eye and sharp point. Take a small stitch through the pattern and both layers of fabric, leaving ½-in. tails. Separate the fabric and snip the threads (see the photo at right). The thickness of the thread holds it in place so you can see the markings from both sides.
- Air/water-erasable pens: Designed to disappear when wet or over time, these felt-tipped pens come in blue and purple, which show up better on some fabrics than others. I use them to mark the positions for buttons and buttonholes. Heat will sometimes set the mark, so remove before pressing.

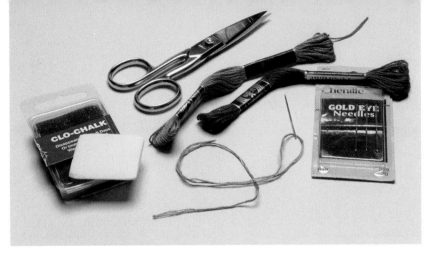

*Transfer markings to the right side of the fabric with tailor's tacks, using embroidery floss and a chenille needle, which has a large eye and a sharp point. You can also mark with Clo-chalk or by making snips.*

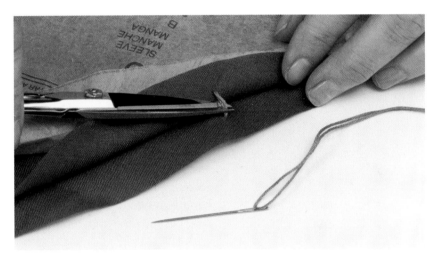

*Tailor's tacks mark both the right and wrong sides of the fabric and will stay in place until you remove them.*

- Snips: Mark centers, foldlines, and notches with ¼-in. snips in the seam. Use caution with a rotary cutter—it is easy to make too deep a cut.

It's much easier to transfer markings just after cutting, but I keep the pattern pieces tacked to a bulletin board for easy reference during construction. Use chalk and dressmaker's pencils to mark seams that will be serged.

# 4 *Fit*

Fitting is a skill you can acquire in a number of ways: in books, videos, in classes for hands-on assistance, and by trial and error in fitting yourself and others. It is an art as well as a skill, and is a fun and creative part of making clothes. Go slowly, adding understanding and skill with each project. Keep a current set of measurements (taken every six months), and make accurate records of changes or problems; you can use the worksheet I have provided on p. 31 or write directly on the pattern tissue. I also keep notes on the back of the pattern envelope, marking the date and any fitting or design changes I made before and during construction.

With your measurements and pattern in hand, it is now time to personalize your pattern to fit you. Fitting is done in stages—if you correct the most obvious problems, you may eliminate minor ones: Lengthen or shorten first, then add enough width so the pattern is long enough and wide enough to fit around you. Add width at the side seams, instead of at the center front or back, to keep neck and design details intact. Once those adjustments are made, you'll do a "tissue fitting" by pinning the main pattern pieces together so you can try it on as if it were a garment. Tissue fitting is a crucial part of the fit and design process because it gives a good idea of the way the garment will fit, and how the design and details look on your figure. After tissue fitting, you'll make pattern alterations and retry the tissue until you have the result you want. I often make pattern changes over a few days to think through the design process. Fitting continues as you sew the garment together, so you can fine-tune fit and styling at every step.

## Proofing the Pattern

Proofing the pattern means making all necessary adjustments to your pattern tissue based on your measurements as they compare to the pattern. Compare your measurements with the pattern, using the

# SAMPLE SET OF MEASUREMENTS

| Measurement | Size 10 Pattern Measurement | You | Ease | Flat Pattern Measurement | Adjustment (+/−) | My Total |
|---|---|---|---|---|---|---|
| High bust | 32½ in. | 33 | 0 | NA | NA | NA |
| Bust | 34½ in. | 38 | 2 in. | 34½ | +6½ | (40) |
| Waist | 25 in. | 29 | 1½ in. | 26½ | +5 | 31½ |
| High hip (from waist) | 34½ in. | 36 | 2 in. | | | |
| Hip | 34½ in. | 42 | 2 in. | 37 | +7 | (44) |
| Back waist length | 16 in. | 17 | 0 | NA | +1 in. | 1 in. |
| Biceps | | 14 | 2 in. | 14 | +2 | (16) |

The high-bust measurement is used *only* to determine pattern size in U.S. patterns.

measurement chart provided in the back of the pattern book, on the pattern envelope, or on the guide sheet for the size you are using. The guide sheet, shown above, compares a sample set of measurements with a U.S. size 10 pattern using the minimum ease. The guide sheet on the facing page is for you to fill in your measurements. Use the guidelines here to help you in completing your guide sheet.

- You: Your measurements.
- Ease: Minimum wearing ease is illustrated in the chart above. You can easily figure design ease for any pattern by subtracting the measurements for the pattern size from the pattern's flat measurement in the bust, waist, hip, and biceps. For example, a size 10 top (bust: 32½ in.), measuring

34½ in. in the bust, has 2 in. of ease.
- Total: Your measurements plus ease.
- Flat Pattern Measurement: Measure your flat pattern at key areas shown in the illustration.
- Adjustment: + or - is the difference between the Total (you + ease) and the pattern measurements. Record the adjustment on the column or directly on your pattern.

## Ease

Ease is the difference between you and the pattern, and is used to create comfort and style. All patterns are designed to have "wearing ease" for comfort (the amount given in the chart above). This is the minimum the garment needs so you can move. "Design ease" is the amount

# YOUR MEASUREMENTS

| Measurement | Pattern Measurement | You | Ease | Flat-Pattern Measurement | Adjustment (+/−) | My Total |
|---|---|---|---|---|---|---|
| High bust | | | 0 in. | | | |
| Bust | | | | | | |
| Waist | | | | | | |
| High hip | | | | | | |
| Hip | | | | | | |
| Back waist length | | 0 in. | | NA | | |
| Biceps | | | | | | |

determined by the designer for the particular style and fashion cycle. Some knit patterns are designed so the finished garment is smaller than the measurements for that size. In this case, the fit is achieved by the stretch of the fabric. By comparing the key bust, waist, and hip measurements with the pattern measurements at those points, you can determine the amount of ease that has been built into the pattern and how much you need to add to or subtract from the pattern so it fits you proportionately.

Do a measurement analysis on your favorite top to see how much ease you like in the hip and bust, and what are your favorite lengths. Measure the garment at the same points (the bust, waist, and hip) as you would on the pattern. Since you are the designer, you can adapt this information to the tops you sew. Remember that the total amount of ease will be added to four seams, so if you need to add a total of 6 in. in the hip, you'll add 1½ in. at each seam. You can add up to 8 in. at the bust and chest without distorting the pattern.

## Flat-pattern measurement

Flat-pattern measurement is a process of measuring the pattern itself at the bust, biceps, waist, and hip excluding seams, darts, tucks, and pleats so you can make a comparison. Some patterns print the finished bust and hip measurements directly on the pattern.

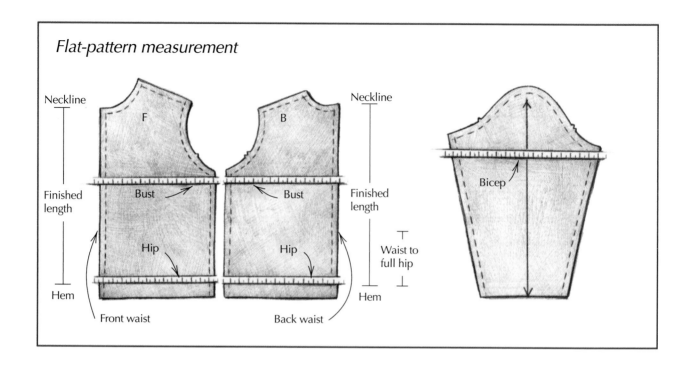

Measure the bust just below the armhole where the garment will be fullest (see the illustration above). Waist measurement is necessary only on fitted garments; in most cases the waist and high hip will be altered proportionately as the hip and bust adjustments are made. For the full hip measurement, measure the distance from your waist to your full hip, then measure the pattern the same distance from the pattern waist. The back waist is taken from the back neck point where the collar rests to the waistline. The waist is usually indicated on the back piece, and can be extended to the front by matching up the side seams and extending the line. The finished length is taken from the back neck point to the hemline.

The biceps measurement is not given on the pattern chart. You must measure the pattern piece to see how you compare. Measure seam to seam across the sleeve at the underarm. The minimum amount of ease is 2 in. at the biceps, so the pattern should measure 2 in. more than your arm so you will be able to "pinch an inch" of fabric. This is an important measurement to consider during fashion cycles that feature slim-fitting sleeves.

Sleeve length and back waist are not so easily determined by measuring. There is no exact way to use a measuring tape to compare the length of your arm with the sleeve length on a pattern. The best way to check sleeve length is in tissue fitting. Once you know how your sleeve

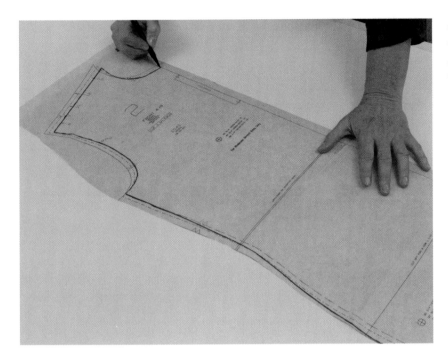

*Multisized patterns allow you to blend size lines to correspond to your measurements. Use your bust size for armhole and shoulder size.*

length differs from a pattern, make that change on all garments you sew. I have seen so many variances in the back-waist measurement that I use it as a starting point only. If you are noticeably long- or short-waisted, make the adjustment indicated by your measurements, then check both front and back while tissue fitting.

## Blending sizes

Multisized patterns have different sizes printed on the same pattern tissue. This may appear confusing at first but can be very helpful if you are one size on top and another size on the bottom. The lines allow you to see how much one size varies from another. Use a colored, felt-tipped pen to mark your pattern

on the size lines that correspond to your measurements. Blend the lines smoothly when going from one size to another. If you are one size in the bust and another in the hip, mark the pattern at those points, then use a hip curve to blend the lines.

## Tools for patternmaking

A collection of patternmaking tools makes this important part of the process easier, more accurate, and a pleasure to do. Just as a chef requires the finest knife honed to a sharp edge, I prefer the finest, professional-quality tools. Each tool has its specific use, so don't substitute one for another:

- Measuring tape that reads from both ends and both sides:

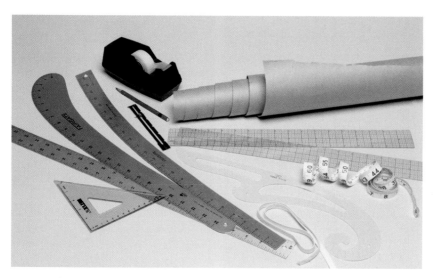

*Having the right tool for altering patterns makes the process easier and gives more professional results.*

You'll use these invaluable tools again and again to refine a roughed-in line or to soften a straight line with a light curve; I keep them close at hand because I use them every time I do pattern work. Curved patternmaking tools are helpful in making clean, curved lines, but it is rare that you'll use them in one long sweep; more commonly, you will use them in sections, moving and adjusting them to maintain the integrity and shape of the original pattern.

- French curve: Look for a dressmaker's French curve; you can also find a smaller version in art-supply stores, but it is designed for graphic arts, not patterns. I use a French curve to reshape necklines, refine sleeves, and whenever I need the transparency to create subtle shaping.
- Paper: Scrap pattern tissue or tissue paper works well. I use medical examination-table paper, which can be pressed, and has a weight compatible with pattern tissue.
- Glue stick, and regular and removable adhesive tape.
- Soft-lead pencil for marking on the pattern.

Additional tools you will need include a right-angle ruler for marking the bias, dressmaker's pencils, chalk, Clo-chalk, and a narrow elastic to mark the waist. This list will grow as you develop your own way of working.

Most measuring tapes are ⅝ in. wide.

- 6-in. gauge: The wide end is ⅝ in. wide.
- 2-in.-by-18-in. transparent ruler: This is essential for creating straight lines, finding right angles, lengthening/shortening, and more. Quilt stores are a good source for finding a variety of lengths and widths.
- Metal measuring stick: I prefer a heavy-duty one that is 1½ in. wide and 48 in. long. Once you use a metal stick, with its clean lines and straight edges, you'll never want to use a wooden one.
- Metal hip curve *and/or* metal variform curve: These professional tools look similar but perform different tasks. Use the hip curve to shape the hip and waist. The variform curve has the shape of the neck, armhole, and a different long curve than the hip curve.

# Pattern Drafting Basics

You will feel confident and enjoy making pattern alterations if you are familiar with a few simple drafting techniques. Lengthening/shortening uses techniques of making parallel lines and making a right angle. Practice making parallel lines using the transparent ruler, which is a technique you'll use again and again to lengthen and shorten, add seams and hems, and create facings and tucks. Draw a fine, straight line, using a sharp soft-lead pencil. Make a second line parallel to the first, using the grid on the ruler for accuracy. Make a right angle by aligning one of the grid lines on the original line, drawing in a second line intersecting at 90 degrees, or a right angle. Most pattern alterations are made parallel to or at right angles to the grain of the pattern piece.

## Adjusting length

Make lengthen/shorten alterations before adjusting the width so you can easily smooth the jog that occurs in the seamlines when you change the length of a garment. Lengthen/ shorten lines on a pattern are positioned to adjust the proportion for long- and short-waisted figures. If your pattern does not have a lengthen/ shorten line, you can add it. If the top has a straight silhouette, you can place that line anywhere in the body of the garment. If there is a defined waist, add or subtract above the waist if you are making this adjustment for a long or short waist. You may want to lengthen or shorten a garment to change the style. In this case, if the garment has a straight body (bust and hip measure are the same), it is fine to add or subtract at the hem. If the hem is shaped and you wish to lengthen or shorten, you can add or subtract a line within the body of the garment to preserve that shape.

After lengthening or shortening a pattern, it is necessary to blend the jog that is created by this alteration (see the detail in the top illustration on p. 36). Mark a spot halfway between the jog edges, then blend in both directions gradually, corresponding to the shape of the pattern. Use a curve stick as needed. If you are going to change the width of the top, make those additional adjustments, then blend all the seamlines in one operation.

***Lengthening*** To lengthen a pattern, cut the pattern apart on the lengthen/shorten line. Attach a strip of scrap tissue along the cut edge of the pattern. Extend the grainline through the scrap tissue. On the scrap tissue, draw a line parallel to the lengthen/shorten line the amount you wish to lengthen the pattern. Align the parallel lines

If you plan to lengthen a top significantly, you may need more fabric. To be certain, do a trial layout of the pattern pieces on a gridded cutting board or paper.

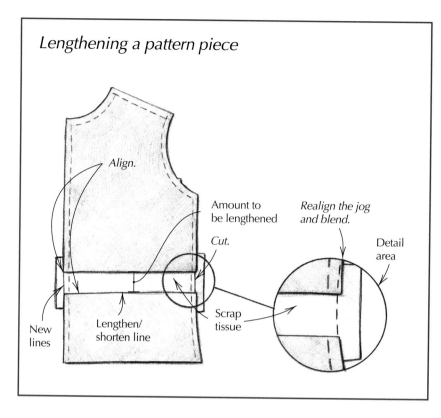

## Lengthening a pattern piece

Align.

Amount to
be lengthened

Cut.

*Realign the jog
and blend.*

Detail
area

New
lines

Lengthen/
shorten line

Scrap
tissue

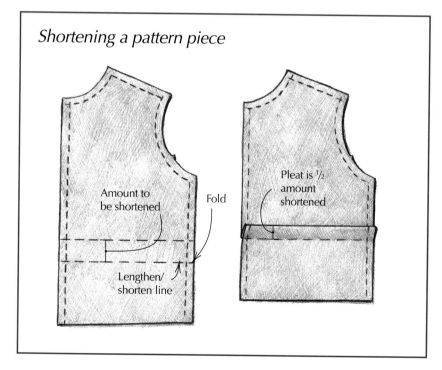

## Shortening a pattern piece

Amount to
be shortened

Fold

Pleat is ½
amount
shortened

Lengthen/
shorten line

and the grainline, and tape or glue the pattern in place (see the top illustration at left).

**Shortening** To shorten a pattern, draw a line parallel to the lengthen/shorten line on your pattern of the amount you wish to shorten (see the bottom illustration at left). Fold the pattern along the lengthen/shorten line. Bring the fold to meet the drawn line. Tape or glue the fold in place. The pleat will measure one half the amount shortened.

## Adjusting width

Adjusting the width is the most common pattern alteration. Adding is more common than subtracting, but you will apply the same principles for increasing and decreasing width at the bust, waist, and hip. Increase or decrease width at the side seams only. If you add width at the center front or back, it will change the size and shape of the neckline and darts will be positioned too far apart.

Mark key points where you are making adjustments to mark the amount you need to adjust the side seams along the tissue at bust, waist, and hip (see the illustration on the facing page).

Once you know how much to add or subtract to assure that the pattern is a proportionate length and large enough to fit around you, you are ready to make

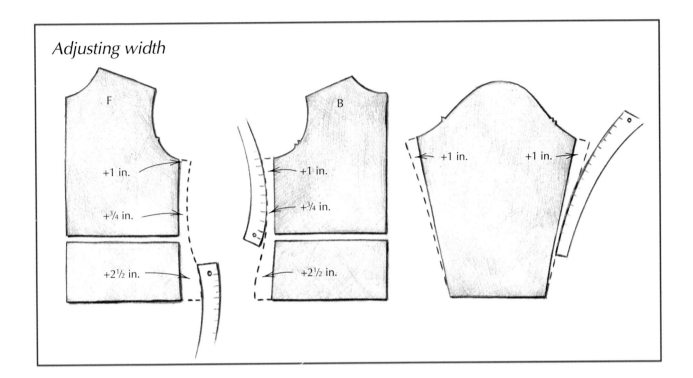

*Adjusting width*

alterations on the pattern tissue. Mark the amount you will add or subtract directly on the key areas of your pattern on the tissue. Add scrap tissue to the side seams as needed.

The total amount to be adjusted is divided evenly among the quarters of the top, so if an extra 2 in. is needed, add ½ in. at each side seam. You can add different amounts at the bust and hip, up to 8 in. (2 in. at each side seam) before the shape of the top becomes distorted.

Connect the key points freehand or by using a curve, blending the corrected amounts into the pattern and maintaining the original shape. Multisized patterns are helpful in adjusting widths and blending the lines. Alter all corresponding pattern pieces to match.

If you add width to the bust, you must add the same amount to each side of the sleeves. Add at the underarm seam, tapering to nothing at the hem.

## Tissue Fitting

Tissue fitting is done after you have altered the flat pattern so you can have a look at the fit, length, and design details in three dimensions. This technique gives you a chance to see how the finished garment will look on your figure. It will take a bit of patience and practice to become adept at pin

Once you have made alterations on the front, you can use a light box or a sunny window to trace the altered cutting line onto the back tissue.

*Tissue fitting takes a bit of practice but is worth the results. You can see fit, dart, neckline and shoulder placement, length, design details, and overall style and silhouette. Pin the sleeve in separately. Slip it on; match and pin at shoulder seam only. Fit sleeve with armhole slightly bent, "walking" the sleeve down your arm.*

fitting, but it is well worth mastering. I never make any garment without tissue fitting first. You'll need a full-length mirror, a large hand mirror, a narrow elastic tied around your waist, good lighting, and time to engage in pattern "play."

## Pinning the pattern together

Pin the altered pattern together, placing pins parallel to the edge along the seams, with seam allowances and darts facing out. If your pattern has curves, like those on princess seams, use tape to keep the tissue from tearing along the seamlines, and clip in the curved areas before pinning. Pin only the front and back main pieces together—no facings, collar, or other small pieces. Then mark the back waist with a large-headed pin. Pin up the hems. Pin the sleeve separately along the underarm, with the seam facing out. If the top is to be very fitted (that is, for a stretchy knit, which is smaller than your body measurements), do not pin the side seams together; just mark the waistline with a pin, aligning the pattern at shoulder, center front and back, and waistline.

## Try on your pattern

Try on the pinned together half-pattern tissue as if it were a finished garment. Wear the undergarments you'll wear with the top; use a shoulder pad if

your pattern calls for one. Begin by placing the shoulder seam along your shoulder. Next, align the center front line with your center front, and position the back waist at your backbone along your waist. Tape the pattern to yourself at center front or neck area, but be sure the top is hanging straight and on grain. Stand back from the mirror to get a full view, and use a large hand mirror to view the back. You'll examine one section of the pattern at a time, systematically studying it from top to bottom (see the photo at left).

**Shoulder** Is the seam straight? Is the shoulder seam along your shoulder point? Is the width of the shoulder in proportion to you? Determine your best shoulder widths from favorite tops and from pin fitting. Further adjustments can be made during construction. Turn the tissue under on the seam to get a clear sleeve-position reading. Shoulder width is an important proportion, and the width can be pared away easily. Burda patterns tend to have broad shoulders, so I often go down a size or two at the armscye when I use them. If the shoulder is too wide, trim from 0 at the armscye notches to the desired amount (usually not more than ¾ in.) at the shoulder (see the top illustration on the facing page).

**Armhole** The depth of the armhole determines the proportion of a garment and how the top will fit beneath a jacket. Measure in a straight line from the shoulder to underarm. Today's clothes average between 8 in. and 11 in. and range from a high set-in sleeve to a dropped sleeve. If you are petite or small boned, you can pare down the depth of the armhole by pleating out ½ in. to 1 in. on the front and back armhole and the cap of the sleeve (see the bottom illustration at right). Draw these lines in the armhole at right angles to the grainline and blend the cutting lines.

**Bust** Check the amount of ease over the bust. Bust darts should point to the fullest part of the bust, ending at least 1 in. from bust point. If the pattern's dart is not right for you, make a mark on the pattern indicating your bust point.

There are two ways to adjust the bust dart: The simplest is to lower or raise the apex point of the bust dart, then reconnect that point with the legs of the dart (see the top left illustration on p. 40). But in some styles it doesn't work easily. If that's the case, then the technique that works the best is to redraw and reposition the entire dart by making a bust box. On a piece of scrap tissue, draw a box around the bust dart on your pattern and trace the dart, then slide it into position (see the top right illustration on p. 40). Tape it in place and reconnect the cutting lines.

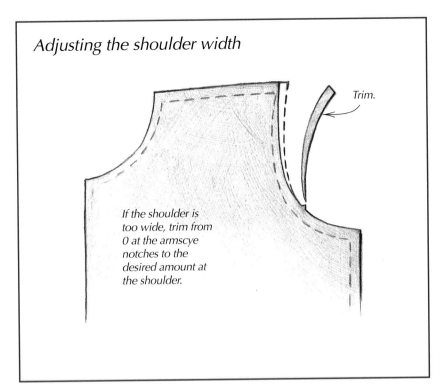

*Adjusting the shoulder width*

Trim.

If the shoulder is too wide, trim from 0 at the armscye notches to the desired amount at the shoulder.

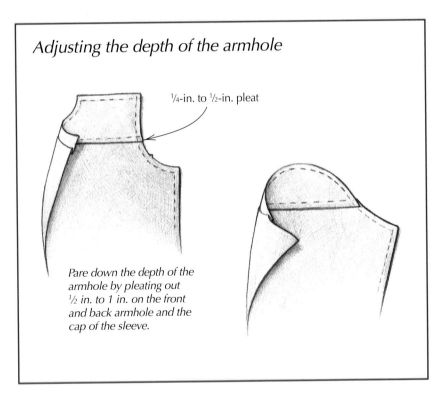

*Adjusting the depth of the armhole*

¼-in. to ½-in. pleat

Pare down the depth of the armhole by pleating out ½ in. to 1 in. on the front and back armhole and the cap of the sleeve.

## Raising or lowering the bust dart

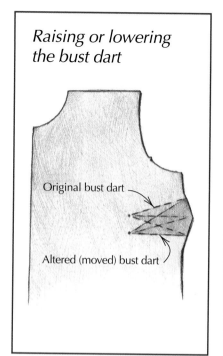

Original bust dart

Altered (moved) bust dart

## Moving the bust dart

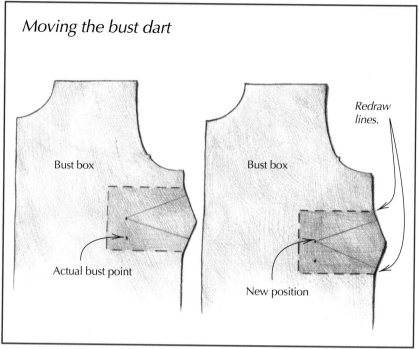

Bust box

Actual bust point

Bust box

Redraw lines.

New position

## Adding a bust dart

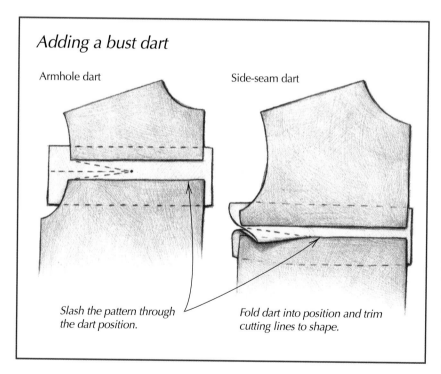

Armhole dart

Side-seam dart

Slash the pattern through the dart position.

Fold dart into position and trim cutting lines to shape.

If you are full busted and there is no dart, you may notice the top is shorter at center front or there are gaps in the armhole. Adding a dart adds depth and shaping to a top, and is much more flattering to a full-busted figure than a flat, unshaped bodice. A bust dart can be added at the side seam or in the armhole (see the illustration at left). You will instantly see a better fit by manipulating a dart in the pattern tissue. Experiment with the size of the dart and to see which position looks better. Because the dart pleats out fullness, you'll need to lengthen the top, solving the too-short-front problem as well. The depth of the dart determines the amount to lengthen. Draw a horizontal line, then slash the pattern through the dart position. Add scrap tissue and lengthen the total amount of the dart you will add. So, if you pleated out a ¾-in.-deep dart, you will lengthen a total of 1½ in. Repin the pattern tissue together, and form the new dart exactly where you want it.

**Princess seams**  Princess seams are shaped to fit the curves of the body, beginning at the shoulder or armhole, extending to the hem. This slimming seam adds shaping while eliminating darts. The two curved seams are made to follow the contours of the body, so careful fitting is essential. Check the fit in the bust during tissue fitting to be sure that the fullest part of the bust coincides with the fullest curve on the princess seam.

It is easy to adapt the shape of princess seams to your figure by reshaping the bust curve of the front side panel. You can raise or lower this curve or make it smaller or larger to fit the contour of your figure. Add scrap tissue and tissue-fit to determine where to add or decrease fullness. By changing the side panel, you are altering the length of the seam, so you will have to alter the center panel as well.

Combine this formula with tissue fitting: Add or subtract ¼ in. from the original line for each cup size larger or smaller than a B on the side panel. Pleat out or lengthen the same amount on the center panel. Mark new stitching and cutting lines at the fullest part of the curve. Redraw the lines, blending into the original cutting lines at the armhole and waist (see the illustration on p. 42).

**Neckline**  Is the neckline flattering? It should lie smoothly along your body. If you are using a facing, the finished edge of the neck will be ⅝ in. from the edge. With a bound neck, the cut edge becomes the finished edge.

**Back neckline**  Begin here by determining the best location of the back neckline for you. Will it fall at the natural neckline or below? Some patterns tell you the distance below the natural neckline. Pin fitting shows where the neck seam lies. Camouflage a dowager's hump or a round back by raising the back neck. If you are using a multisized pattern, it is as simple as using the highest cutting line. Use the grading lines on your pattern as a guide.

**Front neckline**  Do you prefer round or V shape? It is simple to convert a round neck to a V neck. Mark the location of the V while pin fitting; I prefer a gentle curve rather than a straight line. Use a curve stick to connect the shoulder seam to the V point. How deep do you want the neckline? Use the collarbones as a guide—a neckline that traces the edge of the collarbone is flattering. Vogue Patterns are often cut high at center front.

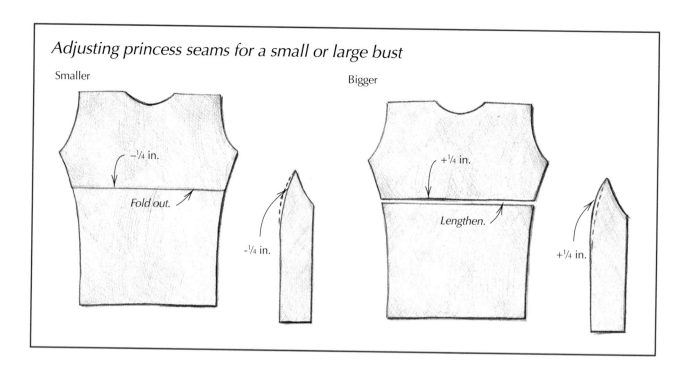

*Adjusting princess seams for a small or large bust*

Smaller

−¼ in.

*Fold out.*

-¼ in.

Bigger

+¼ in.

*Lengthen.*

+¼ in.

If your face is very round, you may prefer the contrast of a V neckline; if your face is angular, a round neck might be a better choice. (Many women can wear both.)

**Width** How far from the center front on a natural jewel neck is *too* wide or *too* narrow for you? Knowing this helps establish your best proportion. If a neckline is too wide, it can broaden the face or upper body; if too narrow, it can form wrinkles at the neck or feel uncomfortable.

Adjust the neckline to flatter your face, to update a look, or to fit under another garment. The three key points—front, back, and shoulder—may be adjusted independently, but front and back must meet at the shoulder. It is common to raise the back neck, widen or narrow the shoulder, and lower the front neck.

If the pattern gapes at the neck, pin a tiny dart in the fitting tissue to indicate how much fullness

should be removed. Remove this "gaposis" from the pattern by slashing and overlapping the total, divided into tiny (⅛ in.) evenly spaced amounts (see the illustration on the facing page). The pattern tissue should remain flat. If it does not, make the slashes longer.

## Tissue-fitting checklist

The following list is a summation of what to check when tissue fitting a pattern.

- Waistline: Is the waist positioned correctly? Is the waist shaping right for your figure?
- Hip: Is the width large enough for the style?
- Length: Is the top the right length? Do you want to

change the shape of the hem or add side slits?

- Pockets: Are they in the right place? Do you want to change or add a pocket?
- Sleeves: Are the sleeves the right length and width and full enough in the bicep? When you have completed your evaluation of the body of the garment and made all necessary changes, slip the sleeve into the armhole, attaching it *only* at the shoulder seam. If you try to pin the entire sleeve in place, the tissue will tear. Check the sleeve length by "walking" the pinned-in-place sleeve down your arm with a slight bend in the elbow. Check the fit at the biceps: You must be able to pinch an inch of tissue to have the minimum 2-in. ease.

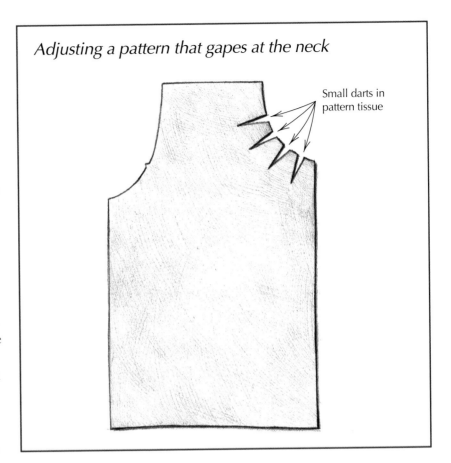

*Adjusting a pattern that gapes at the neck*

Small darts in pattern tissue

## CENTER FRONT NECKLINE

My Aunt Mary was my first sewing teacher. She was a natural and instinctive designer who taught me to "let the fabric tell you what to do." This is one of her unconventional tips: I notice that plain necklines often have just a bit of gap at center front, no matter what other alterations I make. To help a neckline lie flat, redraw the center front fold or seam, paring away ¼ in. at center front, and tapering to nothing 4 in. to 5 in. away. Even though it is traditionally against the rules to alter a garment at center front, this technique is a sure way to correct the gap.

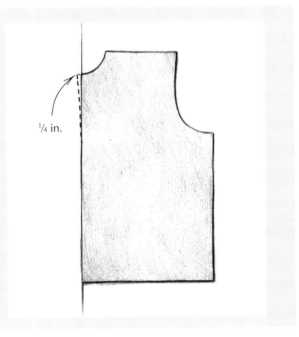

¼ in.

# Pattern Refinements

Once the pattern fits and you have made all the fitting and style changes that show up in tissue fitting, you can go one step further to add shape and refinement. I like to give even the simplest style a once-over to consider any details or additions. Often, this happens the very first time I make a top, and I incorporate these ideas into the next version.

## Lengthening the front on knit tops only

The front of the body is larger than the back, so by making the garment front slightly longer, you'll have a smoother fit. Lengthen the front ½ in. by adding at the bustline, just below the armhole (see the illustration below). For a full bust, add width at the bust by curving (as if there is a dart). Start at 0 at the armhole, increase to ¾ in. at the bust, and taper back to 0 just above the waist. When sewing, ease back to front, distributing ease at the bust.

## Balancing the armhole

Balancing the armhole solves the problem of garments riding toward the back. Burda and some studio pattern companies always add this refinement to their patterns. Many patterns are not balanced, but all styles benefit from it, and the adjustment will soon become second nature in your pattern work. Check the balance of the armhole by placing the garment armhole front and back together, matching at the underarm to see if the depth of the armhole is the same.

If the front and back are the same, the armhole isn't balanced and you need to adjust your pattern. The back should be ½ in. deeper. Add ¼ in. to the back shoulder seam, and trim away ¼ in. from the front. Make the same change to facings.

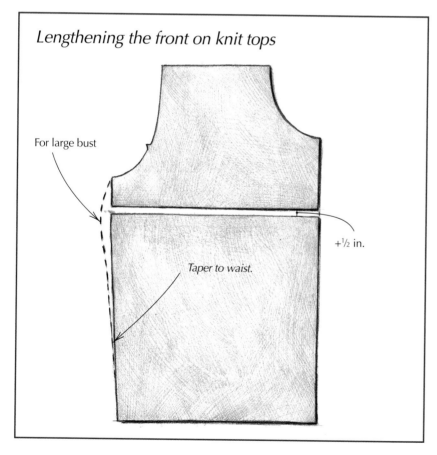

*Lengthening the front on knit tops*

For large bust

Taper to waist.

+½ in.

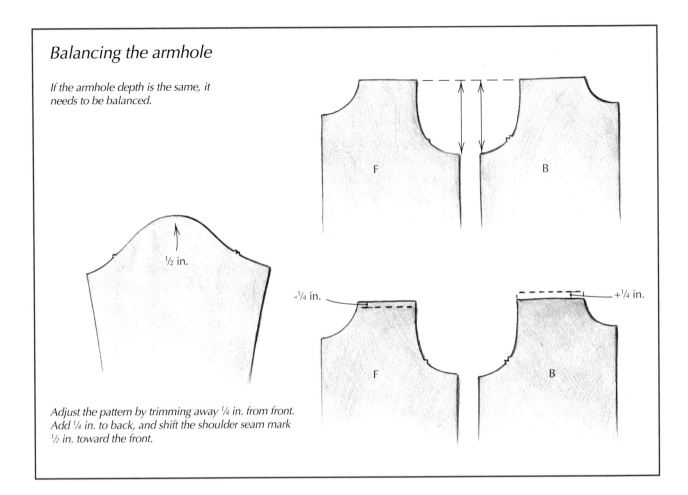

## Balancing the armhole

*If the armhole depth is the same, it needs to be balanced.*

½ in.

-¼ in.

+¼ in.

F

B

F

B

*Adjust the pattern by trimming away ¼ in. from front. Add ¼ in. to back, and shift the shoulder seam mark ½ in. toward the front.*

Once the armhole is balanced, make a small corresponding change to the sleeve. Check the sleeve by folding it in half lengthwise. If the shoulder seam dot is dead center, move it ½ in. toward the front, positioning more ease in the back.

## Sleeve refinements

At this point, you'll be checking the sleeves for fit.

**Dropped shoulders and raglan tops** Dropped shoulders and raglan tops often seem to have too much fabric on the bodice front between the bust and armpit. You can improve the fit by eliminating some of this extra fullness across the chest. I learned this trick from a dressmaker friend who was wearing exactly the same raglan sleeve pattern as I, only hers looked better and had no underarm wrinkles. This optional refinement is done on the pattern front and sleeve *only*.

When pin fitting, mark the pattern tissue at the armpit where the arm joins the body.

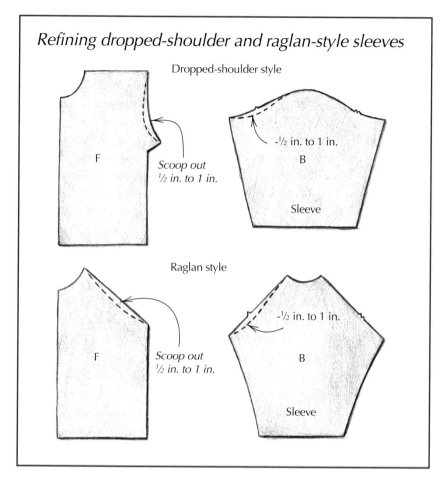

## Refining dropped-shoulder and raglan-style sleeves

**Dropped-shoulder style**

F

*Scoop out ½ in. to 1 in.*

-½ in. to 1 in.

B

Sleeve

**Raglan style**

F

*Scoop out ½ in. to 1 in.*

-½ in. to 1 in.

B

Sleeve

## Making further refinements

*Narrow the wrist width, shape the sleeve, shape the hem, and make a hem facing.*

Wrist width plus seam allowance

5½-in. facing

Curve

Hemline

2-in. hem

This point marks the area where you will scoop out the maximum amount, anywhere from ½ in. to 1 in. On the front pattern piece only, draw a smooth, curved line, using a curved ruler, then trim from shoulder to armhole, scooping out up to 1 in. at the marked point. Make the identical change on the front sleeve (see the top illustration at left).

***Wrist and sleeve width*** The wrist width is too wide on many patterns, especially in larger sizes. Measure the width of your wrist and upper forearm, and determine your ideal sleeve width. Mark the midpoint on the sleeve hem, and add half the new sleeve width plus seam allowance to each side. Redraw the seam to the new wrist width, making a flattering curved shape with a hip curve (see the bottom illustration at left).

***Sleeve hem allowance*** Shape the sleeve hem so it fits neatly inside the sleeve. You can also use this technique to build in the option of a clean, finished, roll-up sleeve by adding a 5½-in. hem facing that is shaped to the sleeve to the sleeve-hem allowance. Fold along hemline and trace off the shape of the sleeve seam, adding tissue at the hem. Add 2 in. for a standard hem, 5½ in. for a roll-up facing.

## Additional refinements

The following three pattern refinements are inspired by fine,

handmade, clothes from the 1930s and '40s. In this period, just before large, ready-to-wear clothing factories became common, many dressmakers and small companies used methods that involved precision and details that eventually would become impractical in large-scale manufacturing. I love to incorporate some of these ideas into my own clothes.

### Sculpt the shoulder seam

I originally saw this technique in a collarless jacket but have used it successfully in tops and T-shirts. It replicates the natural curve of the shoulder by substituting a curved shoulder seam for the straight one found in most patterns. Add a small petal-shaped shoulder pad to enhance the shape and balance the hips. The effect is subtle, very feminine, and flattering.

When tissue fitting, mark the pattern to indicate the spot where your shoulder dips (at the bra strap, about $1\frac{1}{4}$ in. from the neck). Add a piece of scrap tissue to the front and back shoulder. Using a French curve, create a gentle, gradual curve, starting at 0 at the seamline on the neck edge, tapering $\frac{1}{8}$ in. to $\frac{1}{4}$ in. at the curve, for a distance of approximately $1\frac{1}{2}$ in., and raising the cutting line $\frac{1}{8}$ in. to $\frac{1}{4}$ in. for the remainder of the seam (see the illustration at right). Shape both front and back shoulder seam, then shape the sleeve to accommodate this

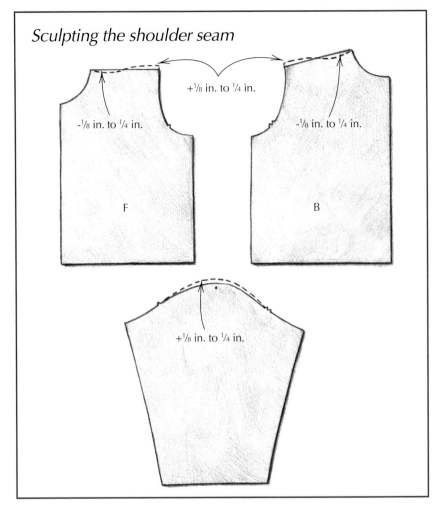

*Sculpting the shoulder seam*

$+\frac{1}{8}$ in. to $\frac{1}{4}$ in.

$-\frac{1}{8}$ in. to $\frac{1}{4}$ in.

$-\frac{1}{8}$ in. to $\frac{1}{4}$ in.

F

B

$+\frac{1}{8}$ in. to $\frac{1}{4}$ in.

extra height by adding the same amount to the cap of the sleeve that you added to the shoulder seam, blending from notch to notch. The secret to success is to blend your curves carefully, then try on the garment before applying the neck finish. Reshape the neck facings to reflect the change made to the shoulder.

### Curve the hem line on long sleeves This refinement reflects that when you stretch your arm out to reach, you need more

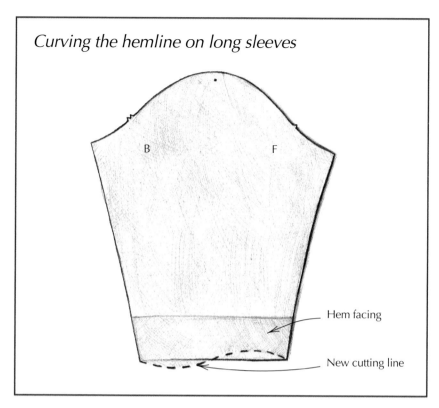

## Curving the hemline on long sleeves

B      F

Hem facing

New cutting line

longer, and is shorter at the front. Using this shape, make a hem facing 2 in. to 3 in. wide.

***Curve a cap sleeve*** Many women prefer the coverage of a cap sleeve, yet often the straight line is not flattering. Put a curve on the hem of a cut-on cap by curving in ½ in. to ¾ in. as shown in the illustration on the facing page. Finish the curved edge with bias facing or binding.

## Overlay patterns to draw comparisons

Once all your work is done on one pattern, you can overlay it on a new pattern. Laying your tried-and-true pattern on top of the new one, match waistline and center, then compare the neck location and width, shoulder width, armhole depth, body shaping, and length. This gives you a point of reference, and it can eliminate some confusion when doing tissue fitting.

# Pattern Work Checklist

Keep this checklist handy when doing your pattern work. It contains all the possibilities for fine-tuning a pattern. Unless specified, all apply to knits or wovens.

- Do lengthening and shortening alterations first. Use ⅝-in. seam allowances and 2-in. hems. On multisized

fabric on the back of the sleeve than on the front. When I learned to sew in the early 1960s, most sleeve patterns were drafted with this curve. It is easy to incorporate into any long sleeve with a cuff or plain hem. If your fabric is firmly woven, make a separate facing instead of trying to hem the curve.

Add a piece of scrap tissue to the hem of the sleeve pattern. Mark the hem into even thirds. At the back third make a mark ½ in. outside the cutting line, and at the front third mark ½ in. inside the cutting line. Using a French curve, starting and ending at 0, connect the marks. The sleeve hem at the back of the arm is

patterns, mark *your* pattern size with a colored pen. If you make changes as you sew, transfer them immediately to your paper pattern. Keep notes on pattern changes and construction on your pattern.

- For knits only, lengthen the front ½ in.
- Add width as determined by your measurements at the hip, bust, waist, and bicep.
- Check that the armhole is balanced. The back should be ½ in. longer than the front. If they are equal, trim ¼ in. from the front and add ¼ in. to the back. Correct the sleeve by moving the shoulder seam dot ½ in. toward the front.
- Adjust the wrist width, and curve the sleeve seam.
- Shape the sleeve hem allowance. *Optional:* Add a 5-in. hem facing for roll-up sleeves.
- Add a curve to the sleeve hem.
- Alter the neckline shape or location as desired. Check the location of back, width, and front depth.
- For body shaping, consider a change if the shape is square or if the hip and bust measure the same. Options are hourglass or tapered at the hip.
- On dropped-shoulder and raglan styles, scoop out some of the fullness across the chest on the front and sleeve pattern front only.
- Curve the shoulder seam.

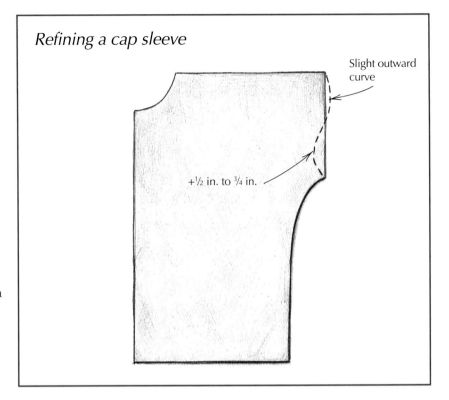

*Refining a cap sleeve*

Slight outward curve

+½ in. to ¾ in.

- Shape the hem. If your hem is a straight line, add ½ in. at the center front and back, tapering to 0 at the side seams. Or create slits, vents, shirttail shaping, or make the front or back longer.
- Allow 1-in. seam allowances at the side seams the first time you use a pattern, just in case.
- Add back or front interest by adding buttons and buttonholes, inserting a pleat or vent, or making a center seam.
- Use seams as design elements. Make a wide- or narrow-exposed French seam. Use flat-felled or topstitched seams.
- For pockets, add an inseam pocket to long tops or tunics.

# 5 *Construction*

All the pattern alterations, refinements, and tweaking are now complete. Fabric and interfacing are cut out and you are ready to sew. I rarely make a pattern exactly as is—I usually change the construction, so this is the time I read through the pattern instructions to determine the construction sequence, which techniques I want to use, and any changes or modifications to make. For instance, I often use a bias binding instead of a facing, incorporate topstitching, or adapt the order of construction to make fitting easier. If you are used to following the pattern directions, mark your pattern to indicate any changes you intend to make. Refer to the construction checklist on pages 62 and 88 before assembling your top.

## Sewing Construction Basics

Maintain the original shape of pattern pieces, control stretch or distortion, reinforce stress points, and prevent fraying by using directional stitching, staystitching, and reinforcing.

### Directional sewing

This is stitching in the direction that does not distort the shape of the fabric piece as you cut, stitch, and press. The curves and angles on a cutout garment are vulnerable to stretching, so you'll want to develop the habit of cutting, serging, sewing, and pressing with the grain. If you run your finger along the cut edge, you'll notice that one direction smoothes the fibers, which is the direction you should sew in, and the other pulls the fibers apart. Usually, working directionally means working from widest to narrowest (see the illustration on p. 52).

### Staystitching

Staystitching is a line of directional stitching done just inside the seamline of a single layer of fabric to stabilize an area that could

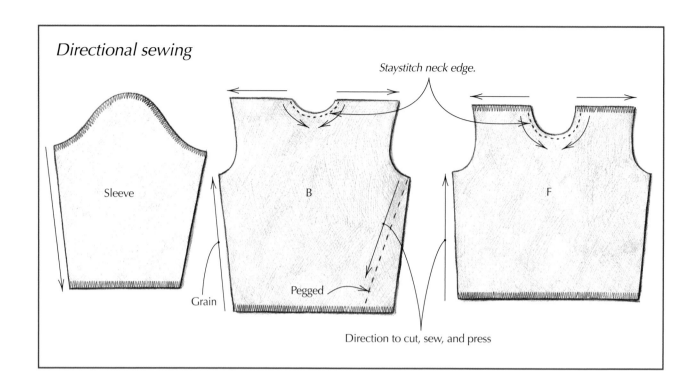

## Directional sewing

Sleeve

Grain

Staystitch neck edge.

B

Pegged

F

Direction to cut, sew, and press

When using staystitch-plus, apply pressure behind or on the back of the presser foot to draw in the fabric.

stretch or distort during construction. Staystitch the front and back neck edges as soon as possible after cutting.

## Reinforcing

Reinforcing is a line of stitching that is right on the seamline, usually in an area that will be clipped or under stress. Stitch 1 in. on either side of the reinforcement point.

## Staystitch-plus

Staystitch-plus (also known as easestitch-plus) is one of the most useful sewing techniques. The staystitch-plus technique is effective in controlling rippling and stretching when sewing a seam or when topstitching. Its

purpose is to ease in an area smoothly and evenly. Like staystitching, it is done directionally, just inside the stitching line. Sewing machines are designed to be used with two layers of fabric, so any time you sew one layer, you'll notice the stitches cause the fabric to draw in slightly. To do staystitch-plus, stitch through one layer of fabric, placing your finger behind or on the back of the presser foot and applying pressure to force a tiny bit more fabric into each stitch (see the photo at left). Ease the fabric through in short segments by stitching a few inches, then raising the presser foot to release the fabric. In order to develop an even, smooth tension when using staystitch-plus, practice on scraps before you stitch on your garment.

I use staystitch-plus to gather in the fullness on flat, dropped sleeves, to ease in princess seams, and when topstitching knits. I never use this technique with a standard set-in sleeve.

## Sewing without pins

Professional factory sewers rarely use pins. I wish I had learned this easy, practical way to sew a seam, using few or no pins when I was learning to sew. Thanks to Margaret Islander for transforming my sewing after 30 years! Begin by practicing on straight seams with little or no ease. Soon you'll be using this factory technique on all your sewing. Once you are used to sewing with few pins, it becomes easier to handle the fabric with none at all.

Sewing with just a few pins or without pins at all takes some practice. Here's how it's done: Place pins directly on the stitching line, positioned so you can pull each pin out (and toss it to a magnetic pincushion or pin it into your wrist pincushion). First, secure the seam by placing one pin at each end. Match notches, pinning within the length of the seam, using as many pins as needed. Control the fabric by forming pleats and sewing a few inches at a time, keeping the edges together and

releasing the pleats as you go. It is natural for the top layer to creep. Control the creeping by holding the two layers up at a slight angle so the bottom layer feeds in at the same ratio as the top (see the photo below). When sewing a seam where one side is smaller (like setting a dropped sleeve or applying neck binding), always stitch with the smaller side on top. The action of the machine eases the two layers together as you sew. You'll need more pins with slippery fabrics and in easing detail areas like setting in a sleeve or stitching around the neck.

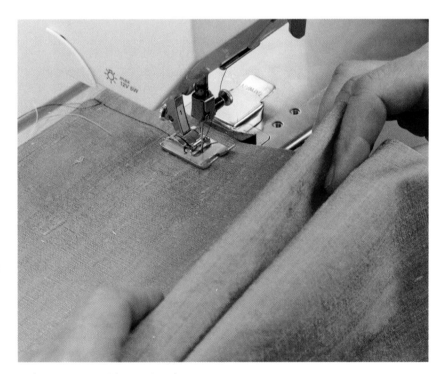

*When sewing without pins, keep long seams in place, forming pleats, and hold the fabric at an angle to keep the top layer from creeping.*

## Seams

Standard seams are sewn right sides together using a ⅝-in. seam allowance. One of my favorite sewing aids is a magnetic seam guide, which acts as a fence to guide the fabric. Even though most sewing machines have lines etched along the throat plate, I find the seam guide to be essential in stitching smooth, straight, even seams.

Your fabric determines the best stitch length. Use a longer stitch when sewing with loosely woven, heavy fabrics, such as hand-wovens, and a shorter stitch when sewing with light or firmly woven fabrics, such as silk crepe. I use European-brand, long-staple, polyester thread for sewing all fabrics. Occasionally, I like to use silk thread when topstitching for a lustrous effect.

After a seam is stitched, it is normal for it to appear puckered. The threads draw up slightly, and any puckering should disappear with pressing. Natural fibers smooth out much more easily than synthetics. After stitching any seam, press the seam flat as sewn to blend the stitches. Then press the seam open.

## Seams for knits

Working with knits has an undeservedly difficult reputation. Even accomplished stitchers claim that knits stretch, curl, ripple, and the hems and edges are difficult to control. Many of the techniques you'll learn here have stemmed from trial and error, heading off trouble, and learning from efforts that simply didn't work. This does not mean that sewing knits is beyond the reach of home sewers; far from it. Sewing with knits is very simple once you know how to finish the edges and control the stretch.

After cutting out your pattern, use the scraps to test needle and thread on your machine. I have found that a standard size 80/12 universal needle (which has a tapered, rounded point) and good-quality polyester thread are the right choice for most light- to mid-weight natural- or mostly natural-fiber knits. I sew most knits using a size 80/12 universal needle with a 2.5-mm stitch length. I stock a variety of double needles with universal and ball points in different sizes and widths.

Skipped stitches may occur with synthetics, with "power" knits that contain a high proportion of Lycra, or with very fine synthetic knits. If skipped stitches occur, try a stretch needle, which comes in size 75/11, or a double needle in widths 2.5 and 4.0. Skipped stitches may only show up on knits when using universal-point double needles, so keep these stretch double needles handy for sewing today's knits. I try to avoid ball-point needles since they tend to leave tiny holes in the fabric that may not be apparent until after the garment is worn or washed. If you are working with synthetic or power stretch knits and are experiencing skipped stitches, then try a fine ball-point needle in sizes 60/8, 65/9, or 70/10. These oddball needles are generally available from a sewing-machine dealer, and you'll need to use a very-fine thread such as a long-staple polyester.

Even though it is possible to serge an entire T-shirt together, you don't need a serger to make beautifully constructed knits. Since they don't ravel, a plain or pinked edge works fine. I like to use a serged edge with knits because it adds a finished look rather than for construction purposes, but a straight stitch and standard 2.5-mm stitch length works great with most knits. For very stretchy knits, use a smaller stitch and the narrowest "baby" zigzag, which "reads" straight and adds stretch. I do not recommend stretching the fabric as you sew, nor do I use the built-in stretch stitches. Both techniques have a tendency to distort the fabric.

## Seam finishes for wovens

Essential seam finishes you'll want to master are French seams, flat-felled seams, and mock flat-felled seams. Use these finishes with light- to mid-weight woven fabrics and straight seams. Flat-felled seams have topstitching and a sporty appearance while French seams are best used for more delicate, feminine garments. Both of these techniques can be used as a decorative element on the outside of a garment. Test each fabric to see which technique works best.

**French seam**  It is important to make a test sample before creating a French seam so you can account for the turn of the cloth, which is the amount of

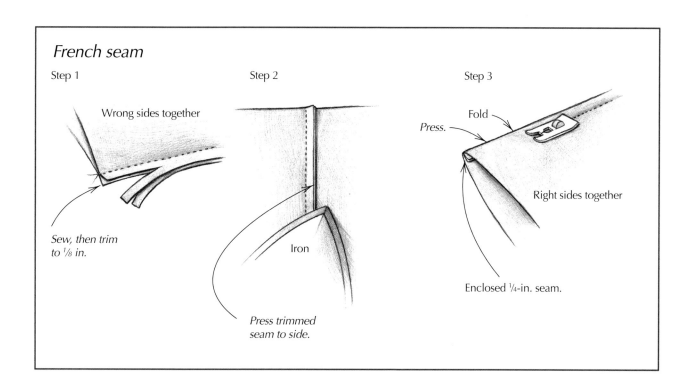

### French seam

Step 1

Wrong sides together

*Sew, then trim to ¹/₈ in.*

Step 2

Iron

*Press trimmed seam to side.*

Step 3

Fold

*Press.*

Right sides together

Enclosed ¹/₄-in. seam.

fabric taken up as you turn and enclose the seam. A ⅝-in. seam is enough for lightweight fabrics. With mid-weight fabrics, French seams are easier to execute by using a ¾-in. or ⅞-in. seam allowance.

1. Stitch a ¼-in. seam wrong sides together. Press flat as sewn. Using a rotary cutter, trim the seam to ⅛ in. (see the illustration on p. 55).
2. Press in one direction, then press right sides together so the stitching line is along the edge.
3. Stitch ¼ in. from the edge.

*Flat-felled seam* This technique is a Japanese dressmaker's variation on the classic flat-felled seam. After you have mastered the classic version, I think you will appreciate this one as well! Make a test sample to see if you want one or two rows of stitching on the right side. The following instructions will result in one row of stitching on the right side. Seam allowances may need to be adjusted for different fabrics: The heavier the fabric, the wider the seam.

1. Prepare the seam for sewing. Press ⁵⁄₁₆ in. (a fat ¼ in.) to the right side of the seam.
2. Trim the same amount from the other side of the seam (see the left illustration on the facing page). With right sides together, place the trimmed edge inside the folded edge, with the raw edge along the fold. Pin as needed and stitch through all

layers, close to the raw edge and even with the fold. Press flat as sewn. Open the fabric flat with the wrong side up.
3. Press the seam to one side, covering the raw edge. Stitch the seam through all layers along the pressed edge and parallel to the first line of stitching. You can adapt this seam finish so one or two rows of stitching show on the right side.

*Mock flat-felled seam* I use this basic seam finish so often I almost take it for granted. It combines a serged edge with a flat-felled seam. It is perfect for flat sleeves, shoulder seams, and some center-back seams. I use it with knits and wovens, straight grain and bias.

1. Serge the edge that will be on top (sleeve cap, front shoulder seam). Stitch the seam, press open, and trim enclosed seam allowance to ¼ in. (see the illustration at right on the facing page).
2. Press to one side so the wider, serged seam is on top.
3. Topstitch the seam from the right side.

## Seam finishes for double knits

A plain, pressed open seam is all you need for stable double knits. Knits that curl should be trimmed or topstitched. Trim by serging close to the stitching line, or stitch a second line ⅛ in. from the seam, and trim or pink.

## Flat-felled seam

Step 1

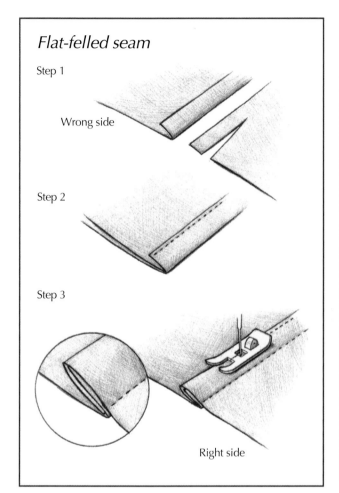

Wrong side

Step 2

Step 3

Right side

## Mock flat-felled seam

Step 1

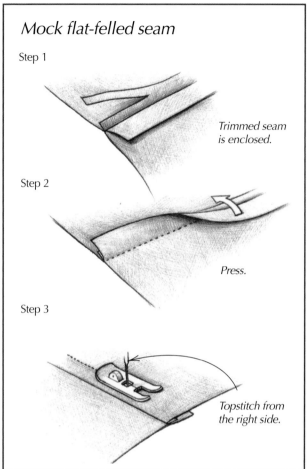

*Trimmed seam is enclosed.*

Step 2

*Press.*

Step 3

*Topstitch from the right side.*

A mock flat-felled seam is perfect for holding seams flat, such as at the shoulder and for dropped- or raglan-sleeve seams.

## Topstitching

Topstitching can call for a heavy thread. Polyester and silk buttonhole thread have a beautiful, ropy look, but if you can't match the color, use two strands of regular thread passed through the tension and thread guides. Use a longer stitch and a topstitching needle, which has a larger eye than a regular needle, to allow the heavier thread to pass through easily without breaking. Topstitching needles come in the same sizes as universal needles; keep an assortment of sizes on hand. I use staystitch-plus when topstitching knits to keep hems from rippling.

## Pressing

One of the secrets to creating beautiful clothing is in the fine art of pressing with a steam iron. Pressing each step of the way

*Pressing tools are the essential ingredient in creating and maintaining finely crafted clothes. From left to right: ham, sleeve board, contoured ham on a ham holder, point presser clapper, iron, and press cloth.*

builds in shape and memory, smoothes out glitches, and "erases" mistakes. Don't take shortcuts here. The iron is to the sewer as a chisel is to a sculptor: You begin with a flat piece of cloth and create a three-dimensional garment.

Always test a scrap of fabric to determine which heat setting to use. You'll also need a clapper/pointer (a hardwood tool for flattening seams) and a tailor's ham, which is a shaped device that is invaluable for pressing curves. A press cloth keeps the surface of the fabric from getting shiny or from burning, and all professionals use them.

A clapper flattens and cools the pressed area, absorbs heat and moisture, and the weight of the tool flattens the seam or dart. For lightweight fabrics, just the weight of the clapper is enough to do the job, but with wool you may need to apply pressure. The ham provides a raised, curved surface that is perfect for shaping necklines, curved seams, and sleeves (see the photo on the facing page). A sleeve board is essential to press detail areas like sleeve seams.

Get into the habit of pressing as you sew. Every time you stitch a seam or dart, first press it flat as it was sewn to blend the stitches, then press it open. Use your fingers and the point of the iron to open the seam. One of the first things I test when working

on a new fabric is how the fabric reacts to pressing on the right side. If the fabric gets shiny or shows the imprint of seams, darts, or serging, do as much pressing as you can on the wrong side, and use a press cloth to touch up on the right side.

Oak-tag templates are perfect for pressing straight, even edges. I use a 2½-in.-by-15-in. template with pencil-marked lines for hems and pockets. I keep different-width templates close to my iron, and I use them frequently.

# Preparing to Sew

When I work on a project I like to get the garment cut, marked, fused, staystitched, and serged in a single time block. After the garment is prepared in this way, I finish the seam edges with the serger.

## Using a serger

The serger, which trims and overcasts the edges of seams in one quick operation, is often the ideal way to finish seams, hems, and facings. It is not necessary to cut seams any wider since the serger knife just trims the ravelly edge of the fabric. Adapt the order of construction when you're using the serger. I like to use it most often as an edge finish but frequently serge the side seams together after they are stitched (and fitted) by using a standard machine.

Before serging, fuse interfacing to facings and edges, and staystitch and reinforce. Do not serge areas that will be enclosed, such as neck edges, and serge using directional stitching whenever possible. Long-staple polyester sewing thread can be used on the serger for most fabrics. For lightweight fabric, use coned serger thread, machine-embroidery thread, or texturized nylon to minimize the thread impression showing on the right side. A three-thread edge is the most versatile of the serged finishes and practically the only one I use.

## Fitting during construction

Fitting and sewing go hand in hand. Wearing the right undergarments, and clothes that go on and off easily, encourages frequent fitting as you sew. Fitting takes place at each stage of construction. Don't rush or skip a step. It is very disheartening to complete the neck only to discover it is the wrong size or shape, or is unflattering. Be prepared to alter and refine at each step. Keep meticulous records and change the paper pattern as you go—that way, the next time you make this pattern, it will go faster.

Alter the garment as you sew, then make corresponding changes to the pattern pieces. The first step is to pin the side seams along the original seam-

lines with the seam allowances to the outside. Evaluate any changes you want to make, and mark with pins where you want to take in, let out, or reshape. If you are alone in the sewing room, this may take more than one try. Take the garment off and repin, placing pins along the new seamline, making these new lines smooth and symmetrical on both sides. Try the garment on again, making changes until the fit and shape please you.

When you are ready to sew, mark the pin positions with chalk, remove the pins, and stitch right sides together. This is one of the times that I draw in my stitching line. If the seam is curved, like the hourglass shaping, use a curve stick (see the photo on the facing page). If the seam is straight, use a straightedge. Do whatever you can to make the stitching lines smooth, even, and symmetrical. Beginners should machine-baste along revised seamlines and try on the garment again. With more experience you can stitch the seam, using a normal stitch length the first time.

On tops with a simple, straight line, alter at the side seams during construction instead of during tissue fitting to see how the fabric looks on the figure. Complete the neck finish, then fit at the side seams directly on the body, making adjustments to the garment and transferring them to the pattern. Experiment to see which garment shape you like best.

Most ready-made tops and many patterns have a straight, boxy cut. The square shape adds bulk, which is OK if you are slim, if you're using fluid fabrics, or if you want a cropped look. I frequently adapt boxy, straight-lined construction patterns and purchased T-shirts in one of the following two ways (see the illustration below right):

1. Shape it to the bust, waist, and hip to look like an hourglass, which works well for hourglass, pear, and some rectangular figures, but does not flatter a wedge or angular figure. This curvy silhouette in a short top that ends at the high hip is flattering to full hips when worn with soft skirts or pants.

2. Taper it at the hip. The pattern is "pegged"; it is narrower at the hem than at the bust. Measure across the pattern at the bottom of the armhole and at the hem to compare. In an oversized fingertip-length top, this flatters most figures as long as there is sufficient ease at the hip. Pegging works best with the hourglass, pear, or overall roundness figure when worn with shoulder pads, and it's perfect for the inverted triangle and rectangle figures. The oversized, pegged top is good with leggings and slim-line pants and skirts.

*Fine-tune side-seam adjustments, using a curve stick to create smooth stitching lines.*

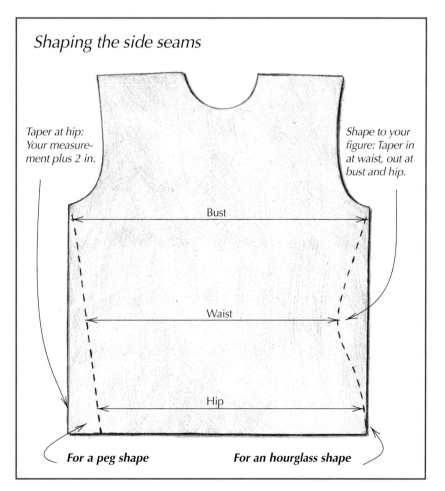

Shaping the side seams

Taper at hip: Your measurement plus 2 in.

Shape to your figure: Taper in at waist, out at bust and hip.

Bust

Waist

Hip

**For a peg shape**      **For an hourglass shape**

# Constructing the Top

After all your careful preparation, this is the moment you've been waiting for when you can thread up your machine and sew.

When all the pattern and design work is complete, begin with the pattern instruction sheet: Consider the construction sequence and if there are any techniques you want to change. In this section, I have included techniques and modifications I use in my own sewing, developed over years of trial and error: For instance, you may decide to use a neck binding instead of a facing, or add a vent or slit. Before you begin sewing, experiment with new techniques, using scraps from your fabric. I make samples before using them in the garment and save them for future reference.

## Darts

Careful marking, stitching, and pressing are paramount. When completed, a well-executed dart will be practically invisible. Place pins along the stitching line with one horizontal pin marking the end of the dart (see the photo on the facing page). Begin stitching from the wide end, backstitching

## ORDER OF CONSTRUCTION FOR WOVEN TOPS

**1.** Prepare fabric and interfacing. Preshrink, straighten the grain, and press.

**2.** Alter the pattern for fit and design.

**3.** Tissue-fit the pattern, making necessary alterations and refinements.

**4.** Cut out the pattern, and transfer markings.

**5.** Test fabric scraps to determine interfacing choice, stitch length, seam treatments, topstitching, binding width, and piping.

**6.** Fuse interfacings, and serge seams.

**7.** Staystitch neck edges.

**8.** Sew shoulder seams. Try on the garment to check the fit at shoulder and neck. This is the point to double-check the fit, shape, and width of the neckline. Adjust if needed. Press the shoulder seam to back and topstitch.

**9.** Finish neck edge by facing, binding, piping, etc.

**10.** Pin the side seams along the seamline with the seams to the outside to check the fit in the body of the garment and the position of the sleeve or armhole.

**11.** Set in the sleeve or finish the armhole. In most instances when sewing tops, I set in the sleeves flat rather than in the round. Pin the side seams with seams to the outside, and try on the garment, checking and fine-tuning the fit. Check the sleeve and hem length. Press up hems while the garment is still flat.

**12.** Sew the side seams, press, and finish. Try on the garment.

**13.** Press hems, and machine- or hand-stitch.

**14.** Complete details like hand stitching, buttons, topstitching, etc. Do the final pressing. Voila! Your top is finished.

*Pull out pins as the dart is stitched, using small stitches at the end of the dart.*

as you begin and removing pins as you come to them. When you are ½ in. from the end of the dart, change to a short stitch length (1.5-mm), and stitch the last few stitches off the edge of the fabric. The shorter stitches increase accuracy and make backstitching unnecessary. Press the dart flat as sewn and to one side over a ham. Press bust darts down and vertical darts to the center.

## Princess seams

Mark dots and notches on both seams. The dots where the seams intersect at the armhole are important. When the dots are matched exactly, the seamlines will intersect right at the armhole, and there will be a small triangle of fabric that can be trimmed away.

To construct princess seams, staystitch the center panel from armhole to just below the bottom notch. Use staystitch-plus (see pp. 52-53) to gather in the curved side panel, which is slightly larger. Stitch with the center panel on top, being careful to keep the underside smooth. Clip the center panel seam allowance only if necessary. Press the curved seam flat as sewn, using a tailor's ham, and press along the seam and in the seam allowance. Press the seam open over a ham, matching the curve of the ham to the curve of the garment.

The outer edge of a self-faced facing is finished before the facing is assembled. Trim seams to ¼ in. and press open.

build on this one. First, let's consider how to make the shaped facing found in so many patterns, then look at variations that can be added or created to make necklines in different shapes and with interesting details.

### Constructing a shaped facing

Facings are used to finish curved and shaped edges like necklines and armholes. A facing is cut to the same shape as the neck edge and along the same grainline. Interfacing is applied to the facing to provide support and body. Don't apply interfacing to the garment as some instructions tell you; the edge may show through to the right side. I prefer to use fusible interfacings whenever possible because the two layers act as one. Always test interfacing on scrap fabric to determine that it is compatible with your fabric. Other options are to use a sew-in interfacing or a second layer of fashion fabric as interfacing (see p. 21).

Preshrink and apply interfacing as described on p. 21. Do not trim away the seam allowance on fusibles as the extra layer stabilizes the neck edge, which can be wobbly if the interfacing *is* trimmed in the seam allowance. Once the interfacing is in place, stitch the facing seams, then trim them to ¼ in. and press open. There are several options to finish the outside edge

## Necklines

A neckline gives a garment character and polish, framing the face and determining the fit and hang of the top. Where a blouse has a collar, the neckline on a top is usually finished with a shaped facing, a bias binding, or a bias facing. One of the first skills a novice sewer learns is how to construct a simple, shaped facing; many other skills

of the facing, but whichever you choose should be invisible from the right side. Finish the edge of the facing by serging, by stitching ¼ in. from the edge, then pinking the edge, or with a self-faced facing.

Make a self-faced facing, using either fusible or sew-in interfacing. Using this method, the fusing is done before the facing is assembled:

**1.** With right sides together, stitch the facing to the interfacing along the *outer* edge of the facing in a ¼-in. seam, using a short (1.5-mm) stitch and size 37 foot, which is ¼ in. wide.
**2.** Trim the seam to ⅛ in. (I use a rotary cutter), and press the seam allowance toward the facing. Press the interfacing in place along the edge, favoring the interfacing to the inside.
**3.** Position the interfacing and fuse from the center outward. Trim any excess interfacing that may have shifted.
**4.** Join the facing pieces together, and trim the seams to ¼ in.; press open (see the photo on the facing page).

**Attaching a facing** Here's a straightforward way to attach a facing.

**1.** Pin the facing to the garment, matching seams, notches, and centers, then stitch (see the top photo at right). I use a smaller stitch (2.0-mm) and a magnetic seam guide to achieve a smooth, curved seam.
**2.** Layer or grade the seams (see the photo below). One of the rules for grading is that the seam that will be next to the outside of the garment is wider, so it acts as a pad—preventing an obvious ridge from showing. Trim the facing seam (which will be on the underside) to a fat ⅛ in., then layer the garment seam to a fat ¼ in. Clip curved seams every ½ in. up to the stitching line. By layering/grading the seams, you eliminate bulk; by clipping, the seam opens up so the facing will turn smoothly. Press flat as sewn, then press the seam toward the facing.
**3.** Understitch from the right side, a scant ⅛ in. from the seam; this technique is used to keep the facing edge from rolling to the outside. Use an edgestitch foot for fast, accurate stitching.

*Stitch with the facing on top (more stable), using a seam guide for precision.*

*Layer the seam, trimming the facing to a fat ⅛ in. and the garment to a fat ¼ in., then clip to the stitching every ½ in.*

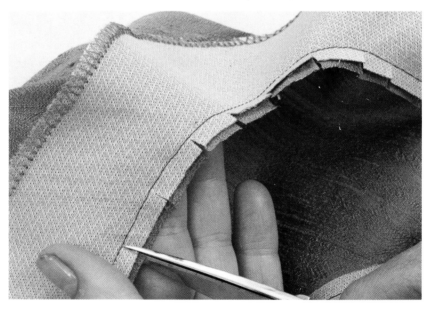

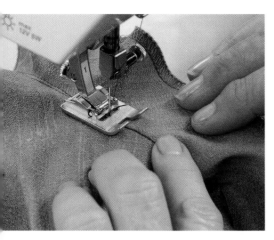

*Understitch on the right side, a scant ⅛ in. from the seam. Use an edgestitch foot for accurate stitching.*

*Pressing the neckline over a ham allows you to keep the shape while favoring the facing to the inside of the garment.*

**4.** Press the facing over a ham, rolling the seam to the inside. Secure the facing by hand-stitching at the seam allowances, by machine-stitching in the well of the seam, or by topstitching from the right side. Do *not* hand-stitch the facing to the garment all along the edge of the facing. The hand stitches are bound to show as the garment is worn.

***Creating facings, and facings as design*** It is simple to create your own facing, whether you want to create a new neckline, make a facing in a different shape or width than the pattern, or make a facing if your pattern does not call for one.

Make a facing duplicating the shape of your neckline (see the photo on the facing page). Place plain paper under the pattern (front and back neck), and trace off the neck curve, extending 3¼ in. along the shoulder seam. Transfer the notches and grain markings. Make the facing width by marking an even distance (3¼ in. is standard) from the neckline curve.

Use facings as a design element by adjusting the width and shape. I like a narrow, 1-in., topstitched facing for silk broadcloth, linen, and stable double knits. The trick is to make a standard, finished, 2½-in. facing, and trim to the narrow width after construction, then finish the outer edge. A deep, back-neck facing creates an interesting topstitching outline, and works well when used with a deep, V-front neckline.

***V necklines*** Deep V necklines require a facing that will "tighten" the neck. Make the facing as described on this page, then cut the pattern piece, trim

*To make a facing, use a seam gauge that duplicates the shape of the neckline.*

the seams ⅛ in., and overlap ¼ in. (see the illustration at right).

V necklines should be staystitched and the V point reinforced immediately after cutting to keep the off-bias neckline from stretching while being handled and stitched. Stay tape keeps the neck from stretching while being worn (see the photo on p. 68).

**1.** Reinforce 1 in. on either side of the V point first, then staystitch from that point on either side up to the shoulder.
**2.** Apply stay tape or a ¼-in. selvage strip from thin lining fabric on V neck along the seamline from within 1 in. of the V to the shoulder seam.
**3.** Hand-baste the stay tape, or hold it in place as you stitch the facing to the garment. Do not tape into the V because it creates

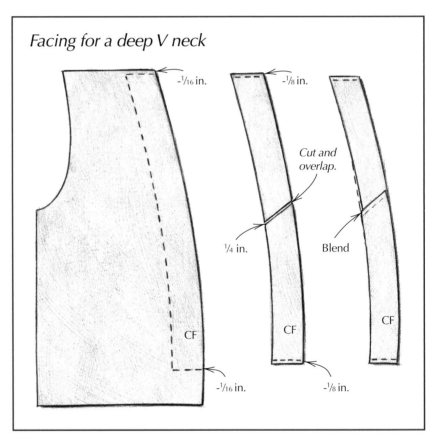

*Facing for a deep V neck*

-¹⁄₁₆ in.

-⅛ in.

Cut and overlap.

¼ in.

Blend

CF

CF

CF

-¹⁄₁₆ in.

-⅛ in.

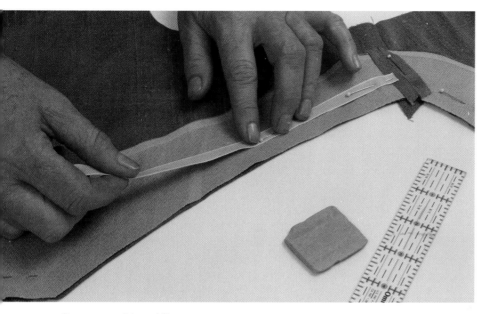

Stay-tape a V neckline to prevent stretching during stitching or in wearing the garment.

edge (see the top illustration on the facing page).

These instructions are for a standard width facing (3¼ in. cut). It will be 1½ in. to 1¾ in. finished, which accounts for the turn of the cloth. See the bottom illustration on the facing page:

**1.** Adapt the shoulder seam by stitching right sides together to 1¼ in. from the neck edge, then backstitch and clip.
**2.** Turn the seam allowance to the other side, wrong sides together, stitching a short, 1¼-in. seam at the neck. This assures that the raw edges will remain hidden on the underside once the facing is in place on the right side.
**3.** Sew facings just as you would if they were on the inside.
**4.** Trim the facing to an even width after the neck edge is finished. (They never come out perfectly even.)
**5.** Understitch toward the body of the garment, *not* the facing.
**6.** Finish the facing edge by turning and edgestitching or binding with bias. Or you can make a clean, turned-under edge by doing a line of staystitch-plus (see pp. 52-53) ¼ in. from the edge, then press under so the stitching is concealed on the underside and edgestitch.

unnecessary bulk, and do not tape around the back neck because it creates a too-tight drag at the neckline.
**4.** Take two stitches across the V, and clip right up to that point.
**5.** Layer the seams, clip the curves, and understitch up to the V point, but not around it because it would cause distorting.
**6.** Press over a ham, rolling seam to the underside, and smoothing and sculpting the V.

***Facings on the outside*** Facings don't have to be on the inside of a garment. Placing the facings on the outside is a trick used in ready-to-wear to create interesting designs. Use your fashion fabric, the wrong side of your fabric, or a contrasting fabric. Vary the width or shape of your facings, use a light padding and topstitching, or add a bias binding or piping along the

***Bias facing*** A strip of bias can be used on necks, armholes, and hems as a narrow, hidden facing that is turned to the inside of the garment. Use a bias strip of self-

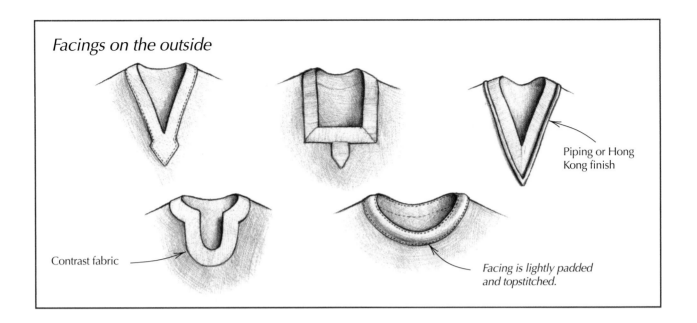

## Facings on the outside

Contrast fabric

Piping or Hong Kong finish

Facing is lightly padded and topstitched.

fabric or lighter-weight fabric. This bias facing can be single or double thickness (see p. 108 for constructing bias binding). The bias facings used on necklines and armholes are narrow, ranging from a finished width of ¼ in. to 1 in. Staystitch the neck before applying the facing.

Apply the bias binding in a 1-to-1 ratio to the edge. Do *not* stretch as you sew. Layer the seams, clip, press, and under-stitch as for a facing. Press the bias facing to the inside over a ham, rolling the seam to the underside. Secure the bias invisibly by hand, or topstitch from the right side of the garment.

**Adding slashes and slits**
Slashes and slits can be incorporated with facings or binding to enlarge the neck

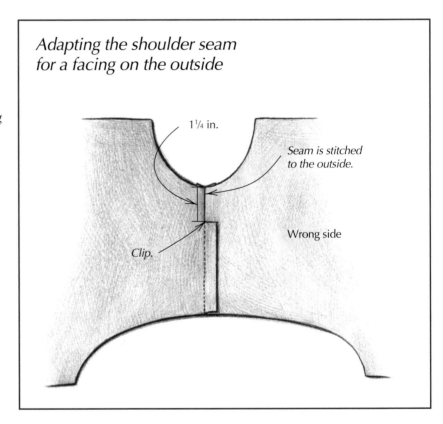

## Adapting the shoulder seam for a facing on the outside

1¼ in.

Seam is stitched to the outside.

Clip.

Wrong side

## Slit/slash neckline styling

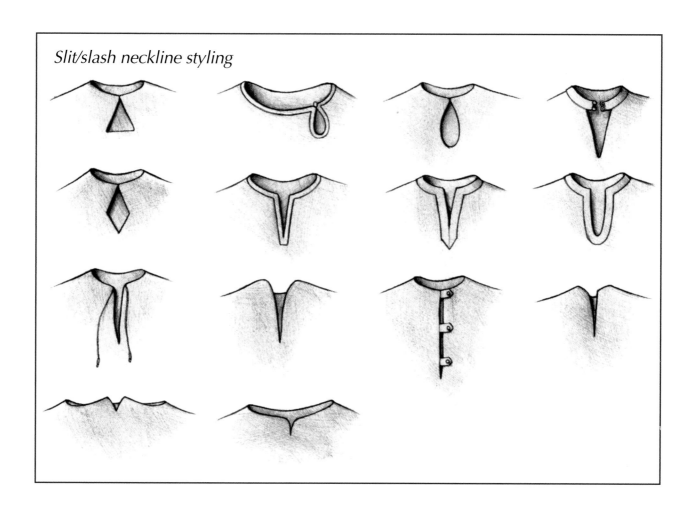

The secret to making a bias facing lie smoothly is to press the bias strip into a curve that duplicates the shape of the neckline before stitching it to the garment.

opening, or create a design detail. It is easy to add a slit to the center front or back. The length can be whatever you choose; 2½ in. to 5 in. is an average amount.

**1.** To make the slit facing, make the width 1½ in. from the center (3 in. total), extending the facing 1½ in. below the bottom of the slit. Curve at the bottom and blend with the neck facing (see the illustration at left on the facing page).

**2.** Mark the center line on the garment and interfaced facing, using silk thread or a chalk

marker. *Do not cut the slash until the facing is stitched.*

**3.** Align the marked center lines on the facing and garment, basting along the slit to hold the layers firmly in place.

**4.** Create a point, a curve, or a square, depending on the shape of the stitching at the end of the slit (see the illustration at right on the facing page):

- For a point, taper the stitching line from ¼ in. each side of the center at the neck edge to ⅛ in. at the point. Stitch, using small stitches at the point, and taking two to three

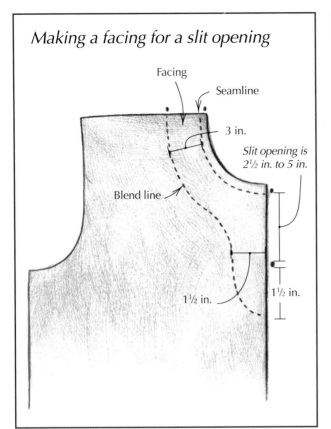

## Making a facing for a slit opening

Facing

Seamline

3 in.

*Slit opening is 2½ in. to 5 in.*

Blend line

1½ in.

1½ in.

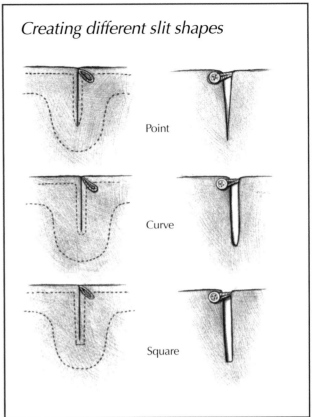

## Creating different slit shapes

Point

Curve

Square

small, horizontal stitches at the point. Clip up to but not through the last stitches.

- For a curve, draw in the shape, making tiny (1.0-mm) stitches on the bottom of the slit in a tight curve. Trim close to the stitching to turn.
- For a square, draw in the square, and stitch the corner using small stitches, taking one stitch diagonally at the corners. Clip into the corners to turn.

**Bound slit** Make a bound slit with ¼-in. bias bindings and a square bottom (see the photo and illustration on p. 72).

**1.** Mark the center of the slit and the bottom. Reinforce along the bottom, using tiny (1.5-mm) stitches, pivoting at the corners.
**2.** Cut two strips of bias, which have been pressed to remove the stretch, 1¼ in. wide and the length of the slit plus 1¼ in. Position the bias strips on the right side of the garment, lining up the cut edges of the strips with the slit center line. Stitch ¼ in. from the center line, backstitching at the reinforcing line.
**3.** Cut along the slit line through the garment fabric only, ending about ½ in. from the end,

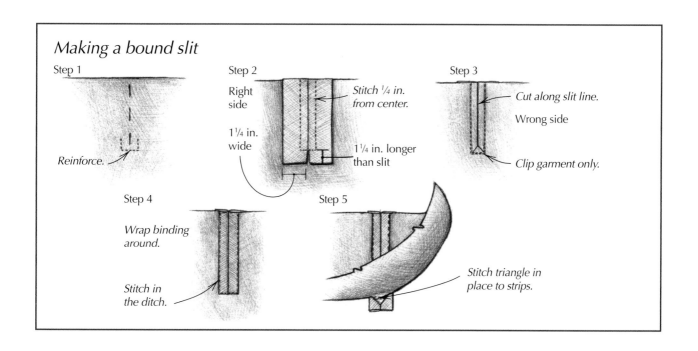

Step 1

Reinforce.

Step 2

Right side

1¼ in. wide

Stitch ¼ in. from center.

1¼ in. longer than slit

Step 3

Cut along slit line.

Wrong side

Clip garment only.

Step 4

Wrap binding around.

Stitch in the ditch.

Step 5

Stitch triangle in place to strips.

*A bound slit is a simple elegant detail to add to a neckline front or back.*

clipping at an angle down to the corners.

**4.** Press, then wrap the binding around evenly, turning the edges under, for an underlap. Stitch in the ditch or slipstitch by hand.

**5.** Finish the bottom of the slit by stitching back and forth across the small triangle and through the binding strips.

**Twisted cowl** Use this easy, soft variation on a turtleneck in knits or wovens, and with any round neckline that slips on easily over your head. The cowl is a rectangle that you can draw directly on the fabric or you can make a paper pattern piece for it (see the photo on the facing page).

**1.** Cut knits with the length of the cowl on the crossgrain, and cut wovens on the bias. The cowl length is equal to the neck seam measurement plus 1 in., but you can vary the width; I have cowls that measure from 6 in. to 15 in.

**2.** Stitch the short ends of the cowl in a ½-in. seam, then press the seam open.

**3.** Finish the long raw edge by serging or turning the edge under ½ in.

**4.** With right sides together, place the seam of the cowl at center back. Stitch one layer of the cowl to the neck, and press.

**5.** Trim the seam to ¼ in.

**6.** Secure the raw edge of the cowl to the inside by offsetting it horizontally 3 in. to 4 in. so the finished effect is soft and twisted.

**7.** Stitch in the ditch or slipstitch by hand.

*The twisted cowl is a softened version of a turtleneck you can plug into a plain neck.*

**Square corners**  Square corners are a signature technique frequently used by designer Issey Miyake to inset a cowl or create a shaped neckline where the front of a garment is set into the back at the neck. This technique only looks hard to construct. Mark and stitch with precision, and you can set in square or triangular angles with ease.

**1.** Mark the two corners that will be joined along the seamline. Reinforce the square angle on the stitching line, and mark the inset along the seamline at the corner.
**2.** Reinforce 1 in. on either side of the square corner, taking one diagonal stitch at the corner (see the top photo on p. 74).
**3.** Clip to the corner. Always work with the reinforced side *up*.
**4.** Align the corners, and pin the two pieces at the corner, distributing the fullness evenly. Place one pin dead center,

perpendicular to the seam, then pin each side along the seamline, with the pins parallel to and directly on the seamline so they can by easily pulled out as you stitch (see the bottom photo on p. 74).
**5.** Stitch along the reinforcing stitching. Pivot at the corner. Leave the needle down, pull out the pin, turn the fabric, and position the fabric away from the presser foot.

## Sleeves

Set in the sleeves after the neckline is completed. Evaluate the fit of the garment and the placement of the sleeve: Visualize the width of the shoulder by turning under the armhole seam at the shoulder to see where the sleeve seam will sit. If the shoulder width is too wide, trim away up to ¾ in. at the shoulder, tapering to 0 at the notches; the front and back

*Mark both intersections of the square corner along the seam. Reinforce and clip to the stitching.*

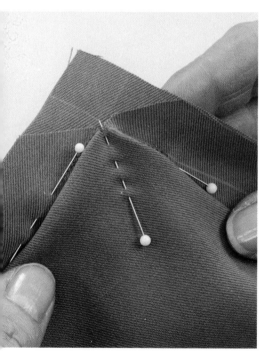

*Match and pin precisely, using the reinforcing as a stitching guide.*

armhole may be adjusted differently. It is not necessary to make any corresponding adjustment to the sleeve cap (see Chapter 4).

***Set-in sleeves*** Notice that a set-in sleeve is shaped with a high cap. The armhole is usually 1 in. to 2 in. smaller than the cap of the sleeve, and the sleeve is eased into the armhole. You'll get a better fit and more professional results if you sew "in the round" for classic, set-in sleeves that sit on or are slightly extended from the natural shoulder line. By understanding the anatomy of the sleeve cap first, you'll find it easier to set in a sleeve with consistent results.

A sleeve cap has two notches on the back of the garment, one

notch in the front. There is more ease on the back of a sleeve than the front. By folding a sleeve in half lengthwise, you can see the difference in shape and size of the cap. Dots and notches match up with corresponding markings on the armhole. The greatest amount of ease lies between the dots. The grain is straight— ½ in. on either side of the dot at the top of the sleeve; very little ease goes here. From dot to notch is the next greatest amount of ease, with a smaller amount from notches to underarm.

To set a sleeve set in the round, first finish the side seams on the garment and sleeves. Easestitch the cap by machine-basting two lines of stitching inside the seamline at ½ in. and ¼ in. from notch to notch using a 4.5-mm to 5-mm basting stitch. With the sleeve side up and wrong side facing you, pin the sleeve to the garment, matching the shoulder, notches, dots, and underarm seam, placing pins perpendicular at notches; setting a sleeve requires a lot of pins. Pull evenly on the basting threads, drawing up the sleeve to fit the armhole. Distribute the fullness smoothly, placing pins along the seamline so you can pull them out as you come to them. Wrap basting threads around the pins at the notches to secure. Stitch along the seamline with the sleeve side up, pulling out the pins as you stitch. If puckers form as you are

*Head off trouble: If puckers form as you are stitching, use your fingers to spread and smooth out the weave of the cloth as you sew.*

*Press a sleeve cap using the shaped edge of a sleeve board.*

stitching, use your fingers to spread and smooth out the weave of the cloth as you sew (see the photo above).

Pressing is crucial when making set-in sleeves, and it is important not to overpress or underpress, allowing the soft ease at the cap of the sleeve to conform to the shape of the body. Place the sleeve cap over the ham or on the edge of a sleeve board, and steam both seams toward the sleeve cap, smoothing along the seam with your fingers. Steam and lightly press the seam, doing most of the pressing from the wrong side (see the photo at right). Touch up from the right side. If you overpress and the sleeve cap looks too flat, press the seam flat as sewn and begin the process again.

Don't trim the seam allowance on a set-in sleeve; the width of the seam fills in the sleeve cap. Serge the edges separately before

construction, or serge the two layers together after the pressing and shaping are complete. I like the minimal effect of pinking just the edges of the sleeve and armhole.

***Dropped-shoulder sleeves*** The cap of a dropped-shoulder sleeve is wide and flat with a small amount of ease. Sew dropped-shoulder sleeves into the garment flat, before the side seams are sewn.

Use staystitch-plus (see pp. 52-53) between the notches to ease in the small amount of ease. Pin the sleeve to the armhole, garment side up, matching the dots and notches; the action of the feed dogs helps ease the sleeve into the armhole. This technique does not work with a set-in sleeve, which has more ease—since you cannot see to control the ease in the sleeve cap, puckers and pleats could form.

When setting in a sleeve, keep the tails of basting thread from tangling by snipping the threads underneath 1 in. from the fabric.

Use a mock flat-felled seam or the Japanese flat-felled seam (see p. 56) with the seam and topstitching on the body of the garment. Use a press cloth when pressing on the right side if your fabric requires it, and topstitch from the right side to get a smooth, professional finish.

***All-in-one sleeve*** Sleeves that are cut all-in-one with the garment are a favorite design of mine, but I have experienced frustration because the angle of the shoulder seam is cut on the "off bias" and stretches as the garment is worn.

One tip to prevent the sleeves from growing is to sew clear elastic as you stitch the sleeve seam. (*Note*: This is the same technique used in stabilizing the shoulder seam on knits, extending the clear elastic all the way down the sleeve seam.) Serge the shoulder/sleeve seam on the front of the garment only. Stitch elastic in a 1-to-1 ratio (no stretching), with the back of the garment up as you sew. Press the seam flat with the front of the garment up, and press the seam open. Trim the back seam allowance to $3/8$ in., then press both seams toward the back. Do not touch the elastic with the hot iron; it will melt. Topstitch the seam allowances toward the back, stitching from the right side $1/2$ in. from the seam. The enclosed elastic will keep the sleeve from stretching.

## Hems

Hems relate to the style and techniques used in the top. I'd use a hand-sewn hem on a silk shell without any topstitching, but I might topstitch a linen top that has topstitched detailing elsewhere. Silk is soft and difficult to control, so is better suited to hand-stitching, while linen is easy to topstitch, and the effect harmonizes with the texture and crispness of the cloth. Consider the width of the hem in relation to the style of the top and the fabric. I use 1-in. to 2-in. hems for most tops; the $5/8$-in. hem indicated on many patterns is too narrow and tends to roll to the outside. On sleeves or when the garment is shaped, make sure the hem is shaped as well, for a hem that is a smaller diameter than the garment creates a struggle and is sure to show.

Shape the hem by folding the pattern piece along the hemline. Duplicate the shape of the garment in the hem; it will appear flared but will fit perfectly into the garment, causing no distortion.

Use a light edge finish for hems. A serged edge is a clean, easy solution for many fabrics, and it should not strike through (show on the right side) when pressed. Machine embroidery thread used in the serger results in a lighter edge than cotton or polyester sewing thread. I rarely use seam tape or add binding to the edge because it adds weight and bulk. A pinked and stitched edge is an honest and minimal hem finish. Use the rotary pinking blade to trim the edge, then stitch ¼ in. from that edge; staystitch-plus can be used if needed. Bias garments need no hem finish since bias does not ravel. Use a template made from an oak-tag file folder to make a perfectly straight and even hem width (see the photo at right).

*Hand-sewn hem* Hand-sewn hems are a sign of finesse and quality clothes; avoid them on garments that will be machine washed or dried. Use a hand-sewn hem on fine-quality garments, especially if the top will be worn over pants or a skirt, or for fabrics that are not suited to machine stitching.

A hand-sewn hem is invisible from the right side. Follow these easy tips for successful hand hemming: Use a single strand of thread in a short length; allow the knot to fall at your elbow when the needle is threaded and ready to sew; use as fine a needle as you can see to thread. I prefer long-staple polyester thread for most hems, though silk thread is perfect because it is smooth, strong, and fine.

This little trick from French couture prevents the drag that causes stitches to show. The secret to invisible hand-stitching lies in three steps:

*Use a template made from oak tag to make a perfectly straight and even hem.*

**1.** Fold the edge of the hem (no matter which edge finish is used) back ¼ in. and apply stitches at this fold.

**2.** The stitch is a version of a simple running stitch, catching the garment and then the fold of the hem, with stitches ⅜ in. to ½ in. apart. Catch just a fiber of the fashion fabric.

**3.** Make easy, not tight, stitches ¼ in. to ⅜ in. long, and form a knot every 4 in. to 6 in. Easy stitches don't show, and the knot assures that your hem will stay up even if a few stitches should get torn with normal wear and tear (see the photo on p. 78).

*Machine-topstitched hem*
Machine-stitched hems are strong and functional. I consider the effect of the width of the

*With the edge of the hem folded back, catch just a fiber of the garment, then the fold of the hem, using easy stitches that are ¼ in. to ⅜ in. apart.*

hem, the thread, and the stitch length carefully. Here are a few techniques I use to ensure a fluid, straight, machine-stitched hem.

- Make a test swatch to assure that your fabric won't stretch.
- Use a template to ensure a straight, even hem.
- Hand-baste hems along the edge, first using a single strand of silk thread, then machine-stitch. This additional step marks the hem edge, and the silk thread pulls out easily.
- Use a clear ruler and Clo-chalk with the basting as a guide, and draw a straight line directly on the right side of the fabric. Clo-chalk is the only product I use to mark on the right side. It vanishes when pressed or washed, or within 24 hours.

- Topstitch from the right side of the garment, because the quality of the stitch is always better on the needle rather than the garment side.

***Hemming vents with a miter*** I like the effect of vents on tops designed to be worn untucked, and add them whether the pattern calls for it or not. This is one of the details I notice in fine ready-to-wear. Most vents are 3 in. to 4 in. long, but you can create interesting details by varying the length, by making the back or front of the garment longer, or by placing the vent at center front or back. Mitering gives a flat, professional look, and by borrowing a technique used in Japanese kimonos, the weight of the fabric in the miter makes the vent hang flat:

**1.** Press up the hem and vent. Open hems out and fold back at the corner of the foldline, forming a diagonal edge, matching the creases. Press along this diagonal line; this will be your stitching line (see the top photo on the facing page).
**2.** With right sides together, stitch along this diagonal line. *Do not trim.*
**3.** Use a point presser to get into the corner and press the seam open. Next, press from wrong side, turn, then press and clap with a clapper to flatten. The fabric will fill up the square corner, adding weight and stability (see the bottom photo on the facing page). Use

To make a mitered corner, pin the corner to the ironing board and fold back the hem matching creases and press along the diagonal line to mark the stitching line.

topstitching to add subtle reinforcing stitching details at the top of a vent.

**Designing vents and slits** I have noticed that in expensive ready-to-wear tops, designers use vents, slits, and topstitching details to add interest and character to the garment. This detail varies with fashion cycles. I keep a notebook of ideas culled from ready-to-wear, and have found some good ideas from Japanese and avant-garde designs. Seek out offbeat garments—I often find great design details on garments I would never wear!

To add a vent or slit to center or side seams, determine the finished length of the vent, and mark on the pattern seamline. Attach scrap tissue and add ⅝ in. to 1 in. to the top of the vent,

Press the seam open over a point presser so the fabric square fills in the corner.

shape the top of the vent in a square or angle, then add width to the seam allowance (see the illustration on p. 80).

For French seams, blend the intersection of the seam and vent, incorporating topstitching.

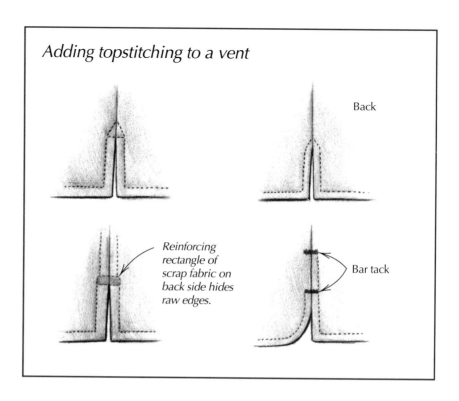

Back

*Reinforcing rectangle of scrap fabric on back side hides raw edges.*

Bar tack

Tuck under the raw edge of the French seam, forming an angle, and baste. Topstitch as shown in the photo on the facing page.

***Pressing hems*** Press all hems after stitching to blend the stitches, and smooth out the hem. Do most of the pressing from the wrong side, and make the final touches on the right side, using a press cloth if your fabric gets shiny from the iron.

## Closures

One of the ways to create exceptional garments is by using distinctive buttons, fastidious buttonholes, and closures that are often the hallmark of expensive ready-to-wear.

***Buttonholes*** Buttonholes must relate in size and placement to the design of the garment, the fabric, and the button. Even experienced sewers confess to experiencing buttonhole-phobia, so here are a few hints I've found helpful in making machine buttonholes:

There are as many ways of making buttonholes as there are sewing machines, and not all machines are user-friendly. If your machine makes less than satisfactory buttonholes, consider purchasing an automatic buttonhole maker, which is a separate attachment that clamps onto the machine and makes buttonholes of a consistent size. Make up a sample swatch with all the sizes so you will know

*Finish the junction of a French seam and vent with topstitching.*

which template fits your button. If buttonhole-phobia persists, try loops instead (see pp. 83-84).

The latest, state-of-the-art sewing machines are so smart they can compute the size of the buttonhole by placing the button onto a screen which "reads" the button, creates the exact-size buttonhole and will repeat it over and over. Whatever means you use to compute buttonhole size, it is always recommended to make a test buttonhole before adding any in your garment.

The main problem I encounter in making buttonholes is when the fabric is not perfectly flat— the top buttonhole often brings trouble. Use a clapper to flatten out the area around the button-hole. If that fails, use a "shim"— a small, folded piece of paper— to make the height even. Test. Test. Test. Practice. Practice. Practice. If you notice your buttonhole is going "off" as you sew, stop immediately, rip it out carefully, and begin again.

Determine buttonhole size by measuring the diameter plus the thickness of the button to determine the inside length of the buttonhole. To figure button size for round or odd-shaped buttons, wrap a strip of paper around the button and shank. Then fold the strip in half to determine buttonhole size.

Interfacing is an essential ingredient behind buttons and buttonholes; the extra layer prevents the buttonhole from stretching and keeps the weight of the button from drooping. Place the grain or the most stable direction of the interfacing parallel with the buttonhole. If there is a fold at the edge, extend the interfacing $1/2$ in. beyond the fold, which creates a soft yet firm edge. If the interfacing ends at the fold, it creates a wobbly edge.

The pattern gives direction and placement of buttonholes, but consider alternatives to give your garment unique character. I rarely use the buttonhole placement guide in the pattern. I wait until the garment is complete to play with the possibilities so I can see the effect on the garment itself. Cluster buttons in groups of two or three, use a series of tiny buttons, try a few large dramatic buttons, or use many buttons close together. I love to use vintage buttons and create a collage effect, combining different but related buttons.

A horizontal buttonhole is the most secure. The end of the buttonhole extends $1/8$ in. beyond the placement line so the button is centered. If there is a vertical band or line in your garment or fabric, or if you are using many small buttons, use a vertical buttonhole. Vertical buttons are placed directly on the placement line.

Mark buttonholes on the right side of the fabric. I use a tracing line of contrasting-color silk thread or Clo-chalk. Silk thread is so fine and slippery, it is easy to remove after stitching, and Clo-chalk is the only product I use to mark the right side of a fabric because it vanishes easily. If Clo-chalk does not show on a particular fabric, I use silk thread.

Experiment with different kinds of threads for machine-made buttonholes. I use long-staple, polyester for most garments, but silk thread makes a subtle, lustrous statement, and machine-embroidery thread makes a fine buttonhole for sheers and delicate fabrics.

Once the buttonholes are complete, press to remove puckering, and seal with a seam sealant to prevent raveling. Cut open using a buttonhole chisel, a small device that easily and accurately cuts the buttonhole opening (see the right photo on the facing page).

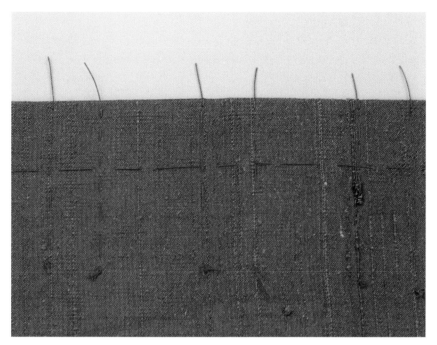

Silk thread marks show up easily on the right side of the fabric, and they are easy to remove after the buttonholes are sewn.

A buttonhole chisel opens the buttonhole with a quick, clean chop.

Place the buttons after the buttonholes are complete. Pin the garment together as it will be worn, aligning the placement line (often the center). For horizontal buttonholes, mark with a pin at the end of the buttonhole; for vertical buttonholes, mark with a pin at the center. Check that all buttons are the same distance from the edge.

**Loops** Loops offer an alternative to buttonholes. A loop is perfect to close a neck opening, and a row of loops adds a fine dressmaker touch. Loops are inserted into a seam, and when complete they should be flat and unobtrusive. Make loops of self-fabric, or use purchased fine, flat, or round braid.

To make narrow, self-fabric loops, cut a strip of bias that is longer than your measurements. The trick is not to try to stitch a narrow tube, but to use the stretch of the bias to create a tiny, bias tube.

**1.** Fold the bias strip in half, right sides together, and stitch ¼ in. from the fold. Widen at each end so the tube will be easier to turn.
**2.** Serge close to the stitching; this trims the seam allowance evenly, and the serged seam fills up the tube. If you do not have a serger, trim the seam to ¼ in.

# ADDING BUTTONS TO A SHOULDER SEAM

Here is how to add a button closing to a shoulder seam.

**1.** Make a full pattern for the front and back pieces (see p. 101). Add scrap tissue to the left front and back pattern shoulder. The cutting line will be the new foldline, and the original seamline becomes the buttonhole/button placement line.

**2.** Draw a new line 1¼ in. from the cutting/foldline; this is the new cutting line.

**3.** Fold the paper along foldline, and cut out the shape of the neck and armhole.

**4.** Cut the interfacing 1¾ in. wide.

**5.** Place buttonholes parallel to the fold.

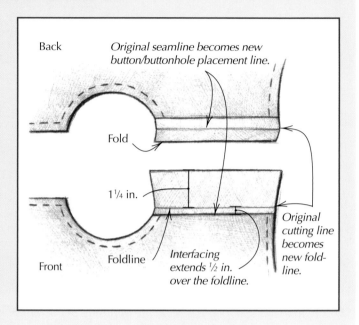

Back

*Original seamline becomes new button/buttonhole placement line.*

Fold

1¼ in.

Front

Foldline

*Interfacing extends ½ in. over the foldline.*

*Original cutting line becomes new fold-line.*

**3.** Turn the tube inside out (see the left photo on the facing page). I use a tube-turning device, which is a narrow wire with a small hook on one end.
**4.** Dampen the tube with a spray mister and stretch (making it narrow and even), pinning to the ironing board until dry (see the right photo on the facing page).

Experiment when applying the loops; you want to have the smallest possible loop to accommodate the button. Here's how to position loops:

**1.** Mark the seamline, and pin one end in place, then move the other end into position.
**2.** Use machine-basting to hold the loop in place until you sew.

**3.** Make the loop larger by making it longer, not by making it stick out farther.

Thread loops are a delicate, nearly invisible way to fasten a small button or a hook. If you want a substantial loop, use buttonhole thread.

**1.** Use a double strand of thread. Wax the thread with beeswax, and press it with a hot iron; this quick step stiffens the thread and prevents tangling. Bury the knot and make two to three stitches, making a bar.
**2.** Cover the bar with blanket stitches placed close together, and make two to three *more* stitches when you have reached the end to prevent slippage.

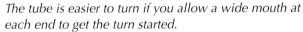

*The tube is easier to turn if you allow a wide mouth at each end to get the turn started.*

*Make the tube skinny and stretch-free by dampening, stretching, and pinning it to the ironing board.*

## Shoulder pads

Shoulder pads have gone from being a '40s vintage look to an '80s fashion-victim look, and have become a fashion option. Today's shoulder pads are discreet and natural-looking, adding just a hint of shape and lift so the garment hangs from the shoulders. Shoulder pads are optional, but if your pattern was designed to add them and you don't want them, you may need to make a simple alteration to eliminate the extra height. Remember, though, shoulder pads not only give shape and definition at the shoulder, but balance out and minimize hips.

I keep a small assortment of shoulder pads on hand (see the photo on p. 86). If your pattern calls for shoulder pads, use them in tissue fitting and as you fit the garment during construction. This may or may not be the pad you finally choose once the garment is finished, but it really doesn't matter at this point. The best time to select a pad is once the garment is complete.

***Types of shoulder pads*** There are two basic types of shoulder pads: one for set-in sleeves and another for raglan, dolman, or all-in-one sleeves. I rarely use a set-in shoulder pad because the edge of the pad creates a visible line when the garment is worn. So after years of having a love-

*Keep an assortment of shoulder pads on hand to try on when you are fitting. Make final shoulder pad decisions when the garment is complete.*

hate relationship with shoulder pads, I've found a petal-shaped, molded style that is perfect in any style sleeve—set-in to raglan. The pad blends easily with your shoulders and adds just a hint of lift, improving the hang and overall effect of most garments. It is so unobtrusive that you can layer one set in a top and another in a jacket without looking like a cross between a turtle and a quarterback. Sew the pad directly into a garment's shoulder seams, or apply a strip of hook-and-loop fasteners (such as Velcro) on one set of pads to use with different garments.

***Positioning a shoulder pad*** One of the reasons I prefer this raglan petal pad is that it can be positioned exactly where you need it. Most people have one shoulder that is different from the other, and this allows for variances in shoulder position.

Try on the garment and place the pads on your shoulders; pin in place along the seamline. If the pads are to be sewn into the garment, note the distance from the edge of the pad to the neck edge. Pads should be sewn an equal distance from the edge, so if one pad is 1 in. from the edge and the other is 1½ in., even out the distance and place both pads 1¼ in. Align the center of the pad with the seamline, and slipstitch invisibly to the seam allowance. If one shoulder curves, place the pad to nest with it. In most cases, the pads will be placed an equal distance from the neck edge. Try them pinned straight with the seam allowance, then adjust as needed.

I use hook-and-loop fasteners, such as Velcro, to attach shoulder pads. Attach the soft side to the shoulder seam. Machine stitching makes the fasteners curl and show, so I prefer to stitch each piece securely by hand. Hook-and-loop fasteners allow you to place the pad exactly where you want it, and you'll end up needing only two pairs of pads in your entire wardrobe—one pair in a light color and one in a dark color.

Eliminate the height added to a pattern for shoulder pads by tapering from 0 at the neck edge and decreasing the height of the pad at the shoulder.

***Covering a raglan shoulder pad with fusible interfacing***  The following is a quick and simple process that works for any style raglan molded shoulder pad. Fusing a cover keeps molded pads intact through the dry-cleaning process.

**1.**  Cut out fusible-knit interfacing, such as Sof Shape. Layer four thicknesses of the interfacing with the stretch going across the pad. Place one pad on the interfacing, and cut around the pad, using a 1-in. seam allowance. Use a rotary cutter with a guide arm. Fold the cut pieces in half lengthwise, trimming so the shape is symmetrical. Mark with a clip at the center.

**2.**  Draw a line along the center of the cover piece and pads, on the top and bottom, with an air-erasable pen.

**3.**  Drape a dart on the top cover piece: Place the pad on a tailor's ham, and center an interfacing piece on top, with the fusing side up. Create a dart over the center of the pad, placing pins as it will be sewn. Mark the shaped darts on two pieces, using a curve stick. Serge the darts or sew them with a straight stitch, and trim to ¼ in.

**4.**  Optional: Apply 3 in. of hook-and-loop fasteners to the darted cover piece (the top). Use the stiffer, hooked side on the pad and the softer, loop side sewn to the seam allowance on your garment. Position the darted piece on the pad to determine placement of the fasteners. Do not extend the fasteners over the curved portion of the pad. Secure the fastener to the interfacing with a glue stick or the fasteners' adhesive. Allow to dry, and stitch the fastener to the interfacing only. Hook-and-loop fasteners are *not* sewn through the pad.

**5.** Fuse and shape the interfacing to the pad. Sculpting while fusing is the secret to getting a pad that retains its shape and appears invisible when worn. Place the pad on a tailor's ham. Center the upper darted cover on the top of the pad and fuse, smoothing out any fullness while building in a curved shape. Then fuse the undarted cover to the bottom of the pad, pressing to retain the curve.

**6.** Finish the edge by serging, or sew along the edge of the pad with a straight stitch, and pink close to the edge. It is easier to retain the curve if you sew with the underside of the pad up.

**7.** Place the completed pad on the small end of the tailor's ham, steam to shape, and let dry.

# Constructing a Knit T-Shirt

If you have never sewn knits, or if you have experienced frustration or fear of them, the following section will take you through the step-by-step process of making a T-shirt, with tips for success. Knits are simple to sew, once you know how to control the neck edge and sew smooth seams and hems. Practice new techniques with garment scraps, and always test seams and topstitching when sewing a new kind of knit.

## ORDER OF CONSTRUCTION FOR KNIT TOPS

**1.** Serge the front shoulder seams and sleeve cap (for dropped-shoulder sleeves, not set-in sleeves).

**2.** Press hems in place.

**3.** Serge or machine-stitch a ¾-in. to 1-in. strip of bias fusible tricot to the hem edges.

**4.** Sew shoulder seam, using clear elastic (on backside). Topstitch the seams toward the back.

**5.** To add neck binding, try on the garment to check neck shape, and adjust as needed. Measure the neck at the seamline to determine the measurement.

**6.** Try on the garment to determine the shoulder width. Adjust as needed.

**7.** To set in sleeves, stitch with the garment (not the sleeve) side up. Try on the garment before pressing, topstitching, or serging. Adjust if needed. Press. Topstitch for dropped sleeves, serge edges together for set-in sleeves.

**8.** Pin the garment together at the side seams, wrong sides together, to check body shape and fit. Adjust fit, mark, and stitch, using a standard machine. Try on the garment one more time.

**9.** Press the hems into place, fusing the interfacing.

**10.** Topstitch the hems from the right side, using staystitch-plus if any stretching occurs, or hand-sew the hems.

**11.** Cover and insert a shoulder pad.

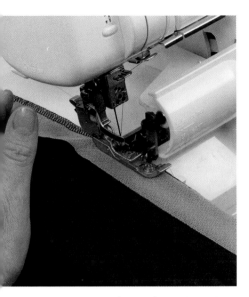

*Serge or straight-stitch a 1-in. strip of Sof Knit along the edge of the hem, with resin side up. A narrower strip will curl.*

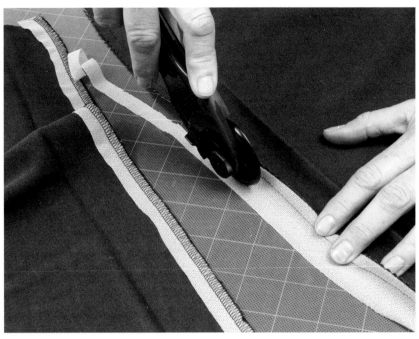

*Trim the interfacing strip to $3/8$ in., using scissors or a rotary cutter.*

## Interfacing the hems

Before assembling your T-shirt, press the hems into place. I use an oak-tag template, 2 in. by 18 in., and press a hem crease in front, back, and sleeves.

To prevent rippling when topstitching the hem in place, try sewing a narrow strip of interfacing to the hem edge, which is easier to do when the garment is flat: Apply 1-in. strips of Sof Knit with a serger or by making a $1/4$-in. straight stitch (see the left photo above). Test to determine if you need to stretch the interfacing or not. If the hem is flared or if the knit stretches easily on the crossgrain, stretch the interfacing very slightly as you sew. Use a 1-to-1 ratio with stable knits. Stitch the right side of the interfacing (sticky side up) to the wrong side of the fabric so when you finally press the hem, the strip will fuse it, temporarily providing stabilization right under the topstitching. Trim the strip to a $3/8$-in. width (see the right photo above). If you're using a straight-stitch finish, pink the hem edge.

## Adding elastic to the shoulder seam

If you are using a serger, serge the *front* shoulder seams and sleeve

*Stitch clear elastic to the shoulder seam with back side up without stretching the elastic.*

cap if your top has dropped sleeves, but not if it has set-in sleeves. This serged edge is an optional seam finish only.

Sew and stabilize the shoulder seam at the same time. Stitch the shoulder seam with the back of the *garment facing up*, stitching a strip of clear elastic into the seam as you sew, without stretching the elastic (see the photo above). Do not apply a hot iron to the elastic or it will melt. Press seam flat (with elastic side down), then open; I use a clapper. Trim the back seam allowance to ¼ in., and press seams toward garment back. Topstitch from the right side.

## Sewing the neckline

Try on the garment. Pin along the side seams, wrong sides together, with the seams to the outside, and try on the T-shirt to check the fit of the neckline.

I prefer a self-fabric bound neck edge, ½ in. to 1 in. wide as shown on the garment on p. 94. Wait until trying on the garment at this stage before cutting the band. By this time you'll know how to handle the fabric, such as its stretch and recovery, whether it curls, whether to make the band single or double, or what new design ideas you may have. If the neckline needs adjustment, it is best to do it now.

## Neck bindings

There are many similarities between woven-bias and knit bindings: Both rely on stretch and recovery, and both curve and mold easily around curved or straight edges. The technique for measuring, cutting, and application is nearly identical. Knit garments can be bound with woven bias, and knit bindings make a good edge finish for wovens. Bindings can match or contrast, be pieced to create patterns or stripes, and be painted, stamped, stenciled, and dyed.

Neck bindings should be not too loose or too tight. A crossgrain,

wrap-around binding draws in the neck edge so it lies flat, which means that the binding must be smaller than the neck edge. If the binding is too loose or the same measurement as the neck, it will stand away from the neck; if it's too tight, it will pucker. Use crossgrain for binding unless your fabric has good stretch and recovery lengthwise. Bias grain on knits is less stable, but it can be used for special effects.

Experiment—every fabric is different, so don't be discouraged if it takes more than one try to get the look you want. Measure around your head so you don't make a neck opening or binding so small you cannot put it on! See pp. 71-72 for how to make a bound-slit neck opening. The following formulas for binding a neck are building blocks for all bindings and for developing other variations.

### Calculate the width of the band

Measurements provide a guideline, but experience has shown me to first cut a wider width (the bands inevitably stretch), then press and trim to the exact width.

Use single-thickness binding with medium to thick fabrics and double binding with lightweight, stretchy, or unstable knits.

For a single binding, measure three times the finished width plus ½ in. for the turn of the

cloth and underlap. For a ½-in. finished width, cut 2 in. wide.

For a double binding, measure six times the finished width plus ½ in. for the turn of the cloth and underlap. For a ½-in. finished width, cut 4 in. wide. Press in half and trim. Use a clear ruler and rotary cutter to trim bands after pressing.

## CHANGING A NECK SHAPE

Here is how to lower, deepen, or make a V neck.

**1.** Fold the shirt in half along the neckline, centering the front and back, and lining up the shoulder seams.

**2.** Draw in the new neckline with a fine-line chalk marker, using a French curve. To create a V neck, use a curve stick, and mark a gentle curve from the shoulder seam to the V point.

**3.** Trim along new line.

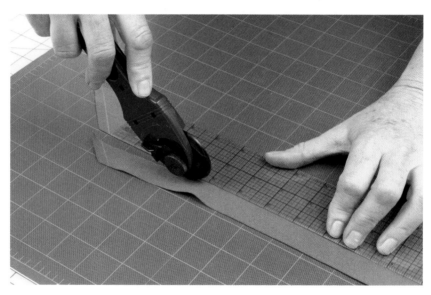

*Trim the binding to an even width after pressing.*

Always cut bindings wider than you think you'll need; it allows for stretch, and it keeps open the option to turn the edge under or leave a raw edge.

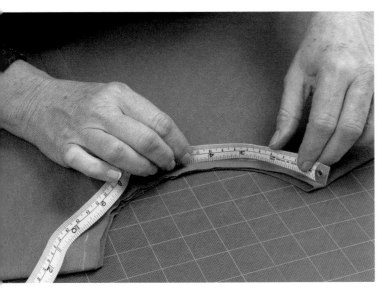

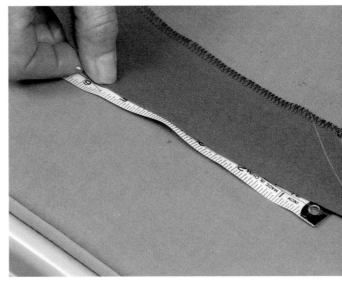

*Measure the neck edge along the seamline with a tape measure on edge, using the seamline as a guide.*

*Use one-quarter of the neck measurement to determine the ratio of binding to neck. Place a test length of binding and measuring tape in a 1-to-1 ratio and stretch the binding to see how much stretch feels right. Too much and the band curls, too little and the neck won't lie flat. In the photo, the binding easily stretches ³⁄₄ in., so make the finished binding ³⁄₄ in. smaller per quarter, or a total of 3 in. smaller than the neck.*

### Calculate the binding length

Measure the neck edge along the seamline with a tape measure, using the seamline as a guide. The binding must be smaller than the neck edge so it pulls the neck edge flat against the body without puckering. After trial and error, I developed this method to get a smooth finish:

**1.** Divide the neckline measurement by four (into quarters)—if the neck measures 24 in., one quarter is 6 in. (see the right photo above).

**2.** Find the ratio by experimenting with a length of binding that is one-quarter the neck size.

Place the measuring tape and the binding side by side in a 1-to-1 ratio.

**3.** Stretch the binding to see how much stretch seems too much, too little, and just right in relationship to the neck edge. It is easy and accurate to find the right ratio by using the fabric itself for comparison. For instance, if the neck measures 24 in. and the binding can be easily stretched ³⁄₄ in. per quarter, then the finished binding will be ³⁄₄ in. smaller per quarter, or a total of 3 in. The binding length is 21 in.

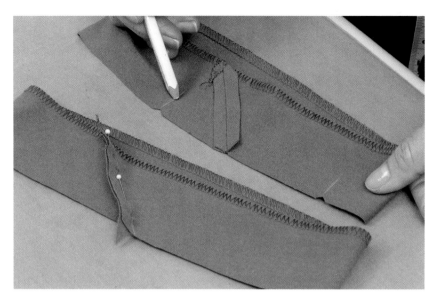

*Mark neck band ends on a 45-degree angle, stitch a ¼-in. seam, and press open. Divide the band in quarters and mark with snips or chalk.*

Adding ¼-in. seam allowances, cut the neckband ends on a 45-degree angle to reduce bulk, and stitch the ends to form a circle. Press seam open.

To apply the neck binding, divide the neck of the garment and the neck binding into quarters, and snip or mark with chalk. Do not use the band's seam as a marker. With the band's seam off-center at the back, match and pin at the markings with the band on top so the feed dog can help ease in the longer layer. Stretching the band slightly as you sew, stitch the seam, then press.

*Pin at quarters and stitch with the band on top, stretching as you sew.*

*Wrap binding around the neck edge and press over a ham, pinning as you press.*

*The finished band lies flat and smooth.*

Use the satin-stitch foot when doing staystitching, staystitch-plus, and using double needles on knit fabrics. Squishy knit fabrics stretch when using the straight-stitch foot, whereas the satin-stitch foot holds the fabric on either side of the stitching so it will not stretch or ripple as you stitch.

Even out the seam allowance width if needed, but *never* clip or grade the seam allowances when binding. You'll end up with an uneven, lumpy band. Wrap the binding to the wrong side, press again, and try on the top. For single binding, either turn the edge under, serge it, or leave a raw edge. On double binding, the folded edge will wrap to the wrong side. Secure the binding by stitching in the ditch from the right side, using an edge-stitching foot, or sew invisibly by hand.

**Turned and stitched neck**  This is a simple, clean, turned, and topstitched finish for armholes and round necks that are large enough to slip on easily over your head. The secret to a smooth, ripple-free edge is staystitch-plus. Staystitch at the neck and armhole, using staystitch-plus in areas that would gap. Serge these edges. Work over a ham and press the edge under, using the staystitching as a guide. Topstitch from the right side, using a single or double needle. Topstitch the armhole after the side seam has been sewn.

## Sleeves

After the neck is complete but before attaching the sleeves, pin the side seams *wrong* sides together and try on the garment to fit. Determine if the sleeve seam sits on your shoulder as you want it. You can see exactly where the sleeve will sit by turning under the armhole edge along the seam. If the shoulder is

# V-NECK VARIATION

To convert a round neckline to a flattering V, mark the desired depth of the V during tissue fitting, then redraw the neckline. See the drawing at right to prepare the V area.

**1.** Measure the neck, including the V, along the seamline, and calculate the length and width of the band as for the round neckline.

**2.** Mark the seamline on the band 1 in. on either side of the V and reinforce. Then divide both the band and neckline into quarters and mark.

**3.** Pin the center-front mark on the band to the V's point.

**4.** With the reinforcing stitching (body side) up, sew for 2 in. on either side of the V's point.

**5.** As you pass the V's point (stitching just inside the reinforcing line), shift the bulk around the needle to continue stitching.

**6.** Sew the rest of the neckband as for a round neck, with the band side up.

**7.** When the band is complete, shape the V by sewing a tiny dart on the inside of the band.

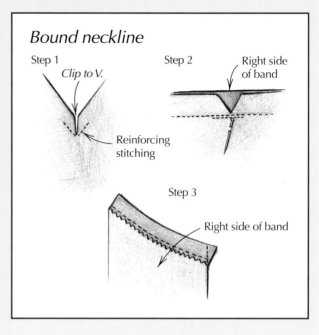

*Bound neckline*

Step 1
Clip to V.

Reinforcing stitching

Step 2
Right side of band

Step 3
Right side of band

*Turned-and-stitched necks stitched with single and double needles. Double-needle stitching has a dimensional trapunto effect.*

*Press the hem in place, fusing the interfacing.*

too wide (I notice this with Burda patterns), trim from 0 at the notches to the shoulder, and make the corresponding change to the pattern (see the illustration on p. 47).

Three pins are all you need when attaching a sleeve: one at the shoulder, and one at each end. Stitch with the garment side up; it simplifies easing. The garment is smaller than the sleeve, so by placing the smaller side up, the action of the machine blends in the extra ease smoothly. Keep the edges even as you sew. Press seam flat as sewn.

For set-in sleeves, press seams toward the sleeve over a ham. Serge the two seams together along the edge once the shaping of the sleeve cap is set. Seams may also be serged separately, pinked, or left plain.

For dropped sleeves, press both seams toward the garment. Trim the garment seam allowance, and finish using a mock flat-felled seam (see p. 56), stitching from the right side of the garment.

Fit one more time before you sew the side seams. Pin the side seams wrong sides together, and try on the garment. Make any necessary changes. These might include making the garment larger or smaller, tapering the sleeves at the wrist (I prefer a narrow 8 in.), adding shaping by curving in at the waist and out at the hip, or tapering in a straight line from the underarm to the hip.

## Stitching the side seams

Machine-stitch the side seams, try it on once more, then serge the edges together in a narrow

## MAKING A JEAN MUIR HEM

I prefer the Jean Muir hem to using double needles. This beautiful, fluid, topstitched hem is so named because it was a favorite of this English designer. It's perfect for wool or rayon matte jersey—the weight of the stitching makes the hem hang beautifully. Use a 2-in.-deep hem with no interfacing, and sew four rows of straight stitching in a short stitch length: one row just at the hem edge (an edgestitch foot helps), a second ¼ in. from the first, a third just catching the top of the hem (no edge finish is needed), and the last row ¼ in. below the third. That's all there is to it!

*The Jean Muir hem is perfect for wool jersey and rayon matte jersey. The four rows of topstitching weight the hem so it hangs beautifully.*

seam. If you do not have a serger, sew the seam, then do another straight stitch ¼ in. away, zigzag next to the stitching, and trim seam to ⅜ in.

### Finishing the hem

For a regular hem, press under, fusing the interfacing strip in position (see the photo on the facing page). For a topstitched hem, topstitch from the right side, using staystitch-plus as needed (see the photo at right). I do not recommend double needles because out-of-control stretching happens easily even with the stabilizing interfacing strip and staystitch-plus.

*Mark the stitching line with Clo-chalk and topstitch the hem from the right side. Staystitch-plus controls rippling.*

# 6 Bias and Surface Design 101

In the fashion world, the bias is spoken of in hushed, reverential terms. Only a few designers have mastered the bias cut. Artist/ couturier Madeline Vionnet is credited with "inventing" the bias cut in the 1920s. Madame Grès, a brilliant and reclusive French designer, worked with individual clients from the '30s into the '70s. Charles Kliebacker, a contemporary American designer-turned-design professor, continues the tradition into the present; he closed his Manhattan atelier in the '80s to teach at Ohio State University. Vionnet developed her prototypes draping on a half-scale dress form mounted on a lazy Susan. All three designers created bias garments by draping fabric directly on a model or on a dress form that was a replica of the client, cutting and constructing one garment at a time.

Bias is the diagonal grain that runs at a 45-degree angle to the lengthwise and crosswise grains. Garments that are cut on the bias have more stretch and are more supple than when the fabric is cut on the lengthwise or crosswise grain. Bias-cut garments appear softer and more fluid, and the fabrics appear "thinner" than the same style cut in the same fabric on the straight of grain. By contrast, the figure can appear round, especially if the fabric is clingy, showing the curves of the body. You can soften the effect of a crisp linen or cotton by cutting it on the bias.

## Bias Shell

Bias garments are a natural for sewers who love the luxury of fine, individually styled clothes. Making bias garments takes a bit more time, a careful selection of fabric, changing the order of construction, and using some different fitting and sewing techniques. Simple styles and foolproof fabrics are like training wheels on a bicycle. Once you are confident about basic sewing, cutting, and fitting skills, you'll enjoy expanding your sewing repertoire to include making bias garments.

Bias garments use more fabric than straight-of-grain garments and are best cut one layer at a time so the grain doesn't become distorted.

*Linen, silk dupioni, stripes, and ikat all take on a fresh dimension when cut on the bias.*

A simple tank or shell is a perfect starting point. The basic shape becomes more fluid, and the fabric takes on a more interesting character by cutting it on the bias. Choose a pattern you have used before. A tank or sleeveless shell with front and back pattern pieces makes the perfect place to begin.

## Fabric choices

Begin with a trip to the fabric store. Take bolts of fabric out and unfurl them. Find the bias by making a "kerchief" fold on a 90-degree diagonal to get a feel for the way fabric responds and feels. Compare different fibers, weights, and textures. Notice how much the fabrics stretch, how a plain weave takes on a new texture, how a twill weave loses its definition, and how

plaids and stripes take on a diagonal dimension. For your first few bias tops, select user-friendly, natural-fiber fabrics with "tooth" such as cotton, linen, silk noil, or wool challis. I look for fabrics with a plain weave, stripes, and minimal texture. Here is a short list of the fabrics I avoid:

- Rayon—it stretches like crazy on the bias and you'll end up with one side of the top growing longer and longer.
- Silkies and polyester—too slippery and hard to handle.
- Twills—they look strange cut on the bias.
- Fabrics that are heavy or stiff like duck or poplin—even the bias can't change them very much.
- Silkies and sheers like crepe de chine, charmeuse chiffon

and georgette are beautiful on the bias, but these hard-to-handle fabrics are not the best place to begin. Move up to silky fabrics once you have conquered the stable ones.

## Selecting and adapting a pattern to bias

Whenever I find a bias pattern, I buy it for my collection, but it is easy to convert a plain-necked (either V or round) top from straight of grain to bias. Tops that have cap sleeves, all-in-one sleeves, dropped sleeves, classic set-in sleeves, or are sleeveless can all be cut on the bias. Whether your pattern is designed to be cut on the bias or not, use the construction techniques and order given in this chapter.

***Tissue fitting and making pattern adjustments***  Alter your pattern so it is the desired length and large enough to fit around your figure at the bust and hip, including ease. Tissue fit your pattern to check the fit and make necessary changes. One secret to success in making bias tops is to allow plenty of ease. I build in more ease than the pattern recommends since bias stretches on the body. If the garment is too tight, it will wrinkle and draw up as you wear it, and you won't feel comfortable or sleek. Don't count on the 1½-in. seam allowances for fitting ease. If you are unsure, make your side-seam allowances

2 in. to 2½ in. so you can easily fit as you sew. If you are large busted, it is well worth adding a bust dart either in the armhole or the side seam. See the chapter on fitting for how to add a bust dart (pp. 40-41).

***Adapting pattern pieces for bias***  Make full pattern pieces for bias-cut garments to preserve the original pattern, and build in wider seam allowances. If you are cutting the front and back with center seams, make left and right pattern pieces, adding seam allowances at center front and back. If you are making front and back without a center seam, make the entire front and back pieces. Use the main pattern pieces *only*, eliminating facings in favor of bias binding.

***Changing the straight of grain to bias***  Use a 45-degree-angle ruler (available at quilt or art-supply stores) to adapt the

Bias garments do not wrinkle as easily as straight-of-grain garments, but they can "grow" on a hanger. Store them folded and flat.

*This ready-to-cut full pattern is marked to match stripes at the side seam.*

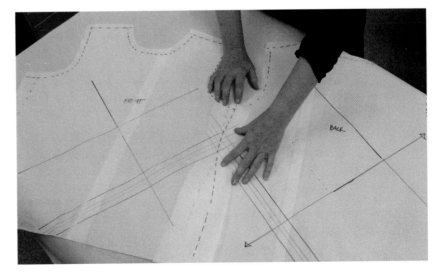

# TO ADD A CENTER SEAM AT FRONT AND BACK OR NOT?

Adding a center seam helps to understand the basic nature of cloth. Lengthwise threads are stronger and greater in number than crosswise threads. Bias garments with the center cut on a fold have the lengthwise grain dominant on one side of the garment and crosswise grain dominant on the other so they will stretch more on one side than the other. This is where thread count, fiber, and construction come into play. Thread count refers to the number of threads per inch.

Back in the 1920s and '30s, European looms could weave fabrics with an equal thread count lengthwise and crosswise. This is impossible today because the old looms were destroyed in the first world war, and it is now too costly. It is the nature of weaving that the lengthwise threads must be finer and stronger than the crosswise/filling threads.

Examine your fabric to see whether there is a discernible difference between lengthwise and crosswise threads. If the fabric is stable (linen, cotton, wool) and constructed so the lengthwise grain is not too much stronger (more threads, stronger threads), you won't notice a thing. If the fabric is constructed so the crossgrain is weaker, there will be a tug of war and the result can be disastrous: One side of the hem will stretch, the neck may lie flat on one side and ripple on the other, and the garment twists on the body.

By creating a center seam, the bias becomes balanced on right and left sides, and these problems disappear. Some designs adapt well to a center seam and some do not. If you don't want seams at center front and back, select a stable fabric with a balanced thread count. In my experience, linen is stable enough to cut the center on the fold, and rayons call for a center seam. V necks work particularly well with a center seam.

---

Fit with plenty of ease unless you want a figure-revealing effect—remember Jean Harlow and her white satin gown that fit like wallpaper on a wall. Even though you have pressed out the stretch, the nature of bias is that the garment will continue to stretch as you wear it.

pattern grainline to bias. Or draw a line perpendicular to the pattern grainline, and fold the tissue in a kerchief fold so the two lines align. The diagonal fold becomes the new bias grainline. Draw the bias line in both directions.

**Adding seam allowances**  Add seam allowances to your adjusted pattern pieces. Bias does not ravel, but when your scissors cut the fabric, the fibers relax and open up, creating a longer cut edge. The cut edge is not an accurate stitching guide, and the weave at $5/8$ in. from the edge can be loose. Use $1\frac{1}{2}$-in. seam allowances on center, side, and shoulder seams. Use $5/8$-in. seam allowances at the neck. Mark stitching lines with thread, tracing paper, or chalk before removing pattern pieces.

**Cutting sleeves**  A bias-cut sleeve is easy to set into a bias top. Cut short, cap, or long sleeves on the bias. If you are cutting a stripe or even a plaid sleeve on the bias, consider adding a seam down the center, of the sleeve, creating chevron or diamond patterns. Placing a center seam on a sleeve creates the same balanced effect as on a garment's body; both sides will drape and feel the same. Use $1\frac{1}{2}$-in. seam allowances on side

*Place a seam down the center of a bias sleeve to create a balanced hand and dramatic effect.*

and center seams, and a ⅝-in. seam allowance at the cap and armhole.

***Figuring yardage*** Bias takes more fabric, and usually fabric is cut in a single thickness. (More on cutting follows.) Once you have constructed your bias pattern pieces, you can use a cardboard cutting board as a guide to figure yardage. Yardage depends on the width of the fabric, the pattern or repeat, and the size of the pattern pieces. Layout must be planned carefully. I guesstimate 1 yard per pattern piece (single thickness), so a long tunic top with sleeves could take as much as 4 yards.

***Piecing*** Piecing is sometimes necessary if the fabric is narrow or because of the size of the pattern pieces. Here are a few tips to make the piecing a part of the garment or placing it where it is not noticeable: In the '30s, designers working with narrow fabrics integrated piecing into the garment's design. I like to position piecing at the bottom of the garment. If only one pattern piece requires piecing, place it on the bottom of the back. If both front and back need piecing, match the size and location at the side seam. It is usually only necessary to piece at one side, but consider piecing at both sides for a balanced and

*Pieced seams must be on the straight of grain. Attach a scrap piece of fabric to the garment with the pattern tissue still pinned in place. Stitch and press.*

*Finish cutting the pieced section.*

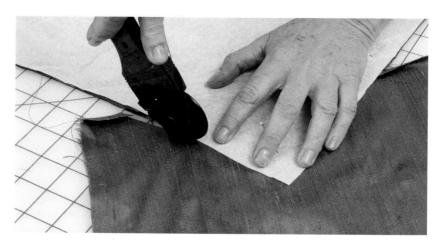

intentional effect. Place the seam where it will be flattering. *Pieced seams must be on the straight of grain.* Use a ¼-in. seam for the garment and pieced section. I like to use the selvage or join on the serger.

**1.** Cut out the pattern piece, ignoring the missing portion and leaving the paper pattern pinned in place.

**2.** Undo pins so you can attach a scrap of fabric to the garment, making sure it is large enough.
**3.** Stitch a ¼-in. seam and press.
**4.** Finish cutting.

## Cutting and layout

Cut the fabric single thickness with pattern pieces at right angles to each other in a mirror image going around the body. Notice in the illustration

*Bias: cutting layout for single thickness*

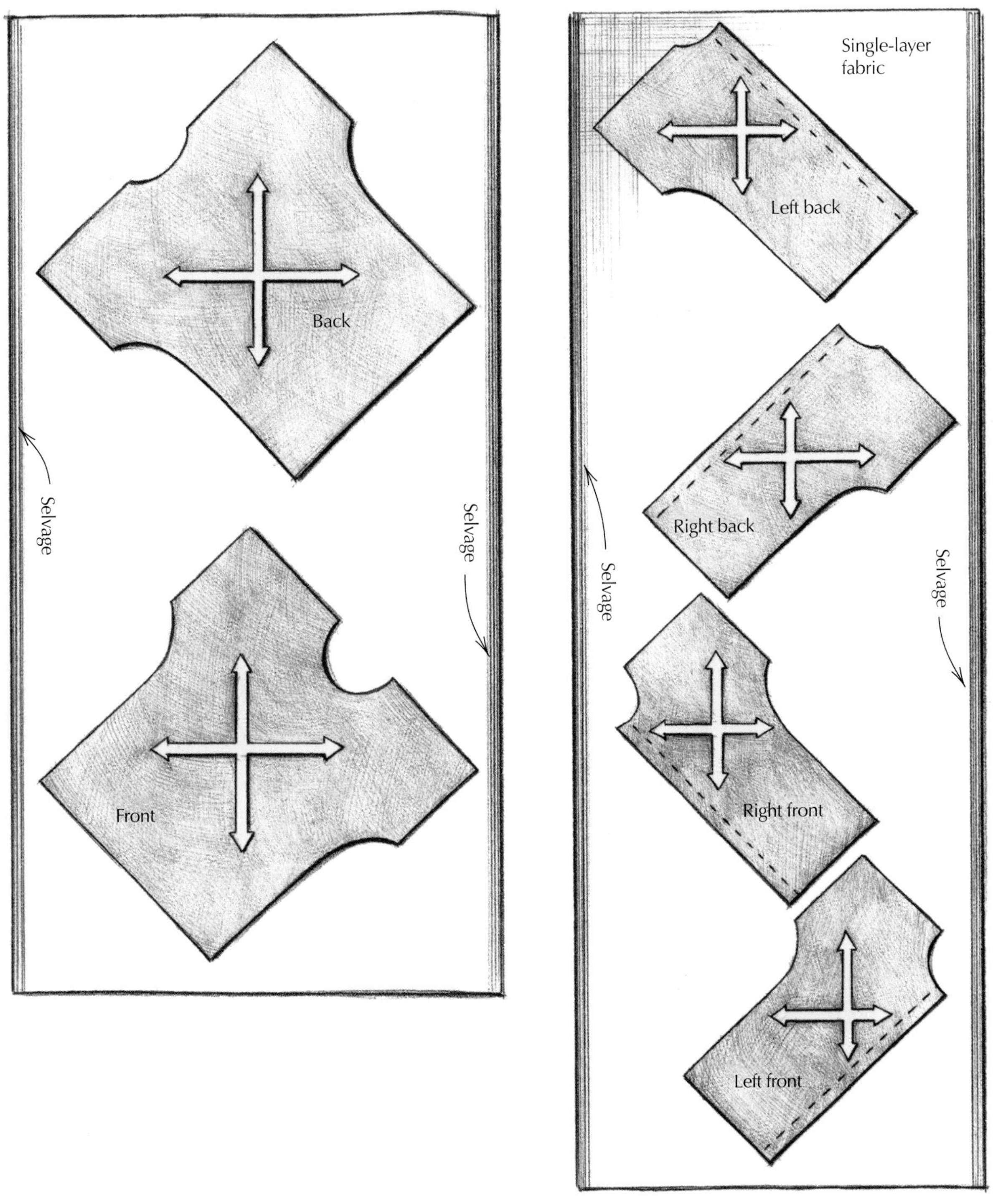

Back

Front

Selvage

Selvage

Single-layer fabric

Left back

Right back

Right front

Left front

Selvage

Selvage

*Bias shell: piecing progression*

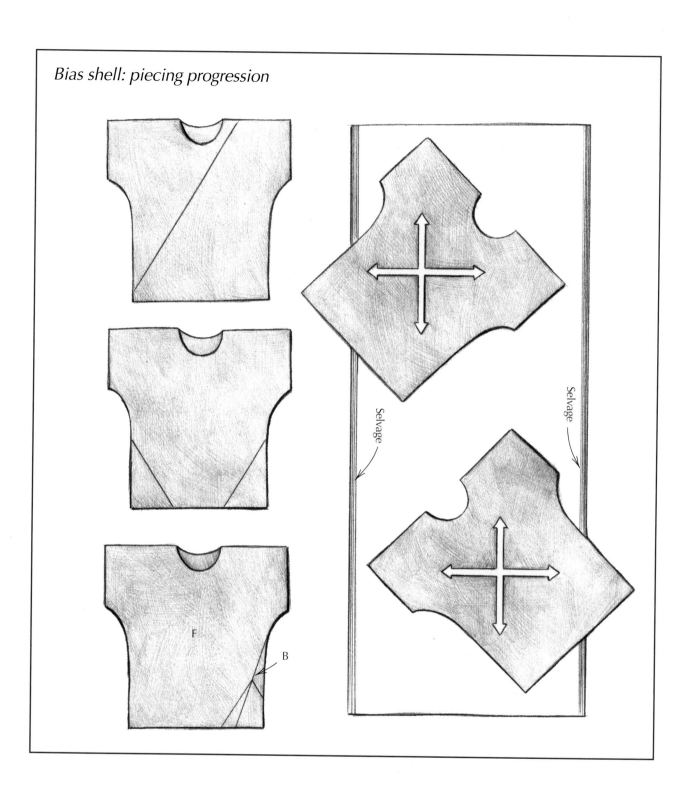

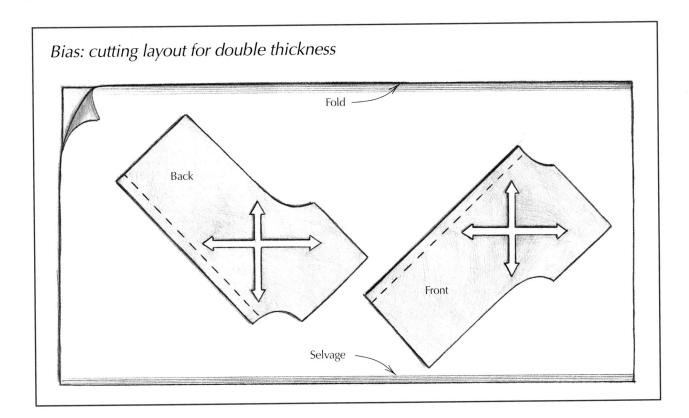

*Bias: cutting layout for double thickness*

Fold

Back

Front

Selvage

on p. 105 how *each piece is going at a right angle to the next going around the body.* This creates a chevron effect, so plaids and stripes may be matched. If your pattern has center front and back seams and your fabric is wide enough, you can cut two layers at once. Whenever possible, I cut all bias garments going in one direction, as if the cloth has a nap.

## Removing the stretch

This step is not necessary for tops made in stable fabrics (linen, cotton, wool, etc.) cut on the bias, but is necessary when working with silky, gauzy, or loosely woven fabrics like chiffon, crepe de chine, georgette, and most rayons. After removing the pattern pieces and before sewing the center-front seam, press the surface of each piece firmly, gently, and evenly top to bottom. The pressing action simulates the effect of wear and of gravity, removing the natural tendency of the bias to stretch. Plenty of residual stretch remains, and the garment has been stabilized.

*Neckline details (from top to bottom): striped knit "double piping" covers the seam of a mock turtleneck top, stencilled corded piping, purchased piping, and bias single binding.*

Facings, even if cut on the bias, tend to create an inner struggle with the garment. *Never* use a straight-of-grain facing on a bias garment. The combination spells disaster!

fabrics, but also consider the design possibilities of unexpected juxtapositions and fabric combinations. Staystitch neck and armhole edges before binding, and remember that the cut edge is the finished edge.

When making a bias top with a V neck and a center front seam, sew the shoulder seams first, apply the neck binding, then sew the center front and back seams after the neck edge is complete (see the photo on the facing page). This assures that the V is perfect and easy to execute.

## Finishing the neck and armhole with bias binding or piping

Bias binding or piping gives a fine finish to neck and armhole edges on bias garments. Bias goes around curves smoothly, and can be molded and shaped; it stabilizes edges and makes interfacings unnecessary.

I use bindings ¼ in. to 1 in. wide or corded piping as shown in the photo above. The weight and style of your top will determine the width of the bindings. Use a single-layer, wrap-around binding with medium-weight fabrics and a double-layer or French binding on lightweight

***Cutting bias strips*** Cut long strips of bias using your scraps after cutting out the garment. I prefer piecing a few long strips to the continuous-bias-strip method. To cut easily and accurately, align the grain on a cutting mat, marking the bias using a 45-degree ruler and metal measuring stick, and cut with a rotary cutter (see the top photo on p. 110).

***Making a French-bias binding***
A French-bias binding is a double binding made using wide bias strip that is folded in half lengthwise, then stitched to the edge and wrapped around so the raw edges are enclosed and finished with the fold on the backside. This finish is perfect with light or fine fabrics like handkerchief linen, and fine and sheer silks. It takes some practice and a bit more skill than a single binding.

To make a single-bias binding, refer to the instructions for binding a knit with crossgrain. The techniques are virtually identical.

Use these instructions for a ½-in. finished French binding. Use a ½-in. seam allowance on the bound edge, and staystitch just inside the seamline. I prefer a single, long strip of bias to piecing.

   **1.** Cut a strip longer and wider than you will need: Bias stretches, and I like to remove the stretch and trim the binding precisely. So cut the width 6 times the finished width plus 1 in. to 2 in. (4 in. to 5 in. wide) to compensate for stretching and folding.
   **2.** Fold the strip in half lengthwise, and press, stretching gently.
   **3.** Measure the strip from the fold three times the finished width plus ½ in. (which is 2 in. in total). This allows for turn of the cloth and underlap. Use a clear ruler and rotary cutter to cut accurately. Allow a bit more for thick fabrics.
   **4.** Open out the binding, and cut one end at a 45-degree angle. Chalk-mark a ¼ in. seam allowance (see the bottom photo on p. 110).
   **5.** Use the directions on p. 92 to determine the finished length of the bias. Remember, the bias should be smaller than the neck seamline. Measure from the

seamline, and mark at a 45-degree angle parallel to the first seam. Add a ¼-in. seam allowance and cut. The angled seams are on the straight of the grain. The angle keeps the finished binding smooth.
   **6.** Stitch short ends in a ¼-in. seam along marked lines, keeping edges even. Press seam open and repress along lengthwise foldline.
   **7.** Divide the bias circle into quarters. Do not use the seam as a mark. Position the seam off center in the back of the garment between the center back and shoulder.
   **8.** Mark the garment neck into quarters and match with markings on the binding. Pin or hand-baste in place.
   **9.** Stitch with the bias on top, using a ½-in. seam. Press flat as sewn.
   **10.** Trim the seam carefully to an even width all around. I have found that no matter how carefully I stitch, this seam will have uneven places.
   **11.** Working over a ham, press the binding toward the raw edges, using a light touch; don't flatten it too much.
   **12.** Wrap the binding around the edge to the wrong side. The binding should cover and overlap the stitching line. Press lightly and hand-baste or pin in the ditch of the seam.
   **13.** Stitch from the right side, by hand or machine, stitching in the ditch with small stitches. Press/steam lightly over a ham.

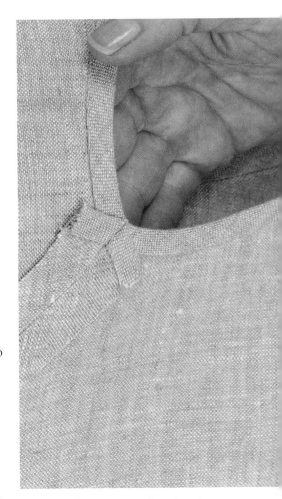

*When making a top with a V neck and center front seam, sew the shoulder seams first. Then apply the neck binding, and sew the center front and back seams after the neck edge is complete, ensuring that the V is perfect.*

*Cut long strips of bias using a 45-degree ruler, metal yard stick, and rotary cutter.*

*Mark the stitching line (¹⁄₄-in. seams) on the short ends with chalk and seam, matching the edges to prevent a jog.*

## Sewing bias seams

When fabric is cut on the bias it opens up and relaxes, so you must compensate by using wider seam allowances, usually 1½ in. Mark seamlines as soon as the fabric is cut. Mark with chalk or thread-trace the seams with silk thread, using a running stitch, knotting the thread every 5 in. After removing the pattern and marking the seamlines, press out each piece to remove excess

# FINISHING THE NECK AND ARMHOLE WITH PIPING

Piping stabilizes the neck and armholes, and adds a subtle design detail to bias or straight-of-grain garments. The neck must be large enough to slip on over the head easily.

Prepare the front and back separately before joining the shoulder seam. Staystitch the edges, then clip to the stitching line every 1/2 in. Serge the edges close to the stitching line, straightening out the seam as you serge. This makes it easy to turn the edge to the inside. If you do not have a serger, trim the seam to 1/4 in. Stitch the shoulder seams, and press. Working on a ham, press the edge to the inside, using the staystitching as a guide.

Make the piping. Cover cording with a bias strip, using a zipper foot. Remove the cording. Serge close to the stitching and reinsert the cording. Hand-baste the piping next to the edge, overlapping the ends. Machine-stitch close to the edge using a zipper foot.

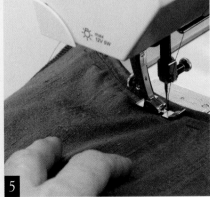

*1. Serge the edge close to the stitching line, straightening out the edge as you serge.*

*2. Press the edge to the inside, rolling the staystitching to the inside.*

*3. It is necessary to remove the cording in order to serge the piping edge; the thickness of the cord won't slide under the presser foot. Serge the edge of the piping, then reinsert the cording.*

*4. Hand-baste the piping, overlapping the ends. Trim the cord ends so they butt together smoothly.*

*5. Machine-stitch close to the edge using a zipper foot.*

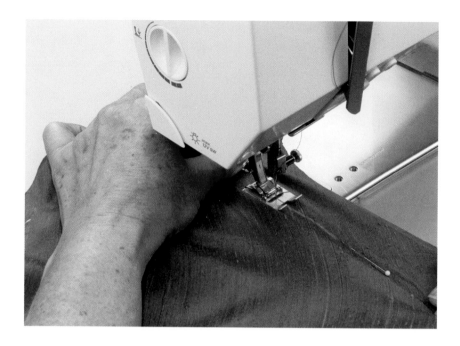

*Stretch a bias seam as you stitch, using the marked seamline as a guide. Stretching keeps the seam from popping when worn.*

Use a glue stick on the piping seam allowance to secure it to the garment; it's easier and more accurate than pins. Keep the glue applicator tidy. Extend the glue ¼ in. to ½ in. from the applicator and apply a thin line of glue along the edge of the seam allowance. You can easily position the piping or adjust it. Allow the glue to dry before stitching. Hand-baste the section where the ends overlap.

stretch. Repin your pattern onto the fabric, adjusting the seamlines if the piece has grown smaller.

Stretch a bias seam as you stitch it on the sewing machine, using a 2.5-mm to 3.0-mm stitch (see the photo above). The seam will look rippled but will press out smoothly. Stretching is essential: It keeps the seam from popping when worn. I have found that stretching as you sew is crucial on vertical seams. Do *not* stretch as you sew the shoulder seams. Once the garment is fitted, trim the seam allowance.

Stitch center seams first, then fit at the side seams by pinning along the stitching line, wrong sides together, and adjust at the

side seams to get the look you want. With challenging fabrics, hand-baste loosely so the seam does not distort, pull up, or shorten.

Bias does not ravel, so seam finishes are optional and unnecessary. I prefer a pinked edge to using a serger, which can cause the edge to ripple and show through to the right side.

## Buttons and buttonholes

Interface behind buttons and buttonholes on bias garments. Use a strip of interfacing with the straight of grain in the direction of the buttonhole to keep the buttonhole from stretching.

*Dyeing and overdyeing fabrics create a range of tones you cannot find in mass-produced fabrics.*

# Further Techniques

Once you have gotten the basics for sewing tops and T-shirts, you can experiment by adding your own one-of-a-kind colors and surface design to your tops. When I couldn't find the colors or images that I wanted, I started reading, taking classes, and experimenting to get what I wanted. It is amazingly simple and so satisfying to add your own signature to the clothes you make.

## Surface Design 101

Sometimes I find a knit I love but the color is not right or the surface seems too flat, or I crave a shot of color in the binding. It is easy and fun to add color and design to knit fabrics by dyeing, painting, stamping, and stenciling. Test. Test. Test. This is play, so let the process lead you, and let mistakes be part of the creative process. I prefer to work with cut-out pieces of the garment rather than with yardage. I pad and protect my work surface with a few layers of muslin, then put a vinyl cover over the entire thing. A lightly padded surface is helpful to get a clean impression from stamps and stencils.

*Dyeing*  If you can bake a cake from a mix, you can dye knits in the washing machine, using grocery-store or procion dyes. Dye whites, pastels, and ho-hum or ugly colors to create a range of rich, subtle tones you won't get

I recently discovered how to do low-water immersion dyeing, following the easy-to-use techniques in Ann Johnston's book *Color by Accident.* You can dye yardage or cut-out garment pieces one or more colors in small containers. Results have an uneven, organic, hand-dyed effect.

*Apply fabric paint to the rubber stamp with a brush and dabbing motion. Stamping takes more paint, stenciling less. You can mix more than one color on a stamp. Be generous with paint, but do not fill up the crevices or the effect will look smeared.*

Procion dyes are also fabric dyes but designed for specific fibers. They require careful measuring and premixing with salt and soda ash, and you can combine and mix colors.

Most washing machines hold 20 gallons of water. I usually use a small-load setting and guesstimate the amount of dye. If you want darker colors with either dyes, use more dye and keep the bath going by resetting the agitate cycle—one to two hours, depending on the depth of color. If you want to keep the dyeing even, add ½ tsp. of calsolene oil per gallon of water. (I do not do this because I like a slightly uneven, hand-dyed effect.) Follow directions for washing the fabric once dyeing is complete. It may take more than one wash to remove the excess dye; wash the fabric in hot water until the water runs clear. Clean the machine when you are finished by running one cycle with detergent and bleach only, then run the next cycle with a load of rags, using bleach and detergent. Exhausted dye is as alkaline as a normal load of laundry, and is not harmful to septic or sewage systems.

any other way. Create a color-coordinated group of fabrics by overdyeing several related colors, textures, or patterns (such as dots and stripes) at once. Use a color wheel to choose the color to overdye; related colors are more likely to please than opposites, which can result in muddy tones. Follow directions for preparing the fabric, and never use utensils you use for cooking or eating. Wear rubber gloves and a dust mask while mixing dye powders.

Grocery-store dyes, the easiest to use, are formulated to color a range of fibers such as wool, cotton, and silk. I've had good results combining colors (like forest green and navy, or red and purple) and by using more dye than the package recommends.

**Stamping** Use purchased rubber stamps or carve your own. Test stamps to be sure you like the impression on the fabric. I use both stamps designed for paper and special stamps for fabric. Bold designs work better than finely detailed ones. Choose stamps with related and harmonious shapes and images. Sometimes using a fragment of the stamp is more pleasing than the whole design. Play!

I use Lumiere metallic paints in #565 Metallic Bronze, #562 Metallic Olive Green, # 141 Metallic Gold, and Neopaque Black JAC 1588. The paints straight from the bottle are too bright, and since I usually want a more antique effect, I mix a drop or two of black with each color. Use a plastic painter's palette to mix the paints because the little wells hold just the right amount.

Have your garment and binding strips pressed and ready before you mix the paints; otherwise, the paints will dry out. Use small, finely textured sponges or a sponge paintbrush, and with a dabbing motion, experiment with the amount of paint that gives the result you want (see the photo on the facing page). Keep cleaning the stamps as you work by dipping them in water, then rubbing gently on a scrubbie, and blotting dry with a rag. If the paint builds up and dries in the grooves of the stamp, it will blur the impression. You can mix several colors on one stamp, but rinse and dry the sponge in between to keep each color pure.

I first experiment on cloth scraps, then lay them out on my garment to plan the final result. It is not necessary for each stamp to be perfect or identical; in fact,

*Layers add dimension. First lay down a metallic monoprint, then the stamp inked in black, and finally a layer of metallic on top with slivers of black showing.*

it is the variety that gives interest and character. When using an image like a spiral, rotate the stamp design a quarter turn each time you place an image next to another to give a random effect. Use the backside of stamps mounted on acrylic to create a monoprint background for the stamp. To do this, apply paint to the flat acrylic side. Apply more than one color to the surface, or lay down color in layers; on dark fabrics use white or light colors, allow to dry, then layer other colors, and finally the stamp on top of it.

***Stenciling*** Stenciling is another easy and effective way to add design and pattern to knits, and it combines very well with stamping. Gather a few appealing stencils, fabric paint

*Stencil "stripes" onto a neck binding. Mark straight guidelines with Clo-chalk and stencil along the lines. A Post-It note mask keeps the rest of the stencil clean.*

and dense sponges or flat-bottomed stencil brushes.

Stenciling takes very little paint; stamping, on the other hand, uses lots. Use a flat plate to hold small amounts of paint. Wad up the sponge and pick up one or more colors. Dab the sponge or brush on the plate to blend colors; don't load up the brush or sponge with paint. Apply even, light coats rather than one heavy coat. Hold the stencil in place and "pounce" the sponge or brush up and down—don't rub or glide because the stencil can shift or paint may seep under the edges blurring the image (see the photo above).

Begin in the center of the stencil and move out to the edges. Experiment: Sponge on more than one color to get shading variations; layer one stencil on top of another; use segments of a stencil; mask out areas, using masking tape or acrylic. When you are satisfied, remove the stencil by peeling up from one corner.

Clean the stencil every few applications to ensure that the back side remains clean. I invest in duplicates of my favorite stencils so I can keep working. With heavy fabrics, you may want to dampen the sponge

*This looks like double piping but is a strip of knit. Raw edges curl to the inside when stretched. Hand-baste down the center, then machine stitch, catching the back side of the neck binding as you sew.*

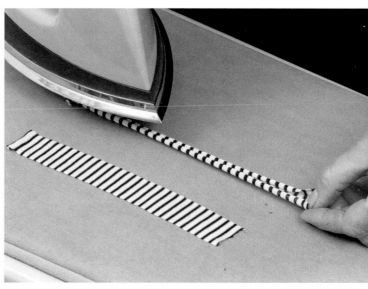

*Stretch the strip of knit fabric, pinning one end, and give it a shot of steam to bring out the curl.*

slightly with water, squeezing it out before adding paint.

Allow the paint to dry 24 hours. Some paints must be heat-set with an iron or press in order to withstand washing and drying, while other paints set over time. So it's best to follow the directions on the package.

## T-shirt trim that curls

I like to take advantage of the fact that many lightweight knits curl to the wrong side along lengthwise cut edges. This trim looks great when sewn in a coordinating striped fabric, a trick I learned from California designer Jean Williams Cacicedo. Cut lengthwise strips 1 in. wide, stretch to curl, and place right side down along a finished neck or sleeve stitching line. Stitch the trim in place down the center of the strip, stretching each cut edge to form a curl, and overlapping ends about 1 in. It looks like a tricky double piping, but it couldn't be simpler to make (see the top left photo above).

When applying curling knit "double piping" trim, hand-baste before you machine-stitch in the ditch to keep the curly trim just where you want it; this eliminates the need for pins.

*The eclectic twin set layers a cardigan over a shell. It is easy to convert any T-shirt into a cardigan.*

Experiment with the stretching and curling of the trim. In some cases it is best to stretch it with an iron to set in the curl; in other cases stretch the strip as it is applied, and give it a shot of steam to set the curl after it is sewn.

## The eclectic twin set

One of my favorite wardrobe staples is a twin set: a knit cardigan worn over a shell/tank and made in the same or related fabrics. I've used cotton/poly/Lycra, velours, fleece, and novelty knits for this versatile combination. The two pieces must fit together, the necklines must nest together, the armhole depth must be compatible, and the weight of the two fabrics must match or harmonize. I've made a summer trio that consists of a sleeveless tank that goes under a short-sleeved cardigan (both cotton/poly/Lycra), and they both slip beneath a long-sleeved fleece cardigan. The autumn version is a short-sleeved velour T-shirt worn beneath a rayon/Lycra, boucle cardigan bound and banded in velour.

Turn any top into a cardigan. Cut the front along the fold or center front line. Finish and

118

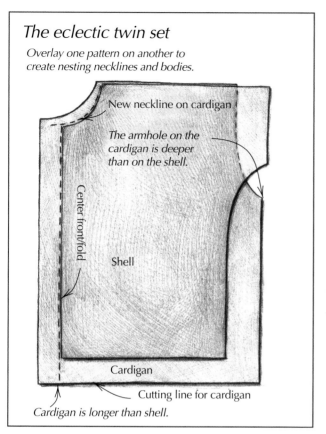

## The eclectic twin set

*Overlay one pattern on another to create nesting necklines and bodies.*

New neckline on cardigan

*The armhole on the cardigan is deeper than on the shell.*

Center front/fold

Shell

Cardigan

Cutting line for cardigan

*Cardigan is longer than shell.*

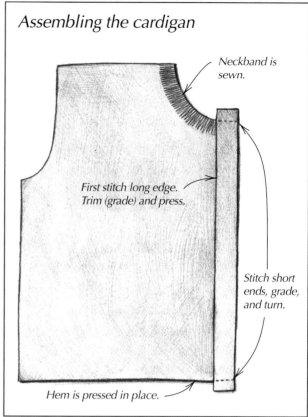

## Assembling the cardigan

*Neckband is sewn.*

*First stitch long edge. Trim (grade) and press.*

*Stitch short ends, grade, and turn.*

*Hem is pressed in place.*

stabilize the front edge with interfaced bands, which are made as follows:

**1.** Cut two bands on the lengthwise grain. A 3¼-in. width results in a band 1 in. wide, and make it the length of the front plus 1½ in.

**2.** Interface the entire band with So Sheer or Fuse Knit cut with the stable grain in the lengthwise direction.

**3.** Apply the neck binding, and press up the hem. Stitch one long side of the band to the front in a ½-in. seam, with ¾ in. extending at top and bottom.

**4.** Trim, grade, press. Stitch the ends, then turn the band to the inside, and secure by stitching in the ditch.

**5.** Apply buttonholes and buttons, with the buttonholes positioned vertically along the front band.

# 7 | *Which Skirt to Make?*

Anyone can sew a skirt, so if you're just learning, a skirt is the perfect starting point. You can get the color, style, and fit you want, and the length that's exactly right for you.

The number of choices in the pattern books may seem overwhelming at first, but there are really only a few skirt styles and silhouettes to choose from. In this chapter, you'll learn how to determine which styles work best on your figure and which styles and fabrics are best for your skill level.

A simple style and a beautiful fabric are the best combination for fast, easy, and successful sewing (just look at the skirts in any Calvin Klein collection). When you want to make a skirt quickly, stay at or just below your skill level and use the techniques and details that you've mastered. If you want to stretch your limits, choose skirts with some new element—a different zipper application, a more fitted style, or a more challenging fabric.

The more difficult and time-consuming skirts to sew are those that are fitted at the waist, high hip, and full hip, or that have more pattern pieces and construction details, such as pleats or pockets.

# Choosing the Best Style

*Begin in your closet. Try on your favorite skirts.
Make notes and take measurements.*

Decide which styles and silhouettes look best on you. What are
the most flattering lengths? Which waistband styles, lengths, and
widths are most comfortable? What is the hip measurement of the
fitted skirt that looks best on you?

Next, take your tape measure to the stores. Try on a variety of
skirts to see what works for you and what doesn't. (I do this at
least twice a year—late August and March are when the stores
have the best seasonal selections.) Again, make notes of the most
flattering lengths, hem widths, waistbands, and so on. Check the
fabric types—this will help you learn which fabrics work best for
which styles. If you find a skirt in the stores that looks fabulous
on you, you'll probably be able to find something similar in the
pattern books.

## What's Best for Me?

Skirt styles fall into a few basic categories: straight, A-line or
flared, gored, pleated/tucked, gathered, wrap, and bias. But how
well a particular style will look on you depends on your figure
type. Some styles look good on almost anyone, while others seem
to suit a particular body shape. The so-called "average" or slim,
well-proportioned figure can wear almost any style of skirt. Four
of the other common figure types and the styles that most flatter
them are described on the facing page.

The chart on pp. 124-127 describes each of the basic skirt styles,
the figure type best suited to each, the range of sewing skills
required, and the recommended fabrics. For easy reference, each
skirt style is coded with the appropriate figure symbols. The page
numbers in parentheses direct you to more detailed discussion of
the suggested style variations and design details.

# FIGURE TYPES

**X or Hourglass**   The hourglass figure looks balanced, curvaceous, and well defined. The shoulders and hips appear to be the same width, and the bust and hips are about 10 in. to 12 in. larger than the waist (an hourglass figure might measure 38-27-38, for example). A woman with this shape can wear both straight and flared styles. If you're full figured, however, you'll look better with straight lines that minimize your curves, such as those on a skirt with vertical seams.

**A or Pear**   On a pear-shaped figure, the shoulders appear narrower than the hips or thighs, the bust is small, and the waist is small in proportion to the hips. If you are pear shaped—most women are—avoid bulky skirts and severe slim-line skirts. Flared, A-line, gored, and bias skirts are most flattering. To camouflage full hips, choose soft, flowing fabrics, soft pleats, and long, graceful skirts.

**H or Rectangular**   The rectangular figure has few curves and not much waistline definition. The shoulders and the hips are similar in width, which makes the figure appear balanced. If you have a rectangular shape, most likely your clothes usually hang well. You can wear skirts that are slim-fitting, as well as ones that are graceful and flowing.

**Y or Wedge**   The wedge figure has shoulders that are broader than the hips, and the upper arms may be heavy. Some women develop a wedge shape as they age; others are born with these proportions. If you have a wedge shape, slim skirts are made for you. Gored and bias skirts are also good choices.

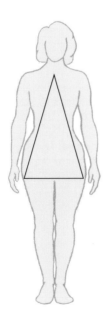

| Hourglass figure | Pear figure | Rectangular figure | Wedge figure |

# STYLES, SKILLS, AND FABRICS

| Skirt types | Style and figure notes | Required skills | Suggested fabrics |
|---|---|---|---|
| **STRAIGHT**<br><br>A straight skirt is cut straight (or tapers in slightly) from the full hip to the hem. | More than any other style, straight skirts reveal the figure. An oversized top worn over a straight skirt, however, works well on figures with proportionally large hips.<br><br>Short straight skirts ending just above the knee are the most flattering. Super-short straight skirts, such as the micro-mini, are best on slim, long-legged figures.<br><br>Long straight skirts can have an air of chic, but look dowdy if they're the wrong length. They're best if they end where the leg begins to taper.<br><br>Some French designers use patterns that are slightly "pegged" at the hem—cut about ½ in. narrower than the full hip at each side seam. A pegged skirt tapers from full hip to hem, creating a curvy, pleasing line for almost any figure that can wear a slim skirt. | Straight skirts fit closer to the body than any other style, so it's important to have some experience with fitting.<br><br>A traditional tailored straight skirt might have darts, soft pleats, curved seams, a zipper, fitted waistband, vent or kick pleat, and a lining.<br><br>**Easy:** A slim skirt with a pull-on elasticized waist-band (pp. 203-205) is an ideal beginner's project. A French vent (p. 186) and lining (pp. 196-199) are optional.<br><br>**Average:** Soft front pleats (pp. 175-177); darts (p. 173), gathers (pp. 178-179), or elastic (pp. 210-212) in the back; machine-stitched zipper (pp. 192-193) at center-back seam; optional French vent (p. 186) and lining (pp. 196-199).<br><br>**Advanced:** Darts (p.173) in front and back; shaped darts for better fit or pockets (pp.180-183); hand-picked zipper (p. 193); lining (pp. 196-199). | For fitted, darted styles, the best fabrics are midweight, sometimes termed "bottom weights" that is, for skirts or pants.<br><br>The best choices in wools are crepe, lightweight gabardine, fine tweeds, and twills. Avoid wool flannel; most kinds are too stiff and heavy for any skirt.<br><br>Other fabrics that work well are linens, silk linen or blends, light tweeds, brushed cottons, and denim-weight cottons.<br><br>For pull-on straight skirts, fabrics should be soft and fluid to avoid excess bulk at the waist and high hip. Silks, wool jersey, challis, and rayon are good choices. |

| Skirt type | Style and figure notes | Required skills | Suggested fabrics |
|---|---|---|---|
| **A-LINE/FLARED**<br><br>An A-line skirt is fuller at the hem than at the waist. | The A-line or flared skirt is probably the best style for most women. It works well on figures with a small waist in proportion to the hips; adds the illusion of a waist on straight up-and-down figures; and may be the only style that works on full-hipped figures.<br><br>Check the shapes of the pattern pieces on the instruction sheet. The skirt should be flared, not rectangular. If the lengthwise grain is at center back or front, you may want to alter it for a more flattering effect.<br><br>Also check the finished skirt width at the hem to be sure it's exactly what you want, based on the measurements you've taken of garments in your wardrobe or in stores. | A-line skirts may be fitted at the waist, high hip, and full hip, which requires skill in fitting. They can also be full with an elasticized waistband—super-easy to sew and fit.<br><br>**Easy:** Full skirt with pull-on elasticized waistband (pp. 203-205); gathers (pp. 178-179) or soft pleats (pp. 175-177); machine-sewn hem (pp. 220-221).<br><br>**Average:** Fitted or partially elasticized waistband (pp. 210-212); zipper (pp. 188-195); pocket detailing (pp. 180-183); curved seams (p. 167).<br><br>**Advanced:** Bias cut (pp. 151-153); lining (pp. 196-199); raised waistband (p. 215); more fitted, but the more fitted the skirt, the more skills are required to make it. | Because A-line skirts are usually flowing, choose fabrics that drape and move nicely.<br><br>For more fitted styles, choose wool crepe, double knits, light gabardine, rayon and silk tweed, brushed denim, suede, silk linen.<br><br>For full, gathered, or softly pleated flared styles, pick silk broadcloth, crepe de chine, rayon, challis, tissue faille, cotton knits, silk noil, wool jersey. |

| Skirt type | Style and figure notes | Required skills | Suggested fabrics |
|---|---|---|---|
| **GORED**<br><br>This style consists of four, six, eight, or more gores shaped to flare from waist to hem.<br><br> | A true classic, the gored skirt is always in fashion. It's also one of the most flattering styles. The vertical lines of a gored skirt create an illusion of height and slimness.<br><br>A gored skirt can be either straight or A-line, depending on the contours of the gores. If you look best in a slim skirt, choose a gored style that's fitted at the waist and hips and that flares near the hemline. If an A-line is best for you, choose a skirt with gores that flare from waist or high hip. Shaped and curvy gores emphasize the hips.<br><br>(See pp. 222-223 for tips on constructing a fitted, lightly fitted, and full gored skirt.) | The more fitted the skirt, the more important your fitting ability. You'll also need accurate stitching and pressing skills to achieve flat, nearly invisible seams. Hems can be sewn by hand or machine.<br><br>**Easy:** Pull-on elasticized waistband (pp. 203-205); additional ease at waist and hips (p. 222).<br><br>**Average:** Lightly fitted skirt (p. 222); invisible zipper (pp. 194-195); machine-topstitched hem (p. 220)<br><br>**Advanced:** Fitted (p. 223); hand-picked or invisible zipper (p. 193 and pp. 194-195); hand-sewn hem (p. 219). | The best fabrics for this style are fluid and drapey.<br><br>Wool jersey, velour, and wool double knits are good for lightly fitted skirts; wool crepe, silk tweed, and fine worsted wool for fitted skirts. Silk crepe de chine and rayon are also good choices.<br><br>Avoid wool flannel and gabardine. |

| Skirt type | Style and figure notes | Required skills | Suggested fabrics |
|---|---|---|---|
| **PLEATED/TUCKED**<br><br>You can vary the size, number and placement of the pleats to create different effects. | Pleats create a subtle vertical line while softening the figure. A skirt with all-around pleats, however, flatters only slim, narrow-hipped figures.<br><br>The position, direction, and depth of the pleats can be varied from those on the pattern to achieve the look that's best for you. Experiment. | **Easy:** Soft pleats (p. 175).<br><br>**Average:** Pressed-down or stitched-down pleats (pp. 176-177).<br><br>**Advanced:** All-around pleats, which are extremely difficult to fit. | Soft pleats require soft fabrics, such as silk and silkies, rayon, and jersey.<br><br>The best choices for pressed- or stitched-down pleats are crisp fabrics, such as light gabardine and menswear worsteds, silk twill, and broadcloth. |
| **GATHERED**<br><br>Gathers emphasize the drape and movement of soft, fluid fabrics. | Gathered skirts visually add weight and bulk to any figure, so choose your pattern and fabric carefully.<br><br>Beware the rectangular-shaped "dirndl" skirt, which is fine for children but frumpy on most women. Check the pattern instruction sheet to make sure the pattern pieces are narrower at the waist than at the hem.<br><br>Carefully position the gathers (pp. 178-179) for the most flattering effect. | Beginners often choose to make a gathered skirt as a first project, but gathers take patience and fussing to get just right.<br><br>**Easy:** Gathers created by an elasticized waistband (p. 203); short spans of gathers.<br><br>**Average/Advanced:** Long spans of gathers; a multi-tiered, Santa Fe–style skirt. | To avoid an unflattering puffy look, use soft, fluid fabrics, such as silk, polyester "silkies," rayon, jersey, and challis.<br><br>If you're unsure whether a fabric is too heavy for a gathered skirt, it probably is. |

# Selecting the Pattern

*Keep it simple. The key to success is to begin with a loose-fitting style and a beautiful fabric.*

As a rule, a garment with fewer pattern pieces requires less time to fit and sew. Scrutinize the illustrations in the pattern books. Keep in mind that each detail—yokes, pockets, pleats, raised waistbands, and intricate seam treatments—adds time and complexity to the project.

Build your skills gradually. With each new garment you make, plan to add another technique or fitting skill to your repertoire. For instance, once you've made a simple, slim skirt with an elastic waistband and a machine-stitched hem, you may want to make the same pattern again, this time adding pockets to the side seams and hand-stitching the hem. Then you'll be ready for a more challenging pattern, say, a darted skirt with a kick pleat and a fitted waistband.

## Beyond the Pattern Envelope

The pattern envelope contains a lot of useful information, but you have to know how to interpret it. Pattern illustrations can be somewhat misleading, because the artists' drawings are much taller and slimmer than most real women actually are. So keep in mind that you'll probably look very different in the skirt than the figure in the sketch. Also, if there's a photograph of a designer original, remember that the pattern company does not buy the original pattern, but rather the right to copy the design, so the cut of the garment won't be exactly the same.

Don't get distracted by details, such as a skirt pocket or the color of the garment in the illustration. Look at the lines of the drawings on the back of the pattern envelope. These will show you the skirt's basic silhouette—that is, whether it is straight, flared, or gathered.

Open the envelope, if the retailer will allow you to, and check the line drawing on the pattern instruction sheet. This is usually larger than the one on the pattern envelope, and the details are easier to see. Also check the shape and grainline position of the pattern pieces.

Check the finished skirt length and width, and compare these to your notes on what looks best on you. Your best lengths may vary, too, depending on the style of the skirt. Length is simple to change, but widths are more difficult to adjust, so you may need to try another size.

Read through the pattern instructions. Be sure you understand or can learn every step. Check the garment details to be sure you are confident you can master them. If not, see if you can simplify the skirt, at least the first time you make it.

## Which Size to Buy?

Choose a skirt pattern based on your full-hip measurement (p. 142), not your waist measurement—the waistline is easier to adjust than the hip. If your upper thighs are larger than your hips (as on a pear-shaped figure), substitute your upper-thigh measurement for the hip measurement when selecting the size.

If the skirt is part of an ensemble pattern, select the pattern size you would normally take in a blouse or jacket. You don't have to buy another pattern for the skirt—simply adjust the skirt pattern to fit. It's much easier to alter a skirt than it is to alter a blouse or a jacket.

While you're searching the pattern books for a skirt, be sure to also check the patterns that show ensembles. You just might find the perfect skirt, as well as a matching jacket or coat.

# 8 Working with Fabrics

It's impossible to select fabric without touching it. When you find a fabric that appeals to you, open it out to the length of the garment to examine its drape and overall effect. Crush it in your hand to see if it wrinkles and if the creases disappear easily. Take the bolt to a full-length mirror and hold the fabric up against you, draping it like a skirt. Stand back and squint to get a different perspective—sometimes a fabric that's appealing at close range isn't when you see it from a distance.

If your skirt will have pleats, fold the fabric to duplicate them. If you want to make a skirt with gathers, scrunch up the fabric to imitate a gathered effect. From these tests, you'll discover whether the fabric drapes smoothly and gracefully (which will flatter the figure without adding bulk) or is stiff and three-dimensional.

When you begin shopping, the fabrics recommended on the back of the pattern envelope are a good starting point. These are the fabrics the pattern designer believes will work best for that garment. Often these recommendations are too generic, however, and make no allowances for the sewer's abilities. The recommendations also fail to take into account that the characteristics of a specific fabric type (such as wool gabardine) can vary greatly. Consult the chart on pp. 124-127 for other suggested fabrics for your skirt style.

# A Glossary of Fashion Fabrics

*Allow yourself time to select just the right fabric—one that you will enjoy sewing and wearing.*

The most common mistake that sewers make is to pair a pattern with an incompatible fabric. If a fabric seems too heavy, too slippery, too wrinkly, too unstable, prone to fraying, or not quite the right color, keep looking. Most sewers have a "little voice" inside that instinctively recognizes when a fabric isn't acceptable. Better to find out before the garment is made than during the project or, worse yet, after the skirt is finished. When you're not sure how a fabric will handle, buy ⅛ yd. to experiment with.

# Foolproof Fabrics

Certain fabrics are like dependable old friends. They are a pleasure to touch, gratifying to sew and press, and they wear, move, and flow beautifully. Natural fibers head the list of foolproof fabrics for skirts.

**Cotton:** *Denim, brushed cotton, chambray, fine poplin, lawn.* Look for long-fiber cottons (the best quality), which can be identified by their beautiful sheen and resistance to wrinkles. A pleasure to sew and press, these cottons last and last.

**Wool:** *Wool crepe, double knits, wool jersey (though not for rank beginners), wool challis.* The weight and drape of wool makes it a perfect skirt fabric. Wool crepe is excellent, as the texture does not add bulk to the figure. It's also easy to press and sew. Avoid wool flannel entirely—it's thick and bulky and doesn't press well.

**Linen:** *Linen blends.* Linen blends well with other fibers. With linen/rayon, for example, you get the best of both fabrics—the drape of rayon and the stability of linen. Moygashel, a brand-name Irish linen, doesn't wrinkle as much as other pure linens. For slim and fitted flared skirts, choose heavy weights. Consider lining your linen skirt, depending on the style.

**Silk:** *Silk linen, silk noil, silk tweed, silk broadcloth.* Silk can be smooth and slippery or have the look and feel of cotton or linen. Until you have more experience, avoid the slippery silks, such as charmeuse, crepe de chine, georgette, and chiffon.

## NEEDLES, THREADS, AND STITCHES

For most skirt fabrics (lightweight to midweight wovens and some knits), a #12/80 universal-point needle is best. With these fabrics, use a good-quality long-staple polyester thread and a 2mm to 2.5mm stitch length (about 8 to 10 stitches per inch).

For very lightweight fabric, such as crepe de chine, use a smaller needle (#10/70) and finer thread—machine-embroidery thread, for example.

With heavy, dense, thick, or textured fabrics, use a longer stitch and larger needle. With denim, for example, use a #14/90 needle. Even if your fabric isn't heavy, because you are stitching through so many thicknesses, you may want to topstitch with a size #14/90 or special topstitching needle.

I baste with silk thread to avoid making indentations in the fabric when I press it before the final stitching.

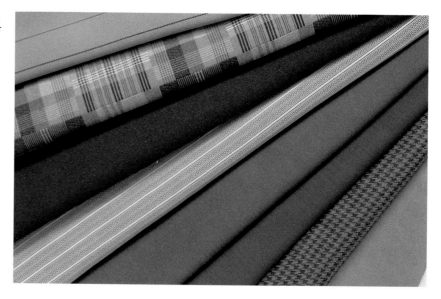

*The feel, weight, and drape of the fabric are essential to the success of your finished garment.*

# Challenging Fabrics

Some fabrics are more challenging to work with because they require expertise in cutting, handling, sewing, pressing, and hand-stitching. To gain some experience gradually, combine a challenging fabric with a simple-to-construct design. For example, try making a simple four-gore pull-on skirt in rayon or silk crepe de chine.

**Rayon:** *A man-made fiber composed of natural materials.* Rayon's soft and drapey characteristics, which give the fabric its appeal, are also what can make it hard to handle. Sand-washed rayons, especially, shift and move easily while they are being cut and sewn. Imported, cottonlike rayons are often more stable and easier to handle than inexpensive, domestic versions. Try the wrinkle test: If the wrinkles fall out after you crumple the fabric, the rayon is probably of good quality and will be easier to sew.

**Polyester:** *A man-made fiber that can look and feel like silk or rayon.* Polyester is difficult to cut, sew, press, and shape. The fiber is so strong that topstitching often puckers. Avoid polyester "silkies" until you're a seasoned sewer, and even then, test the fabric first.

**Wool gabardine:** *Can be firm and crisp or soft and drapey.* Although suitable for a variety of skirt styles, gabardine is a difficult fabric for a beginner to work with because it eases poorly, frays readily, and shows stitching errors. Gabardine also requires expert pressing and topstitching to look its best.

# FABRICS FOR POCKETS, INTERFACINGS, AND LININGS

Once you've found your skirt fabric, select the fabrics for the other items you'll include in the skirt.

**Pockets:** If the skirt fabric is lightweight, doesn't show through from the right side, and won't stick to itself, make the pockets from the same fabric. You can also use the lining fabric to make the pockets.

Pockets may also be made of any strong, slippery fabric or plain-weave cotton in a color close to that of the skirt. Plain broadcloth or cotton twill are also good to use.

If the skirt fabric is a pale color or white, make the pockets of a lightweight lining fabric of nude- or flesh-toned silk or nylon organza.

**Interfacing:** You have a number of choices for waistband interfacing. You don't have to use what the pattern says. Although designed for shirt collars and

*Fusible interfacing creates a stable, crisp waistband.*

cuffs, woven fusible is perfect for waistbands. It creates a crisp finish that holds the waistband's shape. Sew-in interfacing doesn't work as well. There are also waistband styles for which you don't need interfacing (pp. 203-205).

**Lining:** A lining fabric should be thin, strong, and smooth. It should also be compatible with the weight, drape, and care requirements of the skirt fabric. The color should not be visible through the skirt fabric.

If your skirt pattern doesn't include a lining, you need to calculate how much fabric you should buy. The general rule is: double the skirt length. However, it's safer to lay out your pattern pieces on the lining fabric (except for the waistband, which is unlined). For future reference, note on the pattern envelope how much lining fabric you need for the skirt.

Rayon linings are ideal. Not only are they inexpensive, they "breathe" and have excellent draping qualities. They can be difficult to find, however. (Polyester, though less expensive and more available, doesn't breathe well and has only fair draping qualities.)

Silk is the ultimate in luxury. It's expensive, feels marvelous, and can add warmth to the garment. Crepe de chine is an excellent and sumptuous companion to wool crepe or light gabardine. China silk is an excellent traditional lining fabric, but beware of the thin, cheap varieties—with any stress at all (as in a fitted skirt), the seams may pull out.

| Pockets | Waistband Interfacings | Linings |
|---|---|---|
| Plain-weave cotton | Fusible nonwoven, precut | Rayon |
| Plain broadcloth | Fusible woven yardage | Silk |
| Cotton twill | Sew-in woven, by the roll | Crepe de chine |
| Lining fabrics of silk or nylon organza | Elastic and flat-ribbed elastic | China silk |

# Preparing the Fabric

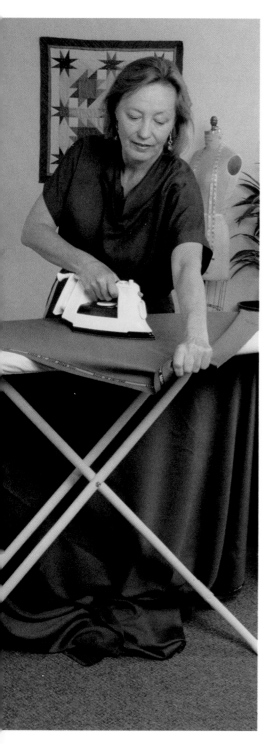

*Prepare the fabric before you sew to ensure that the finished garment will look, hang, and wear well.*

Most fabric will shrink the first time it's laundered, so you should wash or dry clean it before you cut out the pattern pieces. Preshrink using the same method you plan to use to launder your finished skirt. For example, if you'll be washing and drying the skirt by machine, pretreat the fabric by machine. After preshrinking, straighten the grain of the fabric by pulling or pressing to ensure that the finished garment will look its best.

## Preshrinking and Pressing

Washing by hand is often the best way to launder hand-sewn garments. To preshrink the fabric, either wash and dry it by machine this first time only, or wash it by hand. To preshrink by hand, fold the fabric and submerge it in warm to hot water and a little detergent. (The detergent removes the excess dye or finishing substance.) Then rinse and air-dry the fabric.

Undyed white and off-white wools tend to shrink at alarming rates and should always be preshrunk. Lay the fabric on a large terry towel that has just been washed in the machine (the towel should be damp, not sodden). Roll the fabric and damp towel together like a jelly roll, leave them overnight, and, the next day, press the fabric smooth to remove the moisture.

Some fabrics, such as wool crepe, must be dry cleaned. To preshrink the fabric, have the dry cleaner process the piece of fabric just as if it were a garment.

Not all fabrics need preshrinking. Many wools and silks are "needle-ready," and need nothing more than a touch-up with the iron before you lay out and cut the pattern pieces.

Press the preshrunk fabric before you cut out the pattern pieces and hang it on a hanger so it won't wrinkle. Press and hang your pattern pieces, too. They'll be easier to work with.

# Straightening the Grain

Even though fabric is woven straight (with the lengthwise and crosswise threads at right angles to each other), it is often pulled off-grain during the finishing process or as it is wound onto the bolt. If you cut and sew a garment off-grain, it may never hang the way you expect it to.

So, before you lay out your pattern pieces, check that the fabric is on the "straight of the grain," that is, with all edges, selvage, and cross grain straight and at right angles. Make a snip through the selvage about 1 in. to 2 in. from one of the raw edges. Tear the fabric if it tears easily and without distortion, or pull one thread out and cut along the area it was pulled from. (Some fabric stores will do this when you buy the fabric.)

Now fold the fabric in half, with selvages together. Press the fabric and place it on a flat surface. The selvage and cross grain should be straight and at right angles to each other; cross-grain threads should lie on top of one another.

If the fabric is off-grain, pull the fabric firmly from the corners along the bias to straighten it. If you have a lot of yardage, work down the length of the fabric, pulling every 12 in. from corner to corner. This task is easily accomplished with two people, but if you're working alone, you can press the fabric, stretching it along the bias as you work, as shown in the photo on the facing page.

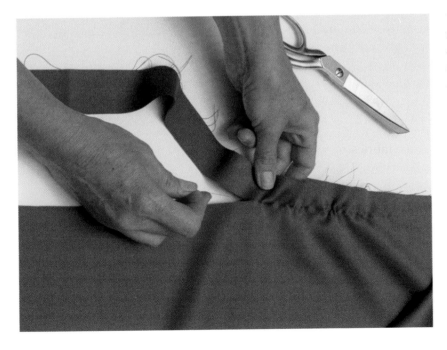

*To find the "straight of the grain," tear the fabric or pull a thread and cut along the crosswise grain. Check that the selvage and cross grain are straight and at right angles.*

# 9 Getting the Right Fit

Part of the fun of sewing for yourself is to get the best fit possible. Fitting is the process of adjusting or altering a commercial pattern so that it will exactly fit the person who will wear the garment. It is rare for anyone to have precisely the same measurements as a commercial pattern, and seldom can a pattern be used straight out of the envelope without changes. Altering and customizing the pattern are as much a part of creating clothes as sewing and pressing are.

Fitting has an undeserved reputation for being difficult. It's not, but it can be time-consuming—up to one-third of the time it takes to construct an entire garment is spent preparing and adjusting the pattern. Once you know how your body differs from the pattern, you can adjust all your patterns for your specific hip or waist measurements, preferred length, or other variations. With all the time you'll invest in perfecting a pattern, it certainly pays to have a collection of favorites that you can use again and again.

Because fitting is a trial-and-error process, it helps to take a fitting class or to have a friend who sews or a professional dressmaker assist you in measuring and basic fitting. Reference books help too.

One of the secrets to success in sewing is the process of "proofing" the pattern. When you proof a pattern, you make certain that the skirt will fit around your body and that it will be the right length. Once that's accomplished, pin the tissue pieces together and try on the pattern to check the style, details, and silhouette. When you have a pattern that's exactly customized to the shape of your body, you're ready to cut out the fabric and begin sewing a garment you can be sure you'll enjoy wearing.

Make it your goal to add pattern adjustment and fitting to your repertoire of sewing skills, expanding your knowledge bit by bit with each project.

# The Basics

*For many people, fitting is a mystery—but it needn't be.*
*There are four basic steps. Take them one at a time.*
*It also helps to have a few tools handy.*

# Four Basic Steps

If you follow these four simple steps before you cut your fabric, any fitting you do during construction will be fine-tuning, not a major overhaul.

**1**. Compare your body measurements to those of the flat pattern.

**2**. Proof the pattern to ensure that the skirt will be the right length and will fit around your body.

**3**. Pin the pattern pieces together as they will be sewn and try on the pattern. Adjust for swayback, round tummy or large hips.

**4**. Make any desired changes to the pattern for pockets, walking ease, linings, or changes in grainline. Pin-fit again if necessary, and transfer any further adjustments to the pattern.

# Tools

Adjusting patterns is much simpler and the results are more professional if you use the right tools. Each tool has its own specific uses for the various patternmaking tasks; none substitutes for another. As you grow more familiar with them, they'll become like extensions of your hands.

Acquire the following, arranged here in order of necessity:

Of course, you'll need a measuring tape and 6-in. gauge.

A 2-in. by 18-in. C-Thru ruler is invaluable for creating straight lines, finding right angles, lengthening, shortening, and more.

A metal hip curve is just right for curving and shaping the hips, waist, and legs. (This professional patternmaker's tool is available at stores that sell patternmaking supplies or from mail-order sources.)

Once you use a metal yardstick you'll never again use a wooden one. It's great for making clean, long straight lines and edges.

There are several additional tools you'll find useful when adjusting your pattern—glue, tape, strips of elastic, tracing paper and pattern tissue, pencils and pens, chalk, Clo-chalk, dressmaker's pencils, right-angle ruler, full-length mirror, hand mirror, embroidery floss and chenille needle, scissors, and appliqué scissors. The list will continue to grow as you find your own way of working.

# Comparing Measurements

*The first step in altering your pattern is to compare your body measurements with the pattern's.*

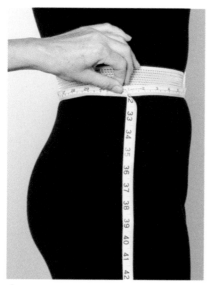

1 *Measure waistline.*

2 *Measure high hip or tummy.*

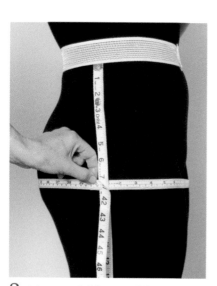

3 *Measure full hip, and from waist to full hip.*

4 *Measure finished length.*

## Measure Your Body

The four critical measurements are the waist, high hip/tummy, full hip, and finished length. Make a note of these. They're essential for altering and fitting your pattern.

When measuring, wear the underclothing and shoes you might wear with the skirt.

**Waist:** Pin a length of wide elastic around your body where you'd like the skirt waistline to be. Measure over the elastic, holding a finger underneath the tape measure to allow an adequate amount of ease **(1)**.

**High hip/tummy:** Check your side view in a full-length mirror and measure your high hip/tummy wherever your figure is largest—between 1½ in. and 4 in. below the waist **(2)**. Be sure the tape measure doesn't rise up slightly at center front. Also measure from waist to high hip.

**Full hip:** Check your side view again and measure around your hips at their fullest point (this is the full-hip measurement). Also measure from your waist to your full hip **(3)**.

**Finished length:** Measure from the waistline at the side seam or front to the desired finished length **(4)**. (Or measure the length of your favorite skirt of similar style.)

# Measure Your Pattern

To make it easier to measure the pattern, take it out of the envelope and spread it out on a flat, uncluttered work table.

**Waist:** Hold the tape measure on its edge (to make it easier to follow the pattern's curves) and measure the waist along the stitching line, excluding seam allowances, tucks, pleats, or darts **(1)**. Pin these in position or simply skip over them when measuring—this will give you the actual measurements of the finished skirt. (Because of the ease built into the pattern, this measurement should be larger than the waist size listed on the pattern envelope.)

**High hip/tummy:** If you have a rounded tummy or high round hips, take an additional measurement 1½ to 4 in. below the waistline of your pattern.

**Full hip:** The full-hip measurement on the pattern will be the same distance from the waist as the measurement on your body. If your skirt has tucks or pleats, pin them into position first to get a true measurement of the finished garment **(2)**.

**Finished length:** Along the skirt's center front or side seamline, measure from the waistline to the bottom edge of the desired hem.

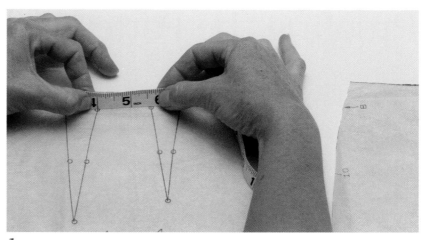

1 *Measure the waistline, excluding the darts, tucks, pleats, and seam allowances.*

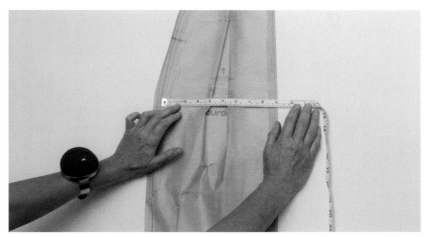

2 *Measure the pattern at full hip with the pleats pinned in position.*

---

## The Four Essential Measurements

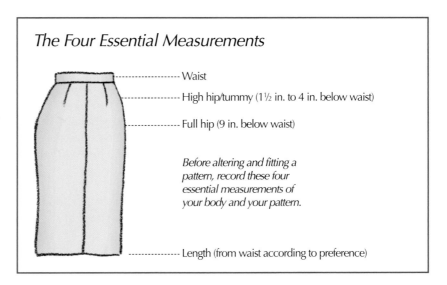

---------- Waist

---------- High hip/tummy (1½ in. to 4 in. below waist)

---------- Full hip (9 in. below waist)

*Before altering and fitting a pattern, record these four essential measurements of your body and your pattern.*

-------------- Length (from waist according to preference)

# Proofing the Pattern

*Adjust the length and width of the flat pattern before you try it on to reduce the amount of fitting you'll need to do later.*

It's more efficient to lengthen or shorten your pattern before you add width so that you'll be working only with the necessary length. You'll also be able to blend the side seamlines easily and accurately as you smooth the jog that often occurs when you change the length of the garment.

If you need to lengthen or shorten your skirt 2 in. or less, simply add or subtract length at the hem. If you need to adjust it more than 2 in., alter the body of the skirt at the lengthen/shorten line.

If your pattern doesn't have a lengthen/shorten line, add one so you will be able to realign the top and bottom halves of the skirt. To do this, extend the grainline; then draw a line at a right angle to it at the point where you want to lengthen or shorten your skirt.

If your skirt is shaped at the hem, as in a gored, flared, or pegged skirt, or if it has a kick pleat, French vent, or hem detail, lengthen or shorten below the full hip so as not to interfere with the design detail.

You may need more fabric if you lengthen or widen the skirt significantly. To find out for sure, do a trial layout of your pattern pieces on paper or on a gridded cutting board.

## Lengthening a Pattern

Cut along the lengthen/shorten line and tape or glue a piece of tissue paper along one cut edge, overlapping the pattern and tissue edges about ½ in. (You can use scrap pattern tissue, as long as it's as wide as the pattern piece and at least 1 in. longer than the amount you're adding to the skirt.)

On the scrap tissue, parallel to the lengthen/shorten line, mark the amount you want to add to the skirt. Extend the grainline through the scrap tissue. Line it up with the grainline on the other half of the skirt pattern and glue or tape the scrap tissue in place.

If you're not also changing the width of the skirt, simply draw the side seamlines on the scrap tissue and blend the seamlines of the skirt halves.

If you are changing the skirt width, make these adjustments (p. 145) and blend all the seamlines in one operation.

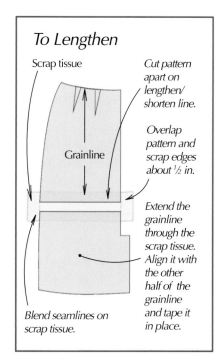

### To Lengthen

Scrap tissue

Cut pattern apart on lengthen/shorten line.

Overlap pattern and scrap edges about ½ in.

Grainline

Extend the grainline through the scrap tissue. Align it with the other half of the grainline and tape it in place.

Blend seamlines on scrap tissue.

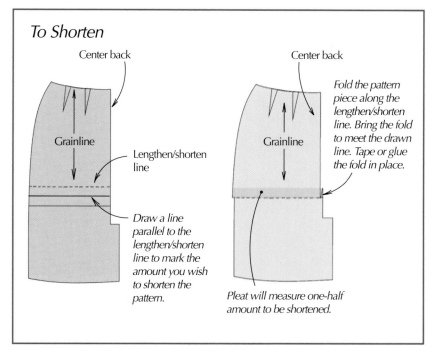

### To Shorten

Center back

Grainline

Lengthen/shorten line

Draw a line parallel to the lengthen/shorten line to mark the amount you wish to shorten the pattern.

Center back

Fold the pattern piece along the lengthen/shorten line. Bring the fold to meet the drawn line. Tape or glue the fold in place.

Grainline

Pleat will measure one-half amount to be shortened.

# Shortening a Pattern

Mark the amount you want to shorten your pattern by drawing a line parallel to the lengthen/shorten line.

Fold the pattern piece along the lenthen/shorten line and then lift the fold to meet the drawn line. Glue or tape the pattern piece in position. The pleat that forms should be half the total amount to be shortened (for example, if you're shortening the skirt 1½ in., the pleat will be ¾ in. wide).

Make width adjustments, if needed, at the hip or waist. Connect and blend the seamlines.

# Adjusting Width

Adjusting width is the most common pattern alteration, and it pays to master it from the start. Increase or decrease skirt width at the side seams only. If you add width at center front or back, the darts/tucks will be positioned too far apart.

Although you'll decrease width less frequently, the same principles apply for both increasing and decreasing. Adjust the side seams on the pattern tissue, drawing in new cutting lines. This will allow you to pin the tissue together along the stitching lines and try on the paper pattern to test the fit.

The total amount of adjusted width should be divided evenly among the quarters of the skirt—if an extra 2 in. is needed, for example, add ½ in. at each side seam.

# CALCULATING PATTERN EASE

Two types of ease are built into the pattern: wearing ease and design ease. Wearing ease is the amount of extra fabric you need to move comfortably in a garment. Design ease is the amount of extra fabric the designer or patternmaker adds to give the garment a certain style and look. The total amount of ease is the difference between the size measurements on the pattern envelope and the actual measurements of the pattern.

For example, the size chart on the pattern envelope or in the pattern book may indicate that a size 10 pattern has a waist of 26 in. and hips of 34 in. The skirt's flat pattern, however, measures 27½ in. at the waist and 38 in. at the hip. This means there is 1½ in. of ease in the waist and 4 in. in the hip, which is standard for a straight skirt.

*Flat-pattern measurement – Envelope measurement = Amount of ease*

To determine the amount of ease in your pattern, measure the flat pattern (p. 143) and compare these figures to the body measurements on the pattern envelope. Write down the amount of ease your pattern allows in the waist, high hip, and full hip. When you adjust your pattern for your body measurements, you want to maintain this amount of pattern ease (as shown in the chart below).

You can add a total of up to 8 in. (2 in. at each side seam) to the waist and/or hip before the shape becomes distorted. If you need to add more width than this, you should use a larger-size pattern.

It's also possible to make varying adjustments to the hip, high hip, and waist. Figures with a rounded tummy or high round hip, for example, may need extra width at the waist as well as at the high hip to achieve a smooth line (pp. 156-157). This is especially true for small-waisted figures (an elasticized fitted waistband, p. 210, works very well on these shapes).

After you've made all necessary adjustments, use 1-in. side seams to build in extra fitting insurance. This will allow you enough extra fabric to alter the skirt while you're

# CALCULATING THE WIDTH ADJUSTMENT

Make a copy of this chart and record your body measurements, the flat-pattern's measurements, and the pattern ease. The chart will help you determine how much to adjust your pattern at each seam for the best fit, while retaining the right amount of wearing and design ease.

|  | Waist | High hip/ tummy | Full hip |
|---|---|---|---|
| Body Measurement | 29 |  |  |
| Plus Ease (as calculated above) | 1½ |  |  |
| Total | 30½ |  |  |
| Minus Flat-Pattern Measurement | 27½ |  |  |
| Adjustment to Pattern (distributed evenly at side-seam allowances) | 3 |  |  |

sewing; the extra seam width can always be trimmed or evened afterward.

Make dots on the tissue with a pencil to mark the amount you need to adjust the side seams at waist, high hip, and full hip. If needed, attach scrap tissue paper to the side seams to add enough width **(1)**. Make sure you maintain the hip ease at your full-hip measurement.

Use a hip curve to connect the dots, adding the same amount you added to the full hip all the way down the seam to the hem, in order to retain the original silhouette of the skirt.

Remember to adjust the waistband pattern piece if you make any changes in the skirt width at the waistline. If you add ½ in. to each of the skirt's side seams, for example, you'll also need to add 2 in. to the waistband by adding 1 in. to each waistband side seam.

As you become more adept at making and fitting skirts, you may prefer simply to chalk-mark the amount that you need to add or subtract directly onto the fabric **(2)**, and cut.

A hip curve will help you redraw the new silhouette of the skirt perfectly.

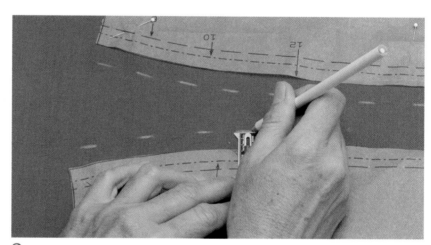

**1** *Add extra width to the side seams of the pattern pieces with tissue paper.*

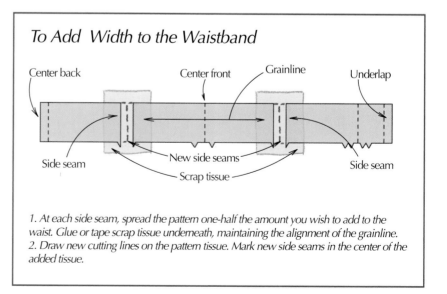

**2** *Mark additions directly onto fabric.*

## To Add Width to the Waistband

Center back   Center front   Grainline   Underlap

Side seam   New side seams   Side seam
Scrap tissue

*1. At each side seam, spread the pattern one-half the amount you wish to add to the waist. Glue or tape scrap tissue underneath, maintaining the alignment of the grainline.*
*2. Draw new cutting lines on the pattern tissue. Mark new side seams in the center of the added tissue.*

# Customizing the Pattern

*A few simple, optional alterations to the flat pattern might make your garment more attractive and comfortable. Consider pockets, linings, and additional walking ease.*

## Adding a Pocket

If your pattern does not have a pocket, borrow one from another pattern. When you find a pocket that works well, copy it and save it for future use.

Position the pocket pattern so it extends into the waistband and mark the opening. If necessary, shape the side seam so it is the same as the side seam on your skirt. (Some skirts are curved to the shape of the hip, others are straight.) Position the pocket pattern on the skirt pattern, aligning them at the waistline, and trace the skirt's side seam onto the pocket.

Transfer the markings for the pocket opening with tiny snips or chalk marks on the wrong side of the fabric.

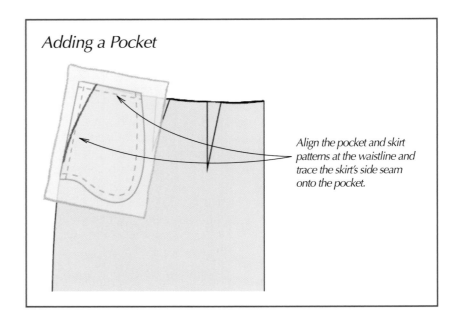

*Adding a Pocket*

Align the pocket and skirt patterns at the waistline and trace the skirt's side seam onto the pocket.

# Adding Walking Ease

Walking ease, a secret of fine dressmakers and never calculated in commercial patterns, is a simple alteration that makes kick pleats, French vents, slits, front openings, button-front and wrap skirts hang perfectly straight. In fact, the straightness is an optical illusion.

When a garment is cut straight, there's a natural tendency for it to hang open at the hem. If you add walking ease, however, skirts appear to hang arrow-straight.

When you add walking ease, you do not change the original grainline of the garment. Make this pattern change after all other adjustments are completed.

The amount of ease is based on the length of the garment and weight of the fabric.

**Kick Pleats, French Vents, Slits** Add walking ease at the front or back seamline, depending on the placement of the kick pleat, French vent, or slit. Add ½ in. for a knee-length (19-in. to 24-in.) skirt, 1 in. for a mid-calf (32-in. to 36-in.) skirt. Add slightly more (⅛ in. to ¼ in.) for heavy or thick fabrics. Adjust the lining pattern too (p. 150).

On the skirt-pattern piece, cut along the seamline/vent fold line from the hem to the waist. Tape or glue a scrap of tissue along one edge. Position the other edge so that the walking ease is added at the bottom of the hem and tapers to nothing at the waist end of the seam.

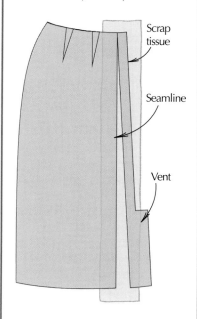

## Adding Walking Ease to a Pleat, Vent, or Slit

Scrap tissue

Seamline

Vent

1. Cut along the seamline/vent fold line from the hem to the waist.
2. Add walking ease at the bottom of the hem by spreading the pattern and adding scrap tissue. Taper the slit in the pattern to nothing at the waistline.

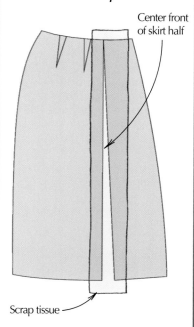

## Adding Walking Ease to a Wrap Skirt

Center front of skirt half

Scrap tissue

1. Cut along the center front, from hem to waist, on both the right and left sides of the skirt.
2. Add walking ease at the hem, tapering the pattern slit to nothing at the waistline. Add ease to a button-front skirt in the same way.

**Other Skirt Styles** For wrap or button-front styles, add ½ in. of ease for knee-length skirts, 1 in. for mid-calf-length skirts. Add the walking ease at the center front, from hem to waist, on both the left and the right sides of the skirt.

If your fabric is a plaid or stripe, or if it has a strong vertical design, add walking ease at the side seams.

For skirts with side buttons, add walking ease at the front and back side seams.

# Adding a Lining

Lining a skirt has multiple benefits: It gives a finished look to the inside of your garment, makes the skirt easy to slide on and off, and helps it stay wrinkle-free. In addition, a lining keeps the skirt fabric from clinging and makes a lightweight fabric opaque.

Even if the skirt pattern includes a lining, I prefer to cut one from the skirt pattern pieces. (For a list of suggested lining fabrics, see p. 135.) Lining fabrics are firmly woven and usually have much less give than the skirt fabric, so don't make the lining smaller than the skirt.

Cutting and constructing a lining is simple and fast. Linings for skirts with special details such as a French vent, however, may require additional adjustments, as shown in the drawing below. When you sew, stitch the lining's side seams slightly narrower (1/8 in.) to allow for sitting room and to keep the seams from pulling out.

Cut the lining so the hem will be at least 1 in. shorter than the skirt, while covering the raw edge of the skirt hem. Different lining-hem finishes may require that you cut the lining to slightly different lengths (pp. 198-199). If you're not sure how you're going to finish the lining hem, simply cut the lining 1 in. shorter than your skirt. Trim as needed.

## LINING A SKIRT WITH A FRENCH VENT

1. To adjust the skirt pattern to be used for the lining, fold the pattern piece back along the seamline and vent fold line. Trace the cut edge of the vent onto the pattern.

2. Add seam allowances by drawing a new cutting line 1 1/4 in. from the traced line, as shown in the drawing. This allows for the skirt's 5/8-in. seam allowance plus the lining's 5/8-in. seam allowance. The skirt and the finished lining will be flush at the vent opening.

3. Now draw the 5/8-in. seam allowance of the lining vent, including the corner, as shown. Don't skip this step. You'll be reinforcing the seamlines at the corner, so you'll want them to be clearly marked.

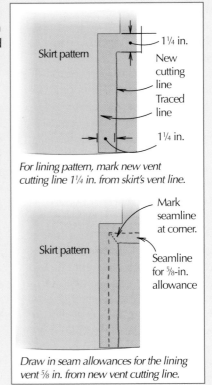

For lining pattern, mark new vent cutting line 1 1/4 in. from skirt's vent line.

Draw in seam allowances for the lining vent 5/8 in. from new vent cutting line.

# Changing the Grainline of a Flared Skirt

The drape and flattering effect of an A-line or gored flared skirt can be changed significantly by repositioning the grainline on the pattern pieces.

Lengthwise grain is often placed at center front and center back of the pattern, on the lengthwise fold, which makes the front and back one pattern piece. This layout is common on commercial patterns because less fabric is required than with other layouts. It's the least flattering, however, as it results in a wide silhouette that broadens any figure and exaggerates a tummy. In addition, the bias at the side seam may stretch, creating an uneven hem.

Two alternate lengthwise-grain positions and one bias-grain position for the same skirt panels are shown on p. 152. Treat both front and back pattern pieces in the same way. Remember that you may need additional fabric if you change the grainline. To figure out the yardage you'll need, do a trial layout on paper that is the width of your fabric or on a gridded cutting board. You can reposition the grainline for any type of fabric.

### Lengthwise Grain in Center of Front and Back Panels
Often used by Ralph Lauren, this cut is very flattering and slimming, especially for the pear-shaped figure. Because the fullness hangs evenly around the skirt, an uneven hem is less likely. This layout is a perfect choice for rayons, knits, or other fabrics that may stretch at the hem.

To alter the pattern, simply fold the skirt panel in half, center seam to side seam. The waist shape will not match, but that's okay. Draw in a new grainline down the center of each panel. (Add seam allowances at center front and back if the original pattern was one piece cut on the fold.)

### Lengthwise Grain Parallel to Side Seam
If the straight of the grain is parallel to the side seam, the skirt's fullness hangs at the center. The center seam is on the bias and may tend to stretch. This styling creates a strong vertical line, which is especially effective with striped fabrics.

This layout broadens the figure and emphasizes a protruding tummy or derriere, but is a good choice for a figure with roundness at the side of the hips—the straight of the grain flattens out the curve.

### Bias Grain
The 45° diagonal line through the lengthwise and crosswise grain of the fabric is the bias. A bias-cut skirt requires more fabric than any of the other layouts, but nothing else has such a beautiful, flowing drape.

The bias cut will reveal curves and bulges, however, and garment construction and hemming take a bit of special care. If you are adapting a pattern with a one-piece front or back to a bias layout, add seam allowances to the center front and back. This way, the garment will hang without twisting to one side.

# Different Grainlines — Different Effects

| **How it's laid out** | **How it looks** | **How it drapes** |
|---|---|---|

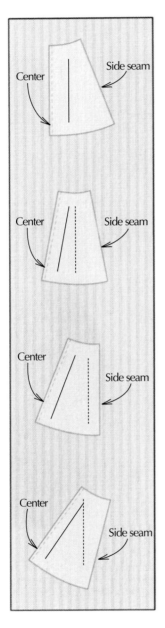

Lengthwise grain in center of front and back (typical in commercial patterns).

Fullness tends to hang at the sides.

Lengthwise grain in center of front and back panels.

Fullness hangs evenly around the skirt.

Lengthwise grain parallel to side seam.

Fullness hangs at the center of the skirt; sides hang straighter.

Bias grain.

Requires more fabric, but has flowing drape.

Original grainline ——————
New grainline --------------------

The simplest way to alter a pattern for the bias cut is to use a right-angle ruler that has a 45° angle marked on it. An alternative is to mark lengthwise and crosswise grains with a C-Thru ruler. Then fold the fabric at a right angle through the intersection of the grainlines so the lines are superimposed on each other. Draw a line along the fold to mark the bias grainline. Mark a second bias grainline at 90° to the first. This way, when you turn over the pattern piece to cut out the second half, you can easily position it.

Place bias-cut pattern pieces on a single layer of fabric, keeping the pattern in a one-way layout, that is, with the nap of the fabric always in one direction. All the hems will be facing the same way.

When cutting two front or back pieces in one layer of cloth, be sure to flip the pattern piece over to cut the second half so that they will be mirror images.

## Finding the Bias Grainline

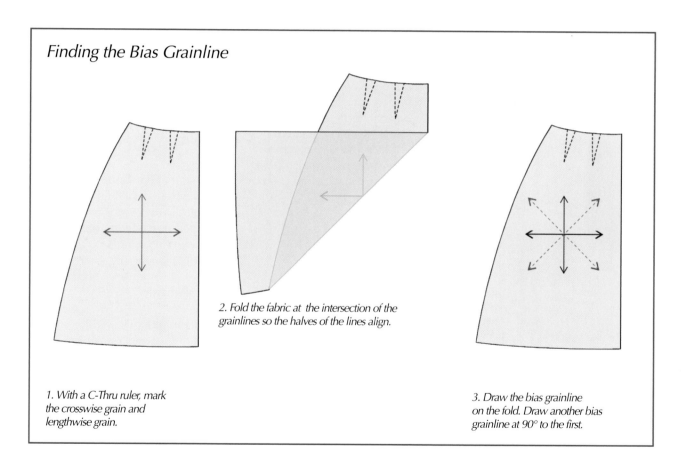

1. With a C-Thru ruler, mark the crosswise grain and lengthwise grain.

2. Fold the fabric at the intersection of the grainlines so the halves of the lines align.

3. Draw the bias grainline on the fold. Draw another bias grainline at 90° to the first.

# Pin-Fitting Adjustments

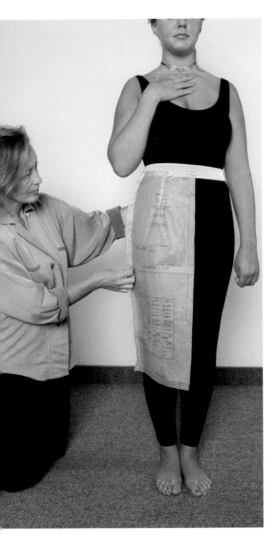

*There's no substitute for pin-fitting your pattern and altering it as carefully as you can before you cut the fabric.*

Once the two-dimensional flat pattern has been adjusted, it's time to have a look at your pattern in three dimensions.

Pin-fitting the pattern on your body, just as if it were the finished skirt, allows you to adjust for aspects of your body profile that are not accounted for by measurements alone. A swayback, a protruding tummy, and a fuller than average derrière, for example, may prevent your skirt pattern from fitting well. These very common adjustments are best made on the pattern tissue, now, before you cut out the garment.

## Try on the Pattern

Pin the pattern together and try it on as if it were the finished skirt. Place pins parallel to the stitching lines along the seams. Pin any darts, tucks, or pleats in position.

Hold the pattern in place at the waistline with a 1-in.-wide length of elastic. Position the center fronts and backs and check the fit, length, and overall styling in a full-length mirror. It takes only a bit of practice to develop an eye for the way the finished garment will look.

Use a large hand mirror to see the back view. A knowledgeable friend is also a great help!

After you check the fit and length, and have made the necessary adjustments, see if the skirt needs an adjustment for swayback or a protruding tummy.

## Adjusting for Swayback

If the skirt needs some adjustment for swayback, you'll find horizontal wrinkles at the center back of the pin-fitted skirt pattern, just below the waistband. Here's how to estimate the amount you'll need to remove at center back for the skirt to lie smoothly.

While pin-fitting, lower the waistline at center back by slipping the pattern slightly under the elastic until the wrinkles are eliminated. Mark the pattern tissue with a pen or pencil right under the elastic at center back. The amount you'll need to remove usually ranges from ¼ in. to 1½ in.

Pin all darts, pleats, or tucks in place. Then draw a new line to eliminate the desired amount of pattern tissue, starting at center back and gradually meeting the waistline at the side seams. The hip curve is the perfect tool for drawing this new waistline. If your skirt has gathers, the line is less critical, so simply draw, freehand, an even, slightly curved line from center back to side seam.

Overlap the pattern pieces for the amount of the adjustment at the center-back seamline, tapering to nothing at the side seams. Redraw the lines for darts, tucks, and the center-back seam. Make corresponding adjustments to the back facing. Avoid the pins and cut along the redrawn waistline.

If you're working without a partner, it may be difficult to determine the exact amount you'll need to remove. That's okay. Estimate now and fine-tune the fit later while you're constructing the garment. You can make this swayback alteration just before you apply the waistband to the skirt, but you may need to shorten the zipper, too. It's easiest to make pattern adjustments before cutting, then double-check them during the garment's construction.

If your skirt has a raised waistband (p. 215), make the swayback adjustment by cutting the pattern back along the waistline, from the center back to 1/8 in. from the side seam.

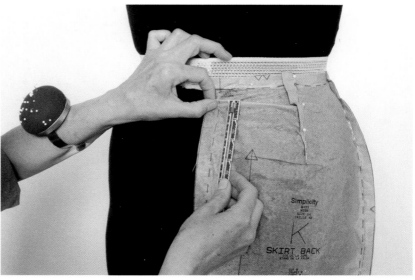

*To adjust for swayback, lower the waistline at center back until the horizontal wrinkles are eliminated. You may need to remove from 1/4 in. to 1 1/2 in. of excess pattern tissue.*

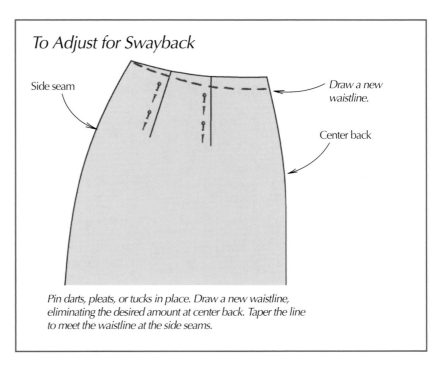

## To Adjust for Swayback

Side seam

Draw a new waistline.

Center back

*Pin darts, pleats, or tucks in place. Draw a new waistline, eliminating the desired amount at center back. Taper the line to meet the waistline at the side seams.*

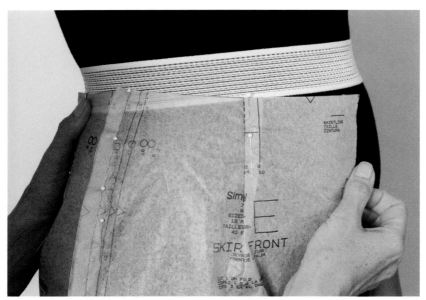

If the pattern piece you're pin-fitting sits below the waistline because of a protruding tummy, you need to add extra length at center front.

# Adjusting for a Round Tummy

To adjust for a round tummy, you usually need to add not only extra width to your pattern (pp. 144-147), but also extra length at center front. When pin-fitting, check that the skirt pattern sits correctly at the waistline. If it doesn't, you'll need to correct it by adding length to the pattern with scrap tissue. This little adjustment can actually minimize the curve visually.

Add enough length so that the pattern meets the waistline correctly and hangs over the tummy smoothly. Exactly how much to add is hard to estimate, but it's best to allow a little extra. Average amounts range from 3/8 in. (which doesn't sound like much, but can make a small tummy nearly vanish) to about 2½ in.

Before you begin, pin any pleats, tucks, and darts in place. Draw a line on the scrap tissue to indicate the additional pattern length at center front and taper to nothing at the side seams. Curve the cutting line slightly outward over the tummy using the hip curve. Trim the tissue with the pleats, tucks, and darts in position.

A figure with a round tummy rarely is flattered by a darted-front skirt. Eliminate the darts and ease the entire amount across the front using the technique known as staystitch plus (p. 174).

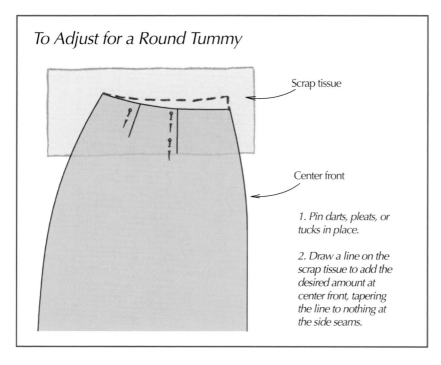

## To Adjust for a Round Tummy

Scrap tissue

Center front

1. Pin darts, pleats, or tucks in place.

2. Draw a line on the scrap tissue to add the desired amount at center front, tapering the line to nothing at the side seams.

# Adjusting for Full-Hip Measurements

The straight darts on a pattern are designed for an "average" full-hip measurement, but you can curve the back darts to the exact shape of your figure. The darts should point toward and end 1 in. to 1½ in. away from the fullest part of the figure. Shorten or lengthen them as needed.

Working from the midpoint of the dart, add or subtract ⅛ in. from each of the original dart lines. Use the hip curve to re-mark the stitching line, beginning and ending at the top and bottom of the dart.

For rounded full hips, scoop in the legs of the darts, allowing ¼ in. of extra fabric in the garment per dart.

For flat or low derrières and narrow full hips, curve the darts out, eliminating ¼ in. of fabric from the garment per dart.

Mark the position of the new end of the dart, and redraw the legs to reconnect them to their original positions at the waist.

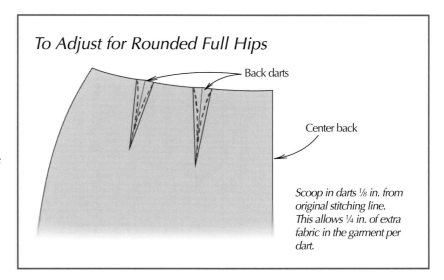

*To Adjust for Rounded Full Hips*

Back darts

Center back

*Scoop in darts ⅛ in. from original stitching line. This allows ¼ in. of extra fabric in the garment per dart.*

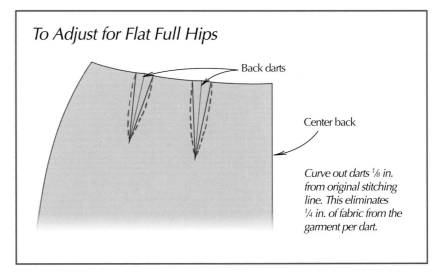

*To Adjust for Flat Full Hips*

Back darts

Center back

*Curve out darts ⅛ in. from original stitching line. This eliminates ¼ in. of fabric from the garment per dart.*

# 10 *Construction Guidelines*

Once you've made all your pattern adjustments, you're probably eager to start sewing. But before you begin, take some time to think through the sewing sequence and plan for any style modifications, details, and finishes you've chosen. Just as an architect needs to understand the whole process of constructing a building, a sewer needs to understand the progression of steps in a garment's construction and how each step leads to the next.

The pattern instruction sheet is your starting point. Read the instructions through and think about the construction sequence. Decide which techniques you want to use and which ones you want to change or modify. For example, you may decide to try a waistband style different from the one provided in the pattern or to change the way you put in the zipper. Also think about topstitching details, seam finishes, and the hem width and finish. If you decide to make any changes in construction techniques or the sewing sequence, write notes to yourself right on the pattern instruction sheet. For easy reference, also note the pages of this book where the techniques you'd like to try are explained in detail.

Before you begin to work on the garment, experiment with scraps of your skirt and lining fabrics. Make sample seams and try different seam and hem finishes. With the thread and needle size recommended for your fabric, test for the best stitch length. Press these samples to determine the best heat setting for your iron. If you're planning to use a fusible interfacing, fuse a scrap of it to your fabric to test their compatibility. Be sure to try any new or difficult technique you'd like to use on your garment ahead of time, and save all your samples for future reference.

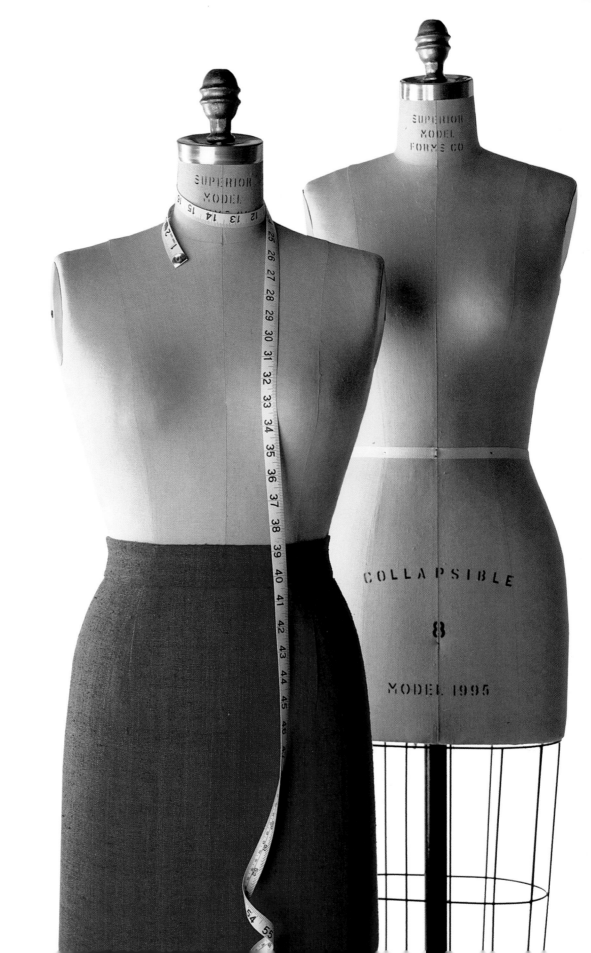

# Construction Chronology

*This sequence illustrates the construction steps for a straight or flared skirt with darts or tucks, pockets in the side seam, a center back zipper, and a lining. It is intended as a guide for developing your own order of construction for sewing your skirt. Following a "generic" sequence such as this is helpful when you add features (a lining, for instance) to a pattern that doesn't have them.*

## Steps in Making a Skirt

Before you begin, read the guidesheet and mark up all pattern, cutting, and construction changes.

**1.** Adjust the pattern for fit and design.

**2.** Cut out all the pattern pieces. Transfer markings to fabric.

**3.** Apply interfacing, as needed, at pocket, waistband, or zipper openings.

**4.** Staystitch interfacing.

**5.** Overlock edges if using serger to finish seams. Apply pockets while serging the side seams.

**6.** Stitch darts or tucks. Apply pockets.

**7.** Stitch center-back seam, forming French vent if there is one. Insert zipper.

**8.** Pin side seams, wrong sides together, vertically along the seamlines. Try on, altering as needed. Stitch side seams. Press. Try on again, fine-tuning for swayback, tummy, and waistline measurements.

**9.** Construct lining: Stitch center back seam, allowing room for zipper and vent opening. Stitch side seams.

**10.** Insert lining. Machine baste at waist, forming tucks at darts. Handsew around zipper.

**11.** Apply waistband.

**12.** Apply closures.

**13.** Hem: Mark, press, trim, pin, and try on. Finish edge, stitch. Press.

**14.** Hem lining, attach at vent.

**15.** Final pressing to finish your skirt.

Replace front darts with staystitch plus

Reinforce zipper opening with fusible interfacing.

Baste centered zipper from right side.

Apply elasticized, fitted waistband.

Turn hem back and catchstitch in place halfway into hem allowance.

Remember to sew a 1-in. seam allowance.

First fitting: Adjust side seams, if necessary.

Reinforce top of vent with fusible interfacing.

Add two rows of topstitching on right side, to reinforce vent.

Construct and insert a lining.

Secure waistband by stitching in the ditch from right side.

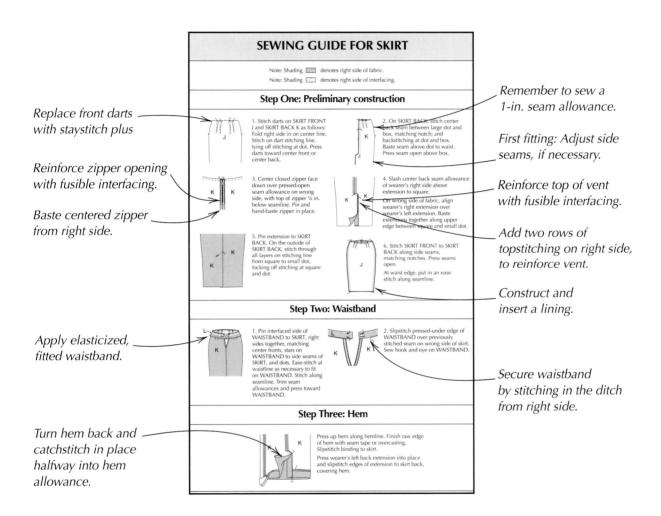

**SEWING GUIDE FOR SKIRT**

Note: Shading ▦ denotes right side of fabric.
Note: Shading ▦ denotes right side of interfacing.

**Step One: Preliminary construction**

1. Stitch darts on SKIRT FRONT J and SKIRT BACK K as follows: Fold right side in on center line. Stitch on dart stitching line, tying off stitching at dot. Press darts toward center front or center back.

2. On SKIRT BACK, stitch center back seam between large dot and box, matching notch; and backstitching at dot and box. Baste seam above dot to waist. Press seam open above box.

3. Center closed zipper face down over pressed-open seam allowance on wrong side, with top of zipper ⅛ in. below seamline. Pin and hand-baste zipper in place.

4. Slash center back seam allowance of wearer's right side above extension to square. On wrong side of fabric, align wearer's right extension over wearer's left extension. Baste extensions together along upper edge between square and small dot.

5. Pin extension to SKIRT BACK. On the outside of SKIRT BACK, stitch through all layers on stitching line from square to small dot, locking off stitching at square and dot.

6. Stitch SKIRT FRONT to SKIRT BACK along side seams, matching notches. Press seams open. At waist edge, put in an ease stitch along seamline.

**Step Two: Waistband**

1. Pin interfaced side of WAISTBAND to SKIRT, right sides together, matching center fronts, stars on WAISTBAND to side seams of SKIRT, and dots. Ease-stitch at waistline as necessary to fit on WAISTBAND. Stitch along seamline. Trim seam allowances and press toward WAISTBAND.

2. Slipstitch pressed-under edge of WAISTBAND over previously stitched seam on wrong side of skirt. Sew hook and eye on WAISTBAND.

**Step Three: Hem**

Press up hem along hemline. Finish raw edge of hem with seam tape or overcasting. Slipstitch binding to skirt.

Press wearer's left back extension into place and slipstitch edges of extension to skirt back, covering hem.

Make sure you understand the instructions on your guidesheet. Remember it's just a beginning. There are many ways to enhance your pattern to get the fit and look you want. Mark your guidesheets with additional steps, reminders for fitting, and techniques to replace the pattern's suggestions.

# Cutting and Marking

*Now you're ready to cut out the pattern pieces and transfer the markings to the fabric. Don't rush this step.*

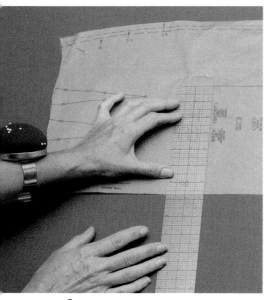

1 *Check that the grainline and selvage are parallel and the pattern pieces are on the grain.*

2 *Mark notches, darts, tucks, and centers with ¼-in. scissors snips.*

Take time and care when cutting and marking. An error of ¼ in. might not seem like much on a pattern piece, but as you cut and mark, your ¼ in. could quickly become an inch.

## Cutting

You'll save time and make fewer mistakes if you cut everything at one time, including the lining and interfacing.

Be precise and fastidious about placing the pattern pieces on the straight of the grain. Use a ruler to check that the grainline and selvage of the fabric are parallel to each other **(1).**

Sharp scissors are fine, but a rotary cutter and a mat will save you some time. Consider using weights, instead of pins, to hold your pattern in place.

## Marking

Mark notches, centers, darts, tucks, etc., with ¼-in. scissors snips whenever possible. They're easy to find, fast to make, and permanent **(2)**. Use the tip of your scissors, not the rotary cutter—it's very easy to cut too deep.

Chalk, tracing paper, and pencils are all designed to mark the wrong side of the fabric. Don't use them on the right side of your garment. (An exception to this rule is Clo-chalk, a white powdery chalk that disappears within 24 hours or as soon as your garment is pressed or laundered.)

You can also use simple tailor's tacks to transfer markings from the pattern to your fabric. These tacks are easily identifiable from either side of the fabric and suitable for any type of marking. They work especially well for positioning darts, pleats, and tucks.

# MAKING TAILOR'S TACKS

Multistrand embroidery floss works well for making tailor's tacks because it's thick and won't pull out readily. I also use a chenille needle, which is sharp and has a large, easy-to-thread eye.

Make one small stitch through both layers of fabric on each pattern mark, leaving at least ½-in. tails at each end (1). Slowly peel the pattern tissue from the tacks without tearing it. Carefully pull open the fabric layers so that there is enough thread between them to clip the tacks and leave tails (2). These tacks on the inside (right side) of the cloth will be more uniform lengths, so you will be able to tell the right side of the fabric from the wrong side at a glance.

To mark any pleats or tucks, try using two different colors of embroidery floss to mark each set. Later, you'll be able to match the sets easily. (See p. 61.)

To mark a dart, make snip marks to mark the tops of the legs. Use tailor's tacks to mark the midpoints and tip of the dart. Then sculpt the dart by connecting the tacks with a hip curve and a fine-line chalk marker (3), and you'll have an easy-to-follow stitching guide.

Don't machine-stitch over tailor's tacks; they can get caught in the stitches and be tricky to pull out. Instead, baste or mark the area carefully, remove the tacks, then stitch by machine.

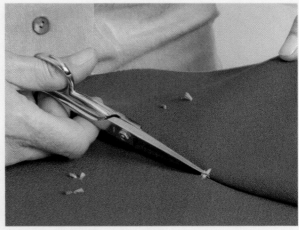

**2** *Pull the fabric apart and clip the tacks.*

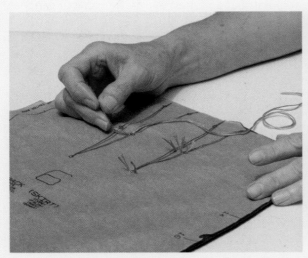

**1** *Mark darts with tailor's tacks, leaving ½-in. tails.*

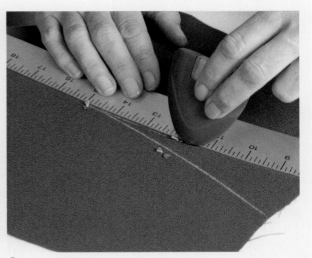

**3** *Use chalk and a hip curve to mark dart lines on the wrong side of the fabric.*

# Pressing

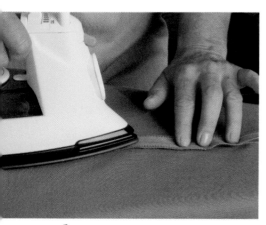

1 *Press the seam flat on the wrong side, holding the seam halves open as you work.*

2 *Press again from the right side, using a press cloth if necessary.*

*Pressing seams and darts is the secret to making clothes that look professional.*

## Tools

The best iron gets hot and stays hot and gives off a good shot of steam. Always test a scrap of your fabric to determine the best setting to use.

You'll also need a clapper/pointer, a hardwood tool for flattening seams and pressing points; a pressing ham, a contoured device that looks like its namesake and is used to shape darts and curved seams; and a press cloth.

Press cloths protect the surface of the garment fabric, and professionals rely on them. Use a cotton, see-through press cloth for cottons, silks, and linens; a specially treated, heavy drill (cotton twill) press cloth and a scrap of wool for pressing wools. The heavy cotton protects the wool fabric, particularly if you are ironing the right side of the fabric, and allows you to press with the iron set at a high temperature. Wool pressed against wool prevents the fabric from flattening and becoming shiny. (Professional tailors often sew a square of wool to one area of the heavy-cotton press cloth in order to have both at hand.)

Test your fabric to see if it can be pressed on the right side. If right-side pressing changes the appearance of the fabric, always use a press cloth. Your fingers are also important pressing tools, especially for fabrics that are slippery or don't hold shape easily. Finger-press all seams before using the iron.

## Techniques

After sewing each seam and dart, press it flat, as it was sewn, to blend the stitches, smooth the fabric, and erase puckers.

Then press the seams open on the wrong side of the fabric. Use your fingers and the point of the iron to open the seam halves to lie flat as you work (1). Press the seam or dart again on the right side of the fabric, using the press cloth if necessary (2).

Unlike ironing, which is a sliding motion, pressing is a lifting and lowering motion.

**3** *Shape curved darts and seams by pressing them over a ham.*

As you work, use the clapper to flatten and cool the pressed area. The hardwood absorbs heat and moisture, and the weight of the tool and the pounding flattens the stitched seam or dart. For some fabrics, such as cottons, rayons, and silks, just the weight of the clapper is enough to do the job; for wools, you may need to apply extra pressure.

Also press back darts and curved seams over the ham to build curves and shape the garment **(3)**. Press front darts over the ham's flattest part to avoid rounding them. Press all vertical darts toward the center of the garment.

After pressing, seams and darts should be so flat they almost disappear. Let the pressed area cool before readjusting the fabric on the ironing board.

## PRESSING THE STRETCH OUT OF BIAS

Before handling any piece of fabric that's been cut on the bias, press the stretch out. This technique is straight from the workrooms of French couture. After pressing, the seams of bias-cut skirt panels can be sewn with minimum distortion. After the garment is finished, the hem will not sag, and the skirt will be less likely to stretch in length and decrease in width.

Position the bias-cut skirt panel on a pressing surface that is long enough for the entire length. Steam-press, and as you do, gently stretch the fabric in the lengthwise direction of the skirt. Begin at one seam and work in radiating parallel lines across the panel to the other seam. Allow the fabric to cool before repositioning it. Repeat the process with all of the skirt panels. The hem may become uneven, but after you've measured it and hemmed it evenly, it will stay even.

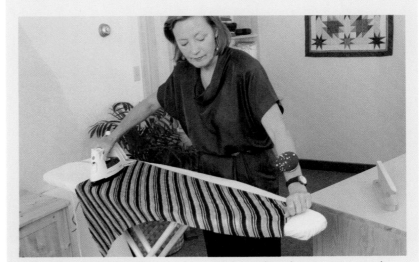

*Steam-press while gently stretching the fabric lengthwise to ensure that the finished garment will hold its shape.*

# Seams and Seam Finishes

*Stitching seams is one of the basic components of sewing. With a little practice, you'll be able to sew perfect straight or curved seams and a variety of professional finishes.*

Before you begin sewing, always test for the best stitch length, needle size, and type of thread for your fabric. Test the stitch length for appearance and strength as well as for ease in ripping. A too-long stitch length uses less thread, but creates a puckered seam.

Keep a supply of different needles on hand and use only the best quality—this is not a place to skimp. Change the needle before you begin each new garment and any time the needle hits a pin (listen for the sound of a blunt or bent needle piercing the cloth).

If you notice skipped stitches, or if the thread keeps breaking or fraying, try a different-size needle. If that doesn't help, try another brand of needle.

*A Hong Kong seam finish, made with China silk, rayon, or silk bias strips, is a flat and elegant binding for hems and waistbands.*

# Sewing Perfect Seams

For smooth seams, always cut, stitch, and press seams in the same direction. For skirts, this usually means working along the length of the garment, from hem to waistline.

To sew long side seams, place pins vertically on the stitching line, positioned so that you can pull them out as you sew. This saves time and—because you're not sewing over pins—it also saves wear and tear on the machine.

Pin the top and bottom of the seam first. Next match the notches, then match or ease the fabric in between. A fabric with "tooth" grabs or sticks to itself and thus requires fewer pins than a slippery fabric that moves and slides. You may need to hand-baste some hard-to-handle fabrics, such as velvet, before stitching.

Most seams are sewn with right sides together, using a ⅝-in. seam allowance. Some machines have this ⅝-in. width marked on the throat plate. A magnetic seam guide, which acts as a "fence" along which you can guide the fabric, is also a very helpful tool (see photo 3 on p. 179).

Always press a seam after stitching and before crossing it with another seam or detail.

Remember, stitching and pressing go hand in hand.

## RIPPING OUT SEAMS

Ripping out seams is an essential part of sewing. Use the narrow point of the seam ripper to break a few stitches on one side of the seam. This frees the thread on the other side so that it can be pulled. Working from one end of the seam to the other, rip just a few stitches, grasp the thread with your fingers, and give it a good pull, disposing of the loose threads as you go.

Another way to rip stitches is to use the point of the ripper to break threads on one side of the fabric every ½ in. to 1 in. along the seam and then pull the long freed-up thread on the other side. (The disadvantage is that on the first side you're left with broken threads all along the seam that need to be removed.)

Never work the curved portion of the seam ripper between the two layers of the seam unless the fabric is heavy and very firmly woven. Otherwise, you're liable to rip the fabric as well as the threads.

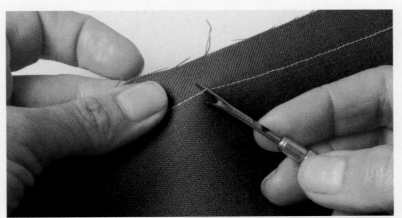

*Break stitches along one side of the seam with the narrow point of the seam ripper.*

*One easy way to finish a seam is with pinking shears. Pink the edges, trimming a small slice of fabric away from the seam allowance.*

## SEAMS FOR BIAS-CUT SKIRTS

Cut, making 1½-in. seams to allow the fabric to relax. Mark the seamline with basting. Press the pieces.

Pin along the marked seamline and try on the garment. Adjust where necessary. You may need to make smaller seam allowances to compensate for the pieces' having stretched slightly in length and contracted in width.

Sew with a slightly shorter stitch length than usual, stretching the fabric as you sew. Because bias does not ravel, you won't need to finish the seams.

# Finishes for Side Seams

Aim for simple, light, unobtrusive seam finishes. Test fabric scraps to see which seam finish is most compatible with your fabric. The seam finish should keep the seam edges from fraying and shouldn't show from the right side. If your fabric doesn't ravel, the best seam finish is none at all.

***Pinked Seams*** Trimming with pinking shears is a classic, honest way to finish a seam (see photo, left). The ultimate in simplicity, it adds no bulk and won't show from the right side. After you sew the seam, trim away the smallest amount of fabric possible.

Test the pinking shears on fabric scraps first. On some fabrics, you can trim both layers of the seam allowance at one time. With other fabrics, to get a clean edge, you must open the seam allowance and trim single layers. Test both methods and compare the results.

Some pinking shears have a notched tip that will cut all the way to the end of the cut. Other brands work best if you don't fully open the shears and if you don't cut all the way to the points. Test to see how deep a cut you need to make to work smoothly.

There's also a rotary cutter with a wavy blade that works well as a pinking tool.

A pinked-and-stitched edge is especially flat and ravel-resistant: Sew a line of stitching 1/4 in. from the edge before the seam is sewn. Pink the edges after seaming, without cutting the line of stitching.

**Zigzag Seams** Zigzag edges are quick and simple finishes. Both are made after the seam is sewn and pressed.

Both finishes have two disadvantages, however. First, the extra stitching and thread can add bulk to thin fabrics, which will keep them from lying flat. Second, these finishes, which aren't found in ready-to-wear, shout "homemade." I generally don't use them, but you might want to experiment with them yourself.

For a zigzag finish, use a stitch of medium width and length. Stitch near the edge, but not along it, and trim close to the stitching. If your machine has this option, try a machine-overcast stitch. Stitch close to the edge so the points of the stitches fall almost at the edge of the fabric.

**Serged Seams** The serger, or overlock machine, has transformed home sewing. Although it doesn't replace a conventional machine, a serger is very useful for quickly cutting and finishing seam edges in one fast and easy operation (above right).

Fuse interfacings to pockets and zipper areas before serging. If your fabric frays easily, serge all around the skirt, but on more stable fabrics, serge only the seams that will be pressed open. Serge the hem after you mark the length and trim to desired width.

When using a serger, it's not necessary to cut wider seams than you normally would. The cutting edge of the serger trims just the ravelly edges before overcasting.

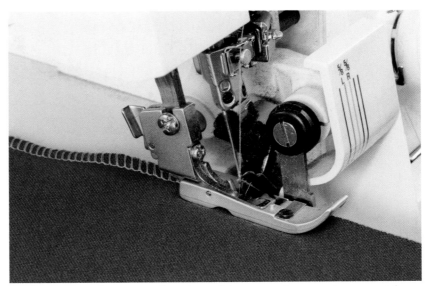

*A serger cuts and overcasts the edges of the seam allowance in one quick and easy operation.*

Use fine, soft thread, machine-embroidery thread, or texturized nylon to minimize the amount of thread impression "striking through" on the right side of the fabric. A 3-thread edge, using long staple polyester or coned "serger" thread, is the most versatile of the serged finishes. Or, if your machine has a 2-thread finish, try that for a flatter edge.

Serge a wide edge on fabrics that are heavy or bulky, and a narrow edge on flat fabrics that are lightweight to midweight.

# Finishes for Hems and Waistband Seams

For a flat and professional-looking finish, you can bind hems and waistband seams with a Hong Kong finish or with a rayon seam binding.

***Hong Kong Finish*** The Hong Kong finish is a simple and elegant touch for medium to heavy fabrics. This flat, narrow binding makes a fine finish for hems or an inside waistband seam on a skirt (see photo on p. 166), but it's too bulky for most side seams.

A Hong Kong finish has two lines of stitching and adds three layers of fabric to the edge. The seam edge is bound in bias strips of a lightweight fabric, such as China silk, rayon lining, silk, or polyester crepe de chine.

For the binding, cut 1¼-in. wide bias strips, piecing the lengths as necessary. Press the bias strips to remove excess stretchability and to prevent them from rippling.

Before you stitch the waistband to the skirt, sew the binding to the seam edge, with right sides together, ¼ in. from the edges. (Bind the hem in the same way after marking and trimming it.)

Trim the seam edge to an even ⅛ in. using sharp long-blade shears or a rotary cutter (**1**).

Wrap the binding around the seam edge and press. On the right side of the fabric, stitch in the "ditch" of the seam of the waistband and the binding—that is, where the two fabrics are sewn together (**2**). For accuracy, use an edgestitching foot with the needle in the center position.

On the wrong side of the fabric, trim the excess binding ⅛ in. from the stitching line (**3**). Bias doesn't fray, so the binding won't ravel.

***Rayon Seam Binding*** A flat woven-tape seam binding creates a dressmaker's touch for bulky and flat fabrics that ravel. Use rayon rather than polyester—it's softer, flatter, and more fluid. With just a bit of practice, you'll find this technique fast and simple.

Rayon seam binding adds less bulk than the Hong Kong finish. It has only one line of stitching and adds only two layers of fabric to the edge. This seam binding can also be used to finish the inside waistband edge and the hem edge.

Press the binding in half lengthwise, making one half slightly wider than the other. Hold the end in place with a straight pin as you work.

Position the narrow half of the binding on top of the right side of the fabric and stitch along this half (**4**). This way, you'll be sure that your stitches will catch the wider half of the binding on the other side of the fabric.

As you stitch along the edge of the binding, pull it slightly toward the fabric with your finger so that it wraps around and encases the raw edge. Press to eliminate puckers.

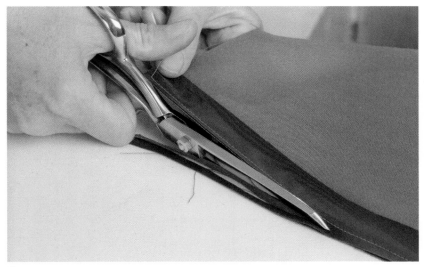

**1** *To apply Hong Kong finish, trim the binding to an even ⅛ in. with shears or a rotary cutter.*

**2** *Wrap the binding around the edge, press, and stitch in the ditch of the seam on the right side of the fabric.*

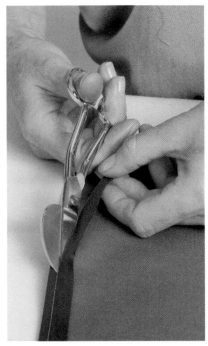

**3** *Trim excess binding on the wrong side of the fabric. Here, the author is using appliqué scissors to get as close as possible to the seam.*

**4** *To apply rayon seam binding, stitch the pressed binding with the narrower half on top of the right side of the fabric.*

# Darts, Pleats, and Gathers

*Darts, pleats, and gathers add dimension to a flat piece of fabric, sculpting and shaping it into curves and contours. With careful fitting, their placements and lines can emphasize and flatter your figure.*

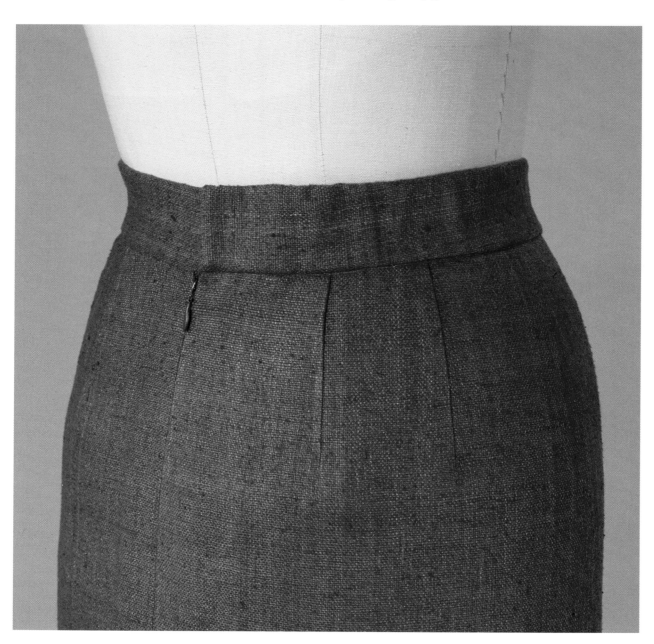

# Darts

Darts are most often used to shape the back of the skirt. A fitted, darted front shows every bump and curve of the body. If you don't have a flat tummy, front darts may not be flattering and can be eliminated with a stitching technique called staystitch plus (p. 174).

When making darts, careful marking and stitching go hand in hand. Position pins all along the stitching line, with one horizontal pin marking the tip of the dart. Make sure that pins are in straight lines along both legs of the dart.

Stitch from the wide end of the dart, backstitching as you begin in order to secure the stitches (1). Remove the pins as you come to them.

When you're ½ in. from the tip of the dart, change to a short stitch length (1.5mm) and stitch the last few stitches along the edge of the fabric. Shorter stitches increase stitching accuracy and make tying knots or backstitching unnecessary. Stitch evenly off the edge to prevent a bubble from forming at the tip of the dart (2).

Sew a smooth and true dart every time by mentally drawing a line from the first stitches to the tip, pointing the machine in that direction. This visualization is helpful even if you've marked the stitching line with chalk.

Press the dart on a ham. A perfectly pressed dart is nearly invisible on the right side of the fabric.

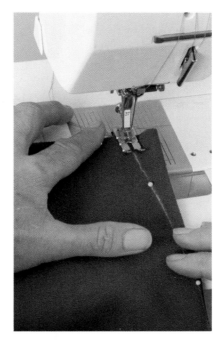

1 *Begin by backstitching at the wide end of the dart.*

2 *When you've reached the tip of the dart, stitch evenly off the fabric.*

# STAYSTITCH PLUS

Staystitch plus (also called easestitch plus) is a machine-stitching technique with a lot of uses. For example, instead of sewing the front darts of a skirt, you can simply ease the fullnessinto the waistband for a more flattering effect. Staystitch plus can be used to ease any skirt to fit into any other waistband.

All sewing machines are designed to sew two or more layers of fabric. Staystitch plus works with the machine's tendency to draw up fabric when sewing one layer.

To staystitch-plus, you stitch through one layer of fabric, applying pressure from behind to force a tiny bit more fabric into each stitch. Position your finger behind the foot to crimp the fabric and ease it through smoothly and evenly. Sew in sort segments, raising foot every few inches to release fabric.

Stitch short segments of fabric—1 in. to 2 in. at a time—then release the piled-up fabric by raising the presser foot **(1)**.

When you're done, the skirt should be nearly equal in width to the pattern piece with the darts pinned into position **(2)**. If you need to ease more fabric, make a second line of staystitch plus just inside the first line.

In order to develop an even, smooth tension while easing the fabric the correct amount, you'll need to experiment and practice.

**1** *As you force more fabric into each stitch by positioning your finger behind the foot, raise the presser foot every few inches to release the eased fabric.*

**2** *After you have used staystitch plus, the garment piece should be equal in width to the pattern piece with the darts pinned in place.*

# Pleats

Pleats add controlled fullness to skirts. They can be soft or sharp, placed all around the waist or hip, positioned in the front and/or the back, or used as details (as a kick pleat, for example).

If possible, make the pleats before sewing the side seams.

Mark the pleats with tailor's tacks (p. 163). Use two colors of embroidery floss: one for the fold of the pleat, the other for the placement line.

**Soft Pleats** Soft pleats must be secured accurately to hang gracefully. Hand- and machine-baste to keep them from shifting during fitting and construction. When the waistband is applied, the pleats are permanently stitched in place.

Pin the pleats into position, aligning the snip marks and tailor's tacks (1).

Hand-baste them securely well above and below the seamline with silk thread. Next, machine-baste them within the lines of hand-basting, above and below the seamline (2).

After stitching the first line of stitching for the waistband, set the pleats by steam-pressing them over the ham.

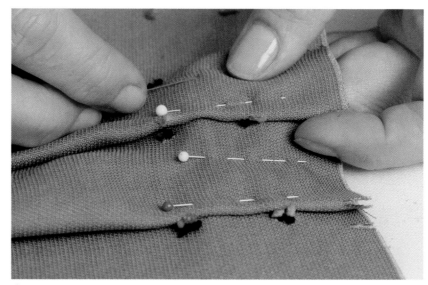

1 *Pin the soft pleats into position, aligning marks and tailor's tacks.*

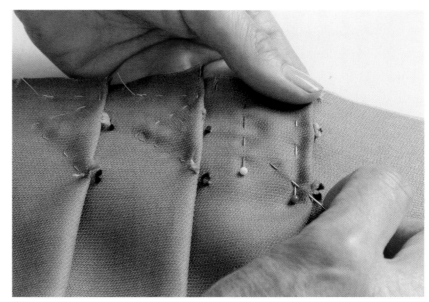

2 *Hand-baste the pleats in position above and below the seamline.*

**Sharp Pleats** Making sharp pleats requires care and accuracy.

Stitching close to the edge of a pleat keeps the pressed edges crisp and lasting, even in soft fabrics. You can edgestitch sharp pleats on the outside and/or inside of the garment. It's crucial to maintain the straight of the grain along the edge of long, straight pleats.

Mark the pleat fold line and placement lines with tailor's tacks every 3 in. to 4 in. Snip-mark at the fabric edges.

Press the pleats into position on a pressing surface long enough to support the length of the garment and wide enough to support several pleats **(1)**.

Hand-baste the pleats with silk thread to secure them **(2)**.

1 *Press sharp pleats into position on a long work surface.*

2 *Hand-baste the pleats securely with silk thread.*

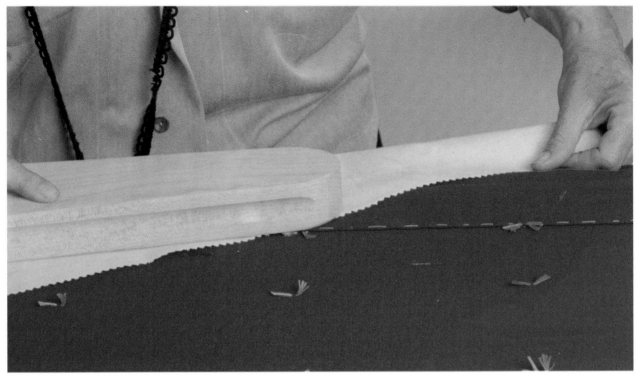

**3** *Use the clapper and a heavy press cloth to sharpen pleats in a pleated skirt.*

Press again on the wrong side of the fabric, using the clapper and a heavy press cloth to sharpen the pleat edges **(3)**. Press again, finishing and touching up, on the right side of the fabric.

For a crisp finish, after the skirt is hemmed, you can edgestitch the inside edge, outside edge, or both edges of the entire pleat, on the wrong side of the garment **(4)**.

Edgestitching adds weight and crispness, and holds the pleats in position. Use an edgestitching foot for greatest accuracy and speed. Always press again after edgestitching.

Another option is to edgestitch just the inside of the pleat within the hem. Again, stitch on the wrong side of the garment to conceal the stitches.

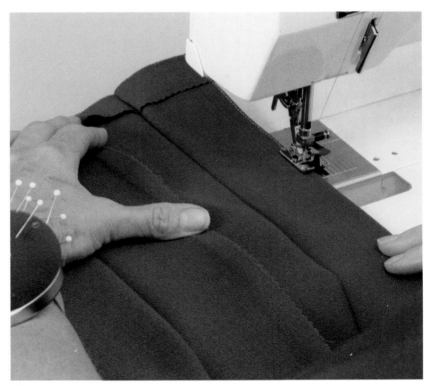

**4** *Edgestitching on the wrong side of the garment holds the crisp pleats in position.*

# Gathers

The best machine gathers imitate finely done hand shirring by creating even, flowing, vertical folds in a soft fabric. This kind of gathering is flattering to most figures. By positioning well-made gathers in the flatter parts of the body, you can create a slimming effect. Poorly done gathering, however, is uneven and lumpy and adds bulk to the figure.

One of the secrets of success is choosing the right fabric. Another is using three rows of gathering stitches rather than the traditional two. Careful stitching, pinning, and seaming are also essential.

On all sewing machines, the bobbin tension is adjusted to create a perfect stitch from the right side, so it's easiest to gather fabric by pulling the bobbin thread. Stitch on the right side of the fabric and use heavier thread in the bobbin to prevent the thread from breaking.

Test for the best stitch length. For even gathers, use the shortest stitch length that gathers with ease—

generally, 3.5 to 4.5mm. Use a longer stitch with heavier fabrics.

If the gathers go all around the skirt, it's best to make them after sewing the side seams. If they don't, you can make them before sewing the side seams.

When making the gathers, stitch three parallel rows $7/8$ in., $3/8$ in., and $1/4$ in. from the edge of the fabric. The row farthest from the edge secures the gathers in position until you attach the waistband. (For smoother gathers in "challenging" fabrics, such as denim, stitch four rows.)

Test your fabric to be sure that the needle holes disappear after you've removed the gathering threads and steamed the gathers. If marks remain, make additional rows of stitching within the seamline to conceal them.

Start and stop stitching each row in the same place. Do not backstitch the ends or you won't be able to pull the threads easily later. Keep threads from tangling by cutting the upper threads 2 in. from the fabric.

Before you gather the skirt to fit the waistband, mark the skirt at center front, side seams, and center back. Also mark the waistband at the corresponding points. Pull the bobbin threads firmly but gently to gather the skirt.

When gathering a lot of fabric, divide and conquer:

- Section the area to be gathered into halves or quarters, marking carefully and clearly with chalk or snip marks. (Pins can fall out.)

- Gather each section separately.

Secure the thread ends by wrapping them in a figure eight around the pins at each end of the lines of stitching (1). Divide each gathered area in half repeatedly, forming small vertical folds, and pin the gathered sections securely with pins placed close together. Use a pin point to adjust the gathers so that they are evenly distributed (2).

The row of stitching that attaches the skirt to the waistband holds the carefully adjusted gathers permanently in position. Stitch on the wrong side of the fabric, adjusting the fabric folds as you work to prevent distortion (3). Stitch slowly. It's inevitable that you'll nick the machine needle with a pin as you stitch, so change the needle when you finish.

Check the evenness of the gathers on the right side of the garment before removing the gathering stitches. Be sure to remove all the threads before pressing—they can create stiffness and bulk in the seam allowance.

Pressing adds a final touch. First, press the seam flat as sewn. Next, work in sections on the wrong side, positioning the gathers over the ham. Set the gathers with steam so they lie even, gently pulling them lengthwise to create parallel folds (4). Be careful not to flatten them as you work.

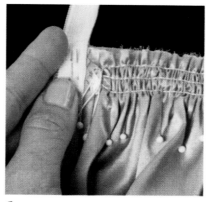

**1** *Secure the gathering threads by wrapping them in a figure eight around a straight pin. Divide and pin each gathered section to form a series of vertical folds.*

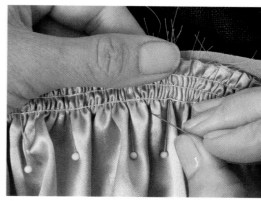

**2** *Adjust the gathers evenly with a pin point.*

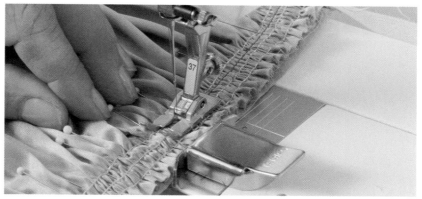

**3** *On the wrong side of the fabric, stitch the gathered skirt to the waistband. A magnetic seam guide ensures a straight line of stitching.*

**4** *Steam-press the gathers lightly over the ham.*

Trimming or grading gathers usually isn't necessary. If you do trim them, however, never trim closer than $3/8$ in. Any more than that and the gathered fabric edges will stand up stiffly, like a crewcut.

# Side-Seam Pockets

*Side-seam pockets, the easiest to sew, are a good
first pocket for the beginner to master.*

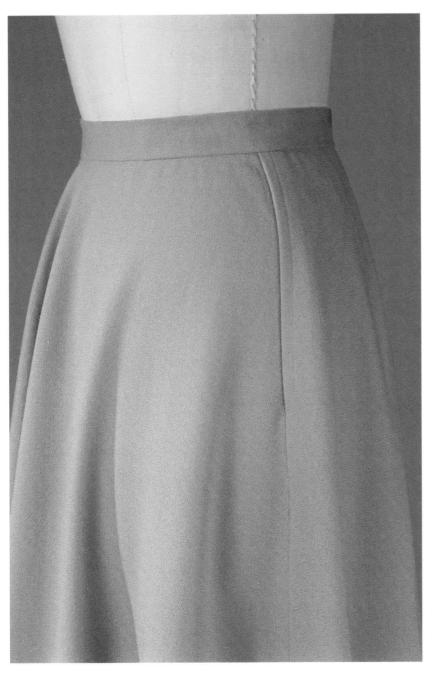

Side-seam pockets work best on semi-fitted, full, and flared skirts with soft pleats or gathers. Don't use them on skirts that are very fitted at the waist and hip, pleated, or cut on the bias, however.

If your pattern does not have a pocket, adding this one is simple. Add 1/8 in. extra at each side seam to make sure that the skirt has enough ease at the hip and high hip to accommodate a pocket. If the skirt is too snug, the pocket openings will gap.

When making a skirt with pockets, pin-fit carefully, baste the pocket opening before stitching, and press the garment well so that the pockets lie smooth and flat without bulges or bulk.

## Construction

You can keep pocket openings firm and stable by reinforcing the front opening with fusible tricot. (You don't need to reinforce the back of the pocket opening because it doesn't get stretched from use.) Mark its placement on skirt front.

Measure from the waist to 1/2 in. below the bottom of the pocket opening. Cut a 1-in. wide strip of fusible tricot to this length for each pocket.

Fusible tricot is stable on the lengthwise grain and won't stretch. (Fusibles do stretch on the cross grain, however, so cut carefully.)

On the skirt front, position and fuse the interfacing over the seam so that it extends ¼ in. beyond the fold of the pocket opening (1). This both strengthens and softens the edge.

Stitch the pocket to the side seam, using a ¼-in. seam allowance. You can also combine straight stitching with serged edges. Press the seam toward the pocket.

Stitch the side seams of the garment, working from the hem, until you reach the bottom of the pocket opening. Backstitch. Don't cut the thread. Instead, lift the pressure foot, carry the thread across, and reposition the needle at the top of the pocket opening (2). Backstitch again and sew the rest of the seam. You can also change to a longer stitch and baste across the pocket opening rather than carrying the thread.

Press open the side and pocket seams as shown in the photo on the following page (3), using the flat side of the ham if the hip area is curved. Use the clapper to smooth and flatten the pocket edges.

Topstitching gives the pocket opening a crisp finish. Mark the topstitching line for each pocket opening on the skirt front with a C-Thru ruler and erasable chalk or silk thread. Or you can simply stitch ¼ in. to ½ in. from the edge of the pocket opening, using the fold as a guide. With a slightly longer stitch, topstitch along the opening, backstitching at each end.

1 Mark notches on pocket and skirt seam.

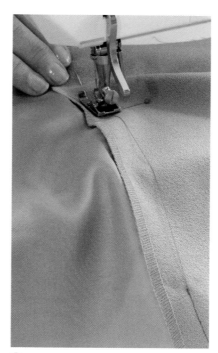

2 When stitching the side seams, backstitch the bottom of the pocket opening, carry the thread across the opening, backstitch the top, and continue the seam.

Working from top to bottom, serge the outside and top edges of the pocket halves. Fuse the interfacing. Then, in one operation, beginning at the hem, stitch and finish the garment's side seams while attaching the pocket.

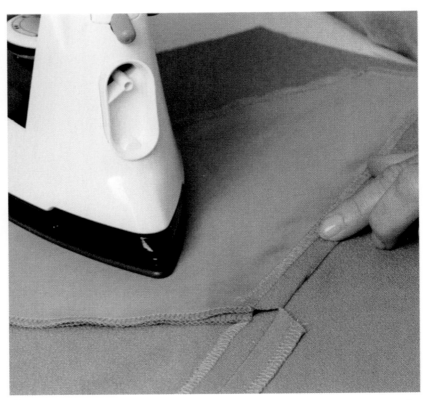

**3** *Press open the side seams and pocket seams.*

**4** *Before stitching the pocket halves together, clip the back side seam on the diagonal and press the back of the pocket to the front of the skirt.*

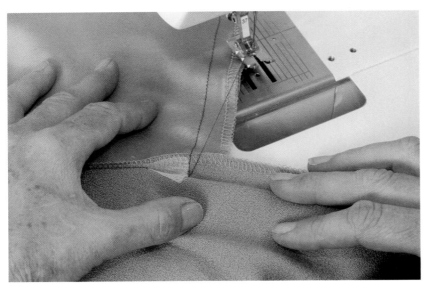

**5** *Sew the pocket together, beginning and ending at the pocket opening.*

Working over a ham, press the back of the pocket toward the front of the garment. Clip the back side seam so that the pocket will fall to the front of the garment easily **(4)**. (Clipping on the diagonal prevents fraying.)

To assemble the halves of the pocket, stitch around the edges, beginning and ending at the backstitching that marks the pocket opening **(5)**. Pinking is a fast, simple solution to finishing the pocket edges if you don't have a serger. Press the finished pocket to the front of the garment.

# SIDE-POCKET VARIATION

This side pocket doubles as a skirt opening. Not only does it eliminate the need for a zipper, it also adds a soft and functional design element. (Ralph Lauren uses side-pocket openings in his skirts.)

To turn a side-seam pocket into a side-pocket opening, make a mark 9 in. below the waist along the long curved edge of the pocket. Reinforce 1 in. on either side of the mark and clip to it, being careful not to cut through the reinforced stitching.

Construct the pockets as described on pp. 180-182, but leave the one on the left side of the garment open

above the mark. Finish this pocket opening by pressing the edge under ¼ in., and then another ¼ in. Topstitch on the right side.

Mark the left side seam on the waistband. Measure the pocket underlap—that is, the top of the pocket back from the side seam to the pocket edge. Add the length of the underlap plus two seam allowances to the finished waistband length.

Attach the waistband as you normally would and add closures (pp. 216-217), positioning them so that when the skirt is closed, the pocket halves align.

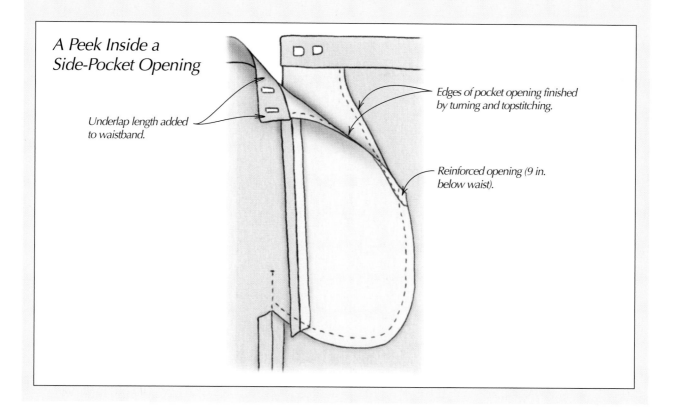

*A Peek Inside a Side-Pocket Opening*

*Underlap length added to waistband.*

*Edges of pocket opening finished by turning and topstitching.*

*Reinforced opening (9 in. below waist).*

# Kick Pleats and French Vents

*Kick pleats and French vents allow you more freedom of movement when wearing a slim-fitting skirt, and they are versatile design details as well.*

Kick pleats are stitched, closed pleats and French vents are faced openings. A kick pleat is positioned at the hemline to make a slim-fitting skirt more comfortable for you to move and walk in. A traditional closed kick pleat can be adapted to an open slit, frequently used by French designers and called a French vent (p. 186).

Keep your eye on the length, stitching, and placement of kick pleats and French vents in ready-to-wear garments so you can adapt your favorite skirt pattern. You can add them to any seam—center back, center front, or side.

Converting a pattern to create a kick pleat or French vent is done in the same way. Determine the finished length of the pleat or vent—don't forget to include the hem length. A good finished standard width is 3 in., including seam allowances. Add a scrap of tissue to the pattern and draw in the pleat or vent, adding the desired length and width to the seamline. The top of the opening can be left square or angled. Mark the seamlines. Make a dot at the top of the opening—this is where the stitching ends for a French vent and marks the pivot point for a kick pleat.

Add the kick pleat or French vent to the pattern first, then add the right amount of walking ease (p. 149).

1 *Apply a square of reinforcement at the top of both sides of the pleat opening.*

2 *Stitch from the square to the end of the extension and backstitch to reinforce.*

# Kick Pleat

Before sewing a kick pleat, always reinforce both sides of the top of the pleat opening to keep the fabric from tearing and the stitches from pulling out.

Position or fuse a 1-in. square of fusible or woven interfacing, a strip of tailor's tape (twill tape), or even a scrap of lining selvage at the top of both sides of the vent opening on the wrong side of the fabric (1). Stitch the garment's seam to the square and press the seam in the direction it's sewn. With small reinforcing stitches, stitch from the square to the edge of the extension and backstitch (2).

Fold back the extension on one side of the seamline and press it. Lay the other extension on top of the folded one, aligning the edges (3). On the topmost layer, make a diagonal clip through the seam allowance to the reinforcement

3 *Fold one extension and press it. Lay the other over it, aligning edges. Baste them into position at top of the extension.*

4 *To secure the open edge of the kick pleat invisibly, catchstitch on the inside of the garment.*

square to keep the garment's seam free and flat. Pin the layers into positon and baste at top along the stitching line.

Lift the garment pieces to double-check the hang of the kick pleat and correct as needed.

Press the skirt's seam open to the opening. To secure the open edge of the pleat, catchstitch on the inside of the garment (**4**) so that the stitches are invisible, or topstitch it on the right side of the garment to add extra detail.

# French Vent

The French vent is easier to construct and less likely to wrinkle than the kick pleat.

The extensions that form a kick pleat or French vent are the same and both are cut and reinforced in the same way. The difference is that on the French vent the extensions are pressed to either side of the opening, rather than overlapped on one side.

After the garment's seam is sewn and pressed, press the opening as shown, allowing the fabric to form straight folds that meet at the center (**1**).

**Mitering the Corner** For a beautiful inside finish, especially in a lined skirt, finish off the French vent with a mitered corner. (Before you try it on your garment, however, I recommend you practice mitering first with paper, and then make two samples with a stable fabric.)

Mark the hem length and fold line of the vent opening (**2**). Turn the marked edges under and press.

At the intersection of the hemline and the vent line, fold the fabric back at an angle, aligning the marked lines on top of each other (**3**). Press the folded corner. Trim a ¼-in. seam allowance (**4**).

Fold the corner again, right sides together, to align the hem line with the vent line (**5**). Machine-stitch along the edge of the layers. Turn the mitered corner to its right side with a point turner and press the corner to form crisp edges.

**1** On a French vent, the extensions are folded back on either side of the opening and pressed.

**2** To miter a corner, mark and press the hem and vent fold line.

**3** Fold the corner back, aligning the marked lines on top of each other, and press.

**4** Trim the folded corner to allow a ¼-in. seam allowance.

**5** Fold again and stitch right sides together. Turn the mitered corner to its right side with a point turner.

# Zippers

*Zippers may be lapped, centered, or "invisible." Conquer the lapped zipper first. It has only one visible line of stitching, and it's perfect for skirts with a side or back opening.*

# Some Tips

• If this is your first zipper, or if you're using a challenging fabric, make three samples before putting the zipper in the garment. Keep the samples for later reference.

• I prefer to make the zipper openings longer than the pattern suggests—9 in. rather than the usual 7 in.

• I also like to use a zipper that is longer than the opening to ensure that the zipper closes in the waistband (especially good for raised and contoured waistbands).The longer opening also makes it easier to get into and out of the skirt. Cut off any excess zipper from the top after sewing the first seam on the waistband.

• Already prepared zippers are sturdier than those sold by the yard. Strong and flexible polyester zippers are preferable to metal ones.

• A zipper foot is essential. It allows you to machine-stitch close to the zipper, whereas the bulky regular foot gets in the way.

• Put the zipper in while the garment is flat. This isn't always the order of construction recommended by most pattern directions, but it's easier. If you're using a side-seam zipper, fit and adjust the side seams before inserting the zipper.

• Contrary to most directions, don't baste the zipper opening closed before you put in the zipper. Simply press the seam allowances under—you'll have more control and you'll be able to make sure the zipper teeth are covered.

• Add interfacing behind the zipper as you would for a pocket (p. 181). This little-known secret makes a noticeable difference. It stabilizes the fabric and makes the final, visible stitching easier.

I recommend a fusible tricot, such as Sof-Knit. Work with ¾-in. strips cut on the straight of the grain to stabilize the fabric and add body, and strips cut on the bias or cross grain for soft shaping. (Keep a supply of scraps on hand to save some time.)

• It's hard to visualize the ⅝-in. seamline at the waistline, so mark it with snips. Beginners may also benefit from marking the seamline along the zipper opening with chalk after the interfacing is fused.

• Press curves on the ham (as on a side-seam zipper, for example) over the flattest curve for subtle, rounded shaping. Press a side seam over a ham; press a center-back seam flat.

## HAND-BASTING

Hand-basting is very effective for holding the zipper in position as you machine-stitch, as well as for marking stitching lines in other parts of the garment.

Use a single strand of silk thread, especially with delicate or slippery fabrics, such as silk or velvet. Silk thread won't show when you press it or leave a trail of fibers when you remove it.

As you hand-stitch, use the basting thread itself as a guide. Hold the thread taut and parallel to the edge of the fold, and sew along it. Machine-stitch next to the hand-basting.

To mark straight stitching lines, use an erasable chalk, such as Clo-chalk, which disappears within 48 hours or washes out. (Always test marking tools on your fabric before you use them.)

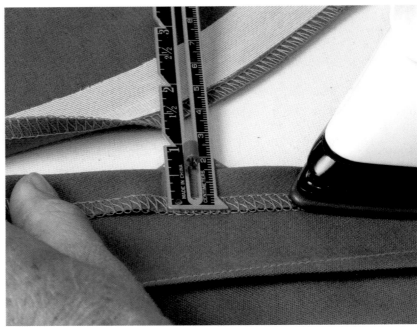

**1** *Fuse interfacing to the zipper's seam allowances. Stitch the skirt's seam to the bottom of the opening.*

**2** *Turn and press the seam allowance for the overlap to a width of ⅝ in.*

**3** *Turn and press the seam allowance for the underlap to a width of ½ in., forming a slight pleat at the bottom of the opening.*

# Lapped Zipper

A lapped zipper laps left over right. An easy way to remember this is to visualize how it will look when finished: On the right side of the garment, the lap that conceals the zipper will be on the left side of the seam.

Snip-mark the seam allowance at the waist. Transfer the mark for the bottom of the zipper opening from the pattern onto the fabric by marking it with a snip at the edge of the seam allowance or with a chalk line.

Apply ¾-in. wide strips of interfacing that are ½ in. longer than the zipper opening. Position them so that they extend beyond the bottom mark for the zipper and ⅛ in. to ¼ in. beyond the seamline into the seam allowance. Fuse the strips to the fabric.

Sew the garment's seam up to the zipper opening, and backstitch to reinforce the end **(1)**. Press the seam open.

Press open the seam allowance for the overlap to a width of ⅝ in. **(2)**. On a side-seam zipper, this is the seam allowance toward the front of the garment; on a center-back zipper, this is the seam allowance on the left side of the seamline.

Press open the underlap seam allowance to a width of ½ in. **(3)**. Form a ⅛-in. pleat at the bottom of the underlap while pressing.

Close the zipper and, with it face up, position the stop ¼ in. to ⅜ in. above the bottom of the opening. Pin or hand-baste the zipper to the underlap, keeping the teeth of the zipper next to the fold. With a zipper foot, machine-stitch from bottom to top, a scant ⅛ in. from the folded edge **(4)**.

With the zipper still closed, pin the overlap in position on the right side of the garment. Be sure to align the snips that mark the seam allowance at the waist **(5)**. The overlap edge should just cover the underlap stitching. Allow extra fabric at the top to accommodate the bulk of the pull tab.

Hand-baste the overlap in position, making sure it just covers the zipper and the pull tab. (It's helpful to pull the tab down a few inches and finish basting with the top of the zipper open.)

Mark and hand-baste the topstitching line slightly to the side of the final machine-stitching line (about ⅜ in. to ½ in. from the folded edge). Check to make sure the basting stitches catch all the layers of fabric and the zipper.

Close the zipper. Starting at the seam at the bottom of the opening, backstitch, then take about five to seven stitches across to the basted line. Pivot and topstitch from bottom to top along the line of basting **(6)**. You can also stitch by hand if you prefer (p. 193).

Avoid a curve in the topstitching around the pull tab by stopping 2 in. from the top of the opening, opening the zipper, and then continuing a smooth topstitching line to the waistline **(7)**.

**4** *Machine-stitch the basted zipper to the underlap using a zipper foot.*

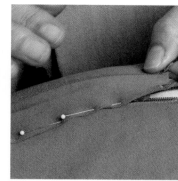

**5** *Pin the overlap in position, aligning the marks for the seam at the waist.*

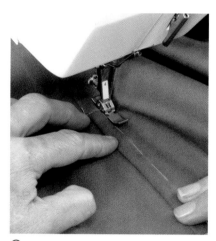

**6** *Hand-baste the topstitching on the overlap, and machine-stitch just outside the basting.*

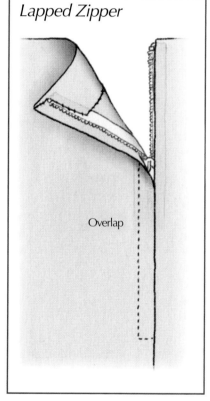

## Lapped Zipper

Overlap

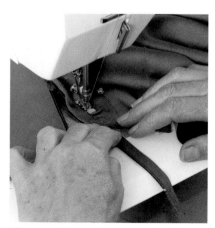

**7** *To avoid an uneven topstitching line at top, open the zipper a few inches and finish stitching in a straight line.*

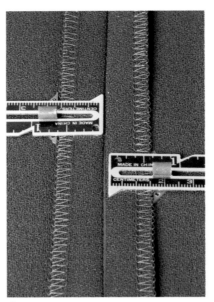

1 *Press ⅝-in. seam allowances on both sides of the zipper opening. (The raw edges of these garment pieces have already been serged.)*

# Centered Zipper

A centered zipper requires skill and precision to sew because it has two lines of topstitching, which must be straight, parallel to each other, and an equal distance from the seam. Symmetrical, centered zippers are a good choice for the back of a skirt.

The topstitching on a centered zipper is a scant ¼ in. to ⅜ in. from the opening. The fabric is slightly raised at the opening because the teeth and pull tab are completely covered when the zipper is closed. As for the lapped zipper, you can stitch by hand or topstitch by machine.

Snip-mark the seam allowance for the zipper at the waist, apply interfacing, and press open the seam at the zipper opening.

Stitch the garment's seam to the bottom of the zipper opening, backstitch to reinforce the stitching, and press the seam open. Press a ⅝-in. seam allowance on both sides of the zipper opening (**1**).

On the right side of the garment, pin the closed zipper through all thicknesses, forcing both sides of the fabric together slightly more than natural to form a ridge (**2**). The heavier the fabric, the more pronounced the ridge will be. When the zipper is sewn in, this

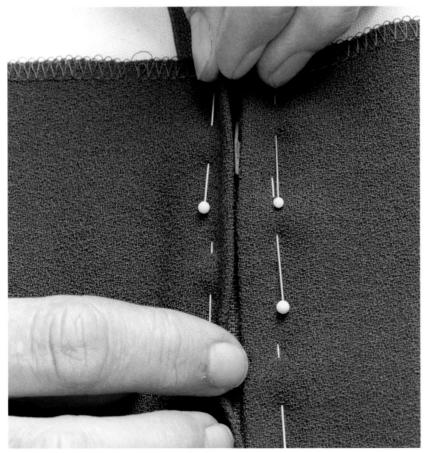

2 *Pin the closed zipper to the skirt opening, forcing both side of the fabric together slightly more than natural, so that a ridge is formed.*

# HAND-PICKED ZIPPER

For a fine custom touch, the final stitching on a centered or lapped zipper can be done by hand with a backstitch.

With a double strand of waxed sewing thread (or buttonhole thread for a more pronounced look), insert the needle through all the layers. Each stitch is formed backward, behind the point where the thread emerges. Make a stitch, then bring the needle through again ¼ in. to ⅜ in. in front of that stitch. From the right side, the stitching looks like tiny, evenly spaced dots in a straight line parallel to the fold.

It takes a bit of practice to develop a consistent, straight stitch length and tension. Try making a long sample before you topstitch the actual garment.

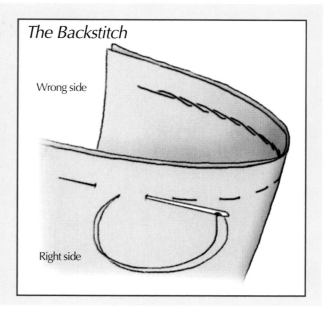

*The Backstitch*

Wrong side

Right side

ridge flattens out and covers the zipper teeth completely. You may need to open and close the zipper and reposition it more than once (double-sided basting tape makes the job easier). Pull the tab all the way up to be sure there's enough fabric to cover it at the waist end.

Hand-baste, just to one side of the topstitching line. With the zipper closed, begin topstitching at the seam at the bottom of the opening. Take about four stitches, pivot, and topstitch along one side of the opening to the waist. Backstitch to reinforce.

Again, begin at the seam at the bottom of the opening and topstitch the other side of the opening, from bottom to top (3). Backstitch.

Press the finished zipper on the right side of the garment, using a press cloth if necessary.

**3** *Begin at the bottom of the zipper opening and topstitch along each side to the top.*

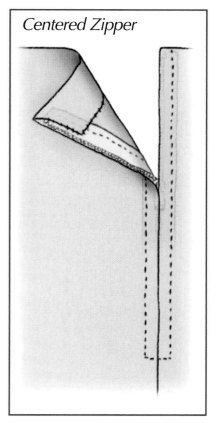

*Centered Zipper*

# Invisible Zipper

The invisible zipper is a specially made, thin and flexible zipper. It can be sewn right into the seam of a garment without topstitching. It's an easy zipper to sew, but if this zipper is entirely new to you, practice before you begin.

Invisible zippers work well with double-knits, velvet, and slippery or unstable fabrics. They're also perfect for bias skirts and for designs that look best without any visible stitching. Interfacing may not be necessary, except with lightweight fabric or bias. To be sure, test first.

You will need a special zipper foot made for invisible zippers and possibly a shank adapter for your machine.

Do not stitch the seam before you put in the zipper. Fuse the interfacing to the seam allowances (p. 190).

Mark the bottom of the opening on the unsewn seam and on the bottom of the zipper. If the zipper is too long, shorten it from the bottom. (The finished zipper will always end up about 1/2 in. shorter than you planned, so allow extra length as needed.)

To shorten the zipper, drop the feed dog and secure the end of the zipper with a wide zigzag stitch. Cut the zipper 3/4 in. below the zigzag stitching **(1)**.

Open the zipper. Working on the wrong side, press the zipper coils open with a warm iron.

With the zipper face down, pin the right side to the right side of the garment. Position the coils on the seamline (the edge of the zipper tape will be a scant 1/4 in. from the raw edge); the bottom of the stop 1/2 in. below the mark for the bottom of the opening; and the top of the tape 1/4 in. below the top edge of the fabric. Working from top to bottom, position the pins so you can easily pull them out as you stitch.

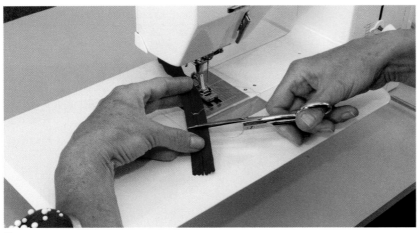

**1** *To shorten the zipper from the bottom, stitch in place, using zigzag stitching with the feed dog lowered, and cut off the excess zipper below the stitching.*

**2** *With the right side of the zipper tape to the right side of the fabric, stitch each half of the zipper from top to bottom.*

(You may want to machine-baste the zipper before you machine-stitch it in place.) If your fabric shifts easily (as do velvet and silkies) or needs matching (plaids and stripes), hand- or machine-baste first.

With the needle centered in the hole in the invisible-zipper foot and the left groove of the foot over the coil, stitch from top to bottom until the foot touches the stop (2). Backstitch at each end.

Close and open the zipper to make sure the stitching is not too close to the teeth, which would prevent it from unzipping easily, or too far away, which would cause the zipper to show.

With the zipper closed, position the right side of the other half of the zipper tape to the right side of the other half of the garment. Make sure the zipper halves align at the top of each side of the garment.

Open the zipper and stitch on the wrong side of the tape with the right groove of the zipper foot over the coil (3). Again, backstitch to reinforce the ends.

Close the zipper. Slide the zipper foot to the left so the needle goes through the outside notch. Holding the end of the zipper out of the way, stitch 2 in. beyond the zipper stop (4). Change back to your regular pressure foot and finish stitching the seam. Press.

Stitch the loose ends of the zipper to the seam allowances to secure them, being careful not to catch the garment. Press.

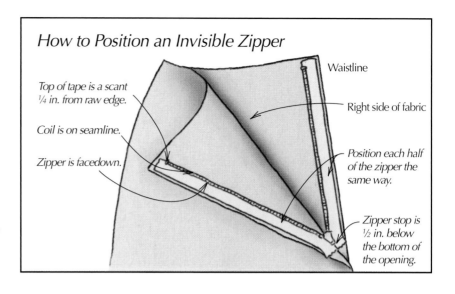

### How to Position an Invisible Zipper

Top of tape is a scant ¼ in. from raw edge.

Coil is on seamline.

Zipper is facedown.

Waistline

Right side of fabric

Position each half of the zipper the same way.

Zipper stop is ½ in. below the bottom of the opening.

**3** *Stitch the right side of the second half of the zipper to the right side of the second half of the garment.*

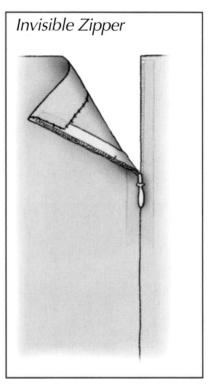

### Invisible Zipper

**4** *Hold the end of the zipper out of the way and stitch 2 in. below the zipper stop.*

# The Lining

*A lining finishes the inside of your garment, reduces wrinkles, and helps the skirt hang well.*

Skirt linings hang free of the skirt and are hemmed separately. They're attached at the waist, and the top edges are concealed by a waistband or facing.

Linings are secured to the garment by hand-stitching around the zipper (and the French vent opening, if there is one).

Sew the lining's side seams on a conventional machine or with a serger. To add a bit more ease, use a ½-in. seam allowance. Stitch the center-back seam, ending just below the zipper opening.

Backstitch to reinforce the ends of the stitching. Press the seams open. If there is a French vent, reinforce the corners and clip diagonally as you did for the garment (1).

Don't sew darts in the lining. Instead, when you baste the lining to the waist, simply position and pin the darts as if they were tucks. The tuck is placed next to the dart, but it folds in the opposite direction to minimize bulk (2).

**1** *If the skirt has a French vent, reinforce and clip the corners of the lining as you did for the garment.*

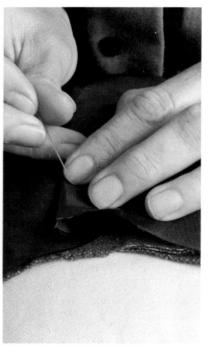

**2** *Don't make darts in the lining. Instead, make a tuck in the lining next to the dart in the skirt, but fold it in the opposite direction.*

## SEW, FIT, AND SEW

One of the secrets to a good fit is to continue to fine-tune the fit as you sew. (For this reason, always wear clothing that you can slip into and out of easily while you're working.)

Construct the front and back of the skirt separately so that you can fit the garment at the side seams.

Pin the side seams along the ⅝-in. seam allowance, wrong sides together, with pins parallel to and along the seamline. Mark the waistline with basting stitches so you can see it clearly. Wearing appropriate undergarments and shoes, try on the pinned skirt. Pin a 1-in.-wide piece of elastic around your waist to simulate a waistband. You can now adjust the side seams to fit your contours.

Let out or take in the seam as needed and try the skirt on again until the fit pleases you. WIth tailor's chalk, mark the alterations on the wrong side of the fabric. Draw a smooth line with the hip curve, making sure both side seams are the same.

The details and constructions methods for your specific skirt style will determine the best times for fitting as you sew. Make notes on the pattern instruction sheet (pp. 160-161).

Check again for swayback and ease at the waist before constructing the waistband or waistline facing. When you're making a classic, fitted waistband, try on the skirt again after the first row of stitching, and once more after the waistband finish is complete.

For skirts with contoured or raised waistbands, apply the facings to the front and back separately so you can fit them as you fit the side seams. This simplifies fitting and construction and makes any additional changes easier.

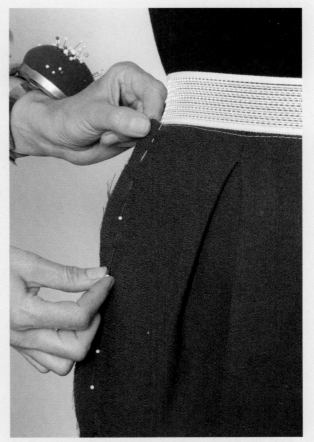

*Fit the skirt at the side seams by adjusting the seam allowances.*

Make all your adjustments, stitch, press, and try on the skirt yet again. It's not uncommon to redo a seam more than once! Continue fitting until you are satisfied.

Fitting is a trial-and-error process. The very best way to understand fitting is to just do it!

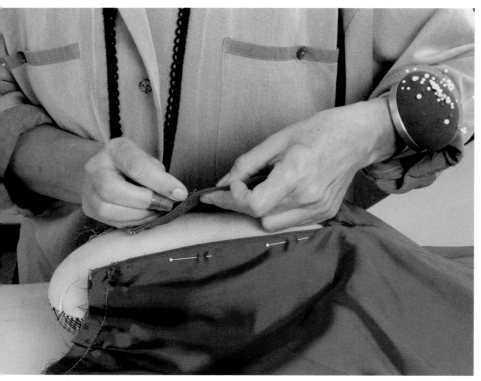

# Attaching the Lining

Insert the lining into the skirt with wrong sides together, and pin the side, center-back, and front seams. Fold tucks in the lining and pin them so they lie in the opposite direction to the skirt darts, as shown on p. 196.

Turn under and finger-press the seam allowance on each side of the zipper opening, making sure the lining won't get caught in the zipper teeth. Slipstitch the lining to the zipper tape (1).

Machine- or hand-baste the lining to the skirt ⅛ in. inside the waist seamline. Baste the lining to the waistband ½ in. from the waistband's edge.

Establish the hem length for the lining. How long you make it depends on how you plan to finish the bottom edge (as described on the facing page). Generally, the lining should be 1 in. shorter than the skirt. Press under the hem.

If your skirt has a French vent, you should have cut the lining as described on p. 36. Turn under and pin a ⅝-in. seam allowance in the lining and slipstitch loosely to attach it to the edges of the vent extensions (2).

1 *Turn under the seam allowances and slipstitch the lining to the zipper tape. Make sure the lining fabric won't get caught in the teeth.*

2 *If your skirt has a French vent, slipsitch the turned-under edge of the lining to the edges of the extensions.*

# Hemming the Lining

There are three options for finishing the hem edge of a skirt lining: serging, turning under, and trimming with lace.

If you decide to finish the edge with serging, be sure to cut the lining 1 in. shorter than skirt.

The hem can also be turned under $1/4$ in. to $1/2$ in., turned again 1 in. to 2 in., and then topstitched. This creates a clean, strong finish. For this treatment, cut the lining the same length as the skirt.

For a simple couture touch, apply lace at the hem with a zigzag stitch (**1**). The lining will look and feel like a built-in slip (this was a signature feature of Jacqueline Kennedy's skirts when she was First Lady). You need to adjust the lining length to compensate for the width of the lace. In other words, cut the lining 1 in. shorter than the skirt length minus the width of the lace.

Trim the excess fabric under the lace close to the stitching (**2**).

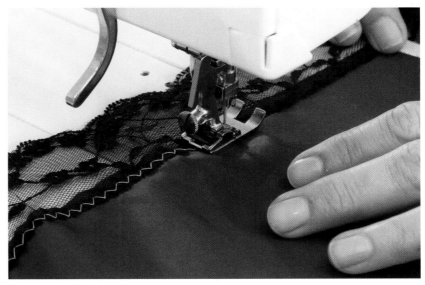

**1** *To add an elegant couture touch, attach lace to the edge of the lining before hemming.*

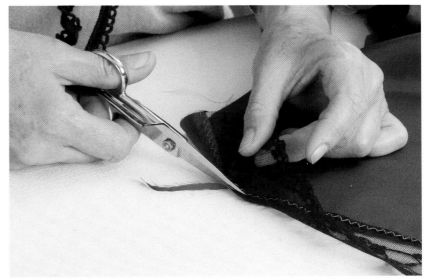

**2** *After you have attached the lace, trim the excess close to the line of stitching.*

# Waistbands

*The waistline of a skirt can be finished in a variety of ways: from the simplest elastic casing to a precisely fitted, multilayered interfaced band.*

# PROFESSIONAL TIPS
# FOR APPLYING A WAISTBAND

Whichever waistband style you choose, the techniques for pinning, stitching, and pressing are the same. Here are some tips for getting frustration-free professional results.

• Pin the waistband to the skirt, right sides together, matching and pinning side seams and centers first. Ease the remaining fabric into the waistband and pin it in place. Position the pins on the seamline so they can be pulled out easily as you sew.

• Stitch with the wrong side of the waistband facing you so it's easier to see and control your work. When sewing a waistband to a gathered skirt, however, stitch with the gathered side up so you can be sure the gathers feed evenly into the machine.

• The waistband is smaller than the skirt, so the action of the machine will do some of the easing for you. If the fabric resists easing, however, hold it at a vertical angle as you sew—a factory trick that makes the job easier.

• Careful pressing is essential to the finished appearance of the waistband. Press the first, and most visible, seam flat as sewn, then press it toward the waistband. Unless the fabric is very heavy, you don't usually need to trim this seam allowance. Use a clapper to flatten as you press, and work over a ham as needed.

• To save time and ensure accuracy in the final stitching, after the ends have been finished, press the waistband as it will be sewn, shaping over the ham. As you press, place pins in the ditch of the seam, catching the back of the waistband, to hold the pressed shape.

• Your pattern will likely tell you simply to turn under the edge of the waistband before sewing it onto the skirt. There are four other, less bulky ways to finish the waistband edge:

1. Use the selvage edge as the finished edge.

2. Serge the edge.

3. Make a Hong Kong edge finish with a bias strip of lining the length of the waistband and 1 in. wide (p. 170).

4. Wrap the edge with a rayon seam binding (p. 170).

Skirts can be made with a pull-on elasticized waistband, which is especially easy for beginners to construct (p. 203); a classic fitted waistband (p. 206); a fitted elasticized waistband (p. 210); a contoured waistband (p. 213); or a raised waistband (p. 215). Some, but not all, require interfacings (pp. 207-209) and closures (pp. 216-217).

Commercial patterns usually provide basic instructions for attaching and interfacing a waistband, but you might want to adapt the pattern for one of these other alternatives.

# Fitting the Waist

A good fit at the waist is crucial to the overall fit and drape of the finished skirt. Ease, the difference between the wearer's body and the amount of fabric in the garment, determines how you will look and feel in the skirt—and ultimately whether or not you will wear it.

Think of your waist measurement, the finished waistband (or facing), and the waist seamline of the skirt as concentric circles, each nesting into the other. The finished waistband is larger than your waist to allow for movement, comfort, and enough room to tuck in a blouse. The waist seamline of the skirt is larger than the waistband so that, when the extra fabric is eased in, the skirt will still flow smoothly over the stomach and hips.

If the fit is right, there's enough ease for you to slip your thumb easily under the waistband. This same amount of ease is added to your waist measurement and determines the length of the finished waistband (excluding the underlap and seam allowances, which are added later).

The amount of recommended ease varies, depending on the style of the waistband and the figure—for example, slim figures generally require less ease than heavy ones. At the beginning of each section on the various waistband styles, you'll find the basic recommendation for the amount of ease for that style for the average figure. Although there are general guidelines, remember that ease is a matter of personal preference. Always measure your body or your favorite skirts to determine how much ease you'd like to have in your finished waistband, and adjust accordingly.

## CHECKING THE FIT

Before you apply the waistband, try on the skirt to double-check the fit of the garment.

Mark the waist seamline by machine-basting the skirt with thread of a contrasting color. Pin a 1-in. to 2-in. wide length of elastic in place as a temporary waistband. Adjust the skirt so that the lower edge of the elastic is positioned along the waist seamline. The elastic "waistband" should rest along your natural waist, with some ease—not too tight, not too loose. Fine-tune the position and fit.

If necessary, at this point, you can adjust for swayback if you didn't alter the pattern when pin-fitting (pp. 154-155).

Now remove the skirt and measure along the waist seamline, excluding the underlap and seam allowances. This measurement should be from 1½ in. to 2 in. greater than the length of the finished waistband. The extra skirt fabric will be eased into the waistband later.

If the skirt's waist measurement is less than 1½ in. or more than 2 in. greater than the waistband measurement, you have several options. You can take in or let out equal amounts of fabric at the side seams. You can also adjust the darts as necessary. If the skirt is too big, you can draw in the extra fabric by running a row or two of gathering stitching (using the next-to-longest machine stitch) and easing evenly. You can also use staystitch plus (p. 174), or a combination of both. If the skirt is big, your waist small, and your hips high and round, a fitted, elasticized waistband (p. 210) also provides a solution.

# Pull-on Waistband

**Amount of Ease:**
*Waistband length: Hip measurement plus 2 in. (plus 1¼ in. for two ⅝-in. seam allowances). The waist seamline should measure 2 in. more than the finished waistband.*

The pull-on waistband is a simple and professional detail that can be used with knits or lightweight wovens. This style of waistband slips on easily over the hips, but doesn't add bulk at the waist. You can even position pleats or gathers where you want them, while retaining the comfort and ease of a pull-on waistband.

Knit ribbing gives the best stretch and the least bulk. You can also use cross-grain knits or lengthwise or cross-grain wovens.

***Measure and Cut*** Cut the waistband to a length equal to your hip measurement plus 2 in. plus two ⅝-in. seam allowances. The extra length will allow for those fabrics with zero stretch— for example, all wovens and some stable knits.

Cut the waistband wider than the finished width, and plan to trim it after you've stitched it to the garment. Knits, in particular, often become more narrow as they are stretched and stitched in place. For example, if I'm using 1¼-in. wide elastic, I cut the waistband 4½ in. wide, which allows for two ⅝-in. seam allowances and about ¾ in. of extra fabric. I trim the waistband to size and finish it after I've sewn the elastic to the seam allowance.

Cut the elastic 2 in. to 3 in. shorter than your waist measurement plus two ¼-in. seam allowances. (I use flat-rib elastic or Ban-rol.)

To assemble the waistband, sew the seams and trim them to ¼-in. allowances. Press them open and topstitch them at center with a wide zigzag stitch **(1)**. This will hold the seam flat and help you identify the garment's center back.

Divide the waistband in quarters, and mark each section. Pin the waistband to the garment, right

**1** *Sew the waistband together and topstitch with a wide zigzag stitch.*

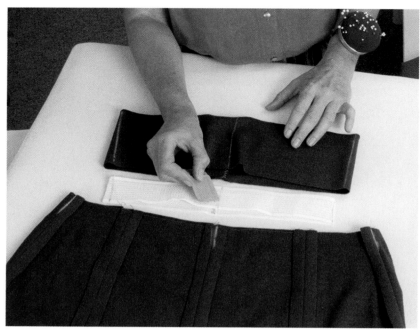

**2** *After dividing the waistband into quarters, pin it to the skirt, matching marks at centers and side seams.*

**3** *Sew the waistband to the skirt, stretching it as needed to fit.*

sides together, at centers and at side seams **(2)**.

Stitch on the wrong side of the waistband, stretching it as needed to fit the garment **(3)**. If the garment is substantially larger than the waistband, on some fabrics (but rarely knits), you may need to use gathering stitches. Press the stitched seams toward the waistband.

Lap the seam allowances of the elastic to form a circle and stitch the ends with a serpentine or zigzag stitch **(4)**. Trim the ends and divide the elastic into quarters, as you did the waistband.

Position the edge of the elastic next to the waistline stitching and pin the elastic to the seam allowance, matching the marks at center front, back, and side seams. Stitch the elastic to the seam allowance with a long, wide zigzag stitch, stretching as you stitch **(5)**.

Wrap the waistband around the elastic. Trim width as needed, but be sure there will be enough fabric beyond the waistline stitching so that when you stitch on the right side, you'll catch the inside bottom edge of the waistband. Finish the waistband edge.

On the right side of the fabric, place pins in the ditch of the seam, positioning them so you can easily remove them as you sew **(6)**. Pin or baste the waistband vertically at each quarter to prevent it from shifting during stitching. On the right side of the garment, stitch in the ditch to finish **(7)**.

Another finishing option is to stitch several rows of topstitching, stretching as you sew. If you plan to topstitch, keep in mind that every row of stitching stretches the elasic about 1 in., so fit the elastic more snugly. Another trick is to use a longer stitch so as not to distort the elastic.

**4** *A wide serpentine stitch will secure the ends of the elastic and keep them lying flat.*

**5** *With the edge of the elastic next to the waistline stitching, stitch with a wide zigzag, stretching as you go.*

**6** *Working on the right side of the garment, place pins in the ditch, catching the inside bottom edge of the waistband.*

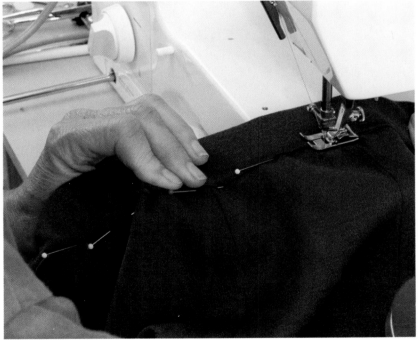

**7** *To finish the waistband, stitch in the ditch, as shown here, or topstitch several rows.*

# MAKE A FITTED WAISTBAND PATTERN

Once you have a comfortable waistband, file its measurements with your patterns. You can also make a permanent pattern piece to use with all your skirts.

To compute the length and width of a custom-fit waistband, start with your waist measurement (p. 142). If your waist measures 26½ in. and you want 1½ in. of ease, your finished waistband measurement is 28 in. **(A)**. If you use ½-in. seam allowances, double that amount **(B)**. The underlap should be at least 1½ in. **(C)**. For this waistband, the total length of fabric to cut is 30½ in.

| | |
|---|---|
| **A.** Finished length (waist measure + preferred amount of ease) | 28 in. |
| **B.** Seam allowances multiplied by 2 | 1 in. |
| **C.** Underlap (measure under fly, pocket extension, or simply use length you prefer) | 1½ in. |
| **Total cut length** | 30½ in. |

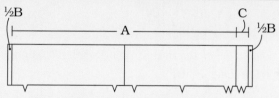

As a rule, waistbands are 1 in. to 2 in. wide. If you want your finished waistband to be 1¼ in. wide, multiply the finished width by two **(A)**. If the front seam allowance is ⅝ in. **(B)**, and you're using a selvage edge, Hong Kong finish, or rayon seam binding, add another ¼ in. to the back seam allowance **(C)**. Always add another ¼ in. for turning under the inside edge of the fabric **(D)**. The total cut width of this waistband is 3⅝ in.

| | |
|---|---|
| **A.** Finished width multiplied by 2 | 2½ in. |
| **B.** Front seam allowance | ⅝ in. |
| **C.** Back seam allowance (Add ¼ in. for selvage edge, Hong Kong finish, or seam binding.) | ¼ in. |
| **D.** Turn of cloth (extra fabric to go up and over the fold) | ¼ in. |
| **Total cut width** | 3⅝ in. |

# Classic Fitted Waistband

**Amount of Ease:**
*Waistband length: Waist measurement plus 1 in. to 1½ in. (plus 1¼ in. for two ⅝-in. seam allowances).*

The fitted waistband is a long rectangle cut on the lengthwise or crosswise grain, interfaced, and fitted with a minimum of ease.

Cutting it on the lengthwise grain with one edge on selvedge provides a finished edge that lies flat on the inside of the skirt. You can also create cross-grain and bias-grain waistbands by piecing at the side or back seams.

If your skirt has a lining, insert it before you construct and attach the waistband.

Use the commercial pattern for the waistband and make any necessary adjustments, or make your own custom-fit waistband. Be sure the body of the skirt is completed and fits well before you cut the waistband—in case any more alterations are needed.

Three interfacing options are described on pp. 207-209. Whichever you decide to use, finish the ends of the fitted waistband as described on p. 216. Apply closures as described on p. 216.

***Marking*** With chalk, pins, or snips, mark the stitching lines, seam allowances, and underlap on the wrong side of the waistband. Match centers, forming a circle. Divide the circle into quarters that correspond to the skirt's center front and back and side seams.

The skirt doesn't divide neatly into four even quarters at the waistline. The back from side to side is ½ in. narrower than the front (this is true for women and men of any size and shape). Adjust the waistband after establishing the garment quarters. Take ¼ in. off the back at each side seam and add it to the center front to compensate for the difference from front to back. Shift the side-seam mark when pinning the waistband in place.

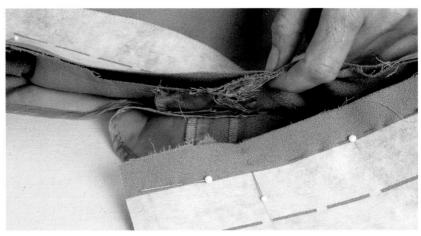

1 *Cut the interfacing to the same length as the waistband, including seam allowances.*

# Three Interfacing Options for the Classic Waistband

Interfacing helps give a garment its shape, body, and support. The two types of interfacing are fusible and sew-in. Woven fusible interfacings designed for men's shirts and sold by the yard make good waistband interfacings.

**Fusible Interfacing** Quick and easy to use, fusible interfacing is applied with a warm iron and requires no stitching. Nonwoven fusible interfacing has no grain. Packaged waistbanding is precut and sold in different widths, according to the width of the waistband. Whichever type you use, always fuse a swatch first to make sure the interfacing and the fabric are compatible in weight.

Precut fusible interfacing is perforated so the stitching lines and fold lines are easy to see; one half is ¼ in. smaller than the other. Cut the interfacing to the same length as your waistband, including seam allowances (1). A small amount of interfacing in the seam will stabilize the end of the waistband.

Position the interfacing on the waistband, wrong side of fabric to adhesive side of interfacing. The narrower half forms the front of the waistband. Be sure the edge of the narrower half is ¾ in. from the raw edge of the fabric to allow space for stitching and for turning the fabric. Mark the seams, centers, and underlap on the narrow half. Fuse the interfacing to the fabric with a warm iron, following the manufacturer's instructions.

Staystitch-plus the skirt to fit the waistband (2). Pin the waistband to the skirt, wrong sides together, matching seams and centers and easing as needed.

With the waistband side toward you, stitch a ⅝-in. seam allowance, just inside the interfacing edge. Press.

2 *Staystitch-plus the waistline of skirt to fit the waistband.*

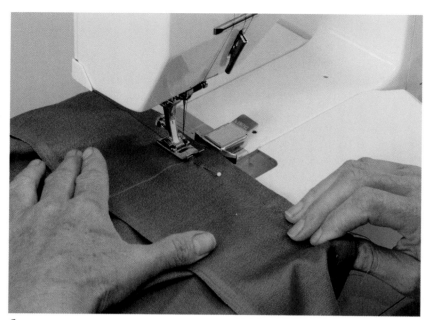

1 Stitch the waistband to the skirt, right sides together.

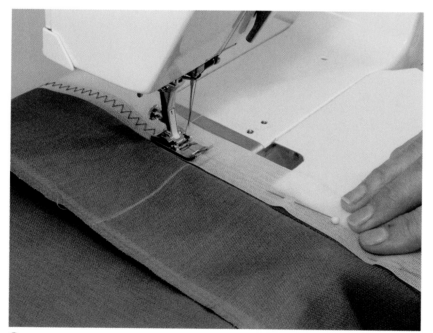

2 Attach Armoflexx to the seam allowance of the waistband with a wide zigzag stitch.

**Sew-in Waistbanding** A woven sew-in waistbanding known as Armoflexx creates a firm waistband and prevents the impression of the seam from showing. It's available by the yard in standard widths. The measurement and application of Armoflexx require a bit more care and skill than fusibles do.

Cut the interfacing to the same length as the waistband. Do not trim away the seam allowances. Even though it seems stiff, Armoflexx can be trimmed to almost nothing next to the seam to help stabilize the ends of the waistband. Transfer the markings.

Pin and stitch the waistband to the skirt with right sides together, matching the seams and centers and easing as needed (**1**). Press.

Match the corresponding side-seam and center marks on the interfacing and waistband. Position the edge of the interfacing next to the stitching line, pinning as needed, and stitch in the seam allowance. A wide, long zigzag stitch holds all layers flat (**2**). Press.

**Layered Interfacing** Both fusible and sew-in interfacings may be applied in single or double layers. I've had better results with fusibles. Sew-ins tend not to lie smooth and flat, but if you prefer to use them, here's what you would do.

Choose two layers of the same material or combine two different types. Although the construction principles are the same for both sew-in and fusible, the preliminary steps vary.

Cut the first layer of interfacing (on the lengthwise or cross grain if it is woven) to the same length as the waistband. Cut a second piece of interfacing on the bias to the same length and the finished width plus ³/₄ in. The bias-cut piece provides stability and softness, and will produce a stable waistband with a soft curve to its upper edge.

**Fusible:** Fuse the larger piece to the wrong side of the waistband. Now fuse the bias-cut piece on top of the larger, so the long front edge is ¹/₈ in. inside the stitching line of the waistband **(1)**. This way, the second layer won't be caught in the stitching and ³/₄ in. will extend beyond the fold for a crisp edge. This technique is best for heavier fabrics; for lightweight fabrics, you can stitch through both layers of interfacing.

**Sew-in:** Hand- or machine-baste the larger piece to the wrong side of the front half of the waistband, ¹/₈ in. inside the stitching line. Baste the second layer to the first, stitching along the fold line and ¹/₈ in. inside all the seamlines **(2)**. If you're using more than one layer of interfacing, trim the seam allowance in the top layer only.

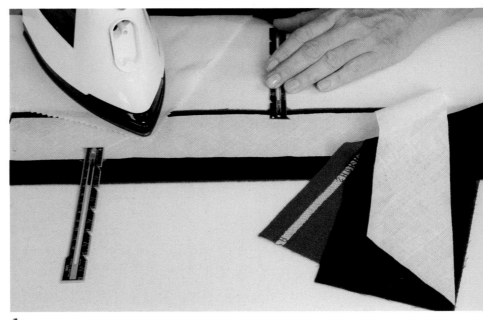

1 *After fusing the first piece of interfacing, fuse the second smaller piece on top of it, inside the stitching line. Use a press cloth if necessary.*

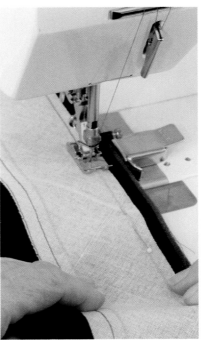

2 *Sew the waistband to the skirt.*

To add an extra bit of "crunch" to either the fusible or sew-in interfacing, machine-stitch two rows, ¹/₄ in. apart, on the back half of the waistband, ¹/₄ in. from the fold line.

# Fitted Elasticized Waistband

**Amount of Ease:**
*Waistband length: Waist measurement plus 1 in. to 3 in. (plus 1¼ in. for two ⅝-in. seam allowances). Skirt waist: The waist seamline of the skirt should measure 1 in. to 3 in. more than the waistband measurement.*

---

A fitted elasticized waistband has style, comfort, and fit, too. It works with any skirt fabric, from crepe de chine to denim. Both the skirt and the waistband have a bit of extra ease, which the elastic draws in.

This waistband is perfect for figures with a small waist and high round hips. It has a slightly puckered,

seersucker appearance when on the hanger, but is flattering on the body. The extra fabric hardly shows and adds no bulk. With this style of waistband, the skirt must have a zipper or a buttoned or side-pocket opening (p. 183).

***Cutting the Waistband*** Cut the waistband, adding 1 in. to 3 in. of ease to the length. The elastic will draw in the extra fabric. Mark the seams, centers, and underlap.

The waist seamline of the skirt should measure 1 in. to 3 in. more than your waistband measurement. Simply cut the waistband to your waist measurement plus 1 in. to 3 in., and then allow for seam and underlap allowances.

Cut the elastic to your waist measurement minus up to 3 in., plus seam allowances and underlap. I recommend Ban-rol elastic or flat-rib elastic, but if you plan to topstitch, use Ban-rol. The dense texture of flat-rib elastic makes it difficult to stitch through.

***Constructing the Waistband*** With right sides together, sew the long edge of the waistband to the skirt with a ⅝-in. seam allowance **(1)**. Press.

Mark the seam allowances, side seams, and front and back centers on the elastic. After you've sewn and pressed the first seam on the waistband, pin the elastic at the marked points, positioning the edge of the elastic next to the waistband stitching line.

Stitch the elastic to the waistband's seam allowance with a long, wide zigzag stitch **(2)**. Stretch the elastic

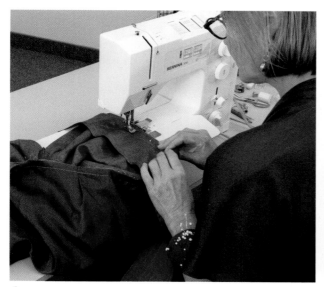

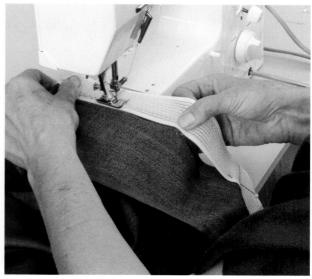

1 *Sew the long edge of the waistband to skirt, right sides together.*

2 *Sew the elastic to the waistband with a zigzag stitch.*

while stitching between the side seams, but not while stitching the underlap or the seam allowances at the ends.

Next, finish the ends of the waistband as described on p. 212. Trim, press, and turn.

Before the final stitching, to keep the top and bottom edges of the waistband flat, slip a small circle or square of fusible web (designed to fuse fabric together, and sold by the yard or in strips) between the back of the waistband and the elastic (**3**). Press and fuse it in place. The elastic has a tendency to roll, and this technique is a bit of insurance to keep the top and bottom edges flat.

3 *Insert and fuse fusible web between the elastic and the back of the waistband to keep the top and bottom edges flat.*

Cut and mark more than one length of elastic, and you'll save time when making your next waistband.

# FINISHING THE ENDS OF A WAISTBAND

1 *Mark the fold line with a snip on both ends of the waistband.*

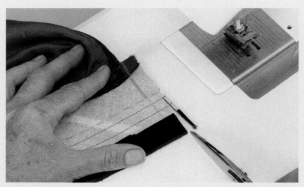

2 *Trim ⅛ in. from the seam allowances at both ends of the inside half of the waistband. Trimming to the fold line "favors" the underside, which means that the ends will naturally roll to the underside of the waistband. Pin the waistband to hold it in position.*

3 *Fold the waistband, right sides together, aligning the edges. Stitch across the waistband ends. Trim the corners, grade the seams, and trim the interfacing from the seam allowance. Press flat. Press open with a point turner.*

4 *Turn the waistband with a point turner.*

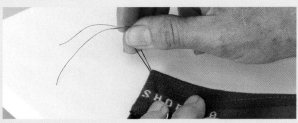

5 *To turn the corner squarely, take a stitch by hand through the machine-stitching (with two strands of thread and no knot) and pull gently. Favor the seam to the underside, and press and pound with the clapper.*

6 *On the right side, pin or hand-baste the waistband in place, catching both halves. Position the pins in the ditch of the seam so you can pull them out easily as you sew. Press the waistband as it will be sewn to make the final stitching easier and more accurate. On the right side of the garment, stitch in the ditch of the seam. Stitch the ends of the underlap together with a narrow zigzag or straight stitch. Be sure both halves of the underlap are caught in the stitching. Press over a ham to reinforce the natural curve of the waistband.*

# Contoured Waistband

## Amount of Ease:

*Waistband length: Waist measurement plus 1 in. to 1½ in. (plus 1¼ in. for two ⅝-in. seam allowances). The waist seamline of the skirt should measure 1 in. to 1½ in. more than the waistband measurement.*

The ultimate in simplicity, the contoured waistband is very complimentary to short-waisted figures. The faced edge of the waistband sits precisely at the waistline, and the waistband facings fit the body's curves. The skirt of Chanel's classic suit—often of thick, nubby wool—has this waist finish, designed to lie smoothly beneath a silk shell.

A contoured waistband facing should measure 1 in. to 1½ in. larger than the finished waist measurement. Staystitch the waistline of the skirt ½ in. from the top edge.

Interface the waistband facings (pp. 207-209). Some body is desirable, but don't use interfacings that are too stiff. You don't need to trim away the interfacing in the seam allowances. Sew the seams, and trim the allowances to ¼ in. Finish the raw edge of the waistband facing with a Hong Kong finish, rayon seam binding, or serging.

Attach ¼-in. twill tape or a ¼-in. selvage strip from the lining fabric as you sew the facing to the skirt **(1)**. This will prevent the

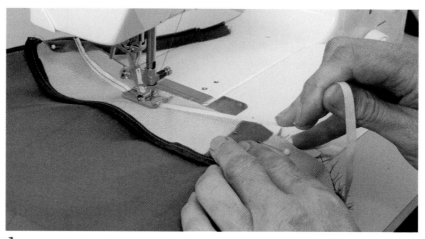

1 *Sew the waistband facings to the skirt and reinforce them with twill tape or a strip of lining selvage.*

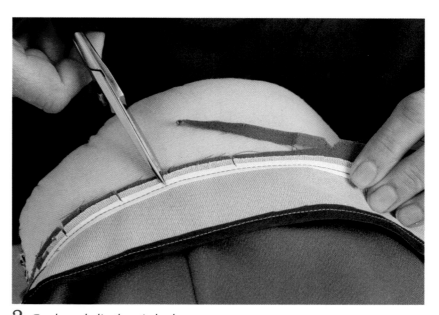

2 *Grade and clip the stitched seams.*

facing from stretching as the garment is worn. You don't need to pin the tape in place first. As you stitch, ease the tape by pulling it slightly. Grade and clip the seams **(2)**.

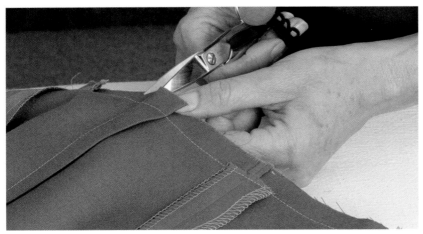

3 *Trim the excess fabric at the waistline so there aren't too many layers.*

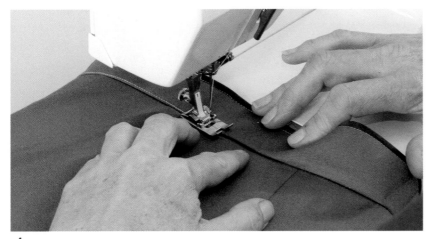

4 *Understitch the facing next to the seam. This helps the facing roll toward the inside of the skirt.*

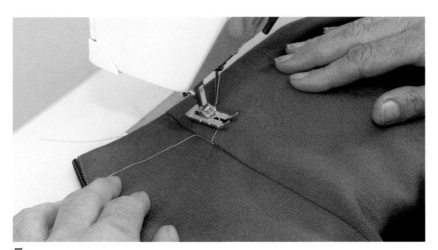

5 *Tack the facings to the garmet at the seams and darts by hand or by machine-stitching in the ditch on the right side of the garment.*

Trim the excess fabric from the darts so there aren't too many layers of fabric at the waistline (3).

Press the seam flat, then press the seam allowances toward the facing. On the right side of the garment, with the facing extended away from the skirt, understitch the facing next to the seam (4). The understitching helps the facing roll toward the inside of the skirt. Press, favoring the facing to the wrong side.

Tack the facings to the garment at the seams and darts by hand or by machine-stitching in the ditch on the right side of the garment (5).

Turn under the ends of the facing next to the zipper and pin them. Slipstitch the facing to the zipper tape. Press the finished waistband over a ham to shape the contour.

### Converting to a Fitted Waist

You can convert the waist treatment of any fitted, darted skirt to a contoured waistband by eliminating the fitted waistband and making facing patterns.

Pin the darts on the front and back skirt-pattern pieces. Mark the pattern 3 in. from and parallel to the waistline edge. (With 5/8-in. seam allowances, the finished facing will be 2 3/8 in. wide.) Extend the skirt grainline on the facing areas and trace two separate facing pieces. Apply the contoured waistband facings as described.

# Raised Waistband

**Amount of Ease:**

*Waistband length: Waist measurement plus 1 in. at bottom of waistband; 1½ in. larger than midriff at top (plus 1¼ in. for two ⅝-in. seam allowances).*

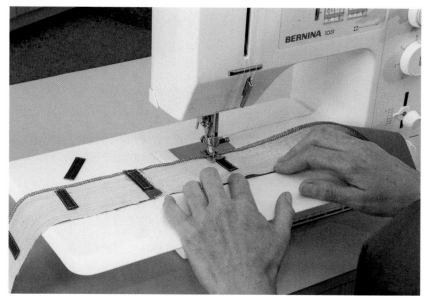

*Cut boning so that it fits just inside the seamlines on the facing, and stitch around each strip.*

A raised, or extended, waistband may extend from 1¼ in. to 3 in. higher than the natural waistline. It isn't separate from the garment, as are other kinds of waistbands; rather, it is cut as part of the skirt panels, then shaped with curves and darts and finished with a separate facing. This style is best for long-waisted figures without much waistline definition or a large bust.

One of the secrets to a crisp raised waistband is to interface the facing as well as the garment. Cut the skirt interfacing using the front and back skirt-pattern pieces, and follow the shaping at the top of the skirt. Cut the interfacing so it is ½ in. wider than the skirt facing. Fuse and position the pieces before marking and sewing darts and tucks.

Use a heavier weight of fusible or sew-in interfacing for the facing than for the skirt. It isn't necessary to trim interfacing in seam allowances.

**Boning** Keep the waistband from crushing or rolling down the waistline by adding boning. Boning, available under the brand name Rigiline, is sold by the foot. It is pliable, soft, easy to stitch through, and comfortable to wear, and it is available in black and white.

Cut a piece of boning for each seam and dart to the height of the finished waistband, without seam allowances.

Sew the boning to the wrong side of the facing at center front and back, at the side seams, and halfway between the centers and side seams. Stitch around all sides of the boning strips (above).

Construct the facings, tape the edges, and attach the facings as you would for the contoured waistband (pp. 213-214).

Closures are optional for a high raised waistband or a contoured, faced waistband. Frequently closures for these waistband styles are omitted in ready-to-wear, but the classic recommendation is a fine metal hook and eye positioned under the zipper to add a bit of extra security.

# Hooks and Eyes

You can close a skirt with buttons, snaps, or hooks and eyes. Buttons are appropriate only if you've used a lightweight interfacing in the waistband—it's difficult to make a good buttonhole through the many layers and uneven thickness at the ends of most waistbands. Snaps have a tendency to pop open under pressure, so they aren't a good choice either. Large hooks and eyes are the most practical hidden fasteners for the overlapping edges on waistbands. They're flat enough to avoid bulk and strong enough to hold up to the firm interfacings and beefy elastics that most waistbands require.

You'll need two sets of hooks and eyes designed for waistbands. Use black metal with dark fabric colors, silver with light.

Hand-sew the first hook ¼ in. from the edge of the waistband overlap (1). With two strands of waxed thread, make small, short stitches next to each other, or use a blanket stitch to form a series of knots to cover the metal. The stitching should not show on the right side of the waistband. Make two small knots in the last stitch to secure the stitching.

Finish by making a tailor's knot, or quilter's knot, in the thread ½ in. from the surface of the fabric. Take a 1-in. stitch next to the hook, between the layers, and tug the thread to bury the knot. Trim the thread end where it emerges from the fabric.

The positon of the first hook determines the position of the corresponding eye. Eyes may be sewn on by hand or machine.

To sew eyes by machine, drop the feed dogs and attach a buttonhole foot (2). Adjust the width of the zigzag to clear the metal and make about 10 stitches through the eye. Finish by positioning the needle in the hole, adjust the stitch, and take three to four stitches in place.

Close the first hook and eye so the waistband is curved, as it will be when worn. Mark and sew the second hook about ½ in. from the edge of the underlap (depending on the length of the underlap) and position the second eye (3). This innermost closure bears most of the stress. Allow a slight bit of slack in the waistband between the first and second sets of closures.

**1** *Attach the first hook with a series of stitches made with waxed thread.*

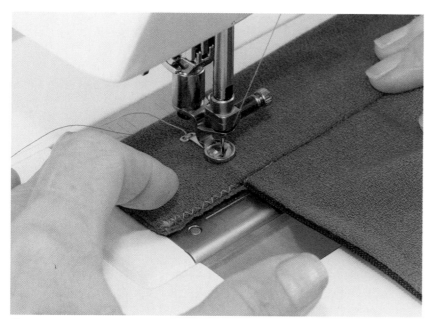

**2** *Attach the eyes with zigzag stitches, using a buttonhole foot.*

**3** *Install two sets of hooks and eyes in the waistband for extra strength. The innermost closure bears most of the stress.*

# Hemming the Skirt

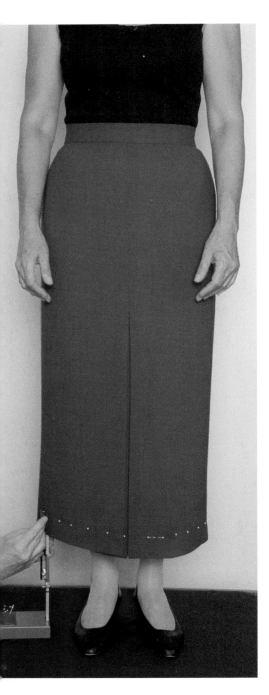

*The hem adds the finishing touch to a skirt. The type of hem you make, its width, and whether you sew it by hand or machine depends upon the fabric, style, and overall design of the skirt.*

The overall effect of the finished hem should be smooth and fluid. The edge needs to be even and parallel to the floor. You can sew a hem by hand or machine, but hand-stitching should be invisible and machine-stitching and topstitching must be straight.

Easing in the raw edge on a flared or shaped skirt prevents the formation of little tucks or pleats that may show through on the right side. Staystitch-plus (p. 174) with a standard straight stitch or use a serger with differential feed to ease and finish the raw edge in one operation.

## Hem Width

The hem width on the pattern piece provides a guideline, but always consider the style of the skirt and the fabric when deciding on hem width. The fabric is really the deciding factor. Some soft fabrics ease well; some firm fabrics may not.

A straight skirt generally requires a 2-in. to 2½-in. hem. Patterns often recommend ⅝-in. machine-topstitched hems for flared skirts. However, a narrow hem may roll to the outside. A slightly wider hem (¾ in. to ⅞ in.) may hang better and is just as easy to make. I prefer flared skirts with hems as wide as 1½ in. to 1⅝ in.

The wider the flare of the skirt, however, the smaller you should make the hem. A smaller hem has less fabric to ease.

## Marking

For accuracy, it's best to have another person mark the hem. The helper should move around the person being measured so the garment won't shift.

Determine the length you want the finished garment to be (p. 142-143). Mark the finished length with a hem marker or a yardstick that has been marked with a piece of masking tape as a guide. Place pins parallel to the floor every 2 in. to 3 in. Pin the front section of the hem to make sure the length is right and double-check the pin positions.

Remove the skirt. Press the hem under, along the pins, removing them as you come to them. Don't try to press to the exact placement of the pins—simply use them to determine a smooth, straight line. Then pin the hem up and try on the skirt again. Adjust the hem as needed.

Measure with a seam gauge, mark the hem to an even width with chalk, and trim evenly along the marked line **(1)**. (Or you can simply serge along the marked line). Trim the seam allowances within the hem to ¼ in. to eliminate unnecessary bulk **(2)**. Finish the raw edge, as described on p. 221.

Press the hem in place by carefully pressing the bottom two-thirds of the hem. This will keep the hem from showing through on the right side of the garment.

**1** *Mark the hem and trim evenly along the marked line.*

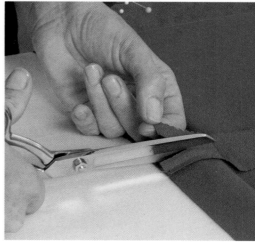

**2** *Trim the seam allowances within the hem to ¼ in.*

# Hemming by Hand

Hand-sewing hems creates softer, less obvious hems, which are particularly well suited for dressier skirts. Some fabrics, like silk, tend to shift, stretch, or distort when machine-stitched, and they're easier to control if they're hemmed by hand.

Silk thread or a long-staple polyester thread are both nearly invisible when stitched. Cotton thread is fine for midweight garments. Use as fine a needle as you can see to thread and a short length of a single strand. The end knot should be just to your elbow when the needle is threaded and ready to sew.

Secure and bury the knot in a seam. Fold the edge of the hem back ¼ in. and stitch along this fold. This prevents the stitches from showing.

**3** *Hem by hand with loose stitches, catching just a fiber of the fabric, and make knots every 4 in. to 6 in.*

Catch just a fiber of the fabric as you stitch (don't worry, it will hold). Make loose stitches ¼ in. to ⅜ in. long and form a knot every 4 in. to 6 in. **(3)**. Loose stitches won't show through; the knots ensure that the hem will stay up even if a few stitches should get pulled out during normal wear-and-tear.

## HEMMING RIPPLE-FREE

Woven fabric is on the cross grain around a hem (and to further complicate things, sometimes it's off bias, too), so it can stretch, pucker, and ripple while you're machine-stitching. To avoid these problems, try these tricks.

1. Stitch with "straight assurance," that is, hold the fabric taut and firm as it feeds through the machine so that the fabric doesn't stretch or ripple. Don't pull the fabric or stop the normal stitching action. (This does not work on knits.)

2. With both hands, pull the fabric at right angles to the needle as it feeds through the machine. This may also help reduce rippling and stretching of the top layer of fabric.

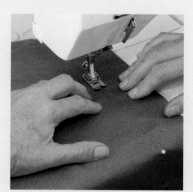

*Apply slight tension to each side of the stitching line.*

# Hemming by Machine

Fine ready-to-wear garments and commercial patterns are using machine-stitched and machine-topstitched hems more frequently. I use them for casual or sporty skirts.

***A Machine-Stitched Hem*** On silky or sheer fabrics, you can get good results with a minimum of frustration by machine-stitching a narrow hem. (Many sewers refer to this as a Calvin Klein hem because it shows up so often in the designer's line.) This hem features three lines of stitching and ensures a clean edge. It works on both the straight grain or bias and is a good choice for skirts in silk crepe de chine, georgette, and chiffon.

On the right side of the fabric, staystitch just within the marked finished hemline. Press along the stitched line. Now switch to an edgestitch foot and two-ply machine-embroidery thread, which is very fine and light.

Position the needle to the left of center and, with the fabric fold against the guide, stitch along the very edge of the underside of the hem. Trim the fabric as close to the stitching as possible with appliqué scissors. Press the fold under slightly—just enough to enclose the raw edge and create as narrow a hem as possible—and edgestitch the hem again on the right side.

A successful hem will have one line of stitching on the right side of the garment and two parallel lines of stitching on the hem. The line of

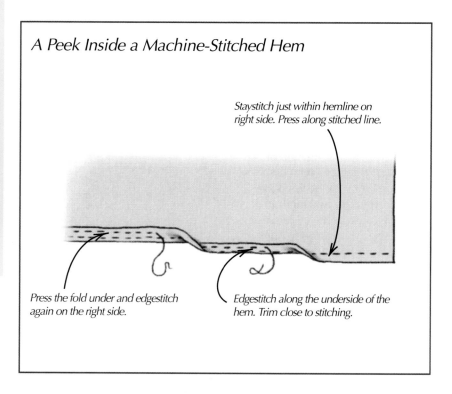

*A Peek Inside a Machine-Stitched Hem*

*Staystitch just within hemline on right side. Press along stitched line.*

*Press the fold under and edgestitch again on the right side.*

*Edgestitch along the underside of the hem. Trim close to stitching.*

staystitching will be enclosed within the fold. Press the garment on the right side.

**Hemming Knits**  Knits demand the durability of a topstitched hem, but the hem can be frustrating to sew because knits stretch more on the cross grain.

Cut a ¹⁄₂-in. strip of bias-cut fusible tricot, such as Sof-Knit. Stitch it to the raw hem edge, wrong side of fabric to right side of fusible (the smooth side is the right side; you'll be sewing with the adhesive side up) **(1)**. On flared skirts, or if the knit is unstable or very stretchy, pull the interfacing strip to stretch it slightly as you stitch. You can also sew in this strip as you serge.

If you haven't serged them, pink the edges close to the line of stitching **(2)**. Fuse the hem into place, positioning it carefully. To secure and finish the hem, topstitch on the right side of the garment using staystitch plus as needed **(3)**.

# Final Pressing

Working on the wrong side of the garment, press the entire skirt and hem. Press only along the bottom edge of the hem, not across its full width—otherwise the impression of the hem might show through to the right side. Touch-up press on the right side of the garment, using a press cloth if necessary.

**1**  *To stabilize a knit hem, stitch a strip of bias-cut fusible tricot to the raw edge.*

**2**  *Pink close to the line of stitching.*

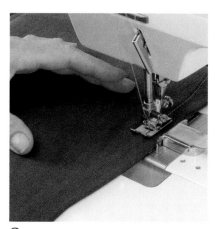

**3**  *Topstitch the fused edge to keep it permanently in position.*

## SIX HEM FINISHES

The best hem finish is one that prevents fraying, yet is so light that it does not add bulk or show from the right side of the garment.

If you own a serger, the **serged edge** (p. 169) is a good finish for both hand- and machine-stitched hems. For a lighter finish, serge with machine-embroidery thread or woolly nylon.

Make a **pinked-and-stitched edge** (p. 168) by stitching ³⁄₈ in. from the raw edge of the hem and trimming as little as possible with pinking shears or the pinking blade on a rotary cutter. You can also combine pinking with staystitch-plus (p. 174).

The **Hong Kong finish** or **rayon seam binding** (p. 170) is best for midweight to heavyweight fabrics. These edge finishes add bulk and may show through to the right side of lighter fabrics. Always test first.

The **turned-and-stitched edge** is suitable for midweight fabrics and crisp sheers with deep topstitched hems. It's also durable and therefore good for skirts that will be laundered.

The **zigzag edge** (p. 169) is fast to make and prevents raveling, but it can add bulk and cause the fabric to tunnel or stretch. For best results, stitch ¹⁄₄ in. from the raw edge and trim after stitching. It's good for midweight to heavyweight fabrics, casual wear, and children's clothes.

# Test Your Skills: A Gored Skirt

*The gored skirt is a true classic—chic and flattering and always in style. Now that you know the many tricks of the trade, try out your professional skirtmaking skills with this easy-to-sew skirt.*

A gored skirt combines the lines of a slim and flared skirt, may be fitted or full, is flattering to almost any size and shape, is comfortable to wear, and easy to fit and sew.

Gored skirts can be shaped in various ways (p.126). The fullness may begin at the waist, the high hip, the full hip, or below the hip.

Choose the fabric weight according to the fit. The most fitted gored skirts are best in fabrics with weight and drape, such as gabardine or wool crepe, or a stable, heavier knit, such as wool double knit or velour. The fullest gored skirts are best in very lightweight fabrics, such as challis and light, fine knits.

In many commercial patterns, the gores are often the same size—for example, you would cut the same pattern piece eight times for an eight-gore skirt. In multiple-size patterns, the extra amounts for the size increments are added to the side panels.

Both fitted and full gored skirts can be seamed on the serger or on a standard sewing machine. Use a separate pull-on waistband and

hem by hand or machine. Here are some tips for constructing a lightly fitted, fitted, or full gored skirt.

## Tips for a Lightly Fitted Gored Skirt

The silhouette of a lightly fitteed gored skirt is similar to a straight skirt, but it allows more ease in movement. It's also slimming and very flattering to a large-hipped figure.

Short to ankle-grazing lengths work well with this style.

Use a commercial pattern for a six- or eight-gore skirt and a heavy, stable, knit fabric—wool double knit, velour, panné velvet, or heavy cotton double knit, for example.

The trick is to cut the pattern two to three sizes larger than your body measurements (p. 142). The heavy knit drags and stretches, so you want extra width to give the illusion of fit, yet enough ease so that the skirt appears to float over the body.

Use standard seams with wool double knit (no other finish is necessary); serged or stitched and zigzag seams with velour or panné, which tends to curl.

Stitch the front and back sections of the skirt together first and adjust the fit at the side seams. The skirt should pull on easily over the hips, so use a pull-on elasticized waistband (pp. 203-205). Hand-stitch (p. 219) or machine-topstitch (p. 220) the hem.

Stitch the side seams last. Before you do, however, pin along the seamlines, wrong sides together. Try on the skirt and adjust the seam width as needed to get the best fit.

## Tips for a Fitted Gored Skirt

Making a fitted fored skirt is the most time-comsuming and difficult of the three possible styles. It is fitted at both the waist and the hip. You can find four-, six-, and eight-gore patterns in this style. The skirt works well in both short and long lengths.

Fit and alter the pattern carefully, allowing the correct amount of ease (p. 146).

Wool crepe or gabardine is a good fabric choice. Sew a standard seam with the edges serged or pinked (p. 168-169).

This is the perfect opportunity to use an invisible zipper at the center back or on a side seam (pp. 194-195). Apply a classic, fitted waistband (pp. 206-207) or a fitted elasticized waistband (pp. 210-211).

## Tips for a Full Gored Skirt

A full, ten-gore skirt is fast and foolproof to make, and very slimming. Cut this style so it is long and dramatic: a 32-in. to 35-in. finished length is average.

The finished skirt is full, but not bulky at the waist and hip. Use a lightweight knit, such as wool jersey, rayon, and Lycra blend; thin, drapey wovens; silk crepe; or the finest challis.

Use any eight-gore skirt pattern in your size. Cut ten gores instead of eight—five for the front and five for the back. (Buy one extra length of fabric to accommodate the two additional gores.)

Serge all the seams or straight-stitch and zigzag (p. 169) or pink (p. 168) the edges. No fitting is necessary. Apply a pull-on, elasticized waistband (pp. 203-205).

Mark the hem, and stitch it by hand or by machine (pp. 219-220). Topstitch if your skirt is made of a knit fabric.

# 11 | *Choosing Your Pattern*

Feeling good can be a direct result of looking good. Few garments are as flattering and comfortable as well-fitting pants. In order to qualify as such, pants must fit to perfection and be flawlessly smooth while you're standing, yet have just the right amount of ease so they are comfortable while you're sitting. And perfect-fitting pants must also allow you to perform all sorts of activities without binding, cutting between the cheeks, riding down in the back, riding up at the ankles, or feeling tight in the waist when you bend over. To top it all off, they must complement your figure!

But fit and comfort are not synonymous. Fit is how your pants look, while comfort is how they feel. When choosing a pants pattern, you should consider the activity for which the pants will be worn. What will be the purpose of these pants? Pants for bike riding will be different than the pants you slip into Monday morning for work. Next, you should consider the style of pants you want. This includes the silhouette—the shape or look pants give your body from a distance (see Figure Silhouettes and Proportions on p. 234)—and structure—the lines within the silhouette formed by the waist treatment, darts, pleats, zipper/closure, gathers, creases, and pockets (see Structural Details on p. 237). Before you can choose a pattern or consider the style of pants you want, though, you need to know differences between the three basic types of pants.

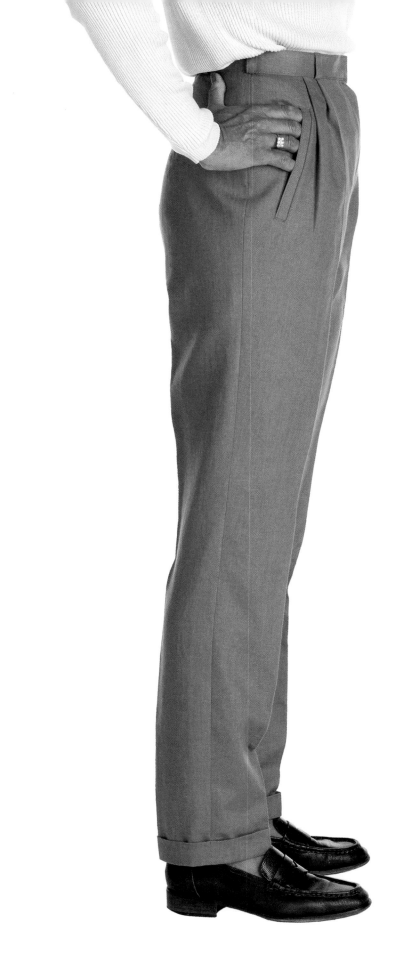

# The Basic Types of Pants

The word "pants" is a generic term that refers to three principle categories of fit between the waist and crotch. Jeans, slacks, and trousers—all pants—look and fit differently. Each is designed with varying amounts of ease to specifically accommodate different activities or purposes.

The distinguishing difference between jeans, slacks, and trousers is the length of the crotch extension (see the illustration below), which affects the way the pants fit or conform to the body (see the illustration on the facing page).

Traditional jeans have the shortest crotch extension because they closely contour the body in front and back. Body shape and figure variances are very visible. Jeans are designed for activities with a lot of movement and where a tight fit

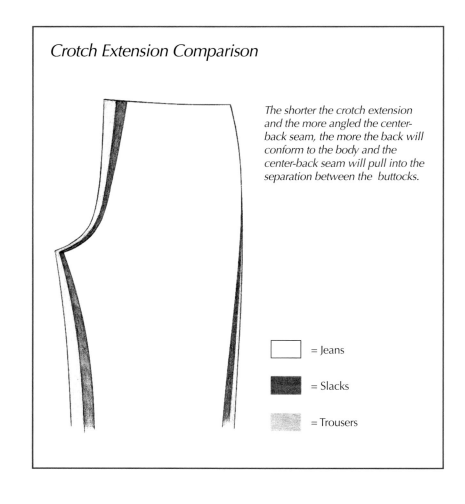

*Crotch Extension Comparison*

*The shorter the crotch extension and the more angled the center-back seam, the more the back will conform to the body and the center-back seam will pull into the separation between the buttocks.*

☐ = Jeans

■ = Slacks

▨ = Trousers

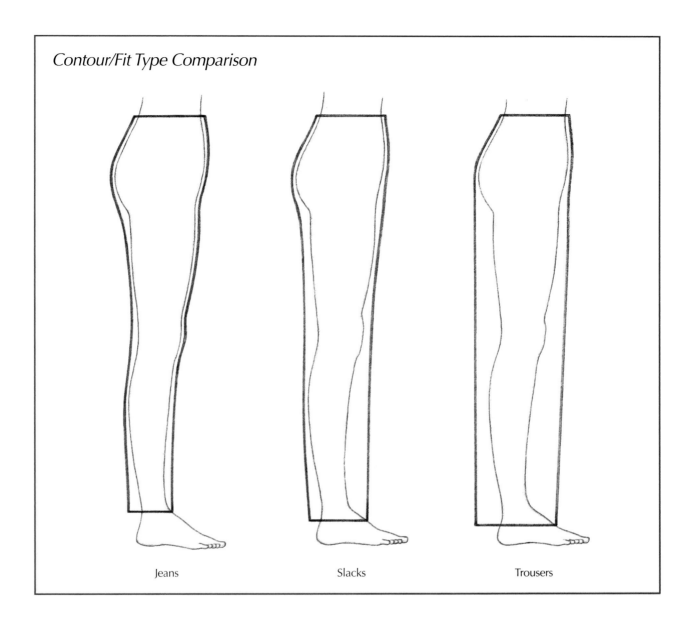

**Contour/Fit Type Comparison**

Jeans        Slacks        Trousers

is needed. Usually described as close fitting, jeans are a fitting challenge.

Slacks have a crotch extension that is longer than jeans but less than trousers. Slacks slightly contour the tummy and buttocks. Body shape is somewhat visible, and the slacks cup under the buttocks. Many pattern companies use this type of pants for their basic fitting shell because it allows you the flexibility to contour the fit closer to jeans or looser like trousers. Slacks are usually described as fitted or semi-fitted (see the left photo on p. 228).

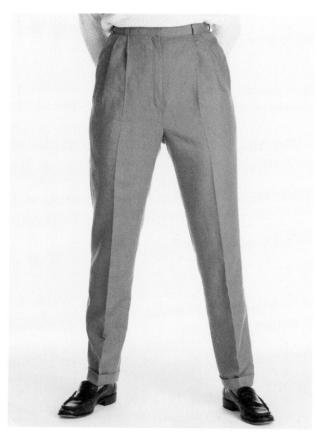

*Slacks are less fitted than jeans but more than trousers. They are a good choice for a basic pattern.*

*Trousers are the longest in the crotch area and the least fitted, making them particularly easy to sew and wear.*

Trousers have the longest crotch extension, conform the least to the contours of the body, and are the easiest pants to fit. They hang straight from the hip. Alterations are usually unnecessary if weight fluctuates slightly. Trousers are usually described as loose to very loose fitting (see the right photo above).

Selecting the correct type of pants pattern (jeans, slacks, trousers) will go a long way toward giving you the silhouette you want, as well as needed comfort. As a rule, the more the pants conform to the body, the harder they are to fit. Because of the basic design differences between the three types of pants, I do not recommend that you take a trousers pattern and try and fit it like jeans, or vice versa. For ease of fitting and sewing, consider choosing a pattern with limited pleats or gathers at the waist and a straight or wide (baggy) leg. Whether you are a beginner or an experienced sewer, this silhouette is complementary to a majority of figure types and is adaptable to all skill

levels, depending on the details you select. If you want to concentrate on fit or if pants are going to be a major staple in your wardrobe (meaning that you will be making more than one pair), consider selecting a basic pattern.

## Basic Patterns

A basic pattern, also known as a master, sloper, block, or foundation, is a simple, semi-fitted pattern with few sewing details. Usually this is a no-frills slack-type pattern. Because of its simplicity, it is used to refine the fit of pants. Once the fitting process has been refined, you emerge with a customized personal master pattern that you can use over and over. By making simple design changes, you can obtain an unlimited variety of styles and details with the assurance of a good fit. Ready-to-wear (RTW) and pattern companies use basic patterns to develop the stylized garments and patterns you buy.

There are many advantages to using a basic pattern. There is no guessing at ease amounts, and the adjustments are the same for each pair of pants you make for the same fit and pattern company. And you have the flexibility to change the style of your pants without being dependent on commercial patterns, so you'll never be out of fashion.

Most pattern companies offer fitting patterns, which include a pants front, back, and waistband. With some simple changes to a fitting pattern (discussed in Chapter 16), you can do your own creative designing with consistent and predictable results. Once you know what changes you need to make on a specific fitting pattern, those changes will automatically apply to every pattern from the same company. Your basic pattern also enables you to compare ease and fit of similarly styled garments from different pattern companies.

## Choosing a basic fitting pattern

If you are an experienced sewer, choose a pattern from the pattern company you normally use. If you've sewn very little, look through the various pattern books and go with the company whose designs appeal to you most. When selecting a pattern, keep it as simple as possible. If no fitting pattern is available, choose a slack-type pants. Details can be added after fitting.

Choose a pattern without pockets. Pants with side inseam pockets are easier to fit than pants with slant or Western-style pockets. This will give you a pattern with a full side front for easier fitting. Two darts or pleats on each side of the front and two darts on each side of the back make it easier to custom fit the pattern.

To determine the skill level needed for your pattern, refer to the terms used by the pattern companies to describe the fitting and sewing levels required to complete the pants. Descriptions of these terms, such as jiffy, beginner's choice, easy, average, and advanced, are found in the back of the pattern book. These are also clues as to the amount of time your pants will take.

## Choosing the correct size

A pattern size is only an estimate of what will possibly fit, and pattern companies don't label pattern sizes the same way. So it's important that you always consult the pattern measurement sizing chart (found on the back of the pattern or in the pattern book) for the pattern company you choose. Keep in mind that you're choosing a pattern size based on what goes into the pants, not based on RTW sizes. RTW has no standards for measurement sizing as pattern companies do. For example, my RTW pants range from size 4 to size 10. I measure for a size 14

If you have flat buttocks and/or thin legs, go down one additional pattern size.

pattern, but generally select a size 12. And I select a size 10 if the pants are described as loose or very loose fitting.

When measuring for a pattern size, do so based on your hip measurement. Snugly measure around the *fullest* part of your hip (the average fullest part is between 7 in. and 9 in. below the waist). Fit is affected by what you wear under your pants, so be sure you measure over under-garments and/or pantyhose. If your measurement is between sizes, choose the smaller size, even though you may be closer to the larger one. For example if your hip measurement is 39½ in., choose a size 14 with a 38-in. hip measurement instead of a size 16 with a 40-in. hip measurement.

Although your hip measurement is 39½ in. and you've chosen a size 14, drop down one addi-tional size to a 12 if you have an average figure and are not unusually full in the hips or thighs. This will prevent you from sewing pants with legs that are too full. If you have a flat buttocks, no buttocks, or thin legs, choose another size smaller, or a 10 in this case. This will eliminate the big legs and bagginess under your buttocks.

The paper pattern will measure larger than your measured size. For example, with 39½-in. hips using a size 14 pattern, the actual hip size of the completed garment may be 43½ in. This

information is frequently printed on the pattern. Because woven fabric pants are not meant to be skin tight, extra room needs to be incorporated in the form of ease.

In simple terms, ease is the difference between your body measurements and the finished pants measurement (includes wearing and fashion ease). When related to the pattern, ease is the difference between the size measurements on the back of the pattern envelope and the actual pattern measurements.

There are two types of pattern ease. The first is wearing ease, which allows a bit of additional room so reasonable movement is possible without constriction. Wearing ease is added in the fitting area (waist, hip, and crotch length). This can vary slightly between pattern companies.

The second type of pattern ease is fashion ease (sometimes called style or design ease). The amount of this ease is added to wearing ease and will vary with each pattern. Fashion ease is recognizable by the use of gathers, pleats, or extra fullness such as flare. You certainly don't need to add fashion ease, but you might be bored if all your gar-ments have the same silhouette. Different patterns that are the same size can measure differently because of the design ease that has been added.

Ease is a personal choice and should be determined in the measuring and fitting process.

## Reading the pattern envelope

Use the pattern envelope to determine how the garment is supposed to fit. Using this information wisely will result in greater satisfaction with the pattern you choose.

**Garment picture and description** The garment picture and description illustrate fabric ideas and drape. Sketches and drawings give you a better picture of the complete silhouette, including such design details as pocket styles, waist treatment, type and location of closure, darts or pleats, and how the pants are expected to fit. Terms such as straight, tapered, or flared are used to describe leg style.

**Fabrics and notions** To achieve the illustrated design, a listing of suitable fabrics, yardage, and notions, such as zippers, buttons, and hooks and eyes, to complete your pants are given.

**Width at the lower edge** The term "width at the lower edge" is used to describe the circumference of one leg at the hem. Compare the circumference with pants you own and like and choose a pattern with a descriptive style closest to the leg width you like. See the chart on the facing page for different lower edge leg widths.

**Finished length** The finished length is measured from side waist to finished bottom edge. This can be easily adjusted if it is different than your personal measurement.

*The pattern envelope is covered with information. Studying it carefully will help you to choose a pattern style that suits you, as well as the appropriate fabric and notions.*

# AVERAGE LEG STYLE WIDTH AT HEMLINE (in inches)

| SIZE | 6 | 8 | 10 | 12 | 14 | 16 | 18 | 20 | 22 | 24 |
|---|---|---|---|---|---|---|---|---|---|---|
| TAPERED | $13\frac{1}{4}$ | $13\frac{1}{4}$ | $14\frac{1}{4}$ | $14\frac{7}{8}$ | $15\frac{7}{8}$ | $16\frac{7}{8}$ | $17\frac{7}{8}$ | $18\frac{7}{8}$ | $19\frac{7}{8}$ | $20\frac{7}{8}$ |
| SLIGHTLY TAPERED | $15\frac{5}{8}$ | $16\frac{1}{4}$ | $16\frac{5}{8}$ | $17\frac{3}{8}$ | $18\frac{3}{8}$ | $19\frac{3}{8}$ | $20\frac{3}{8}$ | $21\frac{3}{8}$ | $22\frac{3}{8}$ | $23\frac{3}{8}$ |
| STRAIGHT | 19 | $19\frac{1}{2}$ | 20 | $20\frac{3}{4}$ | $21\frac{3}{4}$ | $22\frac{3}{4}$ | $23\frac{3}{4}$ | $24\frac{3}{4}$ | $25\frac{3}{4}$ | $26\frac{3}{4}$ |
| SLIGHTLY FLARED | $23\frac{1}{2}$ | 24 | $24\frac{1}{2}$ | $25\frac{1}{4}$ | $26\frac{1}{4}$ | $27\frac{1}{4}$ | $28\frac{1}{4}$ | $29\frac{1}{4}$ | $30\frac{1}{4}$ | $31\frac{1}{4}$ |
| FLARED | 26+ | $26\frac{1}{2}$+ | 27+ | $27\frac{3}{4}$+ | $28\frac{3}{4}$+ | $29\frac{3}{4}$ | $30\frac{3}{4}$ | $31\frac{3}{4}$ | $32\frac{1}{4}$ | $33\frac{1}{4}$+ |

**Pant leg styles**

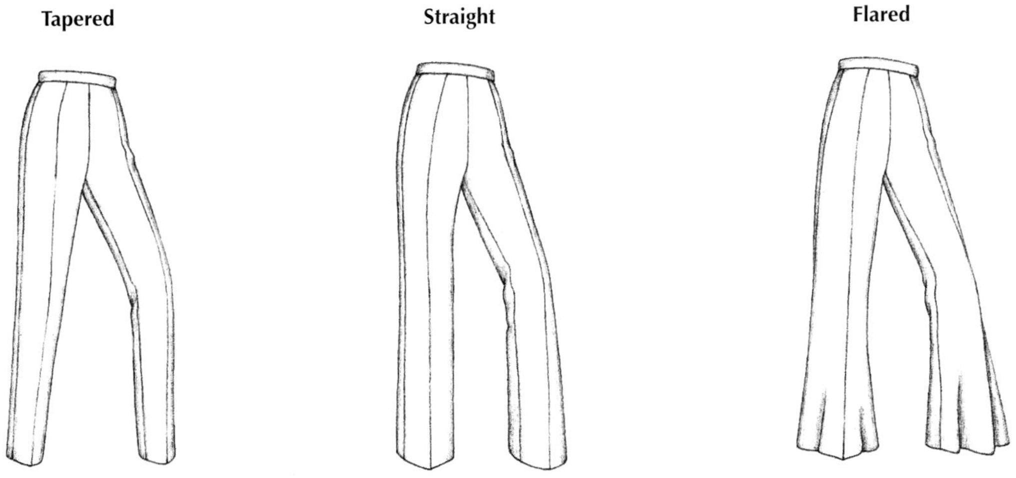

Tapered

Straight

Flared

# FIGURE SILHOUETTES AND PROPORTIONS

| FIGURE SILHOUETTE | OBJECTIVE TO ENHANCE SILHOUETTE | COMPLEMENTARY FIGURE-ENHANCING STYLES | COMPLEMENTARY STRUCTURAL DETAILS (see chart on p. 237) | AVOID |
|---|---|---|---|---|
| HOURGLASS (curvaceous, small waist, proportionately larger hips) | Minimize curves; elongate body | Straight or tapered; cropped; knickers; harem; trousers | Soft pleats; gathers | Patch pockets; horizontal lines at hip |
| TRIANGLE (wider or heavier below waist) | Minimize hips and thighs | Trousers; palazzo; harem; straight leg; raised waist; wide leg | Limited pleats or gathers at waist; creases | Over fitting in hip and thigh area; horizontal seams; gathers, pleats, or eye-catching details at hip; closely contoured styles (traditional jeans); excessively full styles |

**Figure silhouettes**

Hourglass    Triangle    Wedge    Rectangle    Thin    Oval

# FIGURE SILHOUETTES AND PROPORTIONS *(continued)*

| FIGURE SILHOUETTE | OBJECTIVE TO ENHANCE SILHOUETTE | COMPLEMENTARY FIGURE-ENHANCING STYLES | COMPLEMENTARY STRUCTURAL DETAILS | AVOID |
|---|---|---|---|---|
| WEDGE (narrow waist and hips, slender legs) | Widen hip area | Cropped trousers; pull-on/elastic waist; yoke | Wide or full pleats at waist; gathers | |
| RECTANGLE (no waist definition) | Create a more slender shape | Straight leg; cropped; hip yoke; trousers; dropped waist; tapered; raised waist | Soft gathers at waist; pleats | Patch pockets at hips; tight waistbands; spreading pleats; front closures; full gathers |
| THIN (narrow in waist and hips, few curves) | Create more fullness and shape | Flared; palazzo; harem; yoke; draped; wide leg | Patch pockets; horizontal pocket lines; gathers; soft unpressed pleats; cuffs | Tapered, extended vertical lines (creases); vertical welt pockets; excessively long pants; very slim pants |
| OVAL (full in waist and hips with prominent tummy) | Elongate and slim the body | Raised waist; straight leg; wide leg; tapered; trousers | Limited pleats or gathers at waist; creases; back or side closure; slanted or side-seam pockets; piped waist | Details that draw attention to hip area; spreading pleats; horizontal lines; fly zipper or front closure; excessive fullness or gathers |

# FIGURE SILHOUETTES AND PROPORTIONS *(continued)*

| FIGURE SILHOUETTE | OBJECTIVE TO ENHANCE SILHOUETTE | COMPLEMENTARY FIGURE-ENHANCING STYLES | COMPLEMENTARY STRUCTURAL DETAILS | AVOID |
|---|---|---|---|---|
| SHORT LEGS | Lengthen lower torso | Palazzo; wide leg; raised waist; tapered; straight leg; flared | Limited pleats, darts, gathers at waist; fly zipper; creases; vertical seaming (princess line) | Horizontal lines; cuffs; hip yokes; patch pockets; flap pockets |
| LONG LEGS | Shorten lower torso | Yoke; dropped waist | Cuffs; faced waistlines; flap pockets; horizontal yokes | Raised waist; pleats; pants that are too short; creases |
| EXTRA HEAVY | Lengthen and softly define the body | Trousers; wide leg; tapered; straight leg | Slim sewn-down pleats; creases; narrow or inconspicuous waistband | Too tight a fit; poor fit |
| SHORT/PETITE | Elongate the body | Jeans; trousers; tapered; straight leg | Vertical lines: pleats; creases; fly zipper; slant pockets; welt pockets | Too much fullness; pants that are too long; cuffs |

**Pants styles**

Trousers    Palazzo    Wide leg    Cropped    Draped    Harem    Tapered    Straight leg/stovepipe    Flared

# STRUCTURAL DETAILS

| WAIST-TREATMENT OPTIONS | DRAWSTRING OR ELASTICIZED WAIST | FACED WAIST (WAIST EDGE FINISHED) | FITTED WAISTBAND (separate piece usually 1¼ in. wide fitting slightly above natural waist) |
|---|---|---|---|
| | Full; gathered | Raised (above natural waist); yoke (shaped and fitted piece in high hip area); dropped (below natural waist) | Smooth; trousers; jean; dropped; limited pleats or gathers; draped |

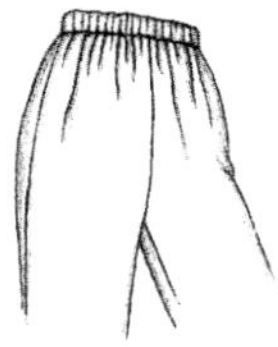

**Raised waist**

**Yoke**

**Dropped waist**

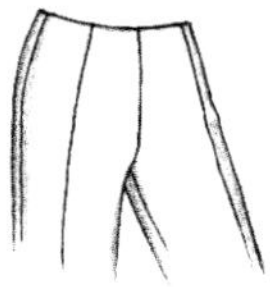

**Smooth**

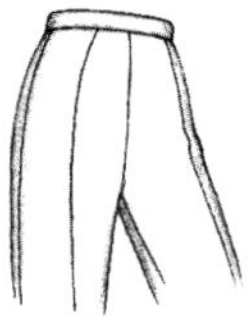

**Trousers**

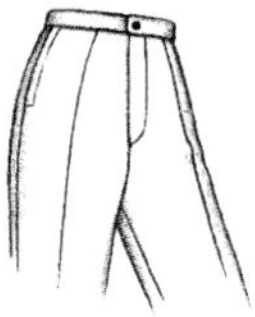

**Jean**

**Dropped waist**

**Limited pleats or gathers**

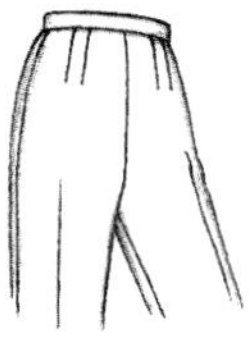

**Draped**

| POCKET OPTIONS | OUTSIDE | INSERTED | WELT |
|---|---|---|---|
| Can be decorative or functional; hidden or eye catching; vertical or horizontal. Depending on shape and placement, pockets can have a strong influence on silhouette. | **Patch pockets** | **Side seam** | |

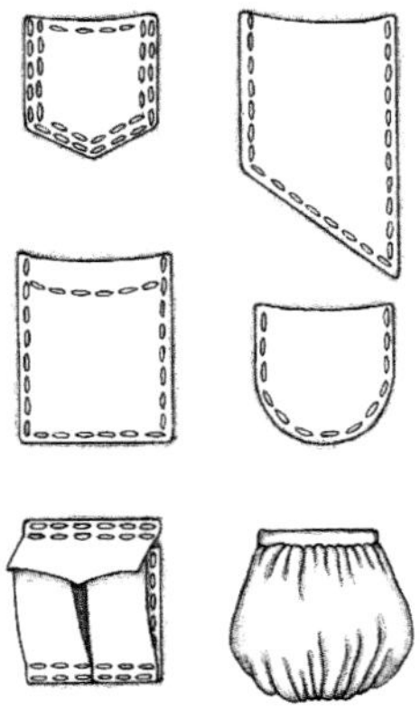

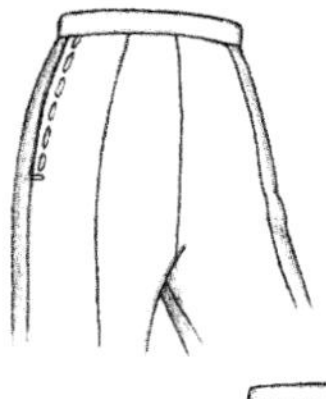

**Slant**

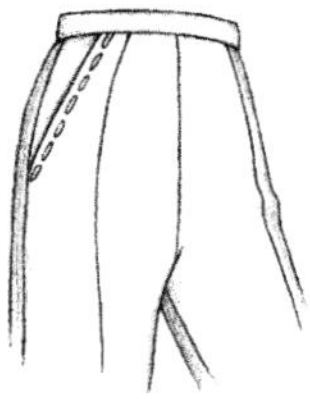

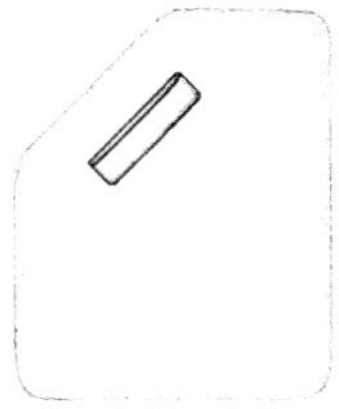

**Welt with flap**     **Bound**

# 12 Choosing Your Fabric

Fabric suitability depends on pattern style and personal silhouette. Weaves and fibers can be mixed together in a mind-boggling number of combinations. In most cases, the wrong fabric rather than poor sewing is responsible for the majority of garment failures.

Your silhouette or visual profile is directly influenced by the characteristics of the fabric you choose. If your goal is to conceal your body contours, look for fabrics that are a medium weight and have a smooth texture and a firm hand. Darker, duller colors visually decrease size and weight. On the other hand, choosing bulky or rough textures, light or bright colors, or shiny fabrics results in visually increasing both size and weight. Soft, stretchy fabrics can be clingy, revealing the contours of the body, or drapable and concealing, depending on the style of pants you've chosen.

When the pants style is created, the designer has specific fabrics in mind that will maintain the style lines of the garment. Every pattern envelope lists suggested fabrics, and although you are not obligated to select one of the recommended fabrics, it is a good starting point. With a basic knowledge of fabric categories, fiber performance, and your personal style (which we discussed in Chapter 11), you will be able to turn beautiful fabric and a great pattern into successful pants.

# Fashion Fabric

In addition to style and silhouette, your fashion fabric should blend or act as an accent color or texture and fit in with your current wardrobe. Wear and care should be compatible with your lifestyle and commitment.

Because natural fibers breathe, or allow airflow through the fibers, they are more comfortable to wear in very warm climates. Wool is a natural insulator. Because of its construction, a series of interlocking scales trap air and hold it while the air is warmed by the body. By choosing a fashion fabric with a high percentage of wool, silk, cotton, or linen, you will add to the wearing comfort and enjoyment of your pants. And you will feel more confident in your pants if you choose a fabric that is consistent with your personal style and image. For example, if you tend to be more conservative and wear classic styles you may not feel comfortable in a flamboyant bright, shiny red print, but better in a muted pumpkin linen.

By following a few simple guidelines your fabric choice will be a success for you and your pants. Look carefully at the pattern envelope for the most suitable fabrics. The first fabric is the best choice based on how the pattern was designed. You can expand your possibilities by choosing fabrics similar to those listed.

Ask yourself if the silhouette pictured calls for fabric that drapes softly, stands away from

*Some patterns call for a crisp linen, while others will only be successful in something with drape, and still others require a stretchy knit. Your fabric choice needs to match your pattern.*

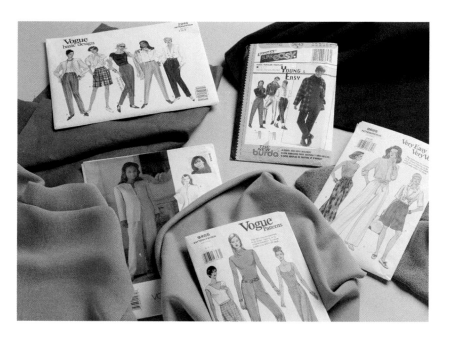

the body, clings closely, or poufs crisply. Your visual interpretation, as well as the list of suggested fabrics, will help you achieve the same silhouette. To do this, whatever fabric you choose must behave in the same way as the suggested fabrics, even if it has a different name or fiber content. Tailored pants styles will usually require crisp fabrics that hold their shape. Fuller styles that may have gathers require a soft fabric with draping qualities.

The following four classifications of fibers are important because they affect the performance, comfort, and care of the fabric. Choosing natural over synthetic fibers is a tradeoff between comfort and care. What you gain in comfort you lose in care.

Fiber types affect how we physically feel in a garment. How we look is equally, if not more, important. How a fabric hangs or drapes on your body can affect your psychological comfort, as well as your silhouette. Poor choices can make your pants uncomfortable to wear and incompatible with your pattern or personal style.

## Natural fibers

Natural fibers are those made from animal or vegetable sources. They include wool, silk, cotton, and linen. Fabrics from these fibers are comfortable to wear

*Whether you choose a fabric that is natural, man-made, synthetic, or a blend, your choice should be guided by your pattern's suggestions, your sewing skill, and the visual profile you want to create.*

because of wicking qualities. Wicking refers to the ability of a fabric to pull moisture away from the body because the fibers can absorb moisture, unlike synthetic fibers. The care of these fibers and their ability to resist wrinkles varies.

## Man-made/ transitional fiber

Rayon is a man-made/ transitional fiber because it is composed of cellulosic fibers whose natural source is wood pulp. The fibers are then chemically processed. Although the rayon fiber is not found in nature, it is derived from a natural source, unlike synthetic fibers, which are derived from chemicals like petroleum and then chemically processed.

## Synthetic fibers

Synthetic fibers are derived from a chemical source and are chemically processed. These fibers include polyester, nylon, acrylic, and spandex. These fibers are less comfortable to wear than natural fibers because they have no wicking qualities and they are prone to static electricity. However, they are machine washable, resist wrinkling, and hold their shape well.

## Fabric blends

Blends combine the best of two or more fibers, resulting in a superior fabric. One such example is a blend of 65% cotton and 35% polyester. The fabric will give you the comfort and wicking qualities of cotton and the wrinkle resistance of polyester. For a fiber to make a significant difference in fabric performance its composition must be 35% to 50% of the fabric. The exception to that rule is spandex. With as little as 3% to 5% of spandex added to a fabric, significant stretch is achieved, particularly in woven fabrics. The look and feel of the woven fabric is maintained, but you get a closer fit with less wrinkling and more comfort. The fabric "gives" and moves with you as you stress it and recovers without bagginess.

## General considerations

Crisp fabrics such as linen, denim, chino, gabardine, ultrasuede, silk pongee, and corduroy are well suited to tailored styles such as classic trousers or slacks that require a fabric that holds its shape and incorporates darts, pleats, or tucks. Soft fabrics such as challis, wool or silk jersey, wool crepe, crepe de Chine, and interlock knits drape softly around the body and make up best in fuller styles or in styles with gathers and few structured lines.

Whether you choose a plain or printed fabric will depend on your pattern choice. The style and the fabric should never compete for attention. Internal pattern details such as pockets, topstitching, and pleats show up better in a plain fabric. A printed fabric works best with a very basic style pants with few internal pattern details.

Easy-to-handle fabrics are those that are firmly woven, are of medium weight, have a smooth texture, and are a solid color or have a small all-over design with no matching required. Construction inaccuracies are less prominent.

The most important consideration when choosing fabric, even more important than fiber content, is the "hand." This is a term used to describe the stiffness vs. softness of a fabric. It refers to the drapability of a fabric: how it will hang and move on your body. Choosing a fabric with the wrong hand means the intended silhouette will most likely be wrong also. Fabric hand is determined by the fiber content, construction (type of weave or knit), and finishes.

When reading the list of suggested fabrics, don't interpret a generic fabric suggestion such as gabardine to mean only wool gabardine. Gabardine refers to a specific type of weave or construction used in all gabardines, whether they are wool, silk, cotton, rayon, or a synthetic. It also implies a suggested weight, hand, or drape of the fabric, in this case, gabardine.

# Lining Fabrics

A lining is a duplication of your pants without a zipper or waistband. If you choose to line your pants, you will be making two separate garments (except for the zipper and waistband). Lined pants are more durable and more comfortable because slippery, smooth fabrics feel wonderful next to your skin. They wrinkle less, and the lining reduces clinging. A lining can also make a sheer fabric more opaque.

Lining fabrics should be lightweight, smooth, soft, and compatible in care with the fashion fabric. They should also be anti-static, wrinkle resistant, and comfortable to wear.

*Lined pants can be more comfortable to wear and feel more luxurious. Choose your lining from rayon, polyester, or silk fabrics. Yardage requirements may be different than for your fashion fabric.*

Consider natural or man-made vs. synthetic fabrics, weighing differences in wicking qualities and compatibility with fashion fabric. If possible, choose a lining fabric with similar wicking characteristics as your fashion fabric for added comfort. Firmly woven fabrics with plain or twill weaves wear better. Finally, the color of the lining should coordinate with the color of the fashion fabric. Good lining choices are lightweight rayon, lightweight polyester, and lightweight silk, such as silk crepe de Chine.

Lining fabrics can be difficult to sew because they are thin, slippery, and difficult to control and because it's hard to prevent puckered seams. Additionally, excessive raveling and improper pressing can present problems to a beginner sewer. Try lining the same pair of pants the second time around, after you have learned basic pants-fitting and construction skills.

# Pocket Lining Fabric

For soft, slippery, durable, and non-bulky pockets, I prefer a stable warp knit or tricot for the pocket lining. You can certainly use your fashion fabric, lining, or pocketing (a durable material made specifically for this). Regardless of which pocket lining fabric you choose, you should face the pocket opening edges to give the appearance that the whole pocket is made from fashion fabric.

# Other Materials

Today there are so many wonderful notions that whatever you need, it's probably available. For every notion there can be several choices. Choosing thread, for example, is no longer a simple matter of color choice. You can choose from silk, silk-finished cotton, cotton polyester, two-ply, three-ply, and top-stitching weights. There are four kinds of zippers, three kinds of tape, and two kinds of coils. So you see it is important to be knowledgeable about what is available, as well as under-standing the type of notion you'll need for your pattern and fabric choice if your project is to be a success. Try different brands of the same product. You may find you like one brand over another. Several times a year, shop the notions department of your favorite fabric store or catalog supplier to see what's new that can make your sewing easier.

## Interfacing

A fitted waistband or waist facing retains its shape better if it is interfaced. Interfacing gives it support and stability so it will not collapse, wrinkle, or curl. Interfacing can be fusible or sew in. Both are available in woven and non-woven types. Many

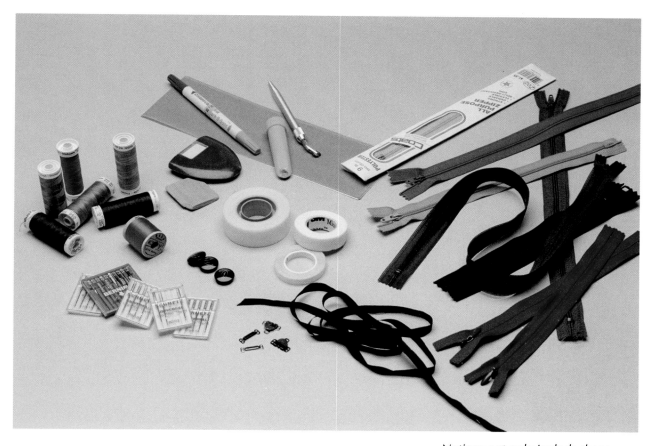

*Notions not only include those things listed on your pattern envelope needed to complete your project but also specialty items that can make your sewing easier, faster, and better.*

fusibles come in precut widths, with perforated foldlines for easy and accurate application, and can be purchased prepackaged or by the yard. Your choice of waist interfacing will affect the comfort and appearance of your finished waist treatment. For comfort, choose a soft interfacing material, such as a fusible, rather than a stiff interfacing, such as Ban-Rol.

## Notions

Consult your pattern envelope for a specific listing of type, number, or sizes of notions. Additional recommendations I

suggest that are not found on the envelope are double-sided basting or transparent tape for pinless zipper applications and a polyester zipper longer than requested because it is easier to install and simple to shorten. If using a metal zipper, purchase the size specified on your pattern envelope.

I prefer using cotton-wrapped all-purpose polyester thread on knits, synthetic fabrics, or blends with synthetics. The thread "gives" with knits without seams popping, and its strength is compatible with synthetic fabrics. I use 100% cotton in size

## MACHINE NEEDLES AND STITCH LENGTH

| FABRIC WEIGHT | NEEDLE SIZE | STITCH SETTING (in mm stitches per inch—spi) |
|---|---|---|
| Lightweight | 60/9 to 70/10 | 1.5mm to 1.7mm/ 15 spi to 18 spi |
| Medium weight | 70/10 to 80/12 | 2mm to 2.5mm/ 12 spi |
| Heavyweight | 90/14 to 100/16 | 2.5mm to 3mm/ 10 spi |
| Very heavy | 100/16 to 120/20 | 3mm to 4mm/6 spi to 8 spi |

50 with natural fibers—I have had fabrics rip before the thread breaks using the all-purpose polyester because the thread is stronger than the fiber when stressed. You can restitch the seam, but repairing the fabric is more difficult.

Simple pants take 125 yards to 150 yards of thread, not including seam finishes or topstitching. Choose a shade slightly darker than your fabric. For multicolor fabric, match the dominant color. Thread weight should be compatible with the fabric for pucker-free seams. For microfibers, use a lightweight or fine thread like two-ply 60 weight.

Specialty needles may be available for your machine for specific fabrics such as natural or synthetic leathers and suedes, microfibers, and denim.

# Fabric Yardage

Pattern yardage requirements for the view, size, and fabric width are calculations, not estimates, and are figured quite close. Therefore, purchase extra fabric if you anticipate pattern adjustments. Purchase two times the intended length-adjustment amount. Width adjustments may require additional width and length, so purchase yardage for a size three to four times larger than you intend to make or ¼ yard to ⅜ yard more if using

45-in.-wide fabric. You can precisely determine the specific yardage required for your adjusted pants pattern by doing a trial layout and marking off 45-in. and 60-in. widths. Then measure the length each requires.

Natural fibers, particularly loosely woven cottons and knits, can shrink. Allow 4 in. to 5 in. per yard for shrinkage for cotton knits and 2 in. to 3 in. per yard for other knits. In addition, allow for straightening of the grain if the fabric has been cut rather than torn. An extra ¼ yard should be enough to straighten the grain.

If you have decided to line your pants and your pattern does not call for lining, purchase fabric according to the 45-in. width yardage chart, or purchase two lengths (your side measurement from waist to floor) to allow for pattern adjustments.

# Processing Your Fabric

Before laying out the pattern, you'll need to pretreat your fabric the same way you intend to care for your pants once they are completed. This is the best way to ensure that your pants will look and fit the same after their first laundering or dry cleaning. Doing this also eliminates future

shrinkage and removes temporary finishes or sizing, thus eliminating sewing problems.

To preshrink or pretreat your fabric, check the fabric care label on the bolt if possible when purchasing the fabric and treat as stated. If you're unable to get the care instructions, here are some general guidelines.

Woven cottons should be washed (by hand or machine) and dried (by line or machine). Cotton knits should be washed and dried several times to maximize shrinkage.

For rayons, linens, silks, and blends, wash using a pH-balanced detergent. I have successfully washed all of these fabrics. However, I caution you to use care and always do a 6-in. by 6-in. sample test. If you don't like the way the sample looks after washing, drying, and pressing, or if it has shrunk considerably, *do not* pretreat the fabric that way. Rayon, linen, silk, and delicate synthetic blends are best soaked in tepid water and mild detergent for 15 to 20 minutes, then line-dried.

For dry-cleanable wool, roll a single thickness of the fabric in an evenly damp sheet (see the photo on p. 248). Let it rest until the wool is thoroughly damp. To dry, lay a single thickness of the wool flat. Another option is to

*If you don't feel like going to the dry cleaner to preshrink your wool, you can roll it up in a damp sheet instead.*

Most washable fabrics can be dry-cleaned. Dry-clean-only fabrics are not necessarily washable. Beware of warnings, special exceptions, and instructions. Be sure to pretreat your linings, interfacing, and any trims, too.

have your dry cleaner professionally steam (no need to clean) your yardage. Do the same for other dry-cleanable fabrics, or thoroughly steam a single thickness of fabric on a flat surface, holding the iron ½ in. above the fabric. Let the fabric rest until it is no longer damp.

## Truing the Fabric

Good fit and professional appearance depend on fabric that has been made thread perfect and trued. Making your fabric thread perfect means that the last crosswise thread at each end of your woven fabric can be pulled all the way across the width without breaking. There

are two methods for making your fabric thread perfect, and both are pretty easy.

The first method you can use is to tear quickly across the crosswise grain. Clip through the selvage about 1 in. Hold the fabric on each side of the clip firmly and pull to tear. Press the torn edge flat. Keep in mind that not all fabrics can be torn.

The second method is to pull a thread. This can be done on any woven fabric without distorting the grain or finish. Clip through the selvage about 1 in. From the clipped area, find a crosswise thread and pull it (it doesn't have to be removed, just dislodged enough to provide a

*You can find the crossgrain of your fabric by clipping into the selvage, pulling a crosswise thread, and then cutting along it. When you pull, be sure to do so gently so that the thread doesn't break.*

line to cut by), as shown in the photo above. Cut along the crosswise thread.

Now true the fabric by folding it in half lengthwise and matching the selvages. The two cut ends just straightened should form a right angle with the selvage. The fabric should be smooth and flat. Natural-fiber fabric can be steamed and gently tapped with the sole plate of the iron in a lengthwise and crosswise direction to achieve this.

Some fabrics acquire a permanent memory and resist alignment. These fabrics can be trued by making a lengthwise fold with selvages together and using an L-square to form a straight crosswise grain. Draw in the crossgrain on the wrong side using a fabric erasable marker or chalk, then cut on this line through both layers of fabric.

Fold knits as evenly as possible, making sure the ribs (comparable to lengthwise grain) are not twisted at the foldline. This fold will act as the straight-grain guide when pinning your pattern.

# 13 Getting the Right Fit

Your appearance is enhanced by how well your clothes fit. Most of us with less-than-ideal figures can direct attention away from figure variations if our clothes fit well. If you follow my fitting process, you will enjoy a sense of accomplishment and feel more self-confident in what you wear. Pants are not difficult to sew. However, fitting them on yourself can be frustrating. Even with a three-way mirror, you may see the problem, but reaching it and knowing how to correct it is another story.

Of all your garments, pants require the most intricate adjustment and fitting techniques. Commercial pattern adjustment lines do not always correspond to your body proportions. The pants can be too big or too small because ease amounts have been interpreted differently by you and by the designer. Your individual figure variances have not been addressed. The result is ill-fitting and uncomfortable pants.

In this chapter, personalizing your pattern and determining ease will be done by calculation instead of guesswork. Follow along as I lead you through the steps of measuring body and pattern so you can determine your fit before cutting your fabric. By working through this process you will be able to measure and adjust any pattern where fit is important.

# Taking and Comparing Measurements

I am about 5 ft. 7 in. Although my back waist length measurement matches the pattern for my size, I am proportionally shorter on top and longer below my waist. Consequently, the length and proportion of a pants pattern is never correct for me. I always need to adjust it in several places. Pattern companies understand we all have curves in relatively standardized places, but the distance between these parts varies from one person to another.

I have taken the same basic style of pants with the same ease, detailing, and amount of darting from different pattern companies and made them up in the full range of sizes. In my fitting classes, it is interesting to see how the same size pattern from one pattern company fits different shapes. Also be aware that using the same size does not guarantee consistency of fit between companies. Having hand-drafted patterns as well as used computer-aided drafting programs, I'm not sure there is a "perfect" pattern. There are always some fitting refinements that can be done.

Pattern companies do not label patterns as thoroughly as I will have you label your pattern. By identifying specific body points and relating them to your pattern, you will have a better understanding of why specific adjustments are necessary and where to make them, regardless of the pattern you choose.

For those of you who've had pants fitting problems and those who have yet to sew your first pair of pants, when you understand why there are differences between your measurements and the pattern's, where they occur on the pattern and body, and how to correct them, you will be more likely to enjoy the measuring and adjusting process because you will then be successful in achieving a good fit. To start this process, you must first mark and measure your body. You will then repeat this on your pattern at the same points/positions as marked and measured on you.

## Preparing to measure your body

Accurate measuring begins with a good foundation. For measuring, wear panty hose over any undergarments you will normally wear under your pants. Wear shoes that have the heel height you most often wear. When measuring, you will need to enlist the help of a friend and gather the following "tools":

## Pants/Body Terminology and Relationship

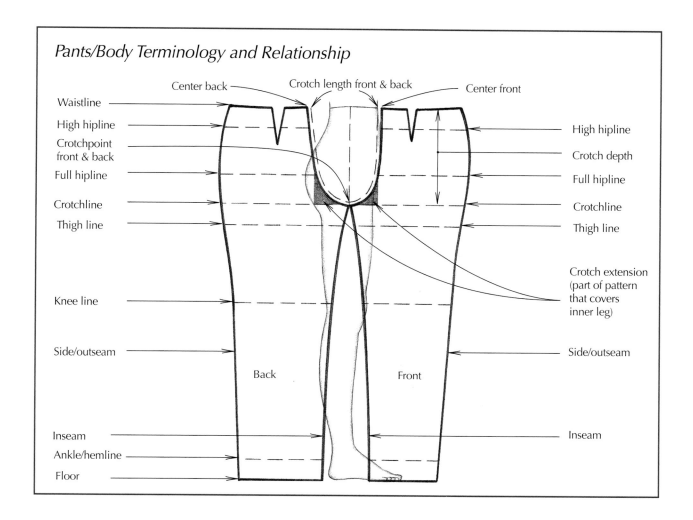

- long mirror
- tape measure
- 4 pieces of ¼-in.-wide elastic that are long enough to fit around your hips
- ¾-in.- to 1 in.-wide Ban-Rol (not elastic) that is 4 in. longer than your waist measurement
- straight pins
- several pieces of ¼-in.-wide masking tape, each about 18 in. long
- Measurement Chart (see p. 254)

## Establishing body reference points

You will now establish five key body reference points: waist, high hip, full hip, thigh, and knee. Later these same five reference points will be established on your pattern. You will then be able to compare your measurements with the pattern's measurements. Differences between your measurements and your pattern's will signal a need for a pattern adjustment. Measurements,

# MEASUREMENT CHART

| | MEASURE-MENTS | 1 BODY | 2 MINIMUM WEARING EASE | 3 DESIGN EASE | 4 I NEED (add columns 1, 2, and 3) | 5 PATTERN | 6 DIFFERENCE (+ you are larger; - you are smaller) | 7 ADJUSTMENT AMOUNT (+ or -) |
|---|---|---|---|---|---|---|---|---|
| LENGTH | 1. Crotch depth | | | | | | | |
| LENGTH | 2. Waist to knee | | | | | | | |
| LENGTH | 3. Waist to floor | | | | | | | |
| WIDTH | 4. Waist | | 1½ in. | | | | | See chart on p. 268, col. 1 or 2 |
| WIDTH | 5. High hip ( ) | | 1 in. | | | | | See chart on p. 268, col. 1 or 2 |
| WIDTH | 6. Full hip ( ) | | 2 in. | | | | | See chart on p. 268, col. 1 or 2 |
| WIDTH | 7. Thigh ( ) | | 2 in. | | | | | See chart on p. 268, col. 3 |
| LENGTH | 8. Crotch length | | | | | | | |

observations, and analysis of your body will help you achieve the best fit (see the drawing on the facing page).

First, have your helper visually divide your side view in half using masking tape. Begin at the waist and go down to knee level (see the left photo on p. 256). This tape should divide your leg in half from waist to hem if the tape were extended that far.

*Waist* Establish your waist position by securing the Ban-Rol around your waist and snugging it to your personal degree of comfort. Pin it securely in place. Make sure the size is also comfortable while sitting. Readjust if necessary. Make sure you have positioned the Ban-Rol where you want your pants waistband to fit. The accuracy of all other measurements depends on the correct positioning of this reference point. Your waist is not

# AN OVERVIEW OF MEASURING AND ADJUSTING PROCEDURES

This is an important and sequential process. Necessary pattern adjustments will be made based on a comparison of personal and pattern measurements. The accuracy and adjustments require that you follow this sequence.

1. Establish reference points on your body.

2. Measure your body. Record on your Measurement Chart.

3. Establish general reference points on the pattern.

4. Establish lengthening/shortening lines on the pattern.

5. Measure pattern lengths and compare them with your length measurements.

6. Make necessary length adjustments.

7. Establish your width levels (distance from waist) on pattern.

8. Measure pattern widths and compare with your width measurements.

9. Make necessary width adjustments.

10. Make refining adjustments that apply based on figure observations.

11. Measure the pattern crotch length.

12. Make crotch length adjustments.

13. True the pattern.

## Body Measurements

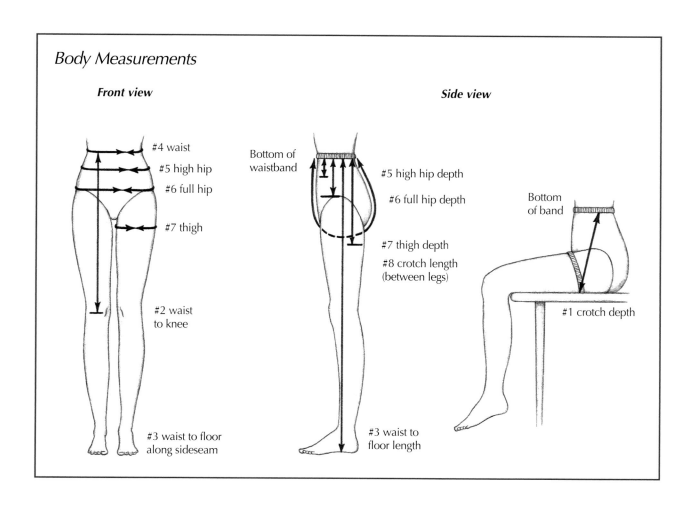

**Front view**

#4 waist
#5 high hip
#6 full hip
#7 thigh
#2 waist to knee
#3 waist to floor along sideseam

**Side view**

Bottom of waistband
#5 high hip depth
#6 full hip depth
#7 thigh depth
#8 crotch length (between legs)
#3 waist to floor length

Bottom of band
#1 crotch depth

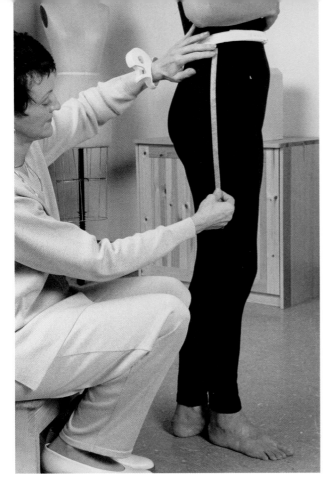

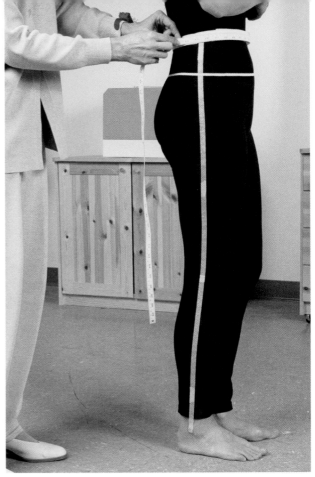

*Before establishing your reference points, have a helper visually divide your side view in half with a piece of tape. This only needs to be done on one side.*

*The waist is measured over Ban-Rol. With elastic, mark the high-hip level parallel to the waist where the tummy protrudes the most at center front.*

necessarily the top band of your panty hose or undergarment. Leave the band in place until all measurements have been completed. Always measure from the bottom of the Ban-Rol.

**High hip** If you do not have a tummy or are not fleshy in the area just below your waist, skip this step. If you are a bit fleshy here, turn sideways and determine the point on your abdomen where your tummy protrudes the most (the apex of

the curve). Mark this point with a small piece of tape. Measure from the bottom of the Ban-Rol at center front to this point. Repeat this measuring and marking with tape the same distance at each side and at center back. Tie a piece of elastic around your waist at this level (see the right photo above). Pin the elastic to your undergarments at these four marks to prevent slippage.

**Full hip** Tie another piece of elastic around your body where

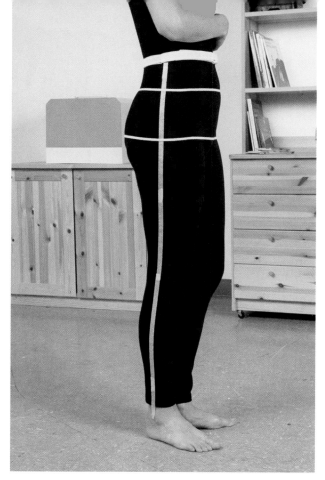

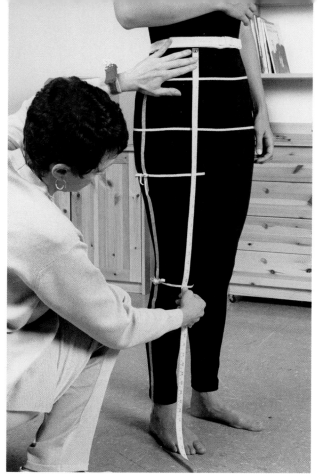

*The full-hip line is parallel to the floor and at the level where the buttocks protrudes the most.*

*The middle of the knee is marked with elastic. The waist to knee measurement is taken down the center of the leg.*

your buttocks protrudes the most. Position the elastic so it is parallel to the floor at the sides and back (see the left photo above). Pin the elastic to your undergarments at front, sides, and back.

**Thigh** Tie the third piece of elastic around one leg where your leg meets your torso.

**Knee** Tie the last piece of elastic around the leg at mid knee.

## MEASURING FIVE REFERENCE POINTS

Use a purchased pair of pants as a guide for fit. Measure them just as you did for your body, in the same places. The more precise you are, the more accurate this fitting tool will be.

To figure crotch depth (measurement #1), measure the side seam from the bottom of the waistband or the natural waistline to the finished hemline. Measure the inseam. Subtract the inseam measurement from the side length. Note measurements for any other areas for which you like the fit. You may use different pants for different measurements. Also note the style of pants for each—jeans, slacks, or trousers.

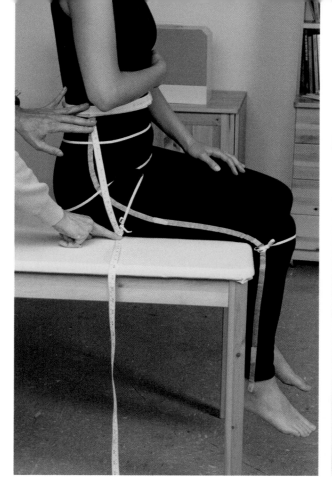

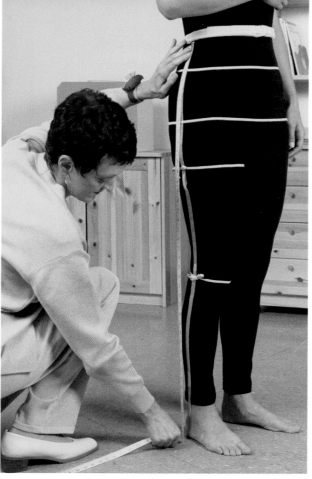

*When measuring crotch depth, sit on a table with your knees against the edge. Measure from the side waist to the point where the thigh elastic meets the table.*

*The waist-to-floor measurement is taken by following the body contour to hip level then dropping straight to the floor. Measure the right and left sides. Record the longer measurement.*

## Measuring length and width/circumference

Length and width measurements are arranged in the order adjustments will be made on your pattern, proceeding from the top to the bottom of the Measurement Chart (see p. 254).

After completing your measurements, you will make all pattern length adjustments except crotch length, beginning first with the crotch depth. An adjustment in the crotch depth will affect all other subsequent pattern length measurements. It is easier and more efficient if you proceed with your adjustments sequentially (follow numbers 1 through 7 in the left-hand column on the Measurement Chart on p. 254). After completing your pattern length adjustments, it's time for the width measurements. They are positioned at the same level (distance from waist) as measured on your body. The final measurement, crotch length, won't be made until after all of the other measurements are made.

**Crotch depth** You will need a table or countertop to sit on for this measurement. Adjust the thigh elastic so it is against your crotch at the inseam. The elastic should be parallel to the floor at the outside leg, so pin here if necessary to prevent movement. Sit up straight on a flat surface so that the backs of your knees are against the vertical edge. Measure on an angle from the side middle-waist marking to where the sitting surface and the elastic meet (see the left photo on the facing page). Record the measurement in column 1 of your Measurement Chart (see p. 254).

**Waist to knee** Measure down the middle front leg to the knee mark (see the right photo on p. 257). Record the measurement in column 1.

**Waist to floor** Measure the side length to the floor following the curve of your body to about hip level, then straight to the floor (see the right photo on the facing page). Measure both sides. Record the longer measurement in column 1.

**Waist** Measure the circumference of your waist over the Ban-Rol. Record the measurement in column 1. It is important to note here that although you may have a measurement of 30 in., that does not mean that 15 in. are proportioned from side to side in the front and 15 in. side to side in the back. You may be proportioned unevenly with, for example, 18 in. in the front and 12 in. in the back. If that's the case, then later, when making a waist adjustment on your pattern, add more width to the front, where it is needed, than the back. This will give a better balance to the side seam. If the adjustment amount is added equally to the front and back, the side seam will pull toward the front about waist level because the front part of the body needs more fabric.

**High hip** If you marked your high hip with a piece of elastic, walk the tape around the body at that level, holding it as you go to prevent it from slipping off the elastic line. Record the circumference in column 1. You should also make a notation of the distance from the waist, in the parentheses in the column titled Measurements (see the Measurement Chart on p. 254).

**Full hip** Repeat the same procedure as for high hip.

**Thigh** Adjust the leg elastic in the thigh area so it is parallel to the floor and around the fullest part. The positioning may be the same or different than when positioned for the crotch-depth measurement. Measure the thigh circumference at the elastic

## PATTERN EASE CHART INTERPRETATION

| PATTERN FIT DESCRIPTION | HIP FITTING EASE INCORPORATED | DESIGN EASE INCORPORATED | TOTAL PATTERN EASE INCLUDED |
|---|---|---|---|
| Close fitting | 2 in. | 0 in. | 2 in. |
| Fitted | 2 in. | 1 in. | 3 in. |
| Semi-fitted | 2 in. | 1 in. to 2 in. | 3 in. to 4 in. |
| Loose fitting | 2 in. | 2 in. to 4 in. | 4 in. to 6 in. |
| Very loose fitting | 2 in. | Over 4 in. | Over 6 in. |

level. Record the measurement in column 1. Measure from the bottom of the Ban-Rol along the side of the tape marking to the thigh elastic level. Make a notation of the distance from the waist in parentheses in the column titled Measurements (see the Measurement Chart on p. 254).

**Crotch length** Measure from the bottom of the Ban-Rol at center front to center back, between your legs. The tape should be lightly touching your body. Record the measurement in column 1.

## Finishing up the Measurement Chart

Having finished all body length and width measurements, you are ready to complete column 4 on your Measurement Chart. All pants patterns designed for woven fabrics incorporate a minimum amount of wearing ease in the hip for movement and comfort. In addition to wearing ease, design ease is added to vary the style or look. Design ease includes extra fullness represented by gathers, pleats, tucks, or flare. For the full hip, refer to the chart above for the amount to enter in column 3—Design ease—of your Measurement Chart. To determine the approximate design ease that has been incorporated into your pattern, read the description on the back of your pattern envelope to give you a fitting clue. Choose the "inch" amount of design ease on the chart that corresponds to the pattern fit description. If there are no clues, carefully look at the style of your pants. Traditional jeans are usually close fitting; slacks are fitted or semi-fitted; trousers are loose; and styles that are very full or have wide legs are very loose fitting.

Put the tape measure around your full hip. To the tape measurement add 2 in. (minimum wearing ease). Then add the design ease amount for your particular pattern as determined on the chart. Is this the total amount of ease (fullness) you want in the hip area? Increase or decrease the amount of design ease to fit your personal preference. Record the amount of design ease you prefer or that corresponds to your pattern's fit description. Keep in mind this is additional ease in excess of the 2 in. you need for wearing comfort. If you change the design ease amount, you may be changing the style of the pants pattern as it was originally intended, in which case you should reevaluate your pattern choice. Trying to change your pattern into something it wasn't originally designed for can create more problems than you want to solve. Once you've determined

the ease measurements, add columns 1, 2, and 3 on your Measurement Chart, and record the totals in column 4.

Take a few minutes to make some observations about your figure. Look at your body from the front or back and side. Check those observations that correspond to your body (see the drawing on p. 262). These observed variances refer to the refining adjustments you need to make to your pattern after all length and width adjustments have been completed. Instructions for refining adjustments are included later in this chapter (see p. 274).

# Establishing Pattern Reference Points

When you have completed marking and measuring your body, you are ready to do these same things on your pattern. Press your tissue pattern pieces with a warm, dry iron. Patterns are generally made and marked in one of the following ways: those that have seam allowances included and the seamline marked; those that do not have seam allowances included and therefore the seamline is not marked; and those that have seam allowances included but the seamline is not marked, as in multisized patterns. Look at your pattern to see if the seamline is

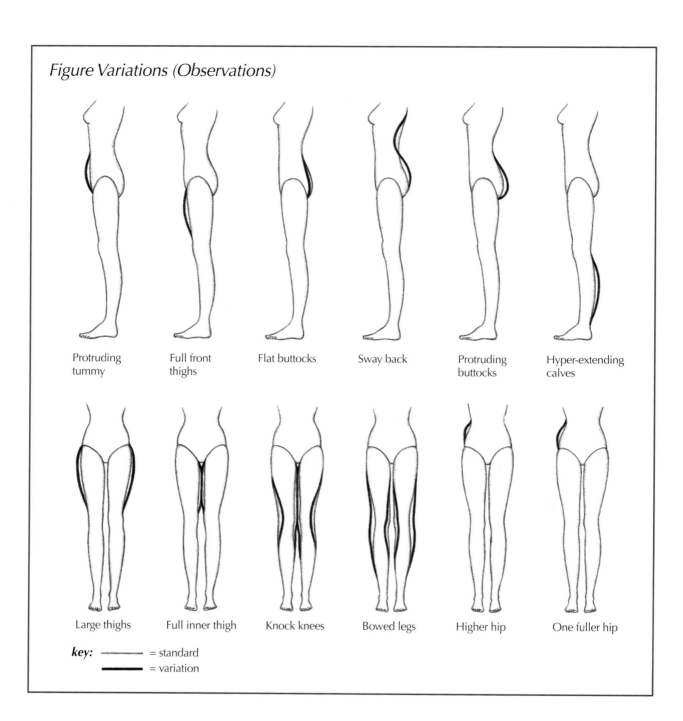

*Figure Variations (Observations)*

Protruding tummy

Full front thighs

Flat buttocks

Sway back

Protruding buttocks

Hyper-extending calves

Large thighs

Full inner thigh

Knock knees

Bowed legs

Higher hip

One fuller hip

**key:** ——— = standard

——— = variation

marked. A broken line inside the pattern cutting line will indicate this.

## Preparing your pattern

If your pattern does not have the seamline marked but does include a seam allowance (usually ⅝ in.), make sure you confirm the amount of the seam allowance by looking on the pattern or in the instructional guide sheet included with your pattern. With multisized patterns, specific pattern pieces are marked with three or more distinctly different cutting lines for each size. Multisizing makes adjusting your pattern somewhat easier because you can transition from one line (size) to another while cutting. For example, if your waist is a size 12 but your hips are a 16, you would gradually cut toward the size 16 cutting line from the waist. Not all patterns come multisized. Therefore, I will guide you through marking similar reference points on your tissue pattern and measuring lengths and widths to determine what adjustments need to be made to correspond to your measurements. This will result in a more precise fit. Learning to do this will enable you to adjust any pattern, multisized or not.

If you have determined that your tissue pattern does not have the seamlines marked but does have seam allowances included, you will need to mark them by hand.

This may seem time-consuming, but it means that measuring your pattern later will be less confusing and easier. If your pattern doesn't include seam allowances or if the seamlines are marked, you can skip marking them in.

Seamlines should be marked along the following pattern edges: waist, side, inseam, and center front and center back through the crotch curve. If your seam allowance is ⅝ in. and your tape measure is ⅝ in. wide, lay it flat against the cutting line of your pattern to quickly mark the seamlines. If using a multisize pattern, use the same size line throughout the marking process. It is helpful to mark the seamlines in red. Dot or dash a line in. If your pattern includes a hem allowance (the amount is printed at the bottom of the pattern), measure up the allowance amount from the bottom edge of the pattern. Draw a line parallel to the bottom. This is the hemline. Extend the grainline arrows on the front and back tissue pattern the full length of the pattern.

To preserve your original pattern, make a copy of it before you start marking your reference points and adjustments on it.

## Marking length reference lines

Not all patterns are identically and consistently marked. Therefore you may find that some of the following lines are already indicated on your pattern and some are not. Draw in the ones you don't have, as instructed, on the front and back pattern pieces.

Establish two pattern reference lines—the crotchline and the knee line. For the crotchline, draw a line from the crotch point to the side of the pattern, perpendicular to the pattern straight grain arrow (grainline). Label it crotchline. The knee line will be halfway between the crotchline and the hemline (if your pattern does not have a hem allowance included, the bottom of your pattern will be the hemline). Draw a line from the inseam to the side, perpendicular to the grainline. Label it knee line. These two lines will be used to determine pattern length measurements #1 and #2.

For pattern length adjustments you need three lines: one above the crotchline, one halfway between the crotchline and the knee line, and one halfway between the knee line and the hemline. The adjustment line above the crotch should be $2\frac{1}{2}$ in. above the crotchline. Establish these adjustment (lengthening/shortening) lines if they are not included on your pattern. They should be perpendicular to the grainline and extend the width of each pattern piece. Label the above-

the-crotchline lengthening/ shortening. Draw in and label the other two adjustment lines.

## Measuring pattern lengths and making adjustments

Pattern length measurements and adjustments must be made now and done one at a time in the order listed on the Measurement Chart so that the pattern width measurements and adjustments will be made at the same level (distance from waist) each was measured on your body.

Record all pattern measurements in column 5 on your Measurement Chart. The procedure will be: measure the pattern, record the measurement, figure the difference between columns 4 and 5, record the difference in column 6. In column 7, record your pattern adjustment amount.

**Crotch depth** To measure crotch depth on the pattern, stand the tape measure on edge. Begin at the waist and follow the side curve of the pattern to the crotchline (see the drawing on the facing page). Once you have this measurement you can figure out the adjustment you'll need to make. Let's use the following example: Your body measurement (column 1) = $10\frac{3}{4}$ in. and the pattern crotch depth (column 5) = $11\frac{1}{2}$ in. That means the adjustment is $-\frac{3}{4}$ in. to shorten the pattern.

# Establishing Pattern Reference Points for Length and Width

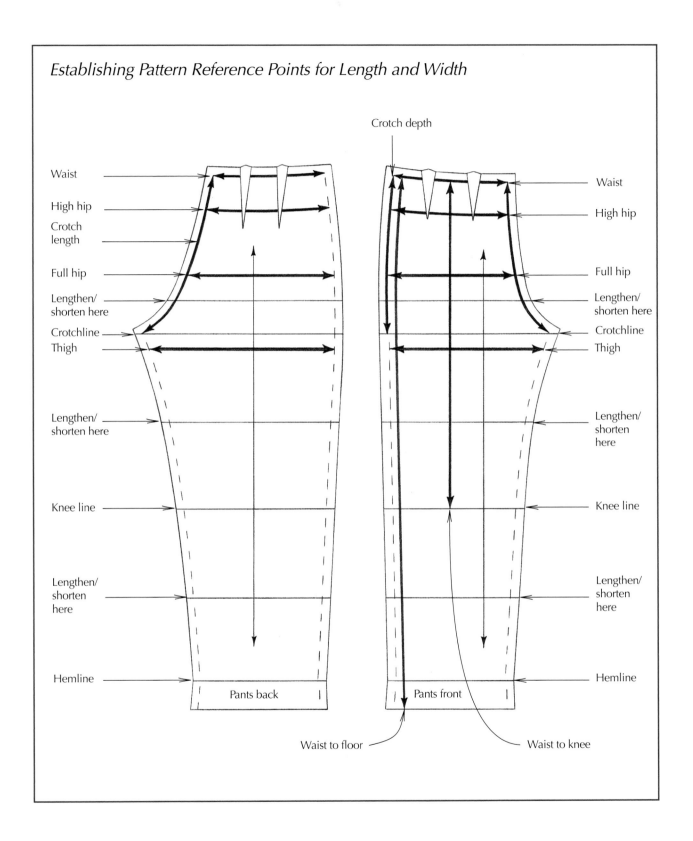

Crotch depth

Waist

High hip

Crotch length

Full hip

Lengthen/ shorten here

Crotchline

Thigh

Lengthen/ shorten here

Knee line

Lengthen/ shorten here

Hemline

Pants back

Waist

High hip

Full hip

Lengthen/ shorten here

Crotchline

Thigh

Lengthen/ shorten here

Knee line

Lengthen/ shorten here

Hemline

Pants front

Waist to floor

Waist to knee

## Shortening (-) Crotch Depth

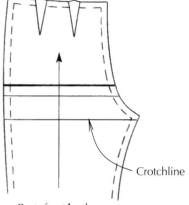

Pants front/back

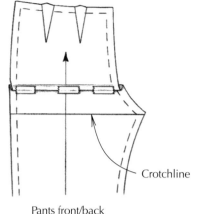

Crotchline

Pants front/back

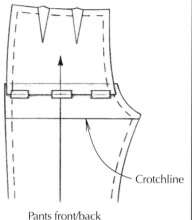

Crotchline

Pants front/back

On the lengthening/shortening line above the crotchline, measure up the amount of adjustment on pattern front and back. Draw a line parallel to the lengthening/shortening line. Adjust by folding or by cutting.

• Crease on the newly drawn line and fold it down to meet the lengthening/shortening line. Tape in place.
OR

• Cut on the newly drawn line and match it to the lengthening/shortening line. Match grainlines and tape in place.

## Lengthening (+) Crotch Depth

• Cut pattern apart on the lengthening/shortening line above the crotchline.
• Place paper under one pattern piece and tape in place.
• Measure from the cut edge of the pattern the amount of the adjustment. Draw a line on the added paper parallel to the cut edge of the taped pattern.
• Extend the grainline onto paper. Match the grainline and cut edge of untaped pattern piece to these lines and tape in place.

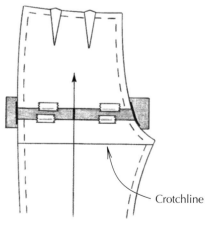

Crotchline

Pants front/back

To shorten the crotch depth, measure up from the lengthening/shortening line above the crotchline the amount of the adjustment (see the drawing above). Draw a line parallel to the lengthening/shortening line. Adjust it in one of the following two ways:

• Crease on the newly drawn line and fold it down to meet the lengthening/shortening line. Tape in place.
• Cut on the newly drawn line and match it to the lengthening/shortening line, aligning the grainlines. Tape in place.

To lengthen the crotch depth, follow these steps (see the bottom drawing on the facing page):

**1.** Cut the pattern apart on the lengthening/shortening line above the crotchline. Tape a piece of see-through paper slightly wider than your pattern and longer than your adjustment to one edge of the cut-apart pattern.

**2.** Using added paper, measure from the cut edge of the pattern piece the adjustment amount, and draw a horizontal line parallel to the cut edge.

**3.** Extend the grainline onto the added paper.

**4.** Match up the grainline on the pattern to the extended grainline on the added paper, aligning the cut edge of the pattern you are joining with the horizontal adjustment line you added (see the photo above). Tape in place.

**Waist to knee** Measure from the waist to the knee line down the center of the front pants pattern (see the drawing on p. 265). Follow the same procedure to shorten or lengthen the pattern as for the crotch depth. The adjustment here is done on the lengthening/shortening line above the knee.

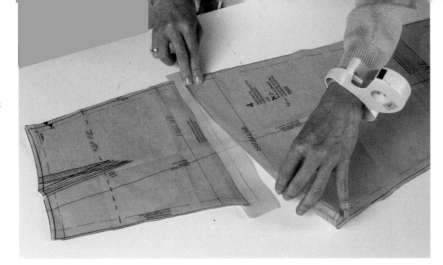

*When making length adjustments, extending the grainline on the added paper makes realigning the pattern pieces more accurate while keeping the cut edges parallel.*

**Waist to floor** Stand the tape measure on edge and follow the side of the pattern from the waist to the bottom of the pattern (see the drawing on p. 265). Note: This measurement includes up to a 2-in. hem, which was allowed for in the body measurement. The finished length will be at the base of your ankle bone. If you want your pants longer, add the increased length amount to the adjustment amount in column 7. The adjustment will be done on the lengthening/shortening line below the knee line. Refer to the crotch depth for adjustment instructions.

## Measuring pattern widths and making adjustments

To accurately measure and adjust pattern widths to correspond to your body measurements, the adjustments must be positioned the same distance from the waist as measured on your body. Along the side, measure and mark the distance from the waist on the

# PATTERN ADJUSTMENT AMOUNTS

*Accuracy is in relation to purpose and provided as a convenience.*

| Difference (Measurement Chart column 6) | Column 1 Side adjustments for 2 in. or less | Column 2 Side, center front, and center back adjustments for more than 2 in. | Column 3 For thighs only: side and inside leg seam |
|:---:|:---:|:---:|:---:|
| INCHES | DIVIDED BY FOUR | DIVIDED BY EIGHT | DIVIDED BY FOUR |
| 1 | 1/4 | 1/8 | 1/4 |
| 1 1/4 | 3/8 | 1/8 | 3/8 |
| 1 1/2 | 3/8 | 1/4 | 3/8 |
| 1 3/4 | 1/2 | 1/4 | 1/2 |
| 2 | 1/2 | 1/4 | 1/2 |
| 2 1/4 | | 1/4 | 5/8 |
| 2 1/2 | | 3/8 | 5/8 |
| 2 3/4 | | 3/8 | 3/4 |
| 3 | | 3/8 | 3/4 |
| 3 1/4 | | 3/8 | 7/8 |
| 3 1/2 | | 1/2 | 7/8 |
| 3 3/4 | | 1/2 | 1 |
| 4 | | 1/2 | 1 |
| 4 1/4 | | 1/2 | 1 1/8 |
| 4 1/2 | | 5/8 | 1 1/8 |
| 4 3/4 | | 5/8 | 1 1/4 |
| 5 | | 5/8 | 1 1/4 |
| 5 1/4 | | 5/8 | 1 3/8 |
| 5 1/2 | | 3/4 | 1 3/8 |
| 5 3/4 | | 3/4 | 1 1/2 |
| 6 | | 3/4 | 1 1/2 |
| 6 1/4 | | 3/4 | 1 5/8 |
| 6 1/2 | | 7/8 | 1 5/8 |
| 6 3/4 | | 7/8 | 1 3/4 |
| 7 | | 7/8 | 1 3/4 |
| 7 1/4 | | 7/8 | 1 7/8 |
| 7 1/2 | | 1 | 1 7/8 |
| 7 3/4 | | 1 | 2 |
| 8 | | 1 | 2 |
| 8 1/4 | | 1 | 2 1/8 |
| 8 1/2 | | 1 1/8 | 2 1/8 |
| 8 3/4 | | 1 1/8 | 2 1/4 |
| 9 | | 1 1/8 | 2 1/4 |
| 9 1/4 | | 1 1/8 | 2 3/8 |
| 9 1/2 | | 1 1/4 | 2 3/8 |
| 9 3/4 | | 1 1/4 | 2 1/2 |
| 10 | | 1 1/4 | 2 1/2 |

pattern front and back for high hip (if measured), full hip, and thigh. Draw a line across each pattern piece at the full hip and thigh that is perpendicular to the grainline and label each line. The high hip cannot be drawn in at this time and will be discussed later.

You are now going to measure the pattern width for the waist, high hip (if measured on your body), full hip, and thigh. These measurements will tell you the size your finished pants will be in these areas before you cut your fabric. Record all pattern measurements in column 5. The procedure is: measure the pattern, record the measurement in column 5, figure the difference between columns 4 and 5, record the difference in column 6, then refer to the chart on the facing page for column 7 adjustment amount.

Since the darts and/or pleats would normally be sewn, they must be folded and pinned closed on the pattern prior to measuring. If your pattern has pleats, check the pattern envelope picture to see how quickly they dissipate down the front into little or no fullness. The fullness should be pinned closed at the waist by matching the pleat lines. Continue pinning the pleat closed down the leg, gradually dissipating the amount taken up by the pleat to zero (usually about crotchline level). Determine this level from

*Before measuring for width, pin darts and pleats closed. Measure between the seam allowances with the tape measure on edge to get an accurate reading.*

your pattern envelope or personal preference. With the darts and/or pleats pinned, draw in the line for the high hip from side edge to center front and center back, keeping distance parallel to waist.

To determine the finished width measurements of your pattern, begin by measuring the waist. Sometimes the finished-garment waist and full-hip size are printed on the front pattern piece, but not always. If not, stand the tape measure on edge and follow the curve of the waist (see the photo above). Add the front and back measurements and multiply by two. Repeat these measuring and recording instructions for the high hip, if measured on your body, and full hip. Total increases or decreases of 2 in. or less will be done equally at the sides on front and back. Increases or decreases of more than 2 in. will be done equally at the sides, center front, and center back.

To make width adjustments easy, use precut widths of adding machine or fax paper when adding extra paper to increase your pattern, or tape your front and back pattern pieces to a large sheet of tissue or sketch paper. In either case, the paper should be several inches larger than your greatest increase to allow for the truing (redrawing) of all pattern lines interrupted in the adjusting process.

Unpin all pleats and darts so your pattern is flat.

The final pattern width measurement will be for the thigh. Measure on the thigh line across the pattern front and back. Add the two measurements and record the total in column 5. Thigh adjustments will be made equally at the side seam and inseam on the front and back of the pattern.

**Waist increase/decrease** If your waist adjustment is a total of 2 in. or less (½ in. or less to each side seam), adjust each side at

waist level (see the left drawing below). Measure out from the pattern edge for an increase or measure in for a decrease. If your adjustment is a total of more than 2 in., adjust at each side, center front, and center back (see the right drawing below).

**Waistband adjustments** For a side-closing waistband with a total increase/decrease of 2 in. or less, add or subtract half the total amount of the increase or decrease at the side-seam marking in the middle of the waistband piece. On the ends, add or subtract one-quarter the

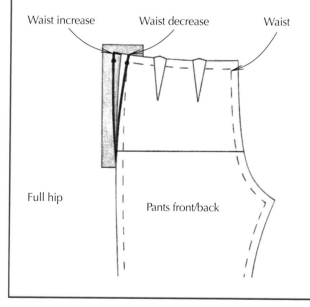

## Waist Increase/Decrease of 2 in. or Less

*Make the adjustment at each side on the front and back at the same level as the waist seam. Measure out from the cutting line for an increase or in onto the pattern for a decrease. The newly drawn line will become your cutting line.*

Waist increase

Waist decrease

Waist

Full hip

Pants front/back

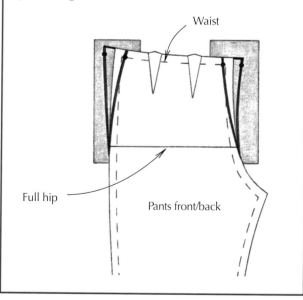

## Waist Increase/Decrease of More Than 2 in.

*If total increase/decrease is more than 2 in., divide the total increase/decrease by 8. Make the increase/decrease at side, center front, and center back. Use chart on p. 268 with Measurement Chart. Newly drawn lines become your cutting lines.*

Waist

Full hip

Pants front/back

total amount at each side-seam marking (see the drawing below).

For a side-closing waistband with a total increase/decrease of more than 2 in., add or subtract one-quarter the total amount of the increase or decrease at the side-seam marking, center front, and center back. On the ends, add one-eighth the total amount at each side-seam marking.

For a center-front-closing/center-back-closing waistband with a 2-in. or less total increase/decrease, add or subtract half the total amount of the increase or decrease at each side-seam marking.

## Waistband Adjustments

**Side-closing waistband**

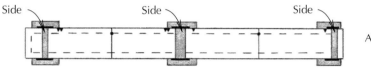

A. For a side-closing waistband with 2-in. or less increase/decrease: Add or subtract one-half the total amount of the increase/decrease to one side seam. On ends (left), add or subtract one-quarter the total amount to each side seam marking.

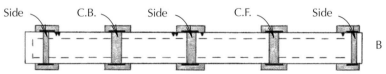

B. For a side-closing waistband with more than 2-in. increase/decrease: Add or subtract one-quarter the total amount of the increase/decrease to one side seam, center front, and center back. On the side with the closure (left), add one-eighth the total amount to each side-seam marking.

**Center-back/ center-front-closing waistband**

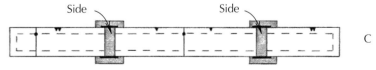

C. For a C.B./C.F.-closing waistband with 2-in. or less increase/decrease: Add or subtract one-half the total amount of the increase/decrease to each side seam.

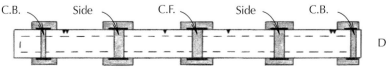

D. For a C.B.-closing waistband with more than 2-in. increase/decrease: Add or subtract one-quarter the total amount of the increase/decrease to center front and both side seams. At center back on each end add one-eighth the total amount of increase/decrease. Reverse this process for a C.F. closure.

## High-Hip Increase/Decrease of 2 in. or Less

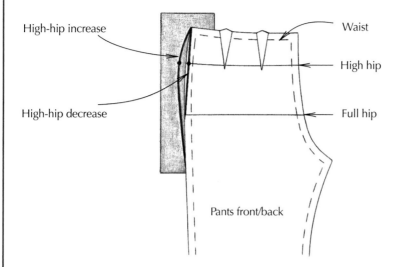

High-hip increase

High-hip decrease

Waist

High hip

Full hip

Pants front/back

*To accommodate a more prominently curved figure just below the waist, add your high-hip adjustment amount from column 7 of your Measurement Chart to the side of the pattern. Add the increase at your personal high-hip distance from waist (amount in parentheses). A newly curved line between the waist and the full hip should incorporate this increase. To decrease, simply straighten the curve between the waist and full hip.*

## High-Hip Increase/Decrease of 2 in. or More

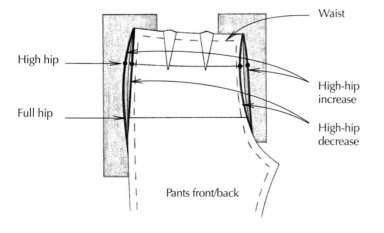

High hip

Full hip

Waist

High-hip increase

High-hip decrease

Pants front/back

*This adjustment will be done the same way as for the 2-in. or less adjustment except in addition to the change made at the side, the adjustment amount from column 7 on your Measurement Chart will also be made at the center front and back. To decrease, simply straighten the curve between the waist and full hip at each side, center front, and center back.*

For a center-back-closing waistband with more than a 2-in. total increase/decrease, add or subtract one-quarter the total amount of the increase or decrease to the center front and each side-seam marking. At the center back at each end, add one-eighth the total amount of the increase or decrease. Reverse the adjustment for a center-front-closing waistband.

***High-hip increase/decrease*** If your high-hip adjustment is 2 in. or less, make an increase or decrease at high-hip level (see the top drawing at left). Usually this type of increase/decrease will accompany a waist increase/ decrease, in which case the blending of your new side line from the waist adjustment will automatically adjust the high hip. Some women may be more fleshy below the waist or have a "roll," which will necessitate a high-hip adjustment. Refer to your Measurement Chart for the amount and placement (distance from waist) of this adjustment. If your adjustment is more than 2 in., adjust at each side, center front, and center back (see the bottom drawing at left).

A decrease in the high hip can cause an undesirable hollow along the side seam. To avoid creating this hollow, your adjustment should only involve straightening the curve at the high hip, not curving inward from the pattern edge.

**Full-hip increase/decrease** If your adjustment is a total of 2 in. or less, follow these steps (see the drawing at right):

**1.** At your marked full-hip level, measure out or in the adjustment amount from column 7 on your Measurement Chart.

**2.** Draw a curved line between the waist and full-hip adjustment. The more the increase, the greater the curve. Blend the line into the edge of the pattern smoothly. This may add a slight amount to the leg width, but it will look better proportionally. There is no increase/decrease in the leg width at the hemline.

If your adjustment total is more than 2 in., follow these steps (see the drawing on p. 274):

**1.** At your full-hip level, each side, center front, and center back, measure out or in from the edge of your pattern the adjustment amount from column 7 on your Measurement Chart.

**2.** Blend a line between the waist, full hip, and the original pattern edge at the hemline. There is no increase/decrease in the leg width at the hemline.

**3.** At the center front and center back, blend a line between the waist and crotch point.

**4.** To balance the leg, draw a new inseam line, beginning at the crotch point. Add the same amount as you added to the side when blending. Taper to edge of pattern at the hemline.

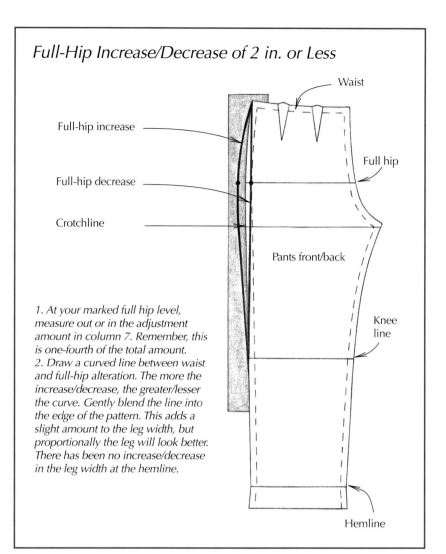

### Full-Hip Increase/Decrease of 2 in. or Less

Waist

Full-hip increase

Full hip

Full-hip decrease

Crotchline

Pants front/back

Knee line

*1. At your marked full hip level, measure out or in the adjustment amount in column 7. Remember, this is one-fourth of the total amount.*
*2. Draw a curved line between waist and full-hip alteration. The more the increase/decrease, the greater/lesser the curve. Gently blend the line into the edge of the pattern. This adds a slight amount to the leg width, but proportionally the leg will look better. There has been no increase/decrease in the leg width at the hemline.*

Hemline

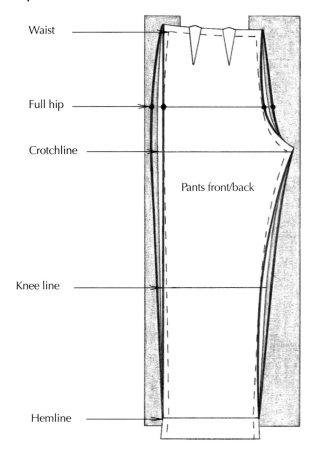

## Full-Hip Increase/Decrease of 2 in. or More

Waist

Full hip

Crotchline

Pants front/back

Knee line

Hemline

*1. At your full-hip distance from waist, measure out or in the adjustment amount from column 7 on your Measurement Chart at the side, center front, and center back.*
*2. Blend a line between the waist, full hip, and original pattern edge at the hemline. No width has been added or subtracted at the hemline.*

*3. At center front and center back, blend a line between the waist and crotch point.*
*4. To balance the leg, draw a line from the crotch point, adding the same amount at the knee that was added at the side and tapering to the hemline so there is no increase there.*

amount at the crotch point that you added or subtracted at the inseam thigh level, tapering to nothing at the hemline (see the left drawing on the facing page).

# Refining Adjustments

Refining adjustments are less common than pattern adjustments but not less important. They address the individual figure variations that you observed on your figure from the front and side (see the drawing on p. 262). These observations should have been checked after your measurements were completed.

Determining if an adjustment is necessary before cutting your fabric will depend on the closeness of fit for your style of pants, as well as the degree of variation. The closer the fit or the more particular you are about fit, the more important these adjustments become. The fit of other pants can give clues about where there are problem areas. Because there are no hard-and-fast rules, judgment is required. Therefore, refining the fit of your adjustments in a trial pair of pants is recommended to learn what amounts are best for you.

Here are some hints for making refining adjustments:
- Always place extra paper, preferably see-through, under cut portions of the pattern.

**Thigh increase/decrease** Add or subtract the adjustment amount at your thigh distance from waist and at the side and inseam of the front and back. Add or subtract the same

## Thigh Increase/Decrease

*Increase or decrease the adjustment amount at your thigh, at the side, and at the inseam of the front and back. You will add or subtract at the crotch point the same amount that you added/subtracted at the inseam thigh level, and taper to "0" at the hemline.*

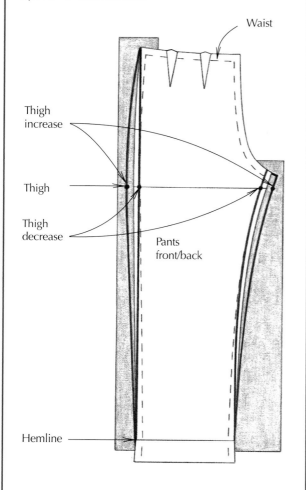

Waist

Thigh
increase

Thigh

Thigh
decrease

Pants
front/back

Hemline

## Full Front Thigh

*Add adjustment increase at your thigh distance from waist at the front seam crotch point and inseam only. Blend a new line along the side seam, adding "0" at the waist and hemline. Blend a new line from the crotch point and thigh line, tapering to "0" at the hemline.*

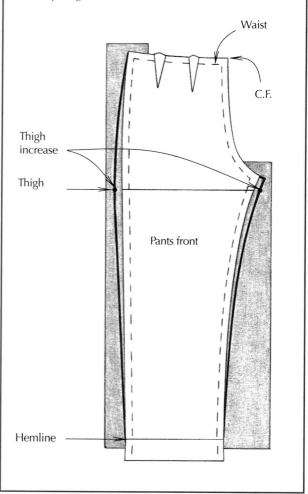

Waist

C.F.

Thigh
increase

Thigh

Pants front

Hemline

- Work on a flat surface that you can pin into, such as a foam, blocking, or ironing board.
- Adjust the pattern by moving or spreading it the needed amount.

- Control pattern movement by pinning the pattern to the working surface/board.
- Tape the pattern in place only after you are satisfied with the adjustment amount and the pattern is flat.

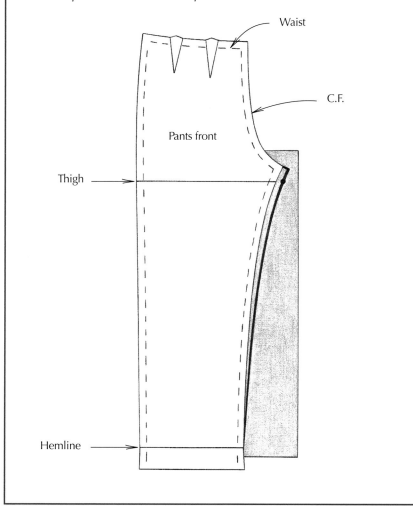

## Full Inner Thigh

*Add the adjustment amount to the inner leg seam at your thigh level. Increase the crotch point the same amount. Taper the new line to "0" at the hemline.*

Waist

C.F.

Pants front

Thigh

Hemline

point the same amount the inseam is increased. Blend a new line along the side, adding nothing at the waistline and hemline. Blend a line from the crotch point and thigh line, tapering to nothing at the hemline.

## Full inner thigh

For a full inner thigh, increase the inseam at thigh level (see the drawing at left). Increase the crotch point the same amount. Taper to nothing at the hemline.

## Protruding tummy

To accommodate a protruding tummy, you'll need to make a few changes. If your pattern has a fly-front zipper extension, cut it off along the center-front line (you will reattach it later). Because the body is curved at the center front, more length and width will be needed. However, little or nothing may need to be added at the side since tummy fullness dissipates toward the side. To adjust for a full tummy, follow these steps (see the drawing on the facing page):

**1.** At the high hip, cut from center front past the dart. Continue to cut but angle up to the side waist. *Do not* separate the pattern pieces at the seam.

## Full front thigh

To accommodate a full front thigh, increase at the front side and inseam at thigh distance from waist (see the right drawing on p. 275). Increase the crotch

## Protruding Tummy

*A tummy needs slightly more length and width at center front.*
*1. Cut horizontally on the high-hip line from center front past the dart or pleat, then angle up to the side waist.*
*2. Cut through the center of the dart or pleat from the waist down to within ¹⁄₁₆ in. of the high-hip cutting line.*
*3. Move the upper portion of the pattern (high hip to waist) up so the spread at center front is about ¹⁄₂ in. Let darts spread open slightly so the cutting line on the upper and lower pattern remains somewhat parallel and the pattern is flat. Redraw the darts, restoring them to their original length.*
*4. Redraw center front, blending a line between the waist and crotch curve.*

Waist
C.F.
High hip
½ in.
Full hip
Crotchline
Pants front

**2.** Cut through the center of the dart(s) to but not through the horizontal high-hip cut.

**3.** Spread the upper part of the pattern (the smaller part) at the center front ¹⁄₂ in.—slightly more for very large tummies, less for smaller ones. A little does a lot. This spreading will cause the center front above the high hip to jut out further, the darts to increase in size, and the front crotch length to become longer. Pin and tape the pattern in place. Redraw darts.

**4.** Redraw the center front. You can make this line an ever-so-gentle curve or keep it straight. If your pattern had a fly extension, make the same spread on it. Pin and tape in place. Then redraw your lines on the center-front fly extension to match the center front of the pants.

## Protruding buttocks

Protruding, or full, buttocks can cause pants to pull and feel uncomfortable in the crotch. Side seams pull toward the back because more width is required

## Protruding Buttocks

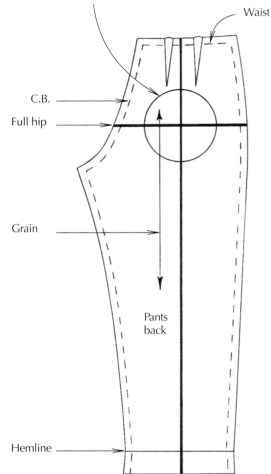

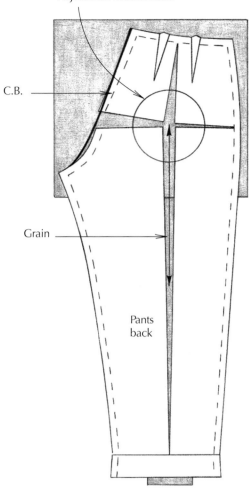

*Adjustment needed here.*

Waist

C.B.

Full hip

Grain

Pants
back

Hemline

*Adjustment needed here.*

C.B.

Grain

Pants
back

Full buttocks need more length at the center back and more width at the full hip.
On the pants back only:
1. Find the center of your horizontal full-hip line.
2. Draw a vertical line from the waist to hem that is parallel to the grainline and passes through the middle hip mark.
3. Cut the hipline from center back to side. Do not separate the pattern pieces at the side.
4. On the center vertical line, cut up to the waist and down to the hem. Do not separate the pattern pieces.
5. Spread ½ in. to 1½ in. on the vertical line at mid hip.
6. Redraw the grainline if needed. Blend the center back line between the waist and crotch curve.

across the back. To fix this problem, the crotch length needs to be increased, as does the width across the back. To make these adjustments on your back pattern, follow these steps (see the drawing on the facing page):

**1.** Find the center of the horizontal line at your full hip and mark.

**2.** Draw a line perpendicular to the full-hip line from the top to the bottom of your pattern, passing through the midpoint established in step 1.

**3.** On the full-hip line, cut from the center back to the side. *Do not* separate the pattern pieces at the side.

**4.** Beginning at the full-hip line, cut up and down the vertical line drawn in step 2. *Do not* separate the pattern pieces.

**5.** On the vertical line, spread the pattern at the full-hip level up to 1½ in. for a very full figure. Spread the lower portion of your pattern at the full-hip line first. Pin, then tape in place. Spread the upper portion the same amount at the full-hip level. The upper portion of the pattern moves up and away from the lower portion so there is a slight angular spread between the mid hip and side on the horizontal cutting line. Pin and tape in place.

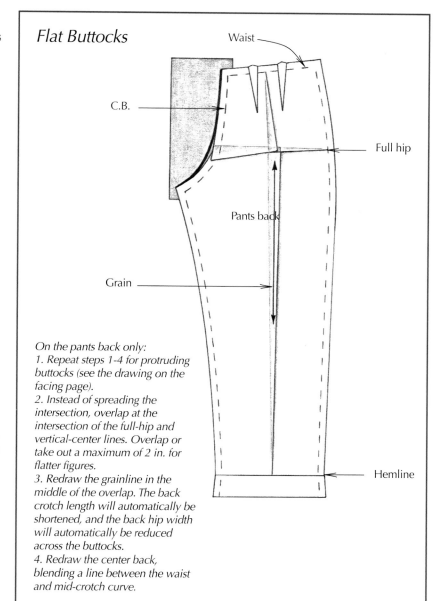

*Flat Buttocks*

Waist

C.B.

Full hip

Pants back

Grain

Hemline

On the pants back only:
1. Repeat steps 1-4 for protruding buttocks (see the drawing on the facing page).
2. Instead of spreading the intersection, overlap at the intersection of the full-hip and vertical-center lines. Overlap or take out a maximum of 2 in. for flatter figures.
3. Redraw the grainline in the middle of the overlap. The back crotch length will automatically be shortened, and the back hip width will automatically be reduced across the buttocks.
4. Redraw the center back, blending a line between the waist and mid-crotch curve.

**6.** Redraw the grainline in the middle of the spread if needed. The back crotch length and hip width has been increased. Redraw center back by blending a smooth line between the waist and midpoint of the crotch curve.

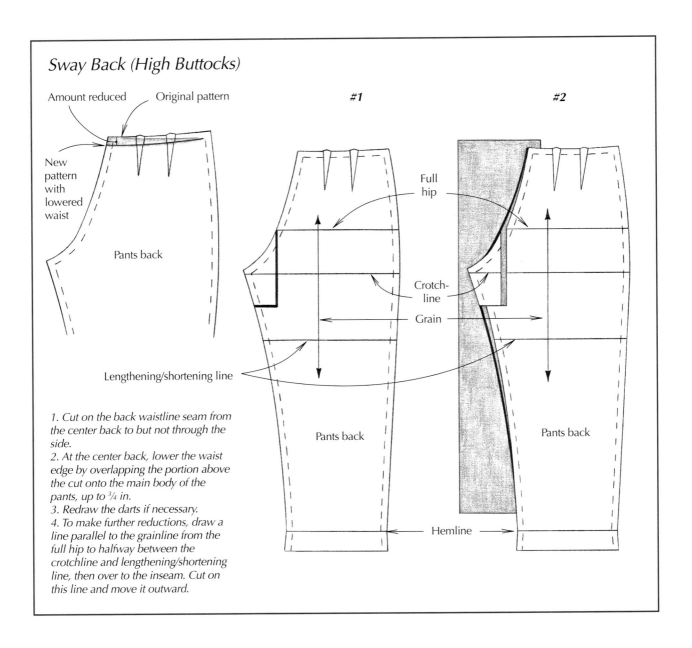

## Sway Back (High Buttocks)

Amount reduced · Original pattern

#1

#2

New pattern with lowered waist

Pants back

Full hip

Crotch-line

Grain

Lengthening/shortening line

Pants back

Pants back

Hemline

1. Cut on the back waistline seam from the center back to but not through the side.
2. At the center back, lower the waist edge by overlapping the portion above the cut onto the main body of the pants, up to ¾ in.
3. Redraw the darts if necessary.
4. To make further reductions, draw a line parallel to the grainline from the full hip to halfway between the crotchline and lengthening/shortening line, then over to the inseam. Cut on this line and move it outward.

## Flat buttocks

Flat buttocks need the opposite pattern adjustment of protruding buttocks. Less crotch length and width across the back is needed to avoid a back leg that is too full and droops under the buttocks. Follow the instructions for protruding buttocks but with

the following differences (see the drawing on p. 279):

1. After cutting on the full hip and drawing a vertical line (step 3 on p. 279), overlap up to 2 in. on the lower portion of your pattern at the full-hip level. Pin and tape in place. Repeat this same overlap on the upper

portion of the pattern at the full-hip level. Pin and tape in place.

2. Redraw the grainline in the middle of the overlap. The back crotch length has automatically been shortened, and the back hip and leg taken in to reduce bagginess.

## Sway back (high buttocks)

With a sway back, the distance between the full hip and waist is shorter at center back than at the sides, so a small fold of fabric just under the waistband but above the high hip will form at the center back. This fold will dissipate toward the side seam. To adjust your pattern to eliminate this problem (see the drawing on the facing page):

1. Cut on the waistline seam from the center back to but not through the side.

2. Lower the waist edge by overlapping the portion above the cut onto the main body of the pants up to ¾ in. Pin and tape in place. If your pattern does not include seam allowances, measure down from center back waist a maximum of ¾ in. Fold dart(s) closed and blend a new line between center back mark and side waist intersection. With dart(s) closed, cut on newly drawn line.

3. Redraw darts if necessary.

4. If more reduction is required, widen the back crotch area. To do this, draw a line parallel to the grainline from the center-back full-hip line to halfway between the crotchline and the lengthening/shortening line, then over to the inseam. Cut on this line and move the piece outward, parallel to the cut to compensate for the shortened crotch length. Pin and tape in place.

## One fuller hip

A full hip, meaning one side of your body is slightly more fleshy than the other, can be accounted for in the fitting process of the fabric pants. Frequently a full hip can add length between the waist and full-hip lines. If diagonal wrinkles are visible between the crotch and high hip on pants in your current wardrobe, follow these steps to make a pattern adjustment (see the drawing on p. 282).

1. Make a copy of the front and back of your pattern from the crotchline up. Because you are changing only one side, you will have the original pattern for the unadjusted side and the adjusted pattern for the fuller hip. Label front and back copy right or left to correspond to the side being adjusted.

2. On the front and back copy draw a line parallel to the grainline between the side and the dart or pleat from the waist

## One Fuller Hip

*Frequently one hip tends to be slightly fuller than the other. The fullness can be adjusted for in the fitting process if it is not excessive.*

*Because this is a change to only one side of the body, make a copy of your pattern from the crotchline up. This way you will have the original pattern for your straighter side and the adjusted one for the fuller side.*

*On the front and back of the side with the fuller hip:*
*1. Draw a vertical line parallel to the grainline between the side and the dart or pleat from the waist to the full hip, then on an angle to the intersection of the lengthening/shortening line and side.*
*2. From the side, cut in on the high-hip line, then up to the waist on the vertical line. Do not separate the pattern pieces at the waist.*
*3. Cut down to the full hip, then over to the side. Do not separate the pattern pieces at the side.*
*4. Spread the side at the seamline by the amount of the adjustment.*

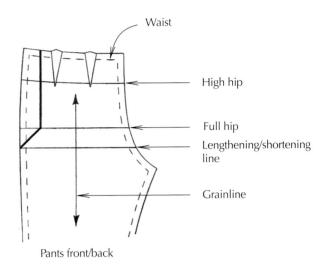

Pants front/back

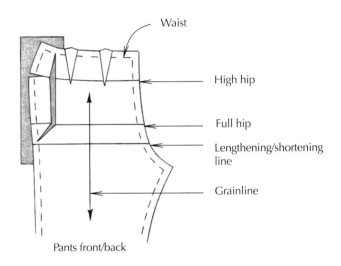

Pants front/back

edge of the pattern to the full-hip line, then on an angle to the intersection of the lengthening/shortening line and side.

**3.** From the side, cut in on the high-hip line, then up to the waist edge and down to the side on the drawn line. *Do not separate the pattern pieces at the side.*

**4.** Spread the side ¼ in. to ½ in. Pin and tape in place. If this is too much spread, it can be removed in the fitting process.

## High hip only

If no wrinkling between high hip and crotch is evident on your current pants, but there is a difference between the waist-to-full-hip measurements of your right and left sides, make a copy of your pattern as in step 1 of the directions for one fuller hip. Continue with the following steps (see the drawing above):

**1.** On front and back at full-hip level, cut in ⅝ in., then up to the waist and over to center front and center back. The cut should be parallel to the pattern edge and ⅝ in. away from it.

**2.** Reestablish your waist level with Ban-Rol. Measure the left and right sides from your waist to the full hip. Use the amount of the difference between the two sides as a guide to spread your pattern in step 3.

**3.** Raise the side at the waist by the amount of the difference between the right and left waist-to-full-hip measurements as determined in step 2. Pin and tape in place. If your pattern does not include a seam allowance, raise the waist at the side equal to the amount of your adjustment and draw a new line between this point and the center front and back.

## Knock knees

If the knees curve in slightly or touch, more width and length is required on the inseam. To make

## Knock Knees

*When the knees curve in slightly, more width and length is required at the inseam than at the side seam.*

*1. Cut on the lengthening/shortening line that's between the knee line and the crotchline. Move the lower portion of the pants leg toward the inseam. The amount will depend on figure deviation.*

*2. To increase the length on the inseam, cut on the lengthening/ shortening line that's below the knee line. Cut up the center of the bottom leg portion. Move half of the leg portion closest to the inseam down to increase the length. You may find ½ in. or less is necessary.*

*3. Redraw the hemline and lower edge of pattern, keeping the lines parallel.*

*4. Redraw the grainlines, extending the lower-leg grain toward the top.*

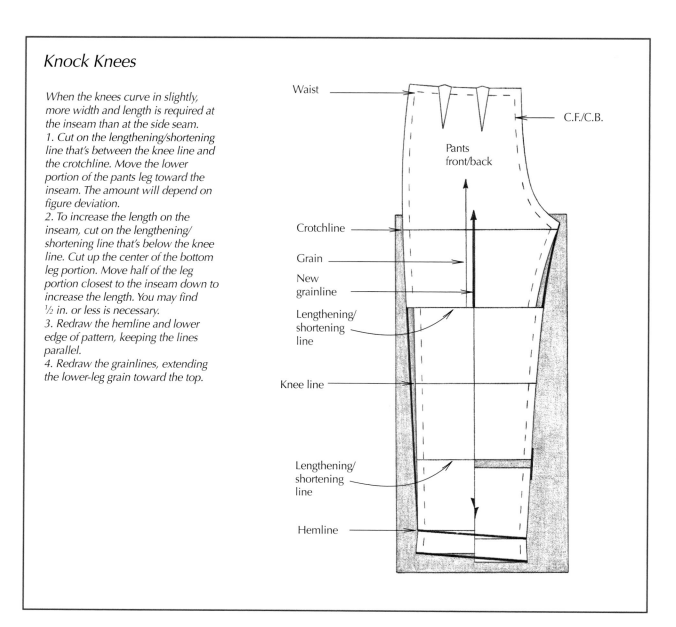

Waist

C.F./C.B.

Pants front/back

Crotchline

Grain

New grainline

Lengthening/ shortening line

Knee line

Lengthening/ shortening line

Hemline

this easy adjustment see the drawing above:

**1.** Cut on the lengthening/ shortening line above the knee line but below the crotchline on front and back. Move the lower portion of the pants leg toward the inseam. Add about 1 in. for knees that are very curved (to

the point of touching), and decrease the amount proportionately the slighter the curve. You may need to add more during the fitting stage. Pin and tape in place.

**2.** To increase the length on the inseam, cut on the lengthening/shortening line

## Bowed Legs

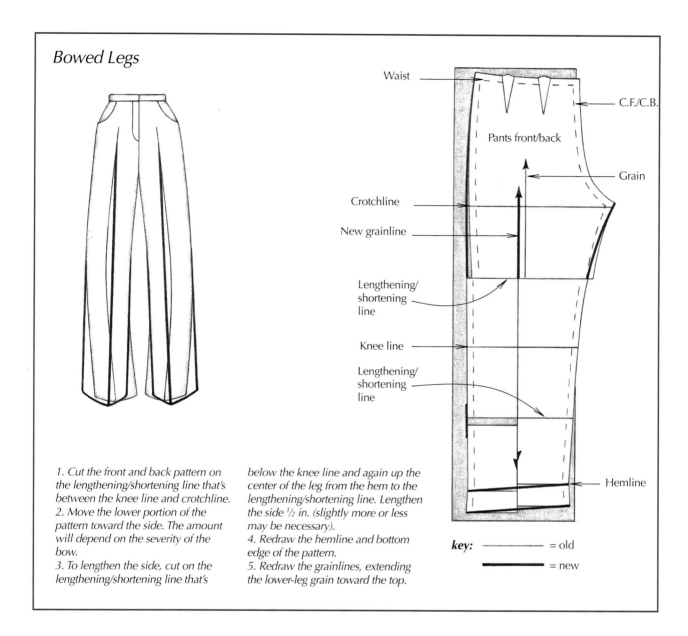

**Waist**

**C.F./C.B.**

**Pants front/back**

**Grain**

**Crotchline**

**New grainline**

**Lengthening/ shortening line**

**Knee line**

**Lengthening/ shortening line**

**Hemline**

*1. Cut the front and back pattern on the lengthening/shortening line that's between the knee line and crotchline.*
*2. Move the lower portion of the pattern toward the side. The amount will depend on the severity of the bow.*
*3. To lengthen the side, cut on the lengthening/shortening line that's*

*below the knee line and again up the center of the leg from the hem to the lengthening/shortening line. Lengthen the side ½ in. (slightly more or less may be necessary).*
*4. Redraw the hemline and bottom edge of the pattern.*
*5. Redraw the grainlines, extending the lower-leg grain toward the top.*

**key:**  —————— = old

■■■■■ = new

located below the knee line on front and back. Cut up the center of the bottom leg portion. Move the leg portion closest to the inseam down + or - ½ in. Pin and tape in place.

**3.** Redraw the hemline between side and inseam and the lower edge of the pattern. Lines should be parallel.

**4.** Redraw the grainline on front and back as one continuous line.

## Hyperextended Calves

*If you have hyperextended calves, you may notice a wrinkling or sagging of fabric just above the back knee. This can also be caused by posture. To correct this problem, try making these changes.*

*1. On the back only, measure up from the lengthening/ shortening line that's between the knee line and crotchline a maximum of ¹/₂ in. Draw a parallel line.*

*2. Crease on the lengthening/ shortening line and bring it up to meet the newly drawn line, or cut on the lengthening/ shortening line and bring the lower portion of the pattern up to meet the new line. Pin and tape in place.*

*3. Draw a line halfway between the lengthening/ shortening line and between the knee line and the hemline.*

*4. Cut on the line drawn in step 3 above, and lengthen the pattern the amount you shortened in steps 1 or 2 above.*

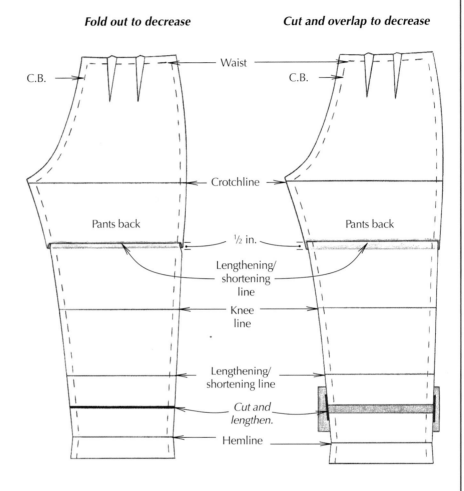

**Fold out to decrease**   **Cut and overlap to decrease**

Waist

C.B.

Crotchline

Pants back

¹/₂ in.

Lengthening/ shortening line

Knee line

Lengthening/ shortening line

Cut and lengthen.

Hemline

## Bowed legs

Legs that curve outward above and below the knee require more width and length along the side. It is the opposite problem of knock knees (see the drawing on p. 285).

**1.** Cut the front and back pattern on the lengthening/ shortening line located between the knee and crotchline.

**2.** Move the lower portion of the pattern toward the side about 1 in. for a severe bow and less for minor curvature. Pin and tape in place.

**3.** Lengthen the side by cutting from the side on the lengthening/shortening line below the knee and down the center of the leg to the bottom of the pattern. Spread the side + or - ¹/₂ in., depending on the severity of the bow. Pin and tape in place.

**4.** Redraw the hemline between the side and inseam. Redraw the bottom of the pattern parallel to the hemline.

**5.** Redraw the grainline so it is one continuous line.

## *Hyperextended calves*

Before doing this adjustment, recheck your side view and make sure you were not standing with your knees locked when the measurements and observations were made. If you have well-developed calf muscles, or if you consistently lock you knees when you stand, you may want to proceed with this adjustment. Here are the steps (see the drawing on the facing page):

**1.** On the back only, measure up from the lengthening/shortening line located between the knee and the crotchline a maximum of ½ in. Draw a parallel line.

**2.** Crease or cut on the lengthening/shortening line and bring it up to meet the newly drawn line to remove the excess. Pin and tape in place.

**3.** Draw a line halfway between the hemline and the lengthening/shortening line just above it.

**4.** Cut on this line, and lengthen the pattern by the amount you shortened above the knee. Pin and tape in place.

# Crotch Length Adjustments

The final pattern measurement and adjustment will be for crotch length (see the drawing on p. 288). If you measured your pattern before completing adjustments to crotch depth, thigh, full front thigh, full inner thigh, full buttocks, flat buttocks, protruding tummy, or sway back, the pattern crotch will have changed and you'll need to remeasure.

Refer to the reference points for pattern crotch-length measurements (see the drawing on p. 265). Stand the tape measure on edge and walk it along the center front and back between the waist and crotch point of the pattern. Add the front and back measurements and record the total in column 5 on your Measurement Chart. Determine the difference between columns 4 and 5, and record it in column 6. The difference is the amount of adjustment that should be recorded in column 7. If the pattern is slightly longer, leave it. If you don't have enough crotch length, you will need to add it now. If you wait until you have cut your fabric, you will be in trouble.

When adjusting for the difference, add up to 1 in. at the center-front waist and 1 in.

## Crotch Length

*If you measured your pattern before you made any adjustments to crotch depth, thigh (front or inner), buttocks, tummy, or sway back, you will now need to remeasure your pattern because your original measurement will have changed.*

*Refigure the adjustment difference. If the pattern is slightly longer, leave it.*

*If you need to add more, add up to 1 in. at center front waist and 1 in. at center back waist. Distribute the difference evenly between the two. Remeasure.*

*If still more is required beyond the maximum that was added above (2 in.), divide the difference between the front and back crotch points.*

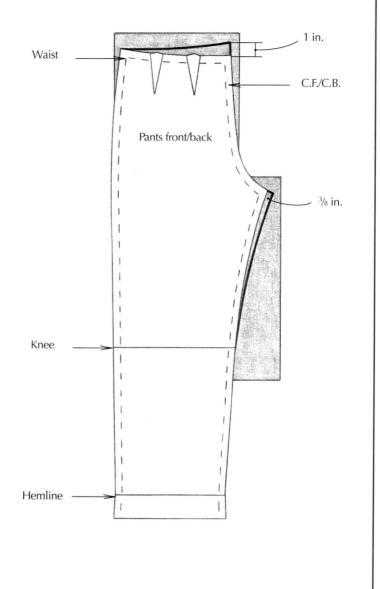

Waist

1 in.

C.F./C.B.

Pants front/back

³⁄₈ in.

Knee

Hemline

at the center-back waist. Distribute the difference evenly between the two. If more length is required than what was added evenly at the center-front and center-back waist, divide the difference between the front and back and add it to each crotch point. For example, if you need to add 2¾ in. to the pattern, add 1 in. at the center front, 1 in. at the center back, ³⁄₈ in. at the front crotch point, and ³⁄₈ in. at the back crotch point.

# Truing Your Pattern

Depending on the amount adjusted, the original smooth and continuous pattern lines can be disrupted. Reestablishing or redrawing these lines is called "truing." Check your pattern edges for lines that are no longer continuous curves or straight lines. You'll develop an eye for this with experience. Use a French curve or a styling curve, such as a Fashion Ruler, to achieve the line that best fits your curves.

When reconnecting a line between two points, you may add or subtract small amounts from your pattern above and below the adjustment points when blending this new line. This is normal, but keep it to a minimum. Because of this blending, any fitting subtleties can be worked out in the first fitting. An abrupt change in a line will create a dramatic bulge or hollow when translated into fabric (see the drawing on p. 290).

In addition to some basic tools such as scissors and tape, you will need the following supplies to true your pattern:

- extra paper around your working pattern to allow room for truing (see the photo above)

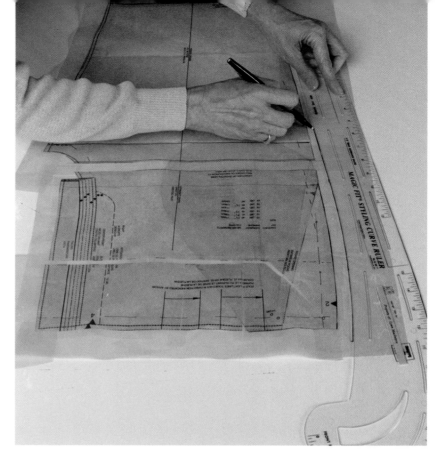

*Don't skimp on tissue when you add it to the edge of your pattern. It will make the truing process easier.*

- a French curve or Fashion Ruler to true the waist, crotch curve, and inseam from the crotch point to knee line, or anywhere an unbroken curved line is required
- a straightedge to true the side from the hip or thigh line (whichever is larger) to the hemline, from the knee line to the hemline on the inseam, and from the center-front/center-back waist to the beginning of the crotch curve
- a pen, pencil, or fine felt-tip marker

Before you begin to redraw the new pattern edges, review the hints at the top of p. 291.

# Three Examples of Truing

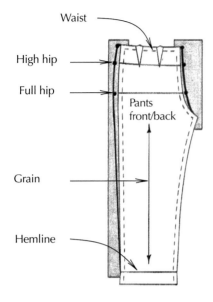

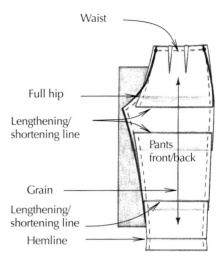

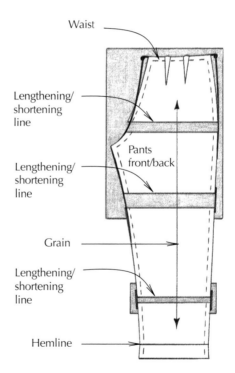

*Where pattern edges have been disrupted by adjustments, redraw the pattern edge so it is a smooth, continuous line.*

*The bold line is a blended line.*

- When truing the waist edge, make sure you fold and pin or tape darts or pleats closed (see the photo at right)
- Adjoining seam edges should be the same length. The inseam edge may differ up to ¾ in. due to easing between the knee and the crotch point.
- Match crotch-point seams and make sure there is a smooth continuous line from the center-front waist to the crotch point to the center-back waist. Reblend through the crotch curve if necessary. Do not change the slope of the curve at this time.
- Make sure all pattern pieces are flat. The only exception is when truing the waist edge where darts or pleats must be folded closed.
- If the grainline has been disrupted, redraw it as a straight continuous line.

# Fitting the Pattern

Having completed the pattern-adjusting process, you are now ready to move into the final phase of preparing your tissue pattern for fitting. Additional seam allowances will be added just in case additional alteration room is needed when fitting your fabric pants.

## Testing the fit

You have several options for testing the fit of your adjusted pattern. You can fit by pinning the pattern together, by making a trial garment, or by altering your fashion-fabric pants.

### Pinning the pattern together

You can only use this first method if your pattern has seam allowances included on it. This method is a good, fast choice for easy-to-fit figures or loose styles. Beware, though, that paper patterns are very fragile and easily ripped unless reinforced with tape, especially through the crotch area and upper inseam. By pinning the pattern together you can check basic length and width fit, but it is difficult to measure comfort through movement. Paper doesn't "give," and because you have only half a pattern, crotch length and sitting comfort are hard to determine. Another drawback is trying to visualize the translation from paper to how actual fabric will hang and shape to the body.

If you do pin-fit, first pin all the darts or pleats closed. Reinforce the crotch curve and upper inseam with tape to prevent tearing. Pin the front and back together at the side and inseams. Clip the crotch-curve seam allowance. Turn up a 2-in. hem allowance. Slip the pinned pattern on one leg, matching the center-front, center-back, side, and waist seams to your body.

*After you have added extra tissue for truing, fold and pin the waist darts or pleats closed before drawing in a new waistline. When unfolded, the edge of the pattern will be the correct shape.*

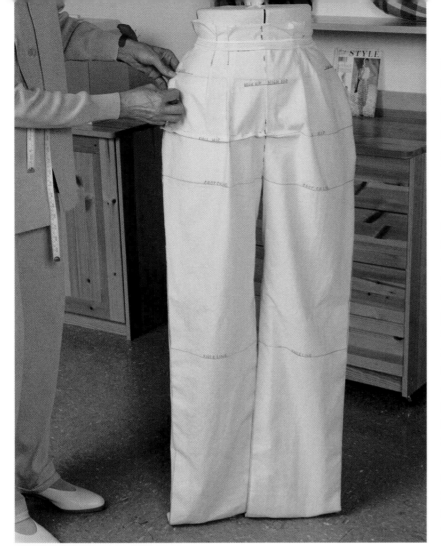

A trial garment made of muslin is a useful fitting tool.

measuring, math, determining ease, or adjusting? If making any new adjustments, make note of the place and amount. Recheck these fitting areas in the fabric pants. Then readjust your Measurement Chart figures.

***Making a trial garment*** Making a trial garment using muslin or an inexpensive fabric similar to what you may choose for a final pair of pants is the second option (see the photo at left). This process is more time-consuming than pin-fitting and is not representative of your actual fabric, but it is a good way to check fit and style and to foolproof several pattern adjustments. Sitting, standing, and movement comfort can be determined. You can also check and recheck fit as many times as necessary, as well as make as many adjustments as needed without concern for the fabric.

Check lengths and widths. Re-pin where necessary if too wide or too long. If the pattern is too small or too short, measure the amount of the needed adjustment. Make adjustments on the pattern. This type of fitting is not intended to get a true fit on close or fitted styles and cannot replace fabric.

Before refiguring adjustment amounts on your Measurement Chart, determine why there is a discrepancy. Did it occur in

***Altering your fashion-fabric pants*** There are several advantages to making your pants in fashion fabric and then checking the fit. First, you can see how your actual fabric looks and drapes. Second, it is easier and faster, especially if you have previously refined your pattern or have few fitting problems. The disadvantages are that some alterations are more difficult and less successful once the fabric is cut out. And making alterations on your fashion fabric may cause the fabric to be overworked. You can damage the fabric, making it

*Increasing the seam allowances will permit you to make alterations easily during the construction process.*

look worn and old before completion. I do not recommend using this method if using expensive fabric unless you have previously thoroughly proofed the fit of your pattern.

The more you demand, the more figure deviations you have, and the closer the fit, the more reason there is to make a trial garment.

## Adding seam allowances

Assuming all measurements, comparisons, and adjustments were made accurately, your garment may still not fit as well as you would like. Although your pants will be statistically correct if you measured and adjusted correctly, it is difficult to account for posture and flesh distribution and how this volume will be taken up in your pants. Therefore, to allow for some alteration room at fabric-fitting time, adjust your seam allowances to the

following minimums on the front and back:

- 1 in. on side seams and inseams
- ⅝ in. at the center front, center back, and through the crotch curve
- 2 in. at the waist edges

You may prefer to add any extra seam allowance to your pattern at this time so you don't forget later when cutting out. If you are a more experienced sewer, add the extra on your fabric when you lay out your pattern.

At this point you have completed your major adjustments, determined as closely as possible by measuring both yourself and your pattern. Recheck your measurements and readjust if necessary. You can take fabric out, but you can't add it back in. Further refining of the fit of your pants (fine-tuning small details) will be done early in the fabric-fitting process.

# 14 | *Refining the Fit*

You are ready to test-fit your adjusted pants pattern in fabric. Only minor changes should be necessary on your fabric pants since major adjustments for measurements were made on your pattern in Chapter 13. Fitting changes made now on your fabric should be transferred to your pattern for a truly personalized custom fit.

Fitting is not an exact science. There is a measure of judgment that only experience can replace. In other words, practice makes perfect, or almost! Whether working with a fitting shell in an inexpensive prototype fabric or fashion fabric you intend to wear, the alteration and adjustment process is done by first pin fitting the fabric on your body, then transferring these alterations through measurements to your pattern and adjusting it. The difficult part is knowing how to transfer these adjustments, when you should make them, and where on the paper pattern to make them.

Pants are a complex problem of translation from a two-dimensional pattern to a three-dimensional garment. Because volume can change the curves and shape of your pants the fit is also affected. Is that 40-in. circumference round, elliptical, oval, more heart shaped, or square?

When fitting your pants, keep in mind the style of the pattern you have chosen. Don't try to transform a loose-fitting trouser style into a jeans fit. The two styles are designed differently from the start. They each fit differently because the purpose and activities each are worn for are very different.

# Analyzing the Fit

Use the illustration on the facing page when analyzing the fit of your pants. Differences will help you determine what refining alterations may be necessary. Check the fit while standing and sitting. Crotch length can vary depending on personal comfort. You should be able to pinch about ½ in. of fabric at the crotch and inseam intersection. Side seams should hang straight down the sides of the legs from the waist to the hemline. There should be sufficient ease at the full hip so you can pinch 2 in. to 3 in. of fabric at the sides (less for slacks). Leg width will vary with hip width. Pants that are too wide can look too large, and too tapered a leg can emphasize the hips.

## Why You May Need to Refine the Fit

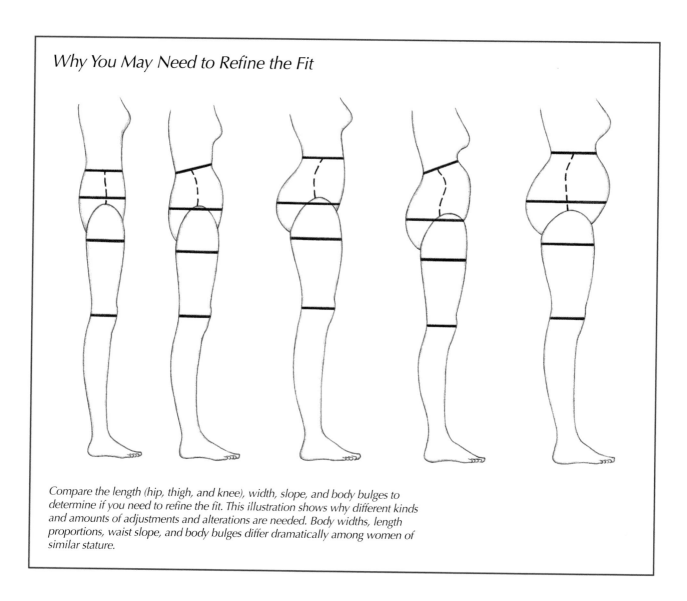

Compare the length (hip, thigh, and knee), width, slope, and body bulges to determine if you need to refine the fit. This illustration shows why different kinds and amounts of adjustments and alterations are needed. Body widths, length proportions, waist slope, and body bulges differ dramatically among women of similar stature.

If you've worked accurately to this point, refining your fit should involve small, subtle changes. Although these changes may seem minor, they are personal changes due to posture, bone structure, or flesh distribution, not style. Some of these changes may be a matter of personal preference rather than a fitting problem. Enlist the assistance of someone else to help in this nip-and-tuck process. Any slight bending or twisting can result in wrinkles, giving you a false sense of the need to adjust. Your pants may look fine to the observer but feel uncomfortable to you.

Some fabrics feel differently, drape differently, and allow a different amount of ease than others. One pair of pants using the same pattern but different fabric than another pair may require some minor changes. For example, on my basic pattern I have two back crotch curves marked, one higher, one lower. When cutting out, I use the higher crotch curve, knowing that when I get the waistband on, I can sew the crotch lower if the fit is too close to my body or if it feels uncomfortable. The two front pleats are made larger or transformed into three when I make my pants in silk instead of wool. Because the bulkiness and draping qualities of fabric differ,

slightly varying the fit, these small changes are not uncommon when fitting your fashion fabric pants.

Small decreases or increases can make a noticeable difference, so work in small increments of ¼ in. for each alteration. Do one alteration at a time. If you notice improvement, it worked!

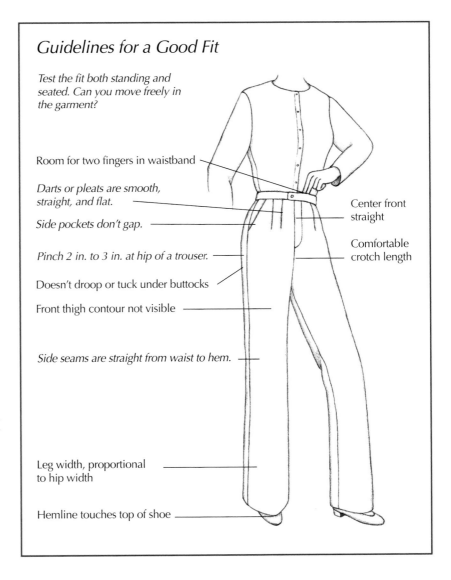

## Guidelines for a Good Fit

Test the fit both standing and seated. Can you move freely in the garment?

Room for two fingers in waistband

Darts or pleats are smooth, straight, and flat.

Side pockets don't gap.

Pinch 2 in. to 3 in. at hip of a trouser.

Doesn't droop or tuck under buttocks

Front thigh contour not visible

Side seams are straight from waist to hem.

Leg width, proportional to hip width

Hemline touches top of shoe

Center front straight

Comfortable crotch length

During the refining process, use different color pens for each fitting to record the amount of change on your Measurement Chart and when making pattern adjustments. That way you can easily identify what changes and the amounts that were made at each fitting. You will end up with a final fit list of adjustments that should be a compilation of your original pattern adjustments and fabric pant alterations. This will be your adjustment guide on future commercial patterns.

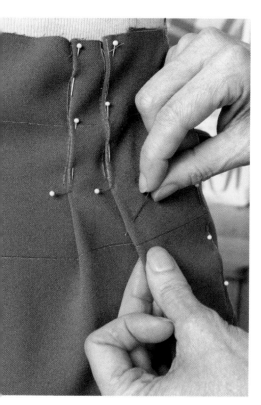

*Pin pleats down to where you want the fullness to disperse before checking the fit.*

# Adding the Third Dimension

You've measured, compared, and adjusted your pattern so it is a two-dimensional statistical representation of your body—leaving no guesswork. Now it's time to add the third dimension: volume. Don't automatically assume that your adjusted pattern is going to be a perfect fit. The next step is to test your adjustments in fabric. As I recommended, if you made your pants out of an inexpensive fabric you can mark on it, pin and sew out unnecessary fabric if the pants are too loose, and sew in additional fabric pieces if an area is too snug, too short, or has an insufficient seam allowance. You can try the pants on as many times as necessary to achieve your perfect fit.

## Factors that affect fit

When fitting your pants there are several factors that affect their fit and feel. These include posture, heel height, under-garments, panty hose, and time of day or month. Try to replicate these factors so that your fabric fitting will be an exact representation of when your measurements were taken. For every fitting problem there can be several solutions. Likewise,

one solution can fix several problems. Don't try and make too many corrections for the same problem at once until you know whether or not there has been improvement.

## Fitting order

In order to fit your fabric pants keep construction as simple as possible by pinning or basting the front and back together. For the sake of comfort when testing movement and sitting room, I suggest basting the front and back together at the center, crotch, and inseams. Eliminate the zipper at this time but leave an opening to get into your pants. Pockets do not need to be incorporated unless they complete the pants front, such as the underlay of slant pockets. Fit first without the waistband. Refer to Fitting Your Pants during Construction (p. 309) for more hints and guidelines when constructing your fashion fabric pants or prototype.

It is best to do fitting in a logical sequence. To avoid over fitting and disrupting the lay of the pleats, pin or baste them down. Begin at the waist and gradually dissipate pleat take-up as you near the crotch level or as pinned on your pattern when

## Fitting Waist, Hip, and Thigh Areas

*Assess the looseness or tightness of fit in the width areas of your pants.*

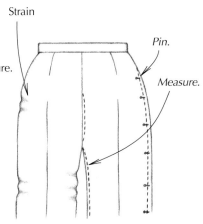

**Decrease**

**Increase**

Looseness · Pin. · Measure.

Looseness · Pin. · Measure.

Strain · Pin. · Measure.

*If your pants are too loose in the waist, high hip, or full hip, pin out the excess at the sides. If the leg is too wide in the thigh area and below, pin out the excess at the side and inseam. If too tight, release the side seams through the waist and hip areas until your pants are comfortable or there are no more horizontal wrinkles evident. Release the side seam and inseam for thigh and leg.*

*Measure the excess pinned out or the amounts released at both side seams on front and back waist and hip areas to determine the **total** decrease or increase amount. Divide this new alteration amount by 4 if it's 2 in. or less, or by 8 if it's more than 2 in. Decrease or increase front and back pattern pieces this new amount (as instructed in Chapter 3) for waist and hips.*

*For thigh and leg, measure the amount of the decrease or increase at the side and inseam front and back to determine the **total** amount of change. Divide this new total by 4. Decrease or increase front and back pattern pieces as instructed in Chapter 3 for thigh increase/decrease.*

you measured it. Then follow this step-by-step fitting sequence.

**1.** Assess whether the waist and hip area is too big or too small (see the drawing above). Take in or let out as necessary on each side to achieve a comfortable,

balanced, stress-free fit. Don't worry about the darts right now. Do not adjust your pattern yet.

**2.** Arrange the pants so the full hip line is parallel to the floor in front and back.

**3.** Fasten a 1-in. elastic band or Ban-Rol at the same waist level as when measured.

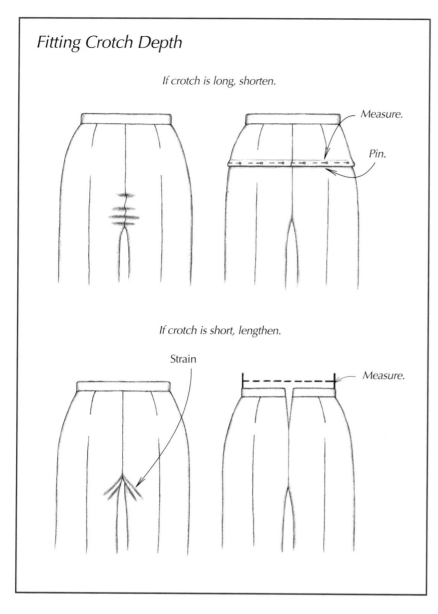

## Fitting Crotch Depth

*If crotch is long, shorten.*

Measure.

Pin.

*If crotch is short, lengthen.*

Strain

Measure.

**4.** Check length proportions beginning with the crotch depth. The intersection of the crotch and inseam should be ½ in. to 1 in. below your body. If too long, pin out the excess as in the drawing above, below the waist but above the crotch line level. If too short, lengthen by dropping the waist. Measure the amount shortened or lengthened and adjust your pattern to reflect these alterations. Refigure the adjustment amount in column 7 on your Measurement Chart. Next check the waist to knee proportion. The knee line mark on your fabric should closely match the front middle of your knee. Pin out the excess if too long, parallel to the floor, between the crotch line and knee line. If too short, measure the distance between the knee line marking on your fabric and your actual mid-knee. Measure the amount to be shortened or lengthened. Adjust your pattern. Refigure the adjustment amount in column 7 as for crotch depth.

**5.** You did a general too big or too small adjustment in step 1 so your pants wouldn't fall off or ride too high. Now refine the circumference fit of the waist, high hip, full hip, and thigh. This may involve taking in or letting out different amounts in each of these areas. It may also be necessary to rebalance the side seams in these fitting areas, especially the waist and high hip. This means that if your front or back half is proportionally larger in any of these areas, you may need to let out or take in different amounts on the front and back seams so the side seam will hang straight and not curve to the front or back where more fabric is needed due to a body bulge. You are contouring the fit to your body, so take in or let out on the side and inseams to achieve the fit and comfort, as well as the personal style, you prefer. Alter leg width from knee line to hem equally at the side and inseam. Measure altered amounts in these areas. Adjust your pattern, then refigure the adjustment amount in column 7 on your Measurement Chart.

**6.** Fit the waistband, altering the pleats or darts as needed. Refining them will be done later.

**7.** Crotch length can be increased or decreased at the center front or back by raising or lowering the waist seam. More specific alterations for excess fullness or tightness in the front or back upper thigh and buttocks can be made by lengthening or shortening the crotch point (see the top drawing at right). Measure the alteration amounts. Adjust your pattern and refigure the adjustment amount in column 7 of your Measurement Chart.

Altering the crotch curve on the front or back may require changing the slope or angle of the curve to fit more comfortably and to reduce wrinkling (see the bottom drawing at right). A bit of testing is required here, so make alterations in small amounts—¼ in. or less each time. The seam allowance will be trimmed later to ¼ in., which will give a slightly looser fit.

**8.** Refine the darts.

**9.** Alter the finished length.

## Fitting Crotch Length

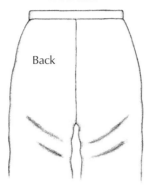

**Decrease**

**Increase**

*If pants sag and wrinkle under the buttocks, reduce the crotch length on the back only. Decreases should be made:*
- *at crotch point on inseam for a flat buttocks*
*OR*
- *at waist for a flat buttocks*

*Increases should be made:*
- *at crotch point on inseam if fabric cups under buttocks*
- *at waist for full buttocks*

## Altering Crotch Curve

*May be done on front, back, or both according to need and comfort.*

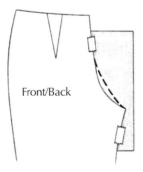

**Raise crotch curve**

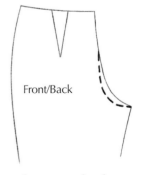

**Lower crotch curve**

*The crotch curve needs to be raised when you have one of the following:*
- *Low full abdomen*
- *Prominent pubic bone*
- *High and/or full buttocks*

*The crotch curve needs to be lowered when you have one of the following:*
- *Excess fabric just above crotch at pubic bone*
- *Low buttocks*
- *Back crotch seam cutting between buttocks*

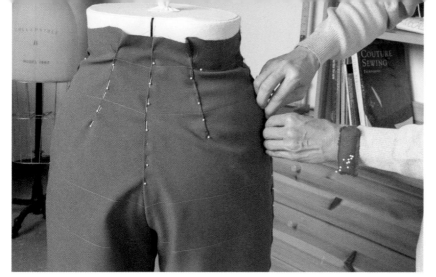

Horizontal wrinkles indicate that the pants are too tight in the high hip area while the diamond-shaped wrinkle in the seat area indicates that the center back seam is too angled and the crotch curve too shallow.

*Postural variation can cause diagonal wrinkles at the back of the leg. Eliminate them by decreasing the length of the back leg above the knee line. Increase the length the same amount below the knee line to keep vertical seams the same length as front.*

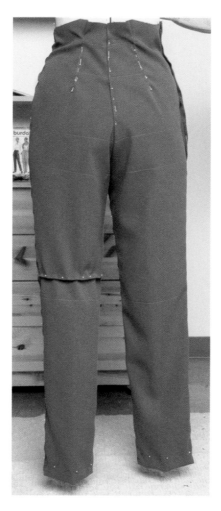

## Read your wrinkles (on your pants)!

Vertical wrinkles mean pants are too loose. Horizontal or diagonal wrinkles mean pants are too tight someplace (see the photos at left). This could involve one alteration or several in different places.

## Guidelines for darts and pleats

Although pleat size is specified on the pattern, the size and number of pleats can be increased or decreased to help fit the waist. The size, number, shape, length, and angle of generic pattern darts can be modified so your fabric is contoured like your body. Darts are one of the most important ways to achieve fit. Darts closest to the side seam are usually shorter and shape the hip curve while darts closest to center front or back provide shaping for tummies and buttocks. If your waist is the same size or larger than your hips, you may not need any darts. A pattern adjustment made in Chapter 13 for crotch depth may signal the need for a dart length alteration. You may need to make some changes to the pleats and darts or to combine these changes with seam alterations to achieve a well-contoured fit. Here are some guidelines for specific problems.

**Fleshy round high hip** A fleshy round hip will require a larger dart. Increase the size of the dart closest to the side seam to give a more rounded effect just below the point. Redraw the dart with an inward curve to allow for greater fullness in the high-hip area. A pleat or side seam alteration may be necessary to compensate for the slight reduction in waist size.

**Flat or concave high hip** This dart alteration requires a smaller dart closest to the side seam to reduce the bulge just below the dart point because the body is less curved. Increase pleats or side seams to take up additional waist increase created by reducing the dart size. Redraw the dart with an outward curve to take out extra fabric fullness created by a flatter body.

**Full or flat buttocks** To create more room for full buttocks, increase the dart closest to the center back. For flat buttocks, less room is required so decrease the dart closest to center back.

**Angle of darts** To create a slimmer look while still doing the same fitting, try angling the back dart(s) parallel to the side seam or center back (see the drawing below). If you change the angle, the dart must still point to the area where the fullness is needed. Reangle the back dart if you changed the angle of the center back seam.

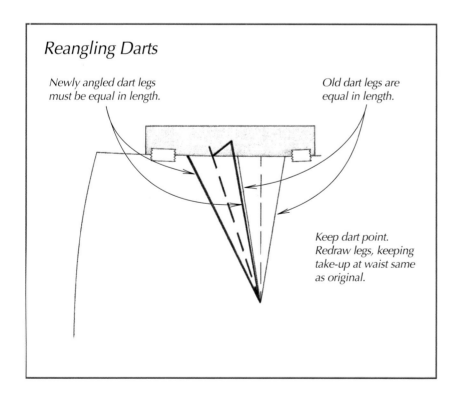

## Reangling Darts

Newly angled dart legs must be equal in length.

Old dart legs are equal in length.

Keep dart point. Redraw legs, keeping take-up at waist same as original.

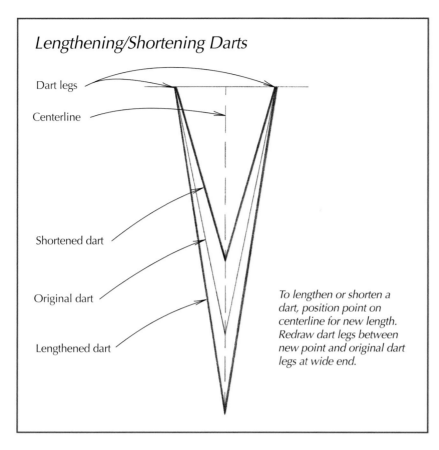

## Lengthening/Shortening Darts

Dart legs

Centerline

Shortened dart

Original dart

Lengthened dart

*To lengthen or shorten a dart, position point on centerline for new length. Redraw dart legs between new point and original dart legs at wide end.*

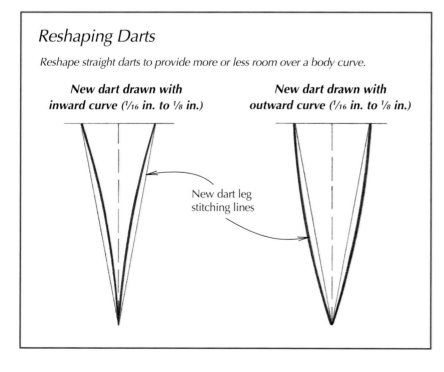

## Reshaping Darts

*Reshape straight darts to provide more or less room over a body curve.*

**New dart drawn with inward curve (¹/₁₆ in. to ¹/₈ in.)**

**New dart drawn with outward curve (¹/₁₆ in. to ¹/₈ in.)**

New dart leg stitching lines

### Excess fabric at end of dart

The problem can be solved by shortening the dart (see the top drawing at left), by decreasing its size, or by reshaping the dart (see the bottom drawing at left). You may need to do all three. If excess fabric still remains, make two smaller darts that total the same width at the wide end as the original single dart.

### Excess fabric in the dart area

Eliminate this problem by increasing the size of the dart, by reshaping the dart, or by lengthening the dart (see the top drawing at left). Sometimes you must apply a combination of these solutions, do all three, or make two smaller darts. For a better fit if you have a sway back, try curving the wide end of the dart outward then gradually curving it inward toward the point.

# Your Permanent Pattern

Now that you have fine-tuned the fit of your pants, check to make sure you have transferred all alterations on your fabric pants to adjustments on your pattern. Column 7 on your Measurement Chart should also reflect these changes. For future reference, make notes on your chart regarding crotch curve alterations as well as what pleats and darts you have changed and how. Your adjusted tissue pattern should now accurately represent

*Make a permanent pattern by tracing your working pattern onto sturdy see-through material, drawing in all reference points and pattern markings.*

the fit of your pants. This pattern can be used to make many pairs of pants, and you'll save a lot of time not having to fit them all. You will also be able to adjust a new commercial pattern based on your revised adjustment record or to apply adjustments to ready-to-wear pants to get a better fit. Keep in mind, though, that not all adjustments are possible once pants are constructed.

You can also use your adjusted pattern to design new style variations. (See Chapter 16 for more on stylizing your pants.)

Once your working pattern is finalized you want to make sure that your pattern will last. Make a clean copy, without all the tape and added paper. There are

specific products for this purpose. They are available in paper, nonwoven material, and plastic and come with various size preprinted grids or plain. I do not recommend fusing your working tissue pattern to more permanent material. If you have used tape, you can end up with a gooey mess on your iron and a ruined pattern. Copy all the grainlines and pattern markings. Indicate all the horizontal length lines such as high hip, full hip, crotchline, kneeline, and hemline. Record the date, your weight, and the pattern name, number, and size.

# 15 Constructing the Pants

You've worked meticulously on preparing and adjusting your pattern to get the perfect fit. Careless fabric preparation or rushed construction can be the cause of poor fit just as much as figure deviations. Each step of the construction process is as important as measuring, adjusting, and altering. Fitting is a continual refining process progressing through construction.

Methods of practical fitting vary greatly. Your objective is to get a picture of the whole situation and assess the fit of your pants as quickly as possible. Fit is affected by the behavior of your fabric. As with the pattern adjusting you did in Chapter 13, fitting is a systematic, sequential process. Whether you jump directly into the permanent construction of your pants or you progressively fit during construction will depend on whether or not you have tested the fit of your pattern. The degree of fit demanded by the style of your pattern also plays an important role in your decision. Unless you have used this pattern before and proofed the fit in an actual garment, I advise first doing some basic, structural-seams-only construction to validate this picture to avoid later ripping out your permanent stitching to make alterations. Pin or base the side, inseams, center front, and back crotch seams to get a general feel for the fit of your pants. Try your pants on. Based on what you see and how your pants feel, you can determine if you need to refine your fit or can immediately begin the permanent stitching and construction of your pants.

I recommend that you resist the temptation to make any further pattern changes other than those that accompany the fitting alterations. You've done the hard part. Now enjoy sewing.

# Constructing Fashion Fabric Pants

Fabric that is pattern ready has been trued, preshrunk, and pressed. Whether working with a prototype or actual fashion fabric, accuracy in cutting, marking, and sewing can affect the fit and the look of your pants. I've listed the general steps for constructing pants to give you an overview of the sewing process. More detailed instructions for each step will follow later in the chapter. I advise consulting your pattern guide sheet sewing instructions because details and processes within differently styled pants can vary. Therefore, the construction order for your pants may be slightly different.

1. Cut the prototype or fashion fabric. Wait to cut the lining until after alterations on the fabric are completed and transferred to the pattern. This saves time so the lining doesn't have to be recut due to fitting alterations.

2. Transfer construction markings, darts, and pleats to the fabric.

3. Sew the darts and pleats.

4. Press the darts and/or pleats.

5. Apply the pockets.

6. Install the zipper.

7. Sew the inseams.

8. Sew the side seams.

9. Stitch the crotch seam.

10. Fit and mark the waistline if not previously done. Fit the waistband.

11. Baste the lining to the pants at the waist edge.

12. Attach the waistband, belt loops, casing, or waist facing (whichever applies).

13. Sew a hook and bar or button and buttonhole on the waistband.

14. Hem and/or cuff the pants. For a prototype, simply pin the hem.

For lining, follow the general construction steps 1 through 4, 7 through 9, 11, and 14. Leave the lining seam open above the zipper installation. For a fly zipper, see p. 330 for special lining preparation.

# Fitting Your Pants during Construction

The following guidelines will help you fit your pants through-out the construction process, just in case minor adjustments need to made. These can apply whether you are using a fashion fabric or a prototype fabric.

- Use a contrasting color thread when basting your seams.
- If this is the first time you have used your pattern, pin or baste the inseam and side seams for easiest adjusting and baste the ⅝-in. crotch seam, leaving an opening at the front or back for trying on the pants (see the photo at right). Pin the opening closed on the seamline.
- Eliminate all details such as pockets and zippers. These are added later once you are sure of the fit.
- Cut the waistband 6 in. longer than your waist body measurement (column 1 on your Measurement Chart), and 3¾ in. wide for a 1¼-in. finished band.
- If working with a prototype fabric for fitting only, mark all personal pattern reference points on the outside of the fabric as well as seamlines so you can pinpoint the location and amounts of alteration/adjustment needed.

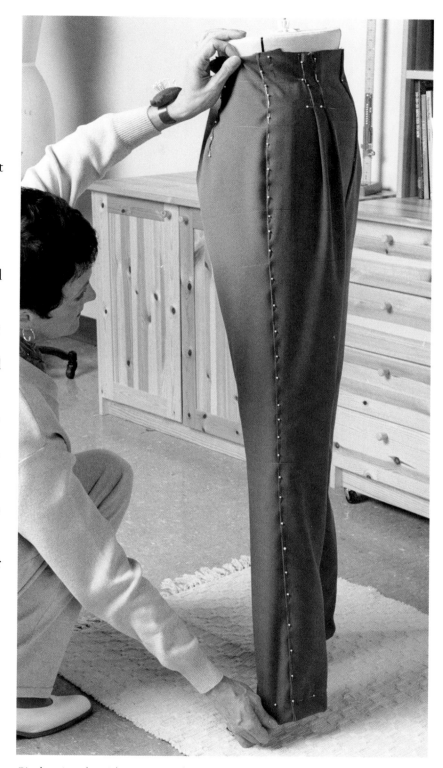

*Pin-basting the side seams and inseams is a quick way to check your fit and make alterations before the final sewing.*

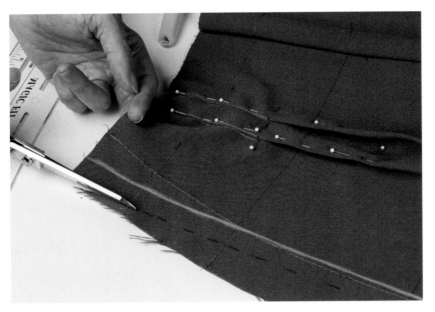

*Recut your seam allowances to an even width after you've made your alterations.*

# Layout, Cutting, and Marking

Many sewers, motivated to see their pants sewn together, hurry through the layout, cutting, and marking process thinking the sewing process is the most important. Nothing can be more misleading. Accuracy and precision begins now with laying out your pattern and proceeds through the cutting and marking. Working carefully now will result in a better-looking and better-fitting pair of pants. Careful preparation of your fabric for the sewing process is time well spent.

## Layout

If your pattern does not have seam allowances included, add them in now. Add a minimum of 1 in. to side seams and inseams and 2 in. above the horizontal waistline on the front and back and ⅝ in. to the center crotch seams. If your pattern has seam allowances included, add enough to total 1 in. on side seams and inseams and 2 in. above the horizontal waistline. This will allow some extra alteration room and can always be trimmed.

On the first page of your pattern guide sheet you will see various cutting diagrams. The pattern is laid on the fabric in these layouts in a particular way. Choose the layout that corresponds to the

- If working with fashion fabric, use a marking procedure that can be easily seen and removed but does not rub off or harm the surface of your fabric.
- Before removing the pins or basting stitches, mark the seamline, making sure all seam allowances are an even width to avoid construction confusion and later misfits.
- Consult the sewing instructions on your pattern guide sheet and the construction sequence specific to your pattern details.

pattern view, size, and fabric width you are using. If you are lining your pants, the lining fabric may be a different width than your pants fabric. If so, a different cutting layout will be used to correspond to your fabric width. Fold the fabric with the wrong sides out and selvages together or as diagrammed in the cutting layout. Usually fabric will be folded along the length, parallel to the selvage. Whenever possible, place pattern pieces going in the same up/down direction. Some fabrics absorb or reflect light differently when viewed from opposite directions (top to bottom vs. bottom to top). A color difference may be noticeable when worn if the pattern pieces are not laid out in the same direction.

Place the pants front and back on the fabric first. Next position the pattern pieces that require a folded fabric edge followed by any remaining pieces. If possible, reserve space along a single selvage to cut the waistband. For pieces that are marked with a grainline arrow, place a pin at one end of the grainline arrow. Measure between the pin and selvage or fold. Pivot the other end of the grainline arrow until it measures the same distance, then pin. Use pins or weights to secure the pattern to the fabric. Precisely measure each piece to ensure straight grain placement.

*Cutting doesn't have to be a chore with the right equipment and comfortable table height.*

## Cutting

As you begin to cut your fabric, here are some suggestions from my experience that help me cut accurately and prevent fabric distortion.

- Handle your fabric as little as possible to prevent stretching.
- Use sharp shears with a bent handle. They allow you to keep the pattern and fabric flat on the solid cutting surface. Do not lift the shears off the cutting surface, and take long, even strokes.
- Hold the fabric down flat with your free hand close to the edge of the pattern to prevent slippage. Use long, firm strokes on straight edges and shortened strokes around curves. A rotary cutter and mat can be used instead of shears.

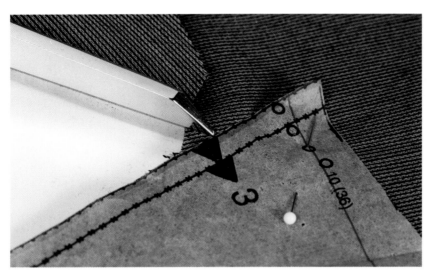
*Cutting out notches away from the pattern provides more seam allowance room for alterations.*

- Cut multiple notches as one. If there isn't room to cut the notches out, designate their position by marking with tracing paper. I prefer cutting notches "out," away from the pattern until I'm sure of the fit (see the photo above). Cutting notches this way is important if you only have ⅝-in. seam allowances. If you cut the V-shaped notch in toward your pattern, you reduce the size of the seam allowance. You compromise the usable amount of seam allowance for alteration purposes if your pattern fit was not previously proofed, as well as the amount left for finishing your seams. If the notch is cut out, away from the pattern, the next time you use it you can mark the notches with a small snip in the edge of the fabric.

## Marking

Pattern symbols are your road map through construction, so marking correctly is essential. Marking is done after the fabric is cut out but before the pattern pieces are removed.

Construction symbols to be marked include dots, stitching lines (such as topstitching line for fly zipper), foldlines, center front line for fly zipper, darts, tucks, pleats, buttonhole(s), and pocket placement lines.

The methods and tools you use to mark depend on your fabric, the pattern symbol, and which side of the fabric that needs to be marked. You can choose from a variety of methods to mark your fabric. The most common are tracing, pin marking, tailor tacks, or baste marking with contrasting thread. Some pattern marking may require two different marking methods and tools to transfer construction marks to your fabric. Most marking is done on the wrong side. Pleats, topstitching, and pocket placement lines can be the exception. Some of the tools you may need include the following:

- Tracing paper and tracing wheel (choose the lightest color paper that is visible on your fabric)
- Dressmaker's pencil or tailor's chalk
- Fabric marking pen that is air erasable and water soluble

*To mark fabric with a tracing wheel, place tracing paper against the wrong side of the fabric and run the wheel along the pattern markings.*

*Clear and accurate markings will make your sewing easier.*

## MARKING HINTS

Regardless of the method and tools you use, the marking method should be readily visible, accurate, and easily removed (or not visible) on the right side of your fabric. Here are some hints.

• Always do a test on both right and wrong sides of the fabric to check for visibility and ease of removal.

• Use a straightedge or French curve for accuracy in marking lines and curves.

• For long lines, mark dots along the line, then connect the marks with chalk, fabric marking pen, or dressmaker's pencil.

• For lines on the right side of the fabric, first mark the line on the wrong side with dressmaker's tracing paper. Then baste on the line to mark the right side (see the photo at right).

• If it is difficult to tell the right side of the fabric from the wrong side, mark the wrong side with a piece of removable tape.

• If the garment piece will be interfaced, mark it after applying the interfacing.

• During construction keep pattern pieces handy for quick reference of pattern markings.

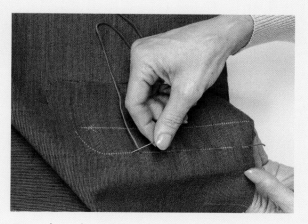

*To mark on the right side, baste from the wrong side in a contrasting color.*

# Lining Your Pants

If you decide to line your pants, the following guidelines will help you get the best results.

- Line only the knee area 5 in. above and below the knee line to prevent baggy knees.
- Lay out, cut, and mark the lining in the same way you did the fashion fabric. Attention to one-direction placement of pieces is not necessary.
- Cut the lining on the crosswise grain (if pattern length permits) to help prevent the pants from stretching.
- If you know the exact finished length of your pants, cut the lining ½ in. longer at this time, or wait and determine the length at the time of hemming.
- Stitch darts and pleats in the lining. When pressing, lay darts in the opposite direction from the fashion fabric to reduce bulk.
- Increase seam allowances by 1/16 in. Sew, finish (if necessary), and press side seams and inseams, leaving the zipper area open.
- Reduce the seam allowance through the crotch curve to ½ in. so the lining doesn't "sit" on top of the fashion fabric.

# Pressing

There are a variety of pressing tools available. Some are basic tools used generally for all types of garment construction. Others are helpful for specific garments or fabrics.

## Basic tools

- Tailor's ham for maintaining the shaping of curved seams and darts
- Seam roll

*Besides general pressing tools, use seamstick, brown paper, and needle board for special pressing problems.*

- Sleeve board
- Point presser/clapper
- See-through press cloth for nonwool fabrics
- Steam/dry iron
- Padded table or board

## Special helpful tools

- Padded seam stick for pressing leg seams open (substitute a heavy cardboard tube in a pinch)
- Needle or Velvaboard for napped fabrics
- Two strips of brown paper that are 2 in. wide and as long as possible to use under seams and darts to prevent the outline from showing on the right side of the fabric, especially on plain dark fabrics and gabardines
- A large press cloth about 15 in. by 30 in. My favorite is fine muslin and ivory wool challis washed several times and sewn together so it is 15 in. by 60 in.

## Techniques

Good pressing throughout construction is as important as sewing straight seams. It is the key to a custom-made look. Maintaining the grain and texture of your fabric as well as shaping it to your body contours assures you of a neat, professional-looking pair of pants.

- Before beginning a project, make up several seam samples and do a test run, varying the iron temperature setting and moisture slightly. See what gives you the best results.
- Press with the grain of the fabric.
- Because you will be pressing during construction, use an up-and-down motion rather than a gliding motion as in ironing.
- Press as you go. Every time the sewing machine touches my fabric I press, even if only to smooth staystitching or basting.
- Make sure you are satisfied with the fit before pressing darts, pleats, or seams.
- After sewing a seam, lay your pants flat and press over the line of stitching. This embeds the stitches into the fabric and smooths the seam before further processing.
- Generally, press seam allowances open and flat unless doing a special type of seam or finish.
- Do not press over pins or basting thread (unless using silk thread).
- Allow fabric to dry thoroughly before handling.
- Press after completing seam finishes or special seams.
- Press on the wrong side.
- Use a press cloth when top pressing.
- Use a ham to shape and smooth darts and to press curved seams.
- If using a napped fabric, always lay the right side against the needle or Velvaboard.

# Seams and Finishes

Plain seams are the backbone of garment construction and are the seams most often illustrated in your pattern guide sheet sewing instructions. Plain seams can require some special handling or finishing and are an essential part of the sewing process. Your pants' durability and appearance are a result of smooth, well-finished seams. When making a choice about which seam finish to use, consider the type of fabric, style and purpose of your pants, sewing equipment you have available, and your time and sewing experience.

## Plain seams

A plain seam is the most common way of joining two pieces of fabric. Many other seams and finishes are derived from it. The edges of the seam allowance are left exposed on the inside of the garment. The edges may be finished to make them more durable or to reduce bulk. Standards for a plain seam are as follows:

- Stitching secured at each end
- Even and accurate seam allowances
- Flat and smooth
- Free of distortion
- Pressed open and flat

## Seam finishes

Seam finishes provide a neat edge and prevent raveling, distortion, or the seam from pulling out. Seams can be stitched and pinked, double stitched and trimmed, serged or overlocked, or bound. Choose the finish that works best with the fabric you have chosen, taking into consideration how much the fabric ravels, how much it will be laundered, bulk, and how much time you have to complete your project. Points to keep in mind when selecting the finish are:

- Location of the seam
- Whether your pants are lined
- Whether your pants will be laundered or dry-cleaned

# Creaseline

Classic pleated-trouser-style pants generally have a pressed-in creaseline, which can be established before construction is started. The front creaseline extends from the hem into the first pleat. The procedure is simple: Fold each front pants leg in half right side out, matching the side seam to the inseam at the hem to establish the midpoint. For darted pants the front creaseline begins 3 in. above crotch level and extends to the hem. The back creaseline extends from the midpoint at the hem edge to the crotch level.

It is more difficult to remove and reestablish the creaseline after your pants are completed. Therefore you should be completely satisfied with the fit and leg width before establishing the creaseline. Any alteration after the creaseline is set could distort it so it would not be centered on the leg.

# Darts and Pleats

Darts and pleats don't present any challenge in the cutting process. Their symmetry in length and width depends on precise marking and sewing.

## Darts

Darts shape straight fabric to fit the curved areas of the figure. They widen at the waist where the fabric width needs to be reduced and taper to a point in the hip area where fabric width needs to be increased. Darts vary in size and shape. It is not unusual to have two darts on the front or back of your pattern, each one a different size and length. Each one is positioned to fit a different curve of the body.

**Directions and marking** Darts are constructed on the wrong side of the fabric. To make it easier to match the stitching lines at the wide end, make a small clip in the edge of the fabric on each marked stitching line. Chalk in a ½-in. line

*If you are sure of the fit, press the creaseline in before construction.*

perpendicular to the point of the dart. This ensures that there will be no guessing about the exact end point.

**Procedure** Fold each dart carefully, matching lines and pin. Begin stitching at the wide end and continue to the point, which is marked by the perpendicular line. Stop at the point with your needle in your fabric and on the edge of the fold. To eliminate a bulge at the dart point, shorten your stitch length to 1 or to 18 to 20 stitches per inch. Take four stitches beyond the marked end line. Stitches should be right along the fold edge (see the left photo on the facing page). Run the last stitch off the fold. Tie several square knots at the point to secure. Clip threads ½ in. from the knot. Press the dart flat as stitched, being careful not to press a crease in beyond the point. Then shape over a ham and press the dart from the wrong side. Darts are usually pressed with the folded edge lying toward the center front or back.

## Pleats

Pleats are folds of fabric providing controlled fullness where you want it. Pleats can be stitched down, crisply pressed, or softly released. The type of fabric you're using will determine whether your pleats are intended to be crisp and sharp or soft and gentle. Pleats work best on light-to medium-weight fabrics. Pleats on heavyweight fabrics tend to be too bulky. A crisp edge can be attained with linen, poplin, flannel, gabardine, crepe de chine, lightweight wool, broad-cloth, or similar fabrics. In some fabrics, a burst of steam without touching the iron to the fabric is sufficient. For a soft look, a delicate touch with the iron is important, or you can allow the pleats to flow without pressing.

### Marking and direction
Transfer pleat line markings to the right side of fabric. Experiment now to see which direction you want your pleats to face: center or side. Try them one way on one side and the opposite way on the other side.

### Procedure
On the right side of the fabric, crease the foldline or leading edge and bring it over in the direction marked on the tissue pattern to meet the placement line (the line the directional arrow points to). Make sure pleat lines are parallel and all edges are perfectly even at the waist edge. Pin in place. Machine-baste at ½ in. and ¾ in. through the double thickness parallel to the waist edge, or machine-stitch (edgestitch) close to the fold edge if desired (see the right photo on the facing page).

# Pockets

No matter what type of pockets your pants have—patch, inserted, or welt—there are some steps you can take to help your pockets hold their shape, look crisp, and contour to your body. First, you should stabilize the pants or pocket by fusing a ¾-in. strip of interfacing over the seamline in the stitching area where the pocket is to be attached. To help prevent stretching, cut the joining edge of an angled pocket on the straight grain or selvage. During application, sew in a ¼-in.-wide piece of stay tape, lining selvage, or silk/polyester ribbon to help maintain shaping. Use a tailor's

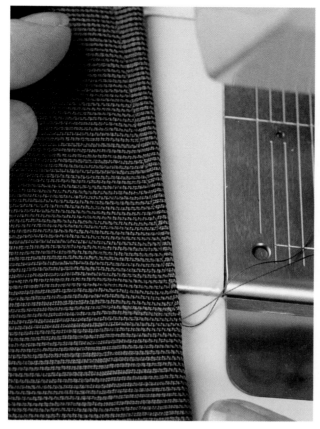

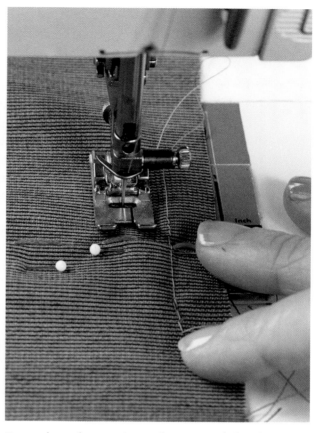

A well-sewn dart is smooth and even all the way down. The chalk mark ensures that darts are the same length.

Baste pleats down twice so they won't shift or become distorted.

ham when pressing slant or inseam inserted pockets to maintain the hip curve shaping. A clapper will help to flatten any bulk. Whenever possible, understitch (as you would a facing) pocket seams where they attach to your pants to help keep edges flat and the seam from rolling to the outside.

The most common type of pocket in pants is an inseam pocket. This style of pocket is inserted in the side seam, and the pocket sack is hidden inside the pants. It is inconspicuous

and the easiest to sew for a beginner. Typically this type of pocket is an extension of the pants and is cut all in one with the pants front and back. However, as an alternate method, some patterns have you cut the pocket as a separate piece. The pocket is cut four times, two times on double-thickness fabric for each pocket in the pants. One pocket piece is stitched to each pants front and back. This is a little more time-consuming than the pocket that is included as part of the main pattern pieces and cut as one.

If your pattern includes either type of inseam side pocket, your pattern guide sheet will instruct you how to sew and finish them. I prefer side-seam pockets that are caught in the horizontal waist seam as opposed to pockets that are cut as separate pieces and attached only to each front and back side seam. Pockets attached at the waist are supported by this seam, preventing them from dragging and distorting the side seams. This is especially important if your pockets are used for something other than decorative purposes.

## Pocket instructions/ procedure

To make inseam pockets or convert ones that are not sewn at the waist, follow these steps.

**1.** If you have a dart or pleat in the area that will be covered by the pocket, pin it closed.

**2.** Place a 15-in. by 8-in. piece of see-through paper over your pants side front and secure with tape or pins. Trace the side edge of the pattern from the waist down 9½ in. Mark two points along this side line, one 1½ in. from the waist and the second 7½ in. from the waist. These marks designate the pocket opening. From the side waist, mark a point 3 in. in toward the center front along the waist edge. The pocket will be 11 in.

at its deepest point and 6½ in. at its widest point. Draw in a completed pocket line beginning at the lowest side mark, sloping down to the lowest point of the pocket, around to the widest, and finishing at the waist mark. Place a notch in the lower portion of the pocket closest to the center front.

**3.** Measure and mark corresponding points on the pants front and back waist and side.

**4.** If constructing the pocket from lining or fabric other than fashion fabric, cut a facing piece from fashion fabric to reduce pocket bulk. This will give the appearance at the pocket opening that the whole pocket has been cut from your fashion fabric. The facing is made from the pocket piece by tracing the side edge of the pocket and extending the tracing a minimum of 2 in. in toward the body of the pocket at the top and bottom. Draw a straight or slightly curved line (a French curve is helpful here), connecting the top and bottom edges. Finish this edge with an appropriate seam finish if needed. This facing edge can be directly topstitched to the pocket. Baste the remaining facing-piece edges to the pocket piece at the side.

## Side-opening pocket

To eliminate the need for a zipper in your pants, you can modify the inseam pocket instructions to create an opening on the left side through the pocket in the following way.

**1.** Increase the width of the pocket 2 in. at the waist edge. The mark on the horizontal waist seam should be 5 in. from the side. Increase the depth 2 in. to 13 in. at the deepest part of the pocket. On the long pocket edge opposite the side seam, measure down 8 in. from the upper edge, and mark a point $5/8$ in. in from the edge. Clip to that point. Form a narrow hem on each pocket piece (fold under $1/4$ in. then $3/8$ in. and machine-stitch) along this edge. This finished edge will remain open and take the place of a zipper opening.

**2.** Complete construction of the side-opening pocket as instructed on your pattern guide sheet for inseam pockets, but leave the long hemmed edge open.

**3.** Stitch the pocket pieces together from the lower dot on the side seam to the clip. Seam-finish the pocket between the dot and side seam as needed.

**4.** Match the side seams and lower edge of the pocket pieces. Stitch the seam between the lower dot and the hem.

**5.** Modify the waistband length. Waistband length will be waist size as fitted, plus two seam allowances and the width of one pocket at the waist edge plus $1\frac{1}{4}$ in. for the closure extension.

# Zippers

When selecting a zipper, it is important to choose the proper length as well as the proper type for the application you intend to use. Although pattern notions often list a 7-in.-long zipper as a requirement, I prefer an opening that's a little longer so I don't have to squeeze into my pants and put stress on the zipper. Therefore I select a 9-in. zipper, set it slightly below the zipper-stop mark, and then shorten it at the top if I am installing a waistband. You can choose from three appropriate types of zippers for pants: conventional, invisible, and special purpose.

## General guidelines for zippers

- Reinforce the wrong side of the seam allowances where the zipper will be installed with $3/4$-in.-wide strips of fusible interfacing slightly longer than the zipper opening.
- Purchase a zipper longer than the pattern calls for.
- Finish seam allowances before starting the zipper.

# SHORTENING A ZIPPER

Zippers can easily be shortened. If the edge will be finished with a waistband, shorten the zipper from the top. If the edge will be finished with a facing, shorten the zipper from the bottom.

## From the top

1. Install the zipper, placing the bottom stop at the desired length.

2. Open the zipper.

3. Stitch a bar tack by hand or machine-stitch over the teeth on one side of the zipper in the seam allowance.

4. Cut off the excess zipper even with the raw edge of the garment.

## From the bottom

1. Close the zipper and measure the desired length. Add 1 in. for an invisible zipper.

2. Zigzag across the coil or teeth 8 to 10 times.

3. Cut the zipper $1/2$ in. below the stitching.

4. Install the zipper.

- Press seam allowances open except for the invisible zipper application.
- Whenever possible, apply the zipper while the garment is flat. If fit is questionable or the garment includes special design features, apply the zipper later or when instructed on your pattern guide sheet.
- Preshrink the zipper unless it is 100% polyester.
- Press the fold out of the zipper tape from the wrong side.
- If you purchased a longer zipper, a portion of the unstitched zipper will hang off the garment above the waist. Follow the instructions for shortening a zipper (see the sidebar above).

## Pinless centered zipper (basted seam method)

This is one of the most used conventional applications. It is easy and appears uniform on the outside of the garment. It is most often used in center front and center back seams. It can emphasize a design feature and is suitable for medium- to heavy-weight fabrics. You'll find $1/4$-in. wash-away double-sided basting tape and $1/2$-in. transparent tape helpful in the construction process. If applying a waistline facing rather than a waistband, use the facing application technique after installing the zipper.

### Installing the zipper

1. Baste the seamline closed from the waist edge to the zipper stop mark. The seam at the waist edge must be exactly even, or one side of the zipper and waistband will be higher than the other.

2. With the zipper faceup, place the sticky side of $1/4$-in. double-sided basting tape on the top side of the zipper. The basting tape should be even with each long edge of the zipper tape. Finger press firmly in place. Peel off the paper layer of the basting tape.

3. Place the zipper facedown on the seam allowance with the bottom stop of the zipper slightly above or below the zipper stop marking. Roll and finger press the zipper down, making sure the zipper teeth are centered exactly on the seamline.

**4.** Attach the zipper foot to your machine. Position the needle to the side of the zipper being sewn (with the needle closest to the teeth and the foot farthest away).

**5.** On the right side, center ½-in. transparent tape over the seam, ending the tape at the pattern zipper stop mark.

**6.** On the right side, begin stitching at the bottom of the tape on the center seam then up each side. Follow the edge of the tape to keep your stitching straight. Move the needle position or the zipper foot to stitch the second side.

**7.** Remove the ½-in. transparent tape. Press the zipper from the wrong side along the stitching lines but not over the zipper teeth.

**8.** From the right side, carefully remove the seam basting.

### Facing a centered zipper after installation

**1.** Pin the facing to the garment edge, right sides together. Turn both ends of the facing back ⅝ in.; trim to ½ in. (see the photo above, background).

**2.** Stitch the facing to the pants. Grade, clip, and understitch the facing seam allowances.

**3.** Turn and press the facing to the inside and slipstitch to the zipper tape (see the photo above, foreground).

*To finish a facing along a conventional zipper opening, fold back the facing seam allowances and pin. Sew the facing to the waist edge. Slipstitch in place, making sure the facing clears the zipper.*

## Fly zipper (basted seam method)

In this application, the front of the zipper laps from the right to the left for women's pants. A fly shield is not necessary on women's pants. If you are installing a fly zipper for the first time, I do not recommend including a fly shield—it makes an easy procedure more difficult.

### Procedure

**1.** Interface the wrong side of the fly extensions with fusible interfacing (see the top photo on p. 324).

*Apply fusible interfacing to reinforce the fabric and provide smooth pucker-free topstitching.*

*With the fronts basted, stitched, and pressed open, measure and mark ½ in. from the center on the left fly extension.*

**2.** Finish the front crotch seam edges and fly extensions if needed.

**3.** Stitch the two pants fronts together on the crotch seam, beginning 1½ in. from the inside leg seam up to a point ¼ in. below the zipper stop mark. Baste the remaining fronts closed on the center front line to the waist edge. Clip the seam allowance to the stitching below the facing extensions so they can be pressed open and flat.

*Stitch using a zipper foot, with the pressed edge aligned with the zipper coil.*

*Stitch the second side of the zipper to the fly extension only.*

**4.** Working from the wrong side, mark a line on the left fly extension ½ in. from and parallel to the center front (see the bottom photo on the facing page). Press only the extension under on this line.

**5.** With the closed zipper faceup, pin the folded extension close to the coil. The zipper stop should be even with the stop mark.

**6.** With the needle to the right of the zipper foot, stitch through the extension and zipper tape only, close to the fold edge, from bottom to top (see the left photo above).

**7.** Open out the pants with the wrong side up, and smooth and flatten the zipper.

**8.** With the zipper facedown, pin the unstitched side of the zipper tape to the unstitched fly extension *only*. Stitch through the middle of the tape and the fly extension only (see the right photo above).

**9.** Turn the garment right side up and smooth the fabric flat. Mark the zipper topstitching line on the right front (as the garment is worn) beginning at a point ¼ in. below the zipper-stop mark. Removable tape, a disappearing marking pen, tailor's chalk, or basting work well for this step. The width of the topstitching line from the center front can vary. I prefer 1 in. to 1¼ in. Place pins through all thicknesses to ensure the fabric stays flat, or make a fly-zipper template and tape to the pants as a guide (see the left photo below).

**10.** With the needle positioned to the left of the foot, topstitch from the bottom to the top on the marked guideline.

**11.** Horizontally bartack at the bottom of the topstitching and seam intersection for about ¼ in.

**12.** Open the basting along the center front.

*For even topstitching on the fly, you can make your own template from the pants pattern. Use a material that is transparent so you can trace the pattern and rigid enough to hold its shape.*

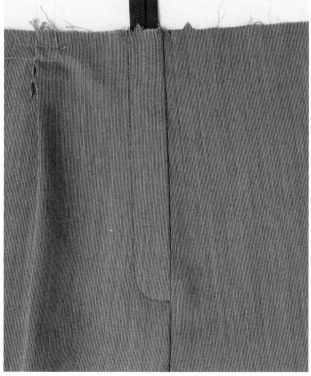

*The finished fly zipper should be even and flat and should not buckle.*

## Invisible zipper (open-seam method)

This zipper is hidden in the seam—only the pull tab shows (see the photo at right). This application does not detract from the fabric or pants style. It is suitable for any weight fabric and any seam where you would put another type zipper. To install this zipper, you'll need a universal invisible zipper foot (a special adapter may be necessary for your machine).

### Procedure

**1.** Open the zipper. With the iron on the synthetic setting, press the coils flat from the wrong side so the two rows of stitching show (see the bottom photo at right).

**2.** Pin the right sides of the zipper and fabric together, with the coil on the seam-line and the top stop of the zipper ¼ in. to ⅜ in. below the seamline.

**3.** Line up the center marking of the invisible zipper foot with the machine needle, or as instructed by the directions that come with the foot. With the right groove of the foot over the coil, stitch the zipper until the foot hits the slider (see the left photo on p. 328). Backstitch.

**4.** Pin the right side of the free zipper tape to the right side of the remaining pants side. Be sure the zipper is not twisted at the bottom. Place the coil on the

*A correctly sewn invisible zipper is just that!*

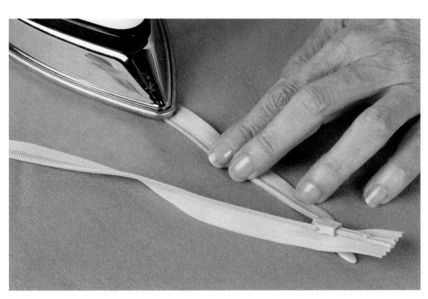

*When ironing an invisible zipper, you will be able to noticeably uncurl the zipper coil.*

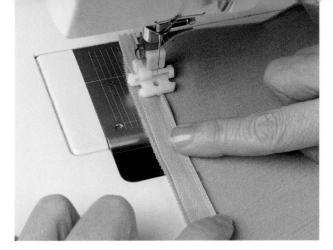

*To sew the first half of the invisible zipper, use the right-hand notch of the invisible zipper foot.*

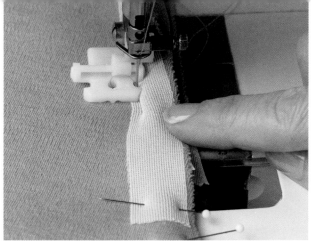

*Without catching the zipper, sew the pants sections together, beginning slightly above and to the left of the last zipper stitching. Note that the zipper opening has been reinforced with fusible interfacing.*

seamline and the top stop the exact distance below the previously stitched side.

**5.** Be sure the center marking of the foot is still lined up with the machine needle. With the left groove of the foot over the coil, stitch the zipper until the foot hits the slider. Backstitch.

**6.** Close the zipper. Slide the foot to the left side so the needle is in the outer notch. Pin the pants sections right sides together along the seam. Pull the end of the zipper out of the way and lower the needle by hand slightly above and to the left of the last stitching. Lower the foot and stitch the seam for at least 2 in. (see the right photo above). Complete the remaining seam with your machine's regular foot.

**7.** Using a zipper foot, stitch each side of the bottom zipper tape to each seam allowance.

### Facing an invisible zipper after installation

**1.** On the facing at the zipper-opening edge, trim off the ⅝-in. seam allowance on both sides.

**2.** Pin the facing and garment right sides together, matching edges at the zipper only.

**3.** Using your machine's zipper foot, stitch ⅜ in. from the edge, parallel to the zipper opening through the facing, zipper tape, and garment.

**4.** Realign the facing, matching seams and waist edge (see the top photo on the facing page). A fold will form at the zipper.

**5.** Pin then stitch the facing to the pants along the waist edge (see the center photo on the facing page). Grade, clip, and understitch the seam allowance (see the bottom photo on the facing page). Press.

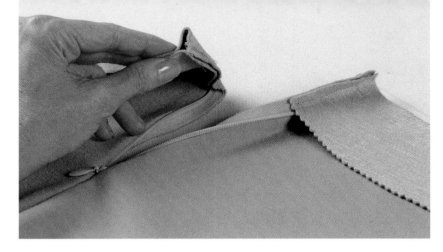

*Realign the trimmed edge of the facing with the zipper edge and stitch. Since the garment is now longer than the facing, a fold will form.*

*Stitch the fold down when stitching the facing to the pants.*

*Grade, clip, and understitch. The result is a neat, clean finish to your invisible zipper facing.*

# Finishing the Crotch Seam

Turn one leg of your pants inside out and the other leg right side out. Slip one leg into the other, making sure right sides are together. Match and pin at the inside leg seam, center front, and center back. Include a piece of stay tape when pinning and stitching the deepest part of the crotch curve (see the photo below). Double-stitch and trim the seam (see "Seams and Finishes," on p. 316) through the deepest part of the crotch curve. Finish the seam allowances above the curve.

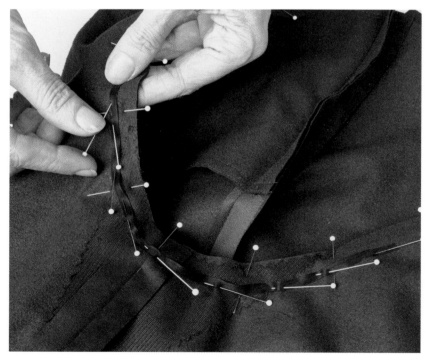

*These synthetic suede pants have a crotch reinforced in two ways: The angles of the pants legs have been reinforced at the crotch point with fusible interfacing, and stay tape is sewn in along the seamline.*

# Attaching the Lining

Lining should be sewn in the same way as the fashion fabric but without the zipper. For the zipper opening, the methods that follow will give you a very neat, clean, professional-looking zipper opening that will be simple to secure to the zipper tape with hand stitching.

## Lining preparation for a fly zipper

When installing a lining in pants with a fly zipper, the zipper is actually off-center while the opening is on center front. Because the lining is retrofitted around the zipper, the finishing at the bottom stop can look less than professional.

These steps will lead you through the process to get a geometrical zipper opening in the lining that is neat, flat, and pucker free from bottom to top. Do not stitch the lining center front crotch seam until after all marking, folding, and trimming is complete.

**1.** On both pieces of the lining mark the center front, bottom zipper stop, and a point ½ in. below the zipper stop.

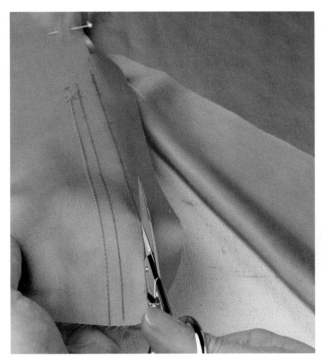

*When all measurements are marked, cut away the left fly extension ½ in. from the foldline.*

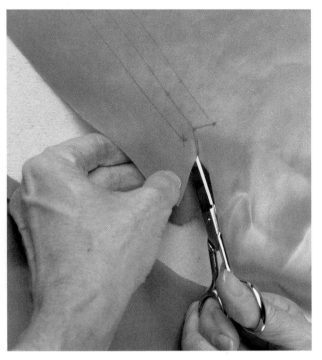

*Clip the right extension from the edge straight across to the mark ½ in. below the zipper stop, diagonally to the center, then diagonally to the bottom of the foldline.*

**2.** On the right side of the fabric and left-hand side of the lining as it will be positioned in the pants, draw a line parallel to and ¼ in. from the center front toward the fly extension. Label this "foldline."

**3.** Trim away the excess fly extension ½ in. from the foldline (see the left photo above).

**4.** Fold the left side of the lining to the wrong side on the foldline.

**5.** For the foldline on the right-hand side of the lining, mark two lines parallel to the center front, ½ in. and 1 in. from the center front toward the *body* of the pants. Extend the 1-in. line so it is ½ in. below the zipper stop mark.

**6.** Beginning at the edge of the fly extension and ½ in. below the zipper stop mark, cut horizontally to the center front, then diagonally up to the midpoint mark and down to the bottom of the foldline, forming a triangle (see the right photo above).

**7.** Beginning at the waist edge, cut on the middle line to the top of the zipper stop (at the point of the triangle), cutting off the excess fly extension.

*Press the triangle and the long edge to the wrong side along the foldlines.*

*With the wrong sides together, stitch the crotch seam with a ⁵⁄₈-in. seam allowance. Stitch a second time using a ³⁄₈-in. seam allowance.*

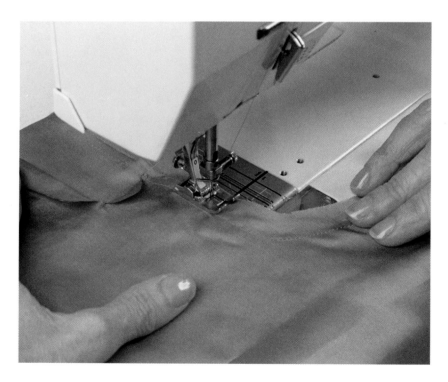

**8.** Fold the remaining fabric to the wrong side on the foldline and press.

**9.** To square off the bottom, fold the triangle formed by the previous trimming to the wrong side and press (see the top photo on the facing page).

**10.** Sew the lining crotch seam with a ⅝-in. seam allowance, stopping the center front crotch seam at a point ½ in. below the zipper stop. Stitch the seam again with a ⅜-in. seam allowance (see the bottom photo on the facing page). Trim close to the ⅜-in. seamline. Press the crotch seam toward the right front.

**11.** Arrange the lining around the zipper slightly back from the coil on either side to avoid catching. Pin (see the top photo at right). Slipstitch in place. Remove the pins and press lightly, being careful not to press over the zipper teeth.

***Lining preparation for other zippers*** For other zipper installations, prepare the lining opening as follows:

**1.** At the zipper stop opening, cut into the seam allowance up to the stitching (see the bottom photo at right). Then cut down at a 45° angle ¼ in. to ⅜ in., forming a triangle.

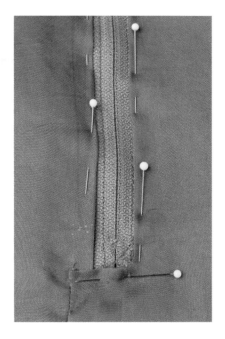

*The finished lining will work perfectly with the off-center placement of a fly zipper.*

*Prepare the lining for a conventional or invisible zipper opening by sewing the lining together up to the zipper stop opening. Clip the seam allowance, then cut down diagonally ¼ in. to ⅜ in. Mark before you cut.*

*With the seam allowance open and the edges turned to the wrong side, pin then press in place.*

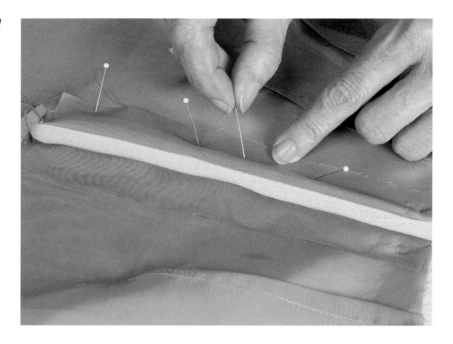

**2.** Turn the seam allowances and small triangle formed to the wrong side. Pin (see the photo above), then press in place. Note: The turned-back seam allowances will be greater than ⅝ in. to allow room around the zipper teeth so the lining won't get caught.

After the zipper opening in the lining has been prepared according to the type of zipper installed, turn the lining inside out. Slip the lining into the pants so wrong sides are together. Match darts, seams, and zipper openings. Pin. Baste the lining to the pants waist edge using a ½-in. seam allowance. Slipstitch the lining to the zipper tape.

# Waistband

The waist finish is an important part of the comfort and appearance of your pants. Finishes will vary with the pattern and current styles, but design principles and basic construction will remain the same. If you are a beginning sewer, it is best to follow your pattern guide sheet. Those more experienced can try some of the variations discussed in Chapter 16 (see pp. 359-365).

Waistband comfort is dependent on proper fit and type of interfacing used. If you have trouble with your waistband curling during wear, consider making the waistband slightly larger or narrower or using a firmer type of interfacing. Fusible

*Ease the waistband by using a large stitch size, then pulling up stitches every few inches with a pin.*

interfacings tend to be softer and more comfortable than the sew-in types like Ban-Rol or Armoflexx. However, the softer interfacings do not hold their shape as well. Professional-looking waistbands should always be an even width, flat and smooth with no bulges, and cut with one long edge along the selvage edge. By cutting the waistband on the selvage, the facing or inside edge of the band is already finished. Unnecessary bulk is eliminated because the seam allowance doesn't need to be turned to the inside of the band. If not cut on the lengthwise grain, the band must be interfaced to prevent stretching.

The following guidelines will aid you in the ease of application of your waist finish and keep it the exact size as when applied throughout the life of your garment.

## Guidelines

The pants waist needs to be slightly larger (by about ¾ in.) than the band. Ease-stitch the pants to fit the waistband. This will pucker the fabric slightly but won't cause gathers. This technique will reduce the size of the pants to fit. With a pin, gently pull up stitches every few inches, taking care not to break the stitching (see the photo above). Evenly distribute ease across the front between the side seams. The amount and placement may vary depending on your figure. If more or less ease is needed, alter at the side seams, pleats, or darts.

I pin-fit the waistband to the garment before attaching it. That way I can determine how much the pants need to be eased to precisely fit the waistband. To ease-stitch the pants, I use a ½-in. seam allowance and a #3 to #4 stitch length (10 stitches per inch), depending on the fabic thickness.

If you're applying a waist facing or if you're not using a stable fusible interfacing, stay the waistline with tape following the directions for staying the crotch seam on p. 330.

## Procedure

The following instructions are for a fitted straight waistband, the most common type of waistband. The waistband will lie flat and provide a clean finish on the inside. The waistband size is usually predetermined by your pattern. However, you can make changes for fitting or style reasons. For the length, use your body measurement or the determined length from fitting, then add two ⅝-in. seam allowances (1¼ in. total) plus a minimum 1¼ in. for the extension (room for a fastener).

A different amount may be needed for a fly zipper depending on how far the zipper is off-set from the center front when installed (this will be a concern only if you modified your pattern for a fly zipper). Make sure the length of your waistband finishes the entire waist edge. Then add two seam allowances and an extension allowance. Add an additional 3 in. to 5 in. for an inseam pocket opening or the width of the pocket at the waist edge. The cut width of the waistband will equal two times the desired finished width plus two ⅝-in. seam allowances.

### Preparing the waistband
**1.** Finish one long edge of the waistband if it's not cut on the selvage.

Fuse the precut interfacing to the waistband using a dampened paper towel over the interfacing.

**2.** Cut the interfacing the length of the waistband (eliminate seam allowances on interfacing if using fusible with Ban-Rol, Armoflexx, or hair canvas).

**3.** Precisely mark ⅝ in. along the long unfinished edge.

**4.** Fuse interfacing to the wrong side of the waistband, aligning the edge with the ⅝-in. seam-line. If the interfacing halves are uneven widths, align the narrower side with the marking. Press for 10 to 15 seconds, overlapping spots slightly as you move the iron. Place a dampened paper towel over the interfacing when fusing (see the photo on the facing page). If you incorrectly position the interfacing with the glue side up, there's no messy iron to clean. It also adds a bit more moisture.

**5.** Mark off the seam allowances and the extension amount.

### Applying the waistband

**1.** Check the fit of the waistband to the pants by pin fitting it first. Adjust the ease on the pants as previously described.

**2.** If attaching belt loops, position them at this time.

**3.** With right sides together, pin the long unfinished edge of the waistband to the pants. Match the marked seam allowance and

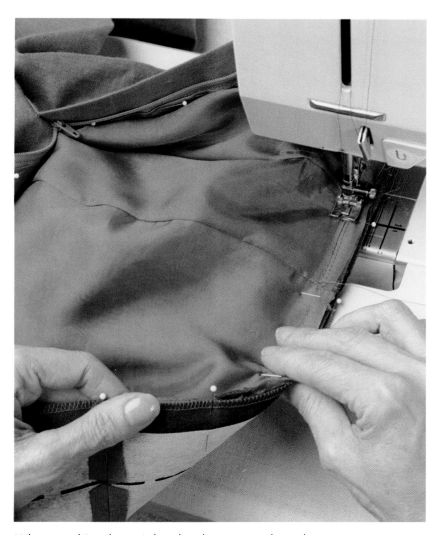

When attaching the waistband to the garment, have the garment on top so you can control the ease and avoid puckers on the garment side.

extension line on the waistband to the pants opening edges.

**4.** With the waistband on the bottom and the garment on top, stitch the waistband to the garment from the zipper opening edge to edge (see the photo above).

**5.** Fold the ends of the waistband in half (perforation

*Cut the corners of the waistband before turning to eliminate bulk.*

*Press the seam toward the waistband, using the end of your ironing board or a tailor's ham to retain the curve of the waistband.*

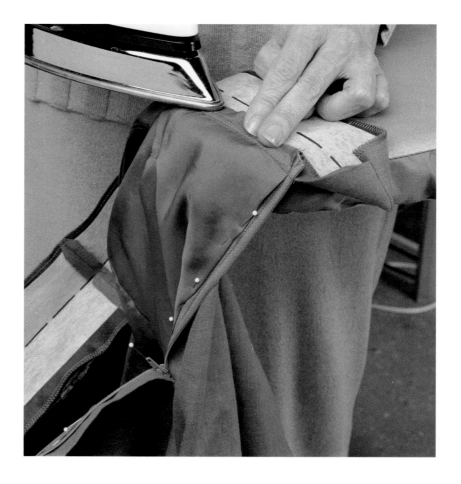

makes this foolproof) with right sides together and stitch each end along the seamline. Trim the seams to $\frac{1}{4}$ in., then cut the corners diagonally (see the top photo on the facing page).

**6.** Press the waist seam toward the waistband (see the bottom photo on the facing page). Then turn the waistband right side out. Pin the waistband in place, making sure it is an even width. Turn seam allowances to the inside of the waistband on the extension end, matching edges. Pin to hold in place. Complete the waistband attachment by edgestitching from end to end on the right side, $\frac{1}{8}$ in. from the waist seam on the waistband. The long, inside, finished edge of the waistband will be caught in this stitching and permanently secured.

**7.** Press over the end of the ironing board or a tailor's ham.

# Closures

Special-purpose waistband hook-and-bar sets are sturdy and well suited for the strain a waistband will get. The number and kind will depend on the length of your extension. The waistband should be secured at the opening edge as well as at the extension end of the waistband. If you prefer a button and buttonhole on a classic band, try my

method. Make a buttonhole, but don't cut it open. Sew the button on top of the buttonhole, and then apply the hook-and-bar closures on the underside. It looks like the real thing, and the closure stays precisely put.

To attach a hook-and-bar set, first attach the hook to the wrong side of the overlap portion of the waistband, $\frac{1}{4}$ in. from the finished open end and centered on the waistband. Attach the hook and bar using a buttonhole stitch. Begin with a single strand of thread and knot the end. At the hook position on the placement side, take a small stitch. Take a second stitch in the same place. When you stitch the hook portion, use a buttonhole stitch and only stitch through the waistband facing. *Do not* stitch through to the right side.

To position the straight bar portion, attach it to the hook with the zipper closed. Lap the overlap portion of the waistband onto the underlap extension portion, positioning the waistband edges evenly as they will be when worn. Make sure the waistband fit is smooth and straight above the zipper.

Find where the straight bar portion lines up on the underlap of the waistband both vertically

## Stitching Hooks and Bars Using a Buttonhole Stitch

*1. Take two stitches on the wrong side of the overlap ¼ in. from the end.*

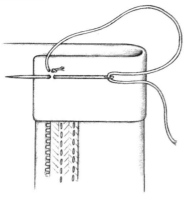

*2. Bring the needle up through the hole of the hook and work a buttonhole stitch, keeping the thread loop under both the point and the eye of the needle.*

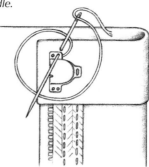

*3. Continue working from right to left until all holes are filled with thread and three sides are secured.*

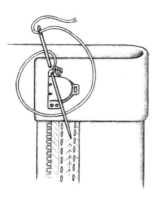

*4. Mark the position of the bar on the underlap extension with pins.*

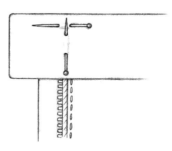

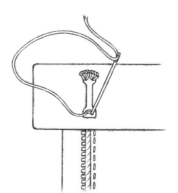

*5. Begin stitching as in step 1. Work using a buttonhole stitch (as shown on top of bar) or in and out as illustrated on the bottom.*

and horizontally, and mark this location with two pins. This is the sewing position for the straight bar. Now unhook the back portion from the hook and position it according to your pin markings. Because there are two holes at each end, you can either stitch around the holes using the buttonhole stitch as before, or as a time-saving technique, you can stitch in and out of each pair of holes. Because this stitching will not show, you can stitch completely through both layers of fabric. You may also stitch the back portion by machine as a timesaver.

# Hems

Whether or not you like your pants to break at the front hemline is a personal preference. The more tapered or tighter the leg is, the shorter the pants can be. Lengthen the hem at the center back leg by ½ in. if necessary to cover the heel of your shoe. Lengthening it more can require a facing. Because the hemline becomes more angled or shaped, it is difficult to turn up a straight 1½-in. hem and have it be flat and smooth. A narrow machine hem, however, is possible. I adjust hem length per pair of pants, that is, according to style, fabric, and shoes of the moment. Besides, it will all change next season. Make notes of what you like and looks best

on you as you make various styles of pants. For cuffs, see p. 369.

A well-finished hem should be inconspicuous on the right side; uniform in width; flat, smooth, not bulky; appropriate in width for your pants' style and fabric; and stitched evenly and securely.

## Procedure

**1.** After determining the length, press the hem to the wrong side. For classic pants with a straight hem, trim the hem allowance to 1½ in.

**2.** Trim seams in the hem allowance to ¼ in. to reduce bulk. Clip each seam allowance to the stitching at the hemline.

**3.** At the side seams and inseams, lengthen the hem by ⅛ in. Even though you're making these areas slightly longer, they will appear the same length due to the slight bulkiness when the hem is finished.

**4.** Apply an edge finish to the right side of the hem allowance. The edge can be stitched and pinked, serged, bound, or edged with seam tape.

**5.** Hand- or machine-stitch in place. If hand hemming, flat stitch or blindstitch the hem edge.

## Setting Creaselines

### Pants with darts

The creaseline in darted pants begins 3 in. above the crotch level and extend through the middle of the leg to the hem.

### Pants with pleats

For pants with pleats, the creaseline will extend from the main front pleat through the center of the leg to the hem.

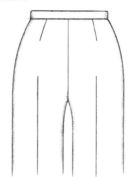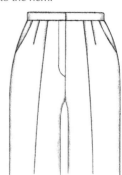

### Front crease for darted trousers

To set the creaseline, fold back the upper leg, matching the inseam to the side seam. Use a steam iron and clapper.

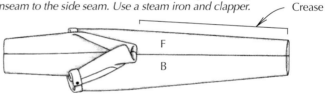

Crease

F
B

### Front crease for pleated trousers

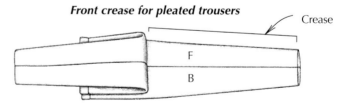

Crease

F
B

### Back crease

Set the creaseline in back as for the front. The creaseline will end at crotch level for both styles.

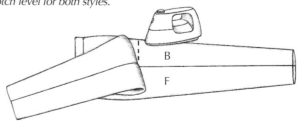

B
F

## Making a French Tack

Stitched and pinked edge

WS lining

WS pants

French tack

1. Bring a single knotted thread up from the wrong side of the pants hem.

2. Take three or four stitches between the garment and the lining hem. Stitches should go in and come out at the same point. Each thread stitch should be about 1½ in. long between the garment and lining.

3. Work a buttonhole stitch over these threads, keeping the stitches close together.

**6.** When the lining hem is finished, it should be ¾ in. to 1 in. shorter than the finished pants length. Finish the raw edge of the hem allowance. Turn the hem to the wrong side and machine topstitch in place.

**7.** Pull the lining legs up through the pants toward the waist. Do a final touch-up pressing on the fashion fabric. Set the creaselines if desired (see the drawing on the facing page).

**8.** Press the hem on the fashion fabric. To prevent a ridge line from showing through to the right side of the fabric, first butt a piece of scrap fabric against the hem edge where it attaches to the garment.

**9.** Attach the lining to the hem allowance with a 1½-in. French tack at the side seams and inseams (see the drawing above).

# 16 Stylizing Your Pattern

A successful design begins with a well-fitting pattern so that no fitting problems are passed on. Because design changes can alter the original fit of your pants to varying degrees, you should be familiar with how your customized pants fit and feel. Study your pattern and note where you have made adjustments, what it looks like, and how it differs from the unaltered commercial pattern you began with.

Before you make any changes to your pattern, always trace a copy onto which you will make your changes, preserving your original for further work and reference. You can enhance or completely change the look of your original pants by executing some of the variations on the following pages. Simple style changes, the addition of design details, and an array of fabrics make for limitless combinations. You may decide to try only one depending on your level of confidence and skill or to combine several into one new pattern.

Analyze your new design carefully and don't get stuck in a fabric rut. It may call for a completely different fabric, maybe one you've never worked with. You're limited only by your imagination and creativity. Have fun! That's what it's all about. If you're unsure, choose an inexpensive fabric on which to experiment or use some of the outdated fabric in your stash. Fabric is a small investment compared to the wealth of knowledge you gain and the pleasure and satisfaction you get from a self-created project.

# Transforming Darts

A basic pants pattern with darts opens up endless design possibilities. Darts shape and fit, but they are not especially beautiful and can be boring after the second pair of pants; however, they can be easily transformed into tuck darts, gathers, pleats, or flare. These options maintain the fitting control of the original dart(s) but look different. The difference between them is how they are marked and sewn.

## Tuck darts

Tuck darts are partially stitched darts. To make tuck darts,

measure the length of the dart(s) to be converted from wide end to point. Divide this distance in half and mark. This mark is where you will stop stitching. Sew as you would a traditional dart, beginning at the widest end and stopping at the midpoint marked (see the drawing below).

## Gathers

Dart-equivalent gathers at the waist are comfortable, not full, give a softer look, and work well for those of us with full tummies or fleshy padding between the waist and hip. The dart(s) can be completely eliminated, but the dart take-up (interior distance between the dart legs) must be accounted for by gathering. The waistline fit will remain the

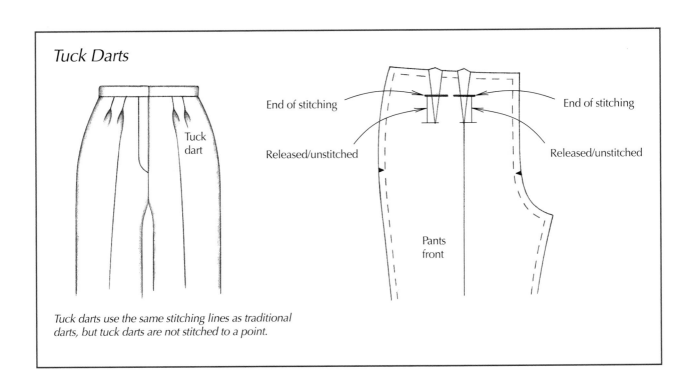

## Tuck Darts

End of stitching

Released/unstitched

Tuck dart

End of stitching

Released/unstitched

Pants front

*Tuck darts use the same stitching lines as traditional darts, but tuck darts are not stitched to a point.*

same. To convert one dart to gathers, place a dot at the wide end of each dart leg (stitching line). The distance between the dots will be drawn up with gathering stitches so the dots meet (see the drawing at right). This gathering is done in the normal construction sequence when it's time to sew the darts. To true the waist edge for gathers, draw a gently outwardly curved line from the side to center front. Repeat for the back if desired.

If there is more than one dart, and the take-up of the darts, as well as the distance between the two darts, is to be gathered (for added fullness), the amount of the additional gathered fullness must be added to the waist, or the waist will be too small. Measure the waist space between the inner legs of the two darts and add this amount to the side waist. To true the pattern, draw a line from the marked waist addition and taper it to "0" at the hip, following the side-seam curve. Repeat for the back if desired.

## Pleats

For a traditional trouser look, convert the front dart(s) into pleat(s). This is a winning style for just about all figure types. An easy way to convert waist darts to pleats during construction is to fold one dart leg over to meet the other on the right side of your fabric at the waist edge.

## Gathers

Single dart converted to gathers

Both darts and space between them converted to gathers

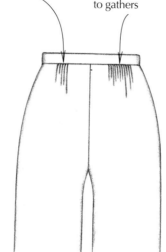

### Single dart converted to gathers

*The dart area below the waist is not sewn as a dart. The area between dots is gathered so the dots meet.*

Gather

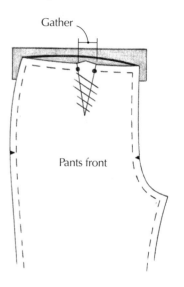

Pants front

**Two darts converted to gathers**

Gathers

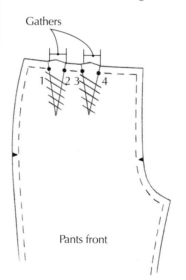

1 2 3 4

Pants front

Gathers

True waist edge

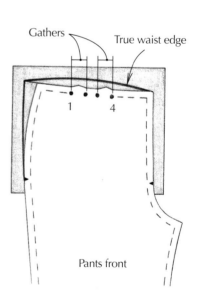

1 4

Pants front

*The area to be gathered will be equivalent to the distance between the darts (dots 1 and 2, and dots 3 and 4) and the garment area between dots 2 and 3.*

*Measure the distance between dots 2 and 3 and add this amount to the side-waist seam.*

*Working with the pattern over a large piece of paper, create a waist pleat by cutting and spreading the front from waist to hem. Work by pinning the pattern to the surface until the spread at the waist is twice the amount of the finished pleat size, then tape in place.*

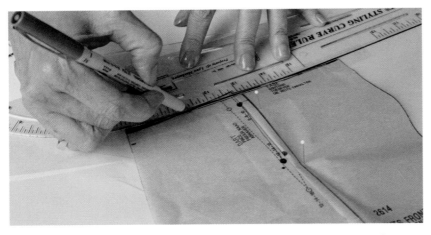

*Redraw and trim the waistline with the new pleat folded and pinned.*

Baste the pleat at the waist seam to hold in place until the waistband is applied.

**1.** For fuller, more generous pleats, modify your front pattern. Locate the dart leg closest to center front. Draw a line parallel to the grainline from the intersection of the waist and dart leg to the bottom of your pattern. Place see-through paper underneath this line.

**2.** Cut from the waist to but not through the hem. Spread the pattern at the waist twice the distance of the desired finished-pleat size. For example, a 2-in. spread will give you a 1-in. finished pleat. If your pattern has only one front dart, incorporate the dart into the pleat by subtracting the dart take-up from the amount of spread. Using the above example, you would spread the pattern 1½ in. if the dart take-up is ½ in. (see the top photo at left).

**3.** The width of the second pleat is the sum of the two dart take-ups. For example, if the take-up of each dart is ½ in. and there are two darts, then the width of the second pleat will be 1 in. To mark the second pleat, begin at the dart leg closest to the side. Measure 1 in. along the waist toward center front and mark.

**4.** Fold and pin each pleat in the desired direction (toward the center front, toward the side, or with each pleat edge to the center of the pleat). With the pleat(s) pinned closed, redraw the waist edge between the side and center front with a gently curved line, as shown in the bottom photo at left. Trim the pattern on the drawn line for the new cutting line. Unpin the pleat(s).

Adding fullness by spreading your pattern, as described here, creates more generous pleat(s) and a bit more fullness in the leg yet gives you the same fit in the waist.

**Hint:** Before attaching the waistband, fold pleats on one side of the front in one direction and in the opposite direction on the other side. See which is more becoming. Once you've decided, fold both the same way and sew on the waistband.

## Flare

One method of creating leg flare is to move the dart(s) to the hem. Dart(s) can be transformed into hemline flare without affecting the fit. A portion or all of each dart(s) can be moved to the bottom of the leg, with the width of the pants leg below the crotch gradually increased. Since the degree of fullness can be controlled when adding this dart equivalent flare, most figure types will benefit from this easy style change.

**1.** Draw a line parallel to the grainline from dart point to hem.

**2.** Cut from the waist to the dart point on one of the dart legs. Cut up from the hem to the dart point but not through it. Keep the pattern flat but do not separate the pattern pieces. Place see-through paper under the pattern. Move one dart leg to the center of the same dart. Tape in

*A transformed waist dart adds considerable flare at the hemline.*

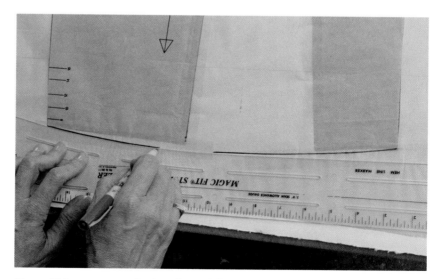

*You will have to true the hemline of flared pants, adding a gentle curve.*

When narrowing or tapering the pants leg, make sure the finished garment measurement at the hemline is equal to or larger than the circumference measurement over your heel and instep. Otherwise, you won't be able to get your pants over your foot.

place. The hemline area will spread open, as shown in the top photo on p. 349. Because only half of the dart was closed and moved to the hem as flare, the remaining half of the dart at the waist will be sewn as a dart. The fit through the waist will be the same as before half the dart was converted to leg flare.

**3.** Redraw the hem edge, incorporating a slight curve, as shown in the bottom photo on p. 349. Repeat for the pants back.

**4.** If more fullness at the lower edge of the pants is desired, transfer the entire width of one or both darts to the hem as flare.

# Changing Leg Width

Whether increasing or decreasing leg width, you'll need to consider style and fit. Pictures or pants you already own can guide your style choice and help you decide how much and where to add or subtract the leg width from your present pattern (see the drawing below). The amount and point where the leg width is increased or decreased can affect the style only or fit and style of your pants. If the increase or decrease in leg width is made below the crotchline, the style is changed but the fit remains unaffected as in tapered, flared,

## Styles of Pants

**Tapered**
Subtract 1 in. from each side. Taper to thigh.

**Straight leg**

**Slight flare**
Add 1 in. to each side. Taper to knee.

**Moderate flare**
Add 2 in. to 3 in. to each side. Taper to thigh.

**Full flare**
Add 3 in. to 6 in. to each side. Taper to crotch level.

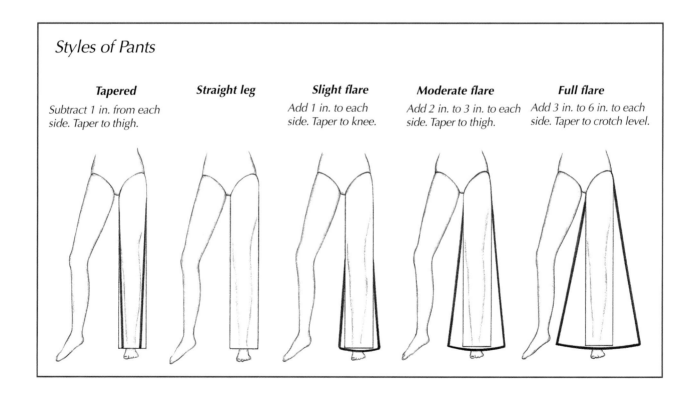

or bell-bottom pants. If a change is made above the crotchline, both the fit and style will be affected as in wide-leg baggies (see the drawing below).

## Flaring and tapering

While flaring is a gradual widening of the leg width, tapering is a gradual narrowing. Leg width can be increased or decreased by adding or subtracting at the side and inseam of the front and back pattern pieces. Both flaring and tapering can begin at the knee, crotch, or above the crotch. The fit of your original pattern, personal preference, and current fashion should guide your choices. Straight or wide-leg pants are becoming on most figures. Flared pants are better suited for women with short, thin legs. Tapered pants look well on a figure with short legs, but they are not as complementary for those who are proportionally larger below the waist, have a flat buttocks, or have thin legs.

The amount of ease included in your pattern at the hip, thigh, and knee areas will determine how much room you have to play with when tapering. If narrowing the leg, pin the original garment where you're planning on making the change to get an idea of the look and fit. The pattern knee circumference should measure 1 in. to 1½ in. more than your bent knee measurement so the knee area isn't too tight when bending or sitting.

I prefer a leg width of 41% (for basic slacks) of my full-hip measurement (about 16 in.). This percentage gives a slight taper to my pants leg without being too narrow and emphasizing my hips. Use this percentage as a beginning guide point for your leg width.

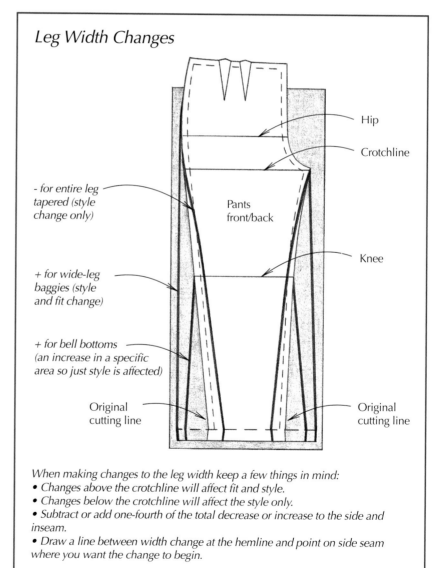

**Leg Width Changes**

- Hip
- Crotchline
- *- for entire leg tapered (style change only)*
- Pants front/back
- Knee
- *+ for wide-leg baggies (style and fit change)*
- *+ for bell bottoms (an increase in a specific area so just style is affected)*
- Original cutting line
- Original cutting line

*When making changes to the leg width keep a few things in mind:*
- *Changes above the crotchline will affect fit and style.*
- *Changes below the crotchline will affect the style only.*
- *Subtract or add one-fourth of the total decrease or increase to the side and inseam.*
- *Draw a line between width change at the hemline and point on side seam where you want the change to begin.*

*Changing the leg width means reshaping the hem allowance at the inseam and side leg. Tape see-through paper at the hemline. Fold the paper toward the pants on the hemline and trim on the side edges of the pants. Unfold and trim at the bottom of the hem allowance.*

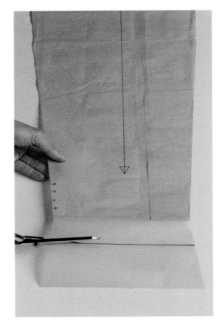

When widening or narrowing your pattern leg width, divide the total amount of increase or decrease by four. Add or subtract one-fourth the total amount of change to the side and inseam front and back pattern at the hemline. If widening, tape a piece of see-through paper 2 in. to 7 in. wide to the side and inseam of the front and back pattern. The width of the added paper should be slightly more than the intended increase. Extend the paper from the lower edge of the hew allowance to the point where you intend the new leg line to blend into your original pattern. If narrowing the leg, mark directly on your pattern.

To complete the new leg line on the side and inseam, draw a line between the newly established width at the hemline and a point farther up the leg. The greater the increase or decrease, the farther up the leg the line can go and the change can begin. If the newly established line extends above the crotchline, the fit will be affected. Below the crotchline only the style will change.

## Reshaping the hem allowance

If you've changed the leg width at the hemline, you will need to adjust the shape of the hem allowance on the front and back pattern. If your pattern didn't include a hem allowance, tape tissue to your pattern at the hemline that is wider than your new leg width and that extends below the hemline several inches. On the tissue, draw a line parallel to the hem-line the amount of the hem allowance (1¼ in. to 1½ in.), or the desired width.

To complete the reshaping, fold the hem allowance to the wrong side of the pattern on the hemline. Pin each side to secure. From the right side of the pattern, cut on the side and inseam new leg line from the hemline up to the point where the line blends into your original pattern. Unfold the hem allowance. If you added the hem allowance as previously described, cut away the excess tissue on the drawn line (see the photo above). You now have your new-leg-width pants pattern and correctly shaped hem allowance to fit the new leg line.

## Pants Go to Any Length

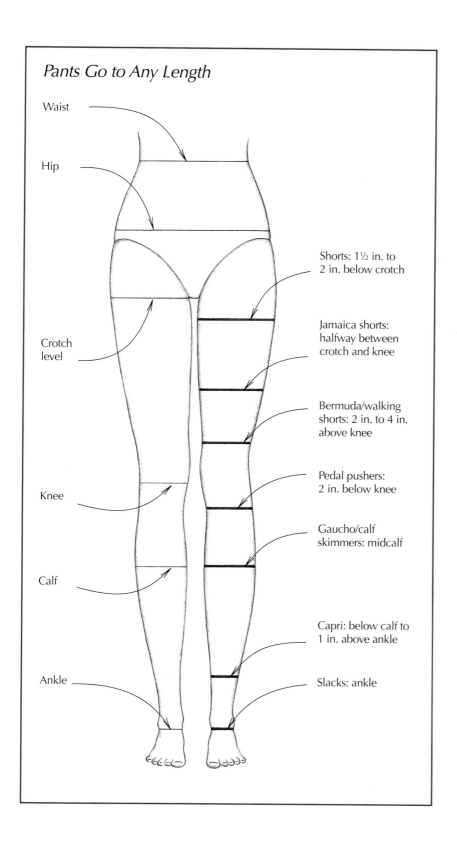

Waist

Hip

Crotch level

Knee

Calf

Ankle

Shorts: 1½ in. to 2 in. below crotch

Jamaica shorts: halfway between crotch and knee

Bermuda/walking shorts: 2 in. to 4 in. above knee

Pedal pushers: 2 in. below knee

Gaucho/calf skimmers: midcalf

Capri: below calf to 1 in. above ankle

Slacks: ankle

# Changing Leg Length

Pants length and names vary from season to season. With a few easy changes you can modify the length of your pattern and be currently fashionable, or adapt your pants for a particular occasion or activity (see the drawing on p. 353).

Depending on the style or leg width of your original pattern, you may need to make a slight width increase or decrease at the inside and side leg to suit personal preference or current fashion. Let your wardrobe or RTW garments be your guide. If in doubt before cutting, allow extra seam allowances as a safety margin until after you have checked the fabric fit and look on your body.

## Converting Pants to Shorts

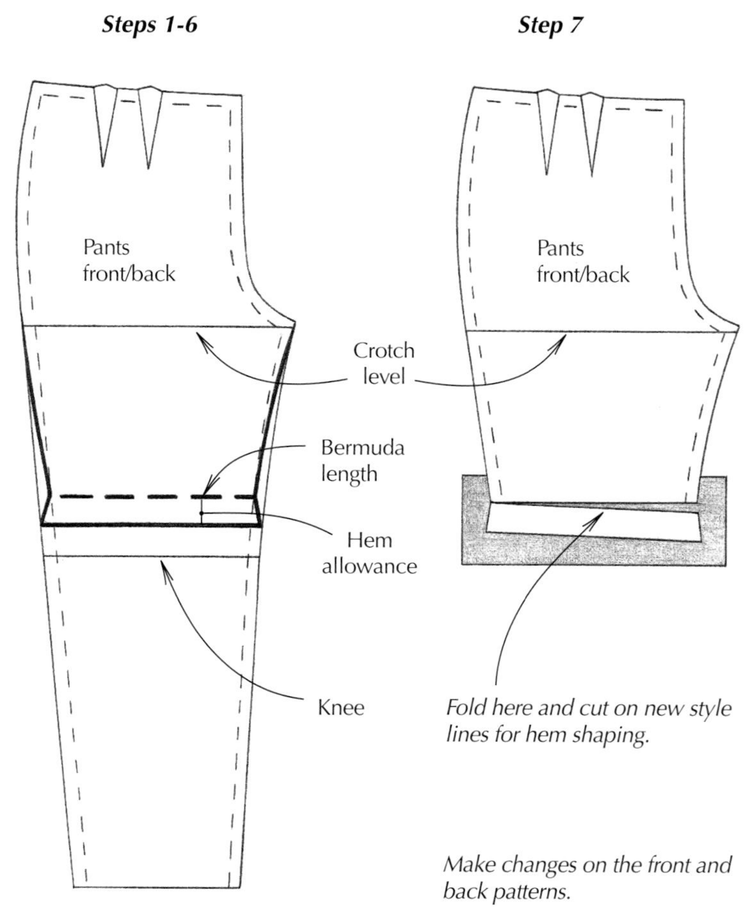

**Steps 1-6**

Pants front/back

Crotch level

Bermuda length

Hem allowance

Knee

**Step 7**

Pants front/back

Crotch level

*Fold here and cut on new style lines for hem shaping.*

*Make changes on the front and back patterns.*

## Converting your basic pattern

**1.** Decide on a new length.

For the front and back repeat the following steps.

**2.** Trace the pattern to its new length.

**3.** At the new length, measure in ¼ in. to 1 in. at the inseam and side leg edges and mark (¼ in. to ⅜ in. for shorts and Jamaicas, ½ in. for Bermudas and pedal pushers, and 1 in. for longer lengths).

**4.** Redraw the inseam and side leg edges to crotch level.

**5.** Add 1 in. to 1½ in. to the finished new length for the hem allowance.

## Raised-Waist Pattern

*Trace the front and back waist seam down the side and center front to the hipline.*

*Flip the pattern, matching the waist seam. Draw in a line 3 in. above and parallel to the waist.*

*The shaded area is the extended pattern on front and back for a raised waist.*

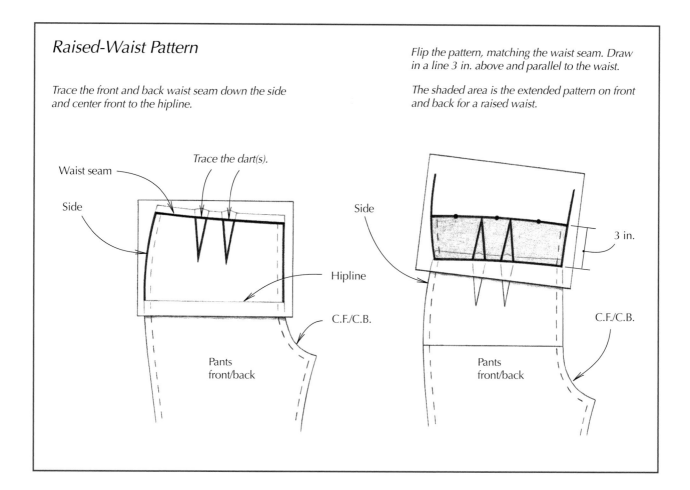

**6.** Fold the pattern to the wrong side along the hemline. Cut along the inseam and side-leg edges for correct hem shaping.

**7.** For lengths above the knee only (shorts, Jamaicas, and Bermudas), you'll need to make a correction on the inner leg so the pants legs will fit and hang better. At the hemline, slash from the inside leg edge to the side edge. Spread the inside leg edge ³⁄₈ in. to ⁵⁄₈ in., tapering the spread to "0" at the side edge.

# Raised-Waist Pants

This style extends 2½ in. to 3 in. above the natural waist and enhances figures with short legs or a long waist/torso. Since this style has no waistband, once the pattern waist is raised, a facing will need to be made to finish the upper edge. Directions are the same for front and back except for the dart(s) as noted.

## Adjusting Darts for a Raised Waist

### Front dart

*For front darts, measure ⅛ in. to each side of the point of the raised-waist dart and mark.*

### Back dart

*Draw in a new raised-waist dart line from ¼ in. on each side of the point to the natural waist level.*

+⅛ in.   High waist                                    +¼ in.

Natural
waist level on
original pattern

*Heavy lines = new dart line for raised waist*

*Regular lines = original dart line as traced on completed pattern*

Because wrinkling and curling of a raised waist may occur, interface with a firm interfacing such as hair canvas. Additional support may be added at the seams and darts by using Rigilene, a polyester sew-through flexible boning, available in black and white.

## Procedure for the pants

**1.** Lay see-through paper over the pants from hipline to waist. Trace the waistline seam from side edge to center front. Trace the side edge and center-front edge to the hipline. Trace the darts (see the drawing on p. 355).

**2.** Remove the paper with the tracings and flip it up so the traced waist seam matches the pattern at the center front and side. Measure 3 in. up from the waist seam into the traced area

and mark with dots. Draw a line through these dots parallel to the waist seam from side to center front to complete the pattern.

**3.** To correct darts for the raised-waist shaping, redraw them as shown in the drawing at left and following these directions: Extend the centerline of the dart(s) into the raised waist, ending at the dart point. On the front dart(s), increase the dart ⅛ in. on both sides of the original dart at the raised-waist dart point. On the back dart(s), increase the dart ¼ in. on both sides of the original dart at the raised-waist dart point.

## Procedure for the facing

**1.** Trace the completed raised-waist pattern on the front and back from the waist seam up (see the drawing on the facing page).

**2.** Fold the dart(s) closed.

**3.** Retrace the pattern piece, blending a smooth line at the high-waist and waist edge. As an option, the center front can be placed on the fold if the opening is at the side or back to reduce bulk.

**4.** Repeat for the back. The center back may or may not be cut on the fold, depending on where the garment opening is.

## Facing for a Raised Waist

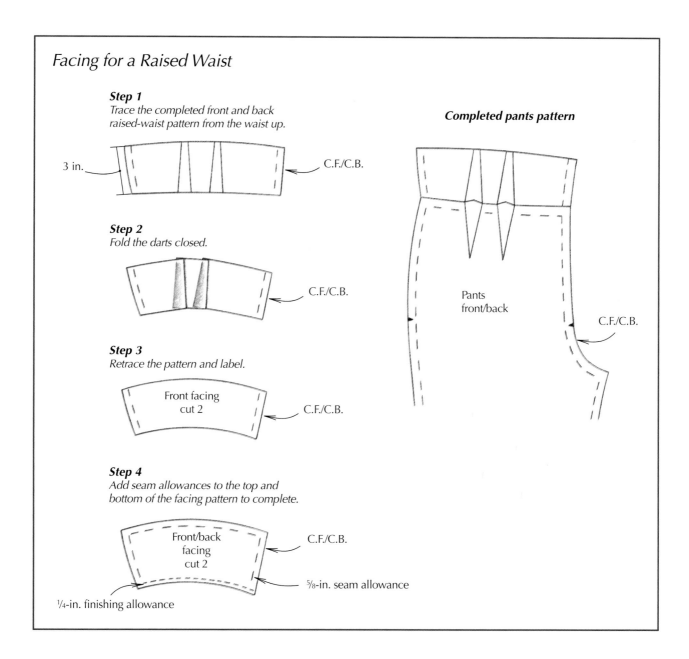

**Step 1**
Trace the completed front and back raised-waist pattern from the waist up.

3 in.

C.F./C.B.

**Step 2**
Fold the darts closed.

C.F./C.B.

**Step 3**
Retrace the pattern and label.

Front facing
cut 2

C.F./C.B.

**Step 4**
Add seam allowances to the top and bottom of the facing pattern to complete.

Front/back
facing
cut 2

C.F./C.B.

⅝-in. seam allowance

¼-in. finishing allowance

**Completed pants pattern**

Pants
front/back

C.F./C.B.

# Pull-On Pants

Because these pants are so comfortable, no one should be without them. You probably own some version of this style with a gathered elasticized waist. Fabric choice as well as leg width can influence how you look in this style. Therefore, begin with a leg width that is not excessively tapered in relation to your hip size. If you have a thick waist, large hips, or a protruding tummy, choose a soft, nonbulky fabric that drapes well, such as jersey knit, wool crepe, challis, rayon, or crepe de chine. The following directions are for a self-fabric fold-over casing. Part of the fun of these pants is their ease of construction—no zipper or separate waistband to apply. If you prefer less fullness at the waist, decrease the amount you add at the waist and add a zipper.

## Converting your basic pattern

**1.** Measure your front and back pattern waist with pleats and darts flat (these will not be sewn), minus seam allowances. Since you're measuring half a pattern, add the front and back measurement, then multiply your measurement by two for the total circumference.

**2.** Tape a large piece of see-through paper under your pattern from the hipline to 6 in. above the waist level. The paper should be several inches wider than your pattern at the center and side.

**3.** Square the center front/back and side of the pattern from full-hip level (or fullest measurement) to waist-seam level.

**4.** Measure and add together the width of the front and back at waist level between the squared lines drawn in step 3. Multiply by two for the total width. Subtract 2½ in. from the total width to account for seam allowances to determine the actual finished garment width. This measurement should be at least 2 in. larger than your largest measurement below your waist. If it isn't, redraw the line between the full hip and waist level, angling it so that the total waist measurement is at least 2 in. larger.

**5.** To form the casing, extend the line drawn in step 3 above the waistline. The extension amount will be two times the width of the elastic plus ¼ in. ease and a ⅝-in. seam allowance.

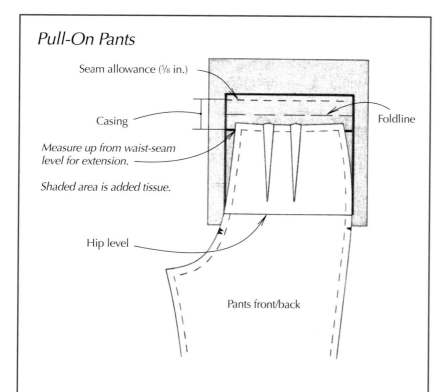

### Pull-On Pants

Seam allowance (⅝ in.)

Casing

Measure up from waist-seam level for extension.

Shaded area is added tissue.

Foldline

Hip level

Pants front/back

*Tape a large piece of see-through paper under the pattern from the hip to above the waist. Square a line from hip to waist level at the front, back, and side(s). Add an extension for the casing above the waist. The amount of the casing should equal two times the width of the elastic plus ¼ in. ease and one ⅝-in. seam allowance.*

For example, for 1-in. elastic, the total extended amount will be 2⅞ in. The foldline will be halfway between the waistline and the seam allowance line.

The length of the elastic should equal the waist measurement minus 1½ in., or whatever is comfortable when the elastic is pulled around your waist, plus an allowance (1 in.) for overlap or joining of the elastic. Use a nonroll elastic in the desired width (¾ in. to 1½ in.).

# Waist Finishes

There are several types of bands or finishes that may fit your particular shape better, be more comfortable, and be complementary to your fabric. This new finish will give your pants a different look, and you may prefer it to the band style that was included with your commercial pattern. In all instances, the construction sequence is the same, but how the waist finish is constructed and applied is different. If you have made a waist-size adjustment on your pattern or a fitting alteration, it may be easier to cut your waistband using your measurement rather than adjusting the pattern piece.

## Considerations

Before designing your new waist finish, you need to do the following:
- Decide where the opening is going to be.
- Decide how much extension (over/underlap) you will need. Front and side closures lap right over left; back closures lap left over right.
- Consider applying preshrunk tape to the waistline to prevent stretching. It should be the length of the waistline seam, without seam allowances, from opening edge to opening edge. It is applied at the same time the waistband is sewn to the pants.
- Determine the finished width.
- Select an appropriate interfacing for reinforcement and stabilization, except for a fully elasticized band.

## Faced finish

A waist facing is an exact copy (without darts) of the edge it is intended to finish. This type of finish is good for rectangular figures, where there is little or no waist definition. It also gives a more pleasing proportion to figures with long legs.

A faced waistline provides a smooth, clean finish that does not extend above the waistline. The facing, which is attached to the right side of the garment and ends up on the wrong side, is usually made from self fabric. If the fashion fabric is heavy or bulky, it can be made from a lighter-weight fabric.

The patternmaking procedure for this type of finish—replacing a separate straight fitted waistband—is the same as for a raised waist (see p. 355), except the facing extends from the waist down 2½ in. Use reinforcing tape in the waistline. If lining the pants, baste the lining to the pants at the waist seam before applying the facing.

## Ribbon Facing

If being comfortable as well as fashionable is your goal, make your waistband narrower or face the waist edge with ribbon to eliminate the tight, bound-in feeling a fitted waistband can cause. A ribbon finish has the look of a faced finish from the outside, but the raw edge of the pants waist is finished with a firm ribbon such as ½-in. or ¾-in. preshrunk grosgrain or precontoured Petersham (available in white or black). The length of the grosgrain or Petersham should be your waist measurement plus 1¼ in.

If lining your pants, baste the lining to the pants-waist seam before applying the ribbon. No taping is required since the ribbon acts as a stabilizer. Trim ½ in. from the garment waist seam allowance, leaving ⅛ in.

Match and pin the edge of the ribbon or Petersham to the fabric edge of the pants waist. Stitch using a ⅛-in. seam allowance and easing the pants to fit. Turn the ribbon to the inside of the pants and tack to the seam allowances at the seams. Wrap ⅝ in. of the ribbon to the wrong side at the zipper opening and tack in place.

## Fitted-contour waistband

This is a separate fitted band that sits above the waist, much like a traditional straight waistband. However, the band is slightly curved. The edge joining the pants is longer than the upper edge, "contouring" better to the shape of the body. This type of band is good if you have a sway back or a small waist in relation to your high hip or buttocks. If the top of your waistbands tend to stand away from your body, try this version. The waistband works with a center-front closing, or it can be adapted for a side closure. For the example that follows and is shown in the drawing on the facing page, the finished width will be 1¼ in., which is the standard width of a straight band.

**1.** On a piece of paper draw a rectangle. The width should be 1¼ in. The length should be equal to your waist measurement (column 1 on your Measurement Chart). Cut out the rectangle on the drawn lines.

## Fitted-Contour Waistband

### Step 1

Draw a rectangle. The width should equal 1¼ in., and the length should equal your waist measurement. Cut out the rectangle.

### Steps 2 and 3

Divide the rectangle into quarters. Label them center front, side seam, center back, side seam, and center front.

C.F.    SS    C.B.    SS    C.F.

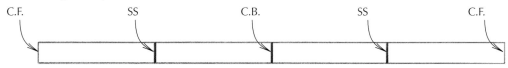

### Step 4

To the left and right of center back, mark six equally spaced lines.

C.F.    SS    C.B.    SS    C.F.

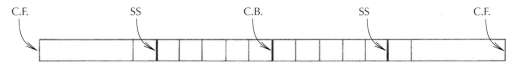

### Steps 5 and 6

Cut on marked lines and spread ⅛ in. Tape in place.

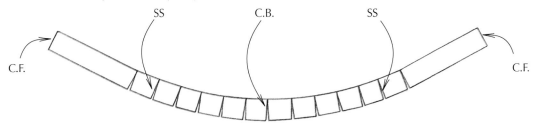

SS    C.B.    SS

C.F.    C.F.

### Steps 7 and 8

Add ⅝-in. seam allowance. Draw a line through center back for grain.

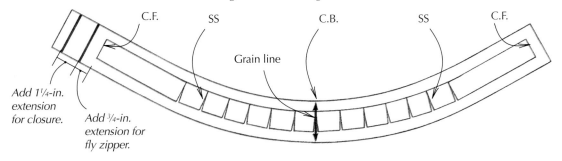

C.F.    SS    C.B.    SS    C.F.

Grain line

Add 1¼-in. extension for closure.

Add ¾-in. extension for fly zipper.

**2.** Fold the rectangle into quarters by first folding the length in half. Then fold the half in half again to create the quarters.

**3.** Mark the center back (the middle fold), side seams (the fold to each side of center back), and center front (the ends).

**4.** To the right and left of center back, mark six equally spaced lines. Four should be between center back and the side seam, one will be at the side seam, and the sixth will be positioned slightly past the side seam toward center front. The spacing between the lines should *look* reasonably balanced. The spaces do not have to be precise. The lines should extend the width of the rectangle.

**5.** Cut a piece of paper 12 in. wide by your waist measurement plus 4 in. For the following steps move to a firm surface that you can put pins into, such as an ironing board. Cut on the lines you have drawn on the rectangle, as well as on center back and the side-seam marks. Cut from one edge to the other, but *do not* separate the pieces.

Place the cut rectangle on the paper and place a pin at the center back edge, which is still attached, and into the working surface to hold in place. Spread the cut edge at center back ⅛ in.

and pin to hold the upper and lower edges. To determine how much to spread each additional cut line, I will use my own example.

My waist measures 27¼ in. Where I attach my band to my pants (the lower edge of my waist) I measure 28½ in. because I begin to curve out immediately below my waist. The difference is 1¼ in. When I wear a fitted straight waistband, it fits my pants but gaps at the top of the center back. I can pinch out a ⅝-in. fold. This is the amount I need to spread the cut edge.

Spread the measurement difference equally between the 12 other cuts and pin in place. The spreads are small, about ⅛ in. or less depending on your measured difference. If you are not sure how much to spread the cut edge, spread it so it is 1 in. larger than the upper measurement of the rectangle (the uncut edge). This measurement can be fine-tuned in subsequent pants.

**6.** Once you have the cuts spread evenly on both sides of center back to equal your larger measurement, tape in place.

**7.** Draw a line from edge to edge though the middle of the spread at center back. For fly zippers, measure the distance between the center front and the zipper teeth on the underlay side of the zipper (½ in. to ¾ in.). Add this amount to the left side of the contoured band. Add 1¼ in. to the right side for an extension closure.

8. Add seam allowances to all edges. Your fitted contour band is now completely customized to your measurements and body contour.

9. Cut two bands from fabric. One will be the outside band, the other the inside or facing. Lay center back on the straight grain. Cut interfacing from the same pattern and on the same grainline if using a woven fabric. One or both pieces can be interfaced depending on the firmness desired.

10. The upper, or narrower, edges of the two band pieces are sewn together. The seams are graded, clipped, and under-stitched. The lower edge is joined to the pants and completed in the same manner as for a straight-fitted waistband.

## Partially elasticized waistband

Do you find your waistline fluctuating and your pants waistband a little too loose one day and too tight another? Help has arrived. This waistband has a smooth look in the front, with shirred elastic at the side back and a smooth center back. Follow these steps to modify your pattern.

1. Determine your largest and smallest comfortable waist measurement. Measure yourself at different times of the day, both sitting and standing, and on different days. Determine the difference between the largest and smallest measurements. For example, if your largest measurement is 32 in. and your smallest is 30 in., then the difference is 2 in. If you divide the difference by four, you will get the amount you should add to the side-seam waist on the front and back. For this example, that amount would be ½ in.

2. Add one-fourth of the total difference (as was just deter-mined in step 1) at the side waist on the front and back pants pattern, tapering to "0" at your full hip depth (see the drawing on p. 364).

3. Measure the width of the side back dart at the waistline seam. The side back dart will be eliminated, but the take up (width between the legs at the waistline) will be added to the back side seam.

4. Cut the original waistband apart at the side seams. Increase each side front one-fourth of the total difference (½ in.). Increase the center-back waistband piece 1¼ in. on each side.

# Pattern Development for Partially Elasticized (Side-Back) Waistband

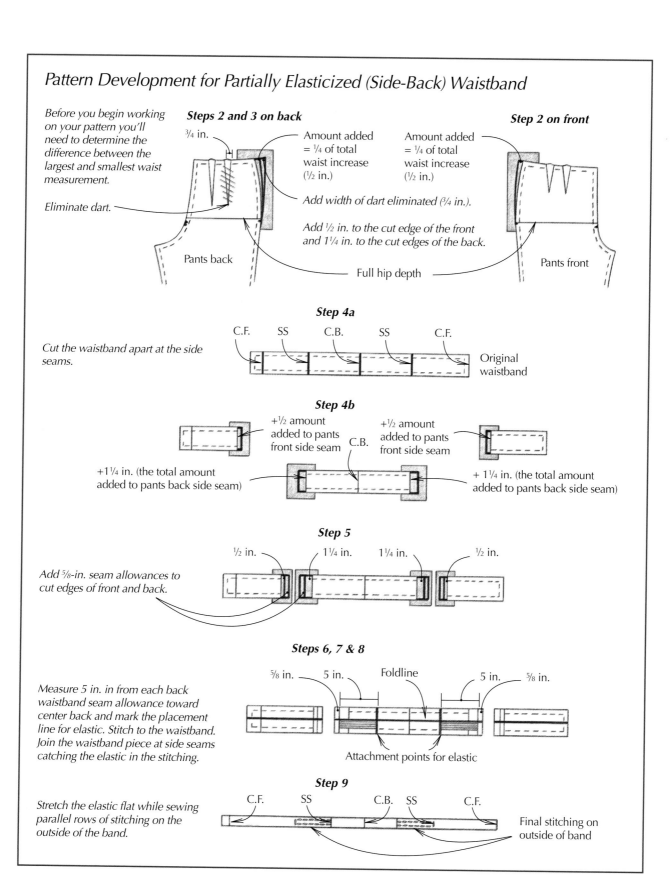

Before you begin working on your pattern you'll need to determine the difference between the largest and smallest waist measurement.

Eliminate dart.

**Steps 2 and 3 on back**

3/4 in.

Amount added = 1/4 of total waist increase (1/2 in.)

Add width of dart eliminated (3/4 in.).

Add 1/2 in. to the cut edge of the front and 1 1/4 in. to the cut edges of the back.

Pants back

**Step 2 on front**

Amount added = 1/4 of total waist increase (1/2 in.)

Pants front

Full hip depth

**Step 4a**

Cut the waistband apart at the side seams.

C.F.    SS    C.B.    SS    C.F.

Original waistband

**Step 4b**

+1/2 amount added to pants front side seam

C.B.

+1/2 amount added to pants front side seam

+1 1/4 in. (the total amount added to pants back side seam)

+ 1 1/4 in. (the total amount added to pants back side seam)

**Step 5**

Add 5/8-in. seam allowances to cut edges of front and back.

1/2 in.    1 1/4 in.    1 1/4 in.    1/2 in.

**Steps 6, 7 & 8**

Measure 5 in. in from each back waistband seam allowance toward center back and mark the placement line for elastic. Stitch to the waistband. Join the waistband piece at side seams catching the elastic in the stitching.

5/8 in.    5 in.    Foldline    5 in.    5/8 in.

Attachment points for elastic

**Step 9**

Stretch the elastic flat while sewing parallel rows of stitching on the outside of the band.

C.F.    SS    C.B.    SS    C.F.

Final stitching on outside of band

**5.** Add ⅝-in. seam allowances to each side front and each side of the center-back piece.

**6.** On the center-back piece, mark off 5 in. from the seam allowance toward center back on each side for the elastic placement.

**7.** The width of your elastic should be the same width as your finished band. Cut a 3½-in. length of Honeycomb or sport elastic (available in ¾-in. to 3-in. widths). This elastic looks like it has separate narrow channels of individual elastic, but it is actually one strip. It retains up to 90% of its stretch recovery when stitched through. Topstitching is done every ¼ in. to ½ in., depending on the width of your waistband. This elastic is especially comfortable at the side waist and looks great on a 2-in.-wide band.

**8.** Stitch a small amount (¼ in.) of elastic in with the side seam allowance when joining the waistband sections together and also at the point about 5 in. toward center back and perpendicular to the foldline (see the drawing on the facing page). **Note:** The elastic acts as an interfacing in the 5-in. area only. You will need to interface the remainder of the band as usual.

**9.** Attach the band as instructed in your guide sheet, matching side seams and stretching the back to fit. Finish the long edge of the facing side as desired or as instructed on your guide sheet. On the right side, evenly divide and mark the space between the fold and the garment seam into several parallel rows. Stretch the elastic flat while stitching through all waistband layers and elastic on marked lines.

# Belt Loops

Decide how many belt loops you want. Four is the standard number, but an additional one at the center back will keep your belt from riding up. Sometimes belt loops are placed in pairs for a decorative effect. If you decide on pairs, make sure you multiply the number of pairs you want by two to get the right number of loops.

**1.** For a standard 1¼-in. finished waistband, begin with a 3-in.-long belt loop that is three times the desired finished width. For example, for four belt loops ⅜ in. wide, you will need a fabric strip 1⅛ in. wide and 12 in. long. Cut the strip with one long edge on the selvage, or serge one edge (see A in the drawing on p. 366).

**2.** Cut a ¼-in. strip of fusible web the length of the fabric strip.

## Making Belt Loops

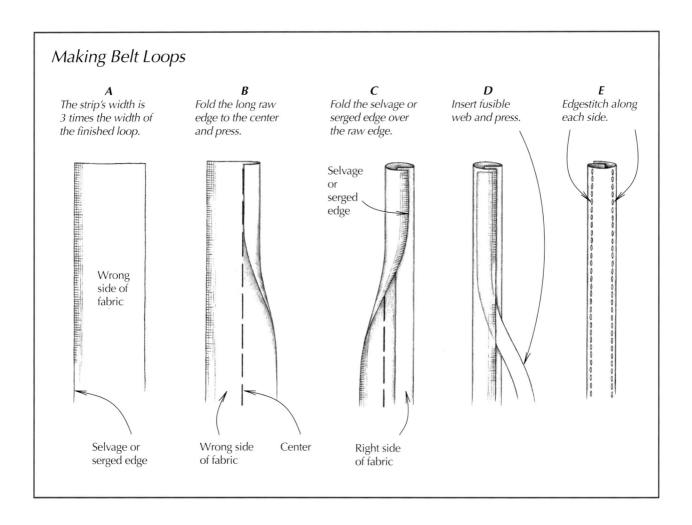

**A**
*The strip's width is 3 times the width of the finished loop.*

Wrong side of fabric

Selvage or serged edge

**B**
*Fold the long raw edge to the center and press.*

Wrong side of fabric   Center

**C**
*Fold the selvage or serged edge over the raw edge.*

Selvage or serged edge

Right side of fabric

**D**
*Insert fusible web and press.*

**E**
*Edgestitch along each side.*

**3.** Fold the fabric strip in half lengthwise and finger crease or lightly press it. (**B**)

**4.** Fold the long raw edge to center and press. (**B**)

**5.** Fold the selvage/serged edge over the raw edge and press. (**C**)

**6.** Tuck the narrow strip of fusible web under the long selvage/serged edge. Press to fuse in place. (**D**)

**7.** Edgestitch each long edge close to fold. (**E**)

Each finished belt loop will be 1¾ in. long with a ⅝-in. seam allowance at each end for attachment.

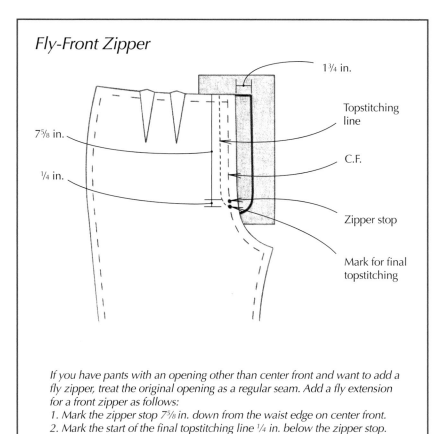

**Fly-Front Zipper**

1¾ in.

7⅝ in.

¼ in.

Topstitching line

C.F.

Zipper stop

Mark for final topstitching

*If you have pants with an opening other than center front and want to add a fly zipper, treat the original opening as a regular seam. Add a fly extension for a front zipper as follows:*
*1. Mark the zipper stop 7⅝ in. down from the waist edge on center front.*
*2. Mark the start of the final topstitching line ¼ in. below the zipper stop.*
*3. Draw an extension that is 1¾ in. wide and parallel to center front from waist to topstitching mark.*

# Fly-Front Zipper

If you have pants with a zipper opening at the center back, you can add a fly-front zipper. Treat the original zipper opening as a regular seam, closing the entire seam when sewing it. To add a fly extension for a front zipper, make the following changes to your pattern, as shown in the drawing above:

**1.** On the pants center front, measure down 7⅝ in. from the waist edge and mark. This will be the zipper-stop mark.

**2.** Measure down ¼ in. from the zipper stop and mark. The final topstitching will begin at the lowest mark.

**3.** Draw a line parallel to center front and 1¾ in. from center front, even with the zipper stop. Draw a curved line to connect this parallel line to the mark ¼ in. below the zipper stop. This extension should be cut for both fronts.

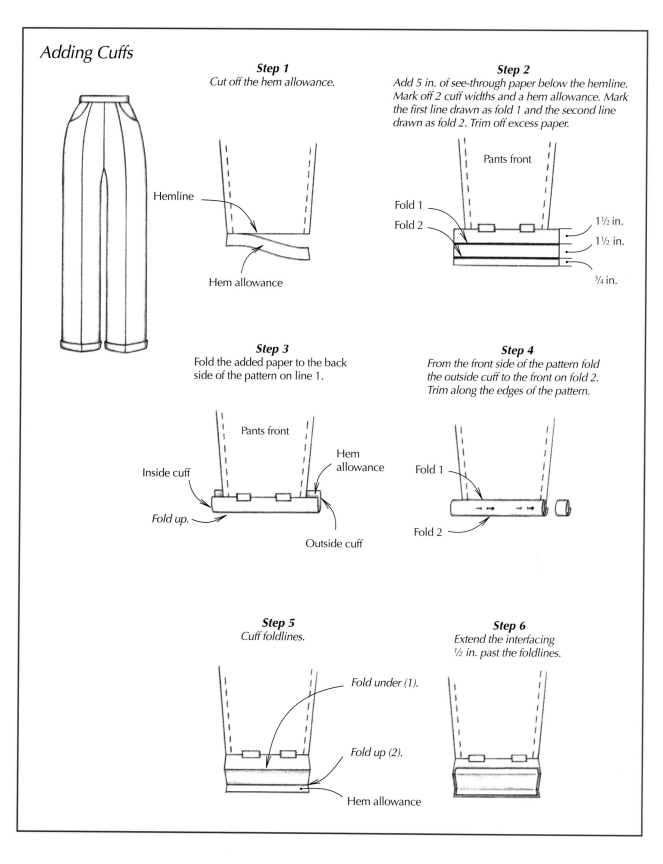

## Adding Cuffs

### Step 1
Cut off the hem allowance.

Hemline

Hem allowance

### Step 2
Add 5 in. of see-through paper below the hemline. Mark off 2 cuff widths and a hem allowance. Mark the first line drawn as fold 1 and the second line drawn as fold 2. Trim off excess paper.

Pants front

Fold 1
Fold 2

1½ in.
1½ in.

¾ in.

### Step 3
Fold the added paper to the back side of the pattern on line 1.

Pants front

Inside cuff

Hem allowance

Fold up.

Outside cuff

### Step 4
From the front side of the pattern fold the outside cuff to the front on fold 2. Trim along the edges of the pattern.

Fold 1

Fold 2

### Step 5
Cuff foldlines.

Fold under (1).

Fold up (2).

Hem allowance

### Step 6
Extend the interfacing ½ in. past the foldlines.

# Cuffs

Repeat steps 1 through 6 for front and back.

**1.** Draw in the hemline (the turn-up line for the hem) at the bottom of the pants front. Cut on the hemline, cutting off the hem allowance.

**2.** Decide on the finished width of the visible cuff (1½ in. is average). Widths vary with fashion. Tape a piece of paper 2 in. wider than the pants-leg width and about 5 in. long to the bottom of the pants leg. Add two cuff widths plus a ¾-in. hem allowance.

**3.** Crease on fold 1 (after the first cuff width), turning the outside cuff and hem allowance end up on the back side of the pattern.

**4.** From the front side of the pattern, crease at the bottom edge of the pattern (fold 2), folding up and bringing the remaining cuff on the back side to the front, leaving the hem allowance on the back side. Pin in place to hold. Trim the excess paper even with the pattern cutting line.

**5.** Unfold for the completed pattern.

**6.** Interface the cuffs with a fusible warp insertion interfacing or a bias strip of woven interfacing. Extend the interfacing ½ in. past the foldlines.

Tack the cuffs to the side and inner leg seams by machine or hand to hold in place.

# Slant-Front Pockets with Optional Tummy-Trim Panel

Once you have determined an accurate waistline fit for your pants and have perfected the side-seam hipline curve, you're ready to incorporate some design changes to transform the look of your pants using your original pattern.

One way is with slant-front pockets (see the drawing on pp. 372-373). The slant-front pocket continues to be popular because of its slenderizing effect on the figure. This classic pocket originates at the side hip. The opening is created by cutting away part of the pants front from the waist to the side seam. Traditionally these two points are connected with a diagonal style line on the front of the pants. The sack of this inserted pocket is hidden on the inside of the pants.

To preserve your original pattern as is and add a second pattern, simply make an exact tracing of the upper portion of your current pattern to a point 2 in. below the crotch-line. This way you can interchange differently styled pants tops without having to retrace the whole leg portion.

1. If you are beginning with a pleated or darted pattern, fold the pattern pleat(s) or dart(s) closed as they would be when the garment is sewn (see step 1 in the drawing on pp. 372-373). Pin or tape them closed. If the darts or pleats are not closed when the pocket pattern is traced, they will be included in the pocket pattern, adding unnecessary bulk to the pocket when sewn.

2. Pin the pattern to your working surface. Place see-through paper over the pants front and secure it with removable tape or pins.

3. Plot and dot on the paper at the following points:
- waist and side intersection
- 4 in. from the side waist toward center front
- 2 in. from the side waist toward center front. This amount is a guideline. Plotting this point more than 2 in. will create a style line that is more horizontal. Plotting it less than 2 in. creates a more vertical pocket line. The more vertical the line, or parallel to the side seam, the more slimming the line.
- 6 in. to 7 in. from the waist along the side edge (for the pocket opening)
- 1 in. below the pocket opening marked above
- a horizontal line from the first dot on the side below the waist to center front

- a line from the waist dot closest to center front, parallel to the grainline, ending at crotch level. Plot a dot where these two lines intersect.
- Number the dots as shown in the drawing on pp. 372-373 (step 2).

4. From dot 4, measure down another 4 in. to 5 in. At this point draw a horizontal line halfway across the pants front, perpendicular to the grainline. This line should not be lower than the crotchline (step 2).

5. Connect dots 1 to 5, tracing the side edge of the pattern, then connect 5 to 6, making sure the deepest part of the pocket touches the lower horizontal line.

Hint: A French curve is helpful to get a smooth, well-shaped curve. Continue by connecting dot 6 to 2, 2 to 3, and 3 to 1, tracing the cutting edge of your pattern. Connect dot 3 to 4 in a straight or slightly curved line (step 5).

6. There will be two parts to the pocket (step 6):
- pocket underlay (dots 1-5-6-2-3-1)
- upper pocket/facing (dots 3-4-5-6-2-3)

The wedge pattern (dots 1-4-3-1) will be used to lay on the pants-front pattern, matching side and waist edges, to cut away that portion of the full front.

**7.** Make the notch markings on the pocket as indicated in step 7 to facilitate matching during construction. The grainline of the pocket is parallel to the pants grainline. Transfer single notch markings on the under-lay side edge to the pants back side edge.

**8.** Lay see-through paper over the pattern and trace one upper pocket/facing and one wedge pattern. Remove all tracings and cut out one upper pocket/facing and one underlay and one wedge pattern (step 8).

**9.** Lay the wedge piece on the pants front, matching side and waist edges. Transfer the single notch marking on the angled edge of the wedge to the pants front. Cut off that portion of the pants-front pattern between dots 3 and 4 (step 9a). Add a seam allowance to this edge (step 9b).

**10.** About midway on the upper pocket/facing style edge, cut across to the opposite edge but do not separate the pieces. Place paper under the cut and spread the edge (between dots 3 and 4) about ¼ in. This will allow some ease in the pocket so it will fit better over the curve of the body and make it easier to use. Slightly more or less ease may be necessary because of the bulk of the fabric or your body shape. Redraw the style line between dots 3 and 4 and the grainline.

Add a seam allowance to style edge (between dots 3 and 4) (step 10).

**11.** The upper-pocket portion of the pocket can be cut from fashion fabric, pocketing, or lining since it will not be seen. If the upper pocket is cut from fabric other than fashion fabric, a fashion-fabric facing can be applied from the style edge 2 in. in, on top of the upper-pocket fabric to reduce bulk. The underlay can also be faced. The exact shape is not important as long as the pocketing fabric is well hidden and is not visible when worn or used. Finish the facing edges that extend into the pocket with a zigzag, clean finish, or serged edge before joining it to the pocket.

**12. To add a tummy-trim panel,** extend the pocket underlay to the front edge of the pattern. The extension length should be about 4¾ in. from the top waist edge (more if you lengthened the crotch depth, less if you shortened it) and should get caught in the center-front seam. This extension can be cut out of any lightweight fabric, stable tricot, power net, or even control-top panty hose (without the elastic band) and zigzagged to the pocket underlay. This will help the pleats lie flatter and prevent spreading if your pattern has been properly fitted (step 11).

## Pattern Development for Slant-Front Pockets

### Step 1

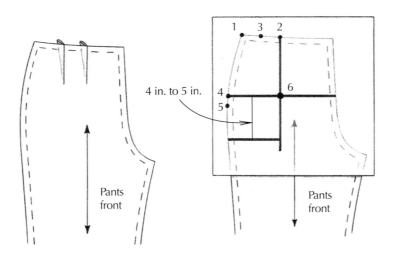

Pants front

### Steps 2, 3 & 4

4 in. to 5 in.

Pants front

### Step 5

Pants front

### Step 6

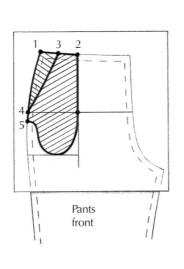

Pants front

### Step 7

Notches

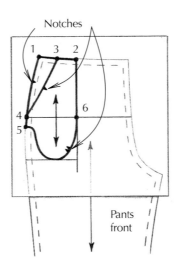

Pants front

### Step 8

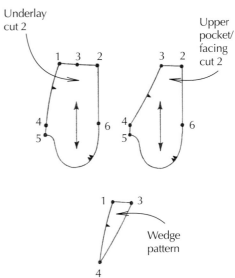

Underlay cut 2

Upper pocket/ facing cut 2

Wedge pattern

= 1-4-3-1 wedge to be cut away from full-front pattern    = 3-4-5-6-2-3  upper pocket/facing

**Step 9a**                    **Step 9b**                              **Step 10**

Seam allowance

Pants
front

Pants
front

Slash

3

4
5

Seam
allowance

*Cut 2.*

## Step 11—pattern for fashion fabric facings

Upper pocket                    Underlay

2 in.                           3 in.

Fashion
fabric

Fashion
fabric

Edge finish
needed

## Step 12—tummy-trim panel

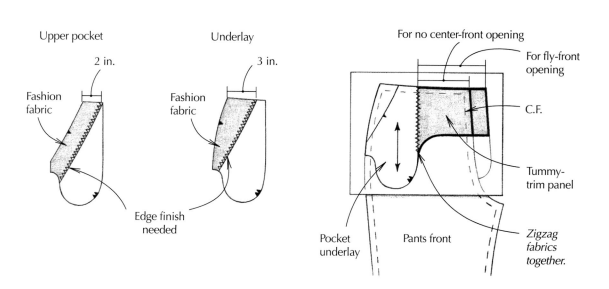

For no center-front opening

For fly-front
opening

C.F.

Tummy-
trim panel

Pocket
underlay

Pants front

*Zigzag
fabrics
together.*

# Index

Index note: page references in *italics* indicate a photograph; page references in **bold** indicate an illustration.